Café

PROGRAMMING

FrontRunner

DAVID H. FRIEDEL, JR.

JOSHUA KERIEVSKY

ANTHONY POTTS

JOHN RODLEY

 CORIOLIS GROUP BOOKS

PUBLISHER	KEITH WEISKAMP
PROJECT EDITOR	SCOTT PALMER
COVER ARTIST	SCOTTSDALE COLOR GRAPHICS
COVER DESIGN	ANTHONY STOCK
INTERIOR DESIGN	MICHELLE STROUP
LAYOUT PRODUCTION	APRIL NIELSEN
PROOFREADER	STEPHANIE HOON
INDEXER	ELIZABETH FRIEDEL

The Coriolis Group, Inc.
7339 E. Acoma Drive, Suite 7
Scottsdale, AZ 85260
Phone: (602) 483-0192
Fax: (602) 483-0193
Web address: http://www.coriolis.com

ISBN 1-57610-003-0 : $29.99

Printed in the United States of America

10 9 8 7 6 5 4 3 2 1

The first guy in the door has to turn on the lights.

That's true whether you're the first member of a team to adopt a new technology, or whether you're doing it all by yourself. Being "first" means that you have no one to ask for help—and that you must find the light switch on your own.

There are undeniable benefits to being a technology frontrunner: Those first in the door can set the standards, test new approaches, and be first to market with major products. There could be millions of dollars lying on the table, waiting for the first hand that learns how to grab them.

We at Coriolis Group Books created the FrontRunner Series so that you'd have help on Day One: the day you bring that new technology product home and crank it up. This will be true even if Day One for you is Day One for the product, too. We've built working relationships with the technology leaders in our industry so that our teams of analysts and writers can be working as soon as new technology is out of the labs. When it comes to a new technology product, you're not all alone anymore. The Front Runner is here to help.

Our goal is to provide you with the best possible information on new technology products the day they're released to the public. Not "soft stuff" or hot air, either—just real, useful, practical information that you can put to work right away. We hope that this book gives you whatever additional power you need to make that final sprint over the line—and on to outstanding success in your study or business.

Jeff Duntemann

Contents

Chapter 4   Java Language Fundamentals   65

Chapter 5 Operators, Expressions, and Control Structures   101

Chapter 9 A Look into the Applet Class 215

Chapter 10 Debugging with Café 251

Chapter 11   Working with Café Studio   279

Introduction

Java is the hottest thing on the Web—and Café is the easiest new way to create Java programs and applets! This book, first in the Coriolis Group's "FrontRunner" series, gives you a fast-track approach so that you can start using Café right away—and become a better Café programmer almost overnight!

This book is organized so that you can use it either as a tutorial or as a ready reference for your Café programming.

If you're new to Java, you should probably just start with Chapter 1 (*Introducing Café) and* read the chapters in sequence. You don't need to know Java; we teach you that along the way, so you'll create working Java programs immediately. As you progress through the chapters, you can apply what you learn to your "real world" programming projects, until finally, at the end, you'll become a master of both Café and Java.

If you already know Java, you can use this book in two ways. Chapters 1, 2, 3, 10, and 11 give you a fast but in-depth tutorial on Café's new features, so if that's what you need, just go straight to those chapters. Later, as you continue to program in Café and Java, you can dip into the book as needed for a refresher or reference information about specific Café and Java features.

But no matter what your level of programming experience, there's one important thing to remember: *have fun!* With this book as your guide, and Café as your development environment, you'll be creating snazzy, innovative Java programs in no time!

Introducing Café

Joshua Kerievsky

Café is an integrated development and debugging environment for Java programmers from novice to expert. In this chapter, you'll get an overview of the powerful features packed inside Café.

Good development environments increase your productivity. Great ones not only increase your productivity but let you do things that would be impossible without them. Symantec's Café is a fairly new product that is already showing signs of greatness.

In the stone age of Java development environments (*that is,* before Symantec's Café was released), developers had to use several different programs to edit, compile, test, and debug their Java applications and applets. This was a workable situation, but when you compare it to what an environment like Café provides, you soon realize how primitive development is without the proper tools.

For many Windows programmers, the proper tools usually come in one integrated development environment (IDE). Such an environment often includes a compiler that burns rubber (rocks, flies, kicks butt, or however you'd like to describe it), a project management system that handles simple or complex builds, a full-featured debugger that is both integrated and graphical, and a help system that knows just about every word, class, and method of a language, developers kit, or API. Café not only provides these features, but offers a wealth of others.

1

A Brief History of Café

Symantec's Café began life in December of 1995 under the name "Espresso." Espresso was a free addition to Symantec's C++ compiler and was designed to make Java applet and application creation both simple and fast. For previous owners of this compiler, the free addition of Java to their familiar C++ environment was a welcome bonus. However, for a growing number of developers who were seeking an IDE for Java, but who did not own Symantec's compiler, the choice was either to buy a C++ compiler or go without an IDE altogether. Many went without.

Meanwhile, Symantec went to work on a Java development environment catered solely to the needs of Java developers. On March 4, 1996, Symantec's Café was released to the world.

Café has now been through two minor releases since Version 1.0 was first announced and shipped. The first of these releases was called Version 1.0.1 and contained some very minor bug fixes. The second release, called Version 1.2 (in a prerelease stage as of this writing) contains some substantial additions to Café's integrated debugger as well as a few minor bug fixes.

Purpose of Café

Café is a sophisticated development tool that has many uses and multiple purposes. It may be used in a variety of ways by a variety of developers to accomplish a variety of tasks. Let's look at some of its key features.

Platform Independent Development

Café is a tool for creating applets and applications that will run on any Java-enabled platforms. These platforms already include Windows 95, Windows NT, Sun Solaris, SGI, Macintosh, and more.

Platform-independent software is what you can produce using Café; but it is not a quality of Café itself. Rather, Café is an optimized 32-bit program, designed specifically for the Windows 95 and Windows NT operating systems.

Support for Expert and Novice Developers

As a development tool, Café is geared for both seasoned professionals and less experienced programmers. It caters to both crowds by serving up tools that automate and simplify certain development tasks while providing robust utilities for getting down and dirty.

Java Education

For those just learning Java, Café comes with a substantial amount of code from which you can learn how to perform many simple and complex tasks. Over 40 sample applets and applications are bundled with Café alone. If you're not sure how to make text or images scroll in Java, you can study and learn from projects like ScrollText, ScrollPic, or ImageTape. If you're looking for some ideas on how to build a spreadsheet, take a look at the sample project, SpreadSheet.

When you use certain Café tools, Café itself generates the Java code for you. This generated code can serve as an excellent teacher. You can learn about form and menu construction, event handling, and how to work with the Frame and Dialog classes. Figure 1.1 is a scene from Café Studio in which a button on a form has been given notice to respond to a user's mouse click, causing Café to generate an empty default handler for the event.

Café also comes with the entire release version of Sun's Java Development Kit (JDK). This means that you have the entire class library source code to learn from as well.

And finally, whether you are new to Java or an experienced hacker, Café's well-indexed online help (which covers both the Java language and the JDK) is an invaluable reference. You can invoke the help system by clicking on an unknown Java word or JDK method and pressing F1.

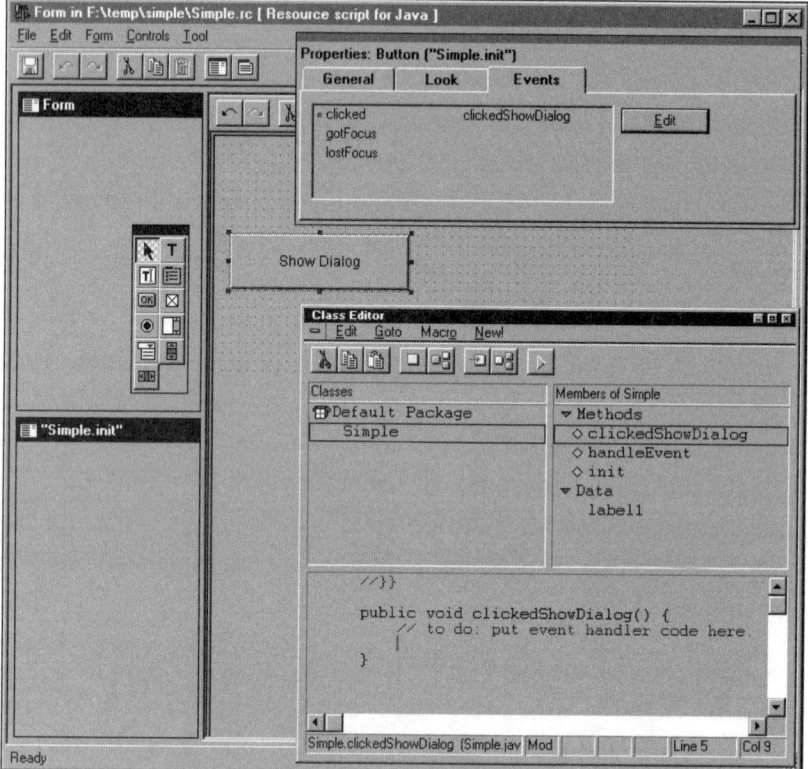

Figure 1.1 **A button called Show Dialog has a "clicked" event associated with it, for which Café generates code that can be edited from within Class Editor.**

Object-Oriented Design and Development

Experienced object-oriented developers will find Café's class management tools, particularly Class Editor and Hierarchy Editor, to be powerful and quite useful. Café lets you navigate and edit your classes (*and* the relationships between them) from several different vantage points. And after making changes to your classes or class hierarchies, Café's parsing technology, continually functioning behind the scenes, updates code and graphical views for you. Figure 1.2 shows you what the Class Editor and Hierarchy Editor look like.

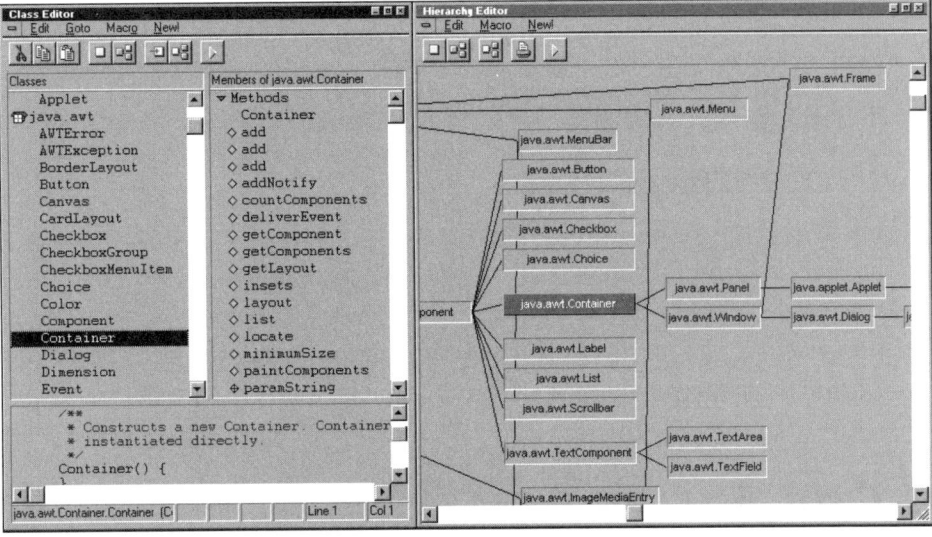

Figure 1.2 Café's Class Editor and Hierarchy Editor.

Easier User Interface Construction

Finally, Café aims to make user interface development in Java a much simpler process. (Figure 1.1 showed you Café Studio in action.) Following in the footsteps of many traditional Windows development environments, Café goes one step further by providing a visual, drag and drop tool for building and editing forms and menus designed to look the same (or very similar) on all Java-enabled platforms.

Café Ingredients

Lets now take a look at some of the many ingredients that make up Café. As a developer, you may find that when you set out to accomplish a certain task in Café, often two or more of the tools we'll explore next will be useful to you in completing your task.

AppExpress

AppExpress is a wizard-like tool that will help you create default applets, standalone applications, and console applications. All you need to do is follow a few simple steps. When you finish, AppExpress will create a Café project for your new applet or application, supply a default form (and *menu*, in the case of an standalone application), and provide you with a default HTML file (in the case of an applet). The AppExpress utility is explained in detail in the next chapter.

ProjectExpress

Like AppExpress, ProjectExpress is a wizard-like tool for easily setting up projects in Café. All you have to do is supply the name and location of your new project and optionally tell ProjectExpress which files to add to your project. You may also control whether or not your project should be automatically parsed by the Café environment. ProjectExpress is explained in detail in the next chapter.

Café Studio

Before Café came along, many Java developers used to complain a lot about the difficulty of building user interfaces using the JDK's AWT, or Abstract Windowing Toolkit. The AWT contains five layout managers that support cross-platform user interfaces but do not make the process of creating these interfaces very easy. For developers used to programming (and designing) in environments like Borland's Delphi, or Microsoft's Visual Basic or Visual C++, giving these developers the JDK's AWT and telling them to design forms was a lot like giving a writer, accustomed to using a word-processor, an old typewriter.

Café changed a lot of that. Café Studio, pictured back in Figure 1.1, is a tool within Café that you can use to visually edit your user interface components. It lets you visually build forms and menus by dragging and dropping components from the toolbar. It lets you select JDK Layout managers for your forms and choose fonts for your labels and text fields. Finally, it makes it easy to associate events with components and drops you into the Class Editor when you want to edit event handling code. Café Studio is covered at length in Chapter 11.

Hierarchy Editor

Café's Hierarchy Editor, pictured back in Figure 1.2, is a very useful tool for viewing and *changing* your class hierarchies. It graphically shows you all of the classes in your project, including the Java system classes (if you choose to see them), and lets you easily find classes in the hierarchy. Additionally, it lets you quickly jump to the source code from a class using either Café's Class Editor or source code editor. The Hierarchy Editor is covered in Chapter 3.

Class Editor

Café's Class Editor, pictured above in Figure 1.2, is an excellent tool for navigating, editing and searching for classes, methods and variables in your projects. It is fully integrated with tools like Café Studio and the Hierarchy Editor and serves as an excellent alternative to the source code editor for writing or editing code. Class Editor is covered in detail in Chapter 3.

Debugger

Café's integrated graphical debugger, shown in Figure 1.3, makes debugging an easy and straightforward affair. The debugger supports some very cool features such as drag and drop and lets you easily navigate your class's ancestors, descendents, and internal data members while you debug. It also lets you control and debug multithreaded code. Café's Debugger is covered at length in Chapter 10.

Programmer's Editor

Café comes with a sophisticated programmer's editor that has support for configurable key mappings, color syntax highlighting, and custom macros. It has full integration with Café's help system and allows you to search for words or expressions across multiple files. The editor also allows you to drag words or highlighted blocks from one location to another and even to other Café windows. The programmer's editor is covered in Chapter 3.

Café's Speed

No one likes to wait for software and Café aims to make you wait as little as possible. This includes when you compile code, change class relationships, test your code and even move from one tool to another within the integrated development and debugging environment. Let's look at some of the features that help make Café fast.

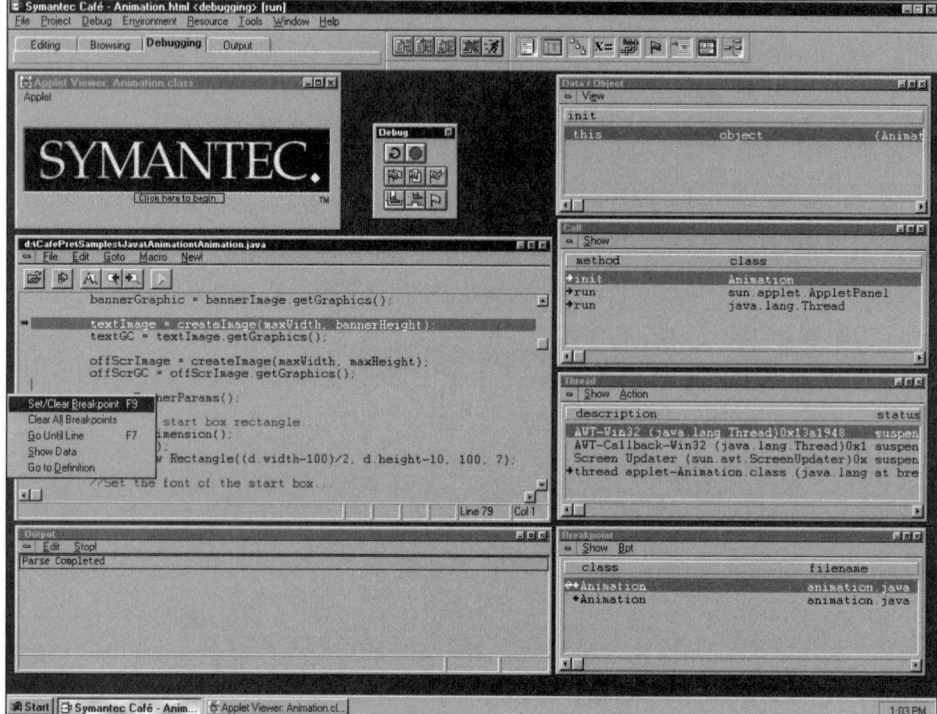

Figure 1.3   Café's Integrated Visual Debugger.

The Café Compiler

The Café compiler is quite simply a speed demon. It compiles code at up to 10 times the speed of the compiler that shipped with Version 1.0 of the JDK.

Whether you're building small applets or large projects, you'll save a tremendous amount of time by simply using the Java bytecode compiler built into Café.

The Café JIT

Since Java is an interpreted language, typically an interpreter is necessary to run Java code. The one problem with interpreters, however, is that they seldom execute code as fast as if the code were already compiled to machine instructions.

A Just In Time compiler is designed to replace the role of an interpreter by compiling pcode into machine instructions at runtime. This usually results in *much* faster performance.

Soon after Symantec released Version 1.0 of Café, they came out with their Just In Time compiler for Java. Called Symjit.exe, this program could run either within Café itself or within the original Sun JDK. As of Prerelease 1.2, Symantec's JIT now comes already integrated into Café. The Café JIT greatly speeds up the execution of Java code and therefore saves you development time.

The Parser

The parsing technology in Café is nothing short of awesome. It enables you to make changes to your classes that will immediately be reflected in Café's various editor windows.

For example, should you decide to change the ancestor of a class using Café's source code editor, you can then click on the Hierarchy Editor window and immediately see your changes reflected. Similarly, if you add, update or delete a method from a class in the Class Editor, the change will be made immediately within the source code editor.

Café's parser thus supports real-time updates which, by not requiring you to re-compile your code, saves you time when editing you project.

The Café Debugger

When you want to find bugs in your code quickly (and who in their right mind would want to find them slowly?), the best tool to use is a full-featured debugger.

Sun's jdb, the debugger that ships with Version 1.0 of the JDK, is a functional debugger, but is a bit slow because it's written completely in Java. It runs as a command-line utility in text mode and requires you to learn a number of keyboard commands in order to use it.

By contrast, the visual debugger that is integrated into the Café environment, pictured earlier in the chapter in Figure 1.3, is simple to use and will not slow you down. It starts quickly, lets you easily add or delete breakpoints (as of Prerelease 1.2, even during runtime!), and lets you click on variables or objects to inspect values. There are so many more speed enhancements in this debugger (like remembering your breakpoints after you shut down Café) that you will have to go to Chapter 10 to learn about them.

Workspaces

The Café environment supports the idea of separate workspaces for different development activities. The initial four workspaces that come with Café are called "Editing," "Browsing," "Debugging," and "Output." You can customize these default workspaces or create your own new ones. Figure 1.4 shows you Café's four workspaces and the process of creating a new workspace.

New workspaces show up as new tabs on the workspace toolbar. Having multiple, pre-configured, workspaces can improve the speed at which you develop and debug your projects. You can learn more about creating and maintaining workspaces in Chapter 3.

Project Management

Whether you're building a small or large-scale project, a Java applet or application, Café's project management system keeps track of all your source code and resources for you. Figure 1.5 shows you Café's Project window for the samples applet, ThreadX.

Figure 1.4   Creating a new Workspace in Café.

Name	Ext	Path	Date	Time	Parsed	
ThreadX.html	.html	F:\Dev	3/3/96	19:52:24	N/A	
AnimationPanel.j.	.java	F:\Dev	5/1/96	16:00:07	Yes	
ThreadX.java	.java	F:\Dev	5/1/96	16:00:57	Yes	
ThreadX.rc	.rc	F:\Dev	3/3/96	19:52:08	N/A	

**Figure 1.5   Café's Project Management System: The Project window for sample
applet, ThreadX.**

Café's project management system coordinates the building of project code and lets you easily control which files may or may not be parsed by Café's parser. Compared to compiling your project's source files manually, using Café's project management system saves you a lot of time.

Café Support

Like any non-trivial product, Café has many windows, utilities, settings, and unique qualities. Although the product's extensive context-sensitive help for the Café environment as well as the Java language and JDK may help answer many of your questions, you may still encounter situations that you don't understand or problems for which you cannot find a solution.

This is where the Internet can play a *major role* in helping you. To get your Café questions answered quickly, you'll often find that by posting a message to the appropriate news group, your answer will arrive sooner than you think. This is particularly true for Java, since it has become such a popular language across the globe.

The following are two places that you may go to look for help on Café. Note that with newsgroups, you may often find the answer to your question by simply reading the questions and answers previously posted by other developers.

comp.lang.java

By far the largest online meeting room and discussion area for Java developers is the newsgroup called comp.lang.java. This new group easily receives close to 1,000 messages a day from developers around the world.

A number of tech gurus from Symantec often follow the messages on comp.lang.java. These folks do a wonderful job of responding to questions about Café on the newsgroup. If you have a question, and it is specifically about Café (as opposed to just being about the Java language) include the word "Café" in the subject line of your message to the newsgroup. You're quite likely to hear either from another user of Café or from someone at Symantec within a short period of time (often within a day or two, and sometimes within the hour!).

Symantec's Java Central

Symantec maintains a Web site devoted exclusively to Café and Java. It is shown in Figure 1.6. You may visit this site for the latest information about Café or to download the latest updates to the product. Symantec's Java Central is a place to learn about other interesting Java related sites, discover books about Java, and sign up to receive information from one of Symantec's mailing lists.

Visit the two following URLs to stay informed on the latest developments at Symantec:

```
http://www.symantec.com
http://cafe.symantec.com/
```

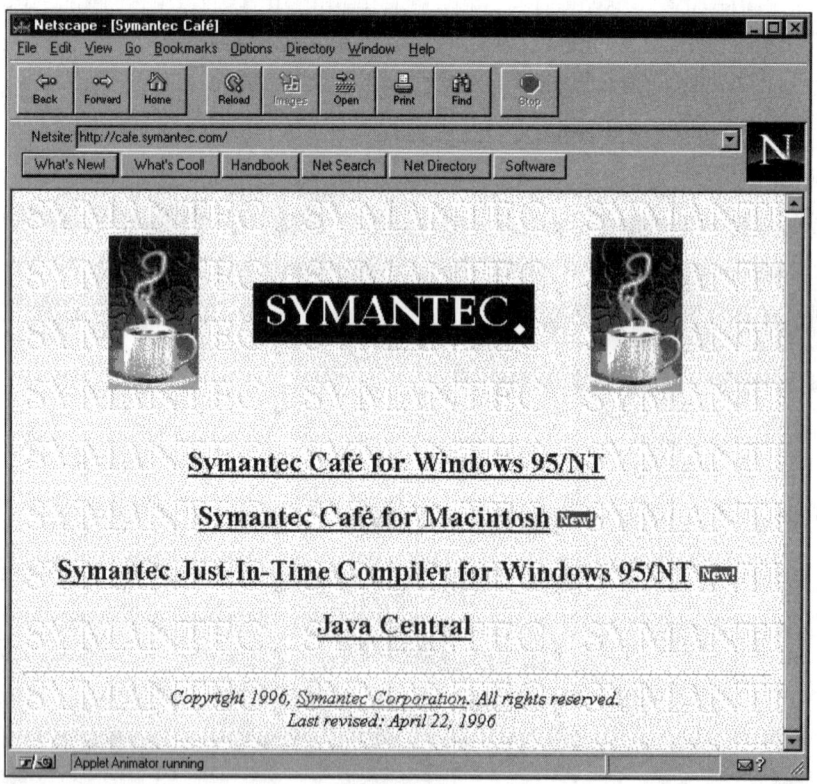

Figure 1.6   Symantec's World Wide Web site for information and updates to Café.

Enter the Café

We've come to the end of this brief overview and introduction to Symantec's Café. You are now ready to enter the Café! This means that you will learn to maximize your productivity as you develop projects using the many tools and features packed into Café's IDDE or integrated development and debugging environment.

There is a lot to discover in this development tool! Thus far, you've only gotten a taste of what Café can do for you. In the chapters that follow, you will get hands on experience using this product to its limits. When you are finished with the book, you will find that your productivity will have increased several times over and you will have a thorough knowledge of an excellent development tool.

If you're already an experienced Java developer, get ready to enter the Café and streamline your productivity as a Café developer.

If you're new to both Java and Café, get ready to make rapid progress as you steadily learn about Java programming while you gain control over the Café environment and its powerful set of tools.

Writing Your First Java App with Café

2

Joshua Kerievsky

Two express trains run through Symantec's Café: AppExpress and ProjectExpress. In this chapter you'll learn how to use these tools to rapidly create your own projects, applets, and applications.

Rapid application development, or RAD, has been a buzzword of the software industry for many years. Developers have argued over the meaning of the word, and scores of companies have claimed that their products supply RAD (at least according to *their* definitions). But however *you* decide to define the term, you'll also be the judge of whether a product truly improves your efficiency and helps you develop projects faster.

Of all the tools and utilities that come bundled with Café's IDDE (Integrated Development and Debugging Environment), you might find that two in particular provide a good deal of RAD, namely, AppExpress and ProjectExpress. These little agents (wizards, helpers—whatever you wish to call them without having a lawsuit on your hands), make starting a Java project *so simple* that creating one from scratch will seem like a thing of the past.

The Café agents essentially need to know some basic information about your new project, applet, or application. You provide this information in a series of dialog boxes. When you've supplied all the necessary information (and as we'll see this can be as bare-bones or as substantial as you like), Café goes to work to create a number of files. The generated files can range from Java source code files to miscellaneous Café project and resource files to simple HTML files.

While there is some overlap in the role of ProjectExpress and AppExpress, the goals of the two agents *do* differ. The former can be used to set up a new Café project that can contain older source files while the latter can be used to produce new Java applets, applications, or console applications. The overlap occurs in the role of ProjectExpress. When you are creating a new project using ProjectExpress, you can also specify whether you wish to create either a Java applet or application. As you learn more about the nature of these two agents, you'll be able to best determine which one to use when.

Let's now begin by seeing how to use the agents to build your first Java applet and application. We'll also explore the functionality of AppExpress and ProjectExpress as we proceed through these examples, and we'll even pay some brief visits to Café Studio and Café's Class and Hierarchy Editors.

Jello World!

If you've read enough software books by now, you might have created enough "Hello World" applications to last you a lifetime. Though we are by no means going to break with tradition in this book, we will honor the trend of late to put a "J" before just about *anything* related to Java and call our first program "Jello World."

Building the Applet

We'll use AppExpress to create "Jello World!"

Open the Tools menu and select AppExpress. You'll be presented with the opening screen of AppExpress, pictured in Figure 2.1.

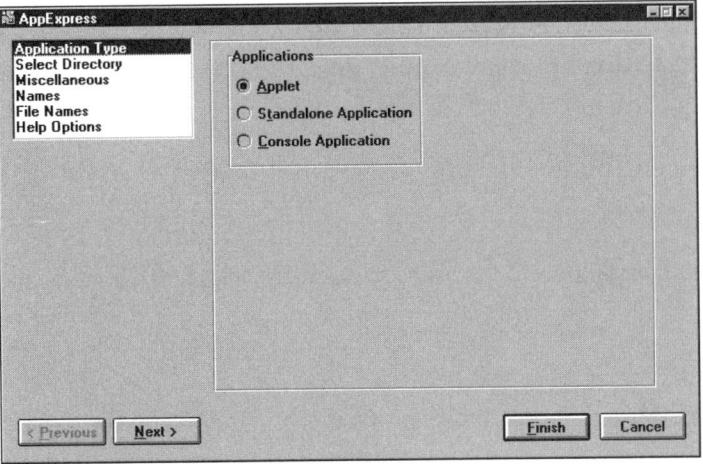

Figure 2.1 **Using AppExpress to create an applet.**

Notice that there are six steps listed in the upper-left-hand pane of AppExpress. These six steps correspond to six dialog boxes contained within AppExpress. You do not have to perform all six steps to finish creating an applet or application. Some of the steps, as you'll see, are optional or simply display some project-related information.

The first step, called Application Type, prompts you to select whether your new project will be an Applet, a standalone application, or a console application. Keep this set on "Applet."

Now, either click on the next step, called "Select Directory," or click the "Next" button on the bottom of the dialog box. Both methods will get you where you want to go.

You're now prompted to supply a directory for your new applet. Choose an empty directory or create a new one by clicking on the button, "Create New Directory..."

Click on the next step, called "Miscellaneous." In this step, the most important item in the dialog box is the Project Name. The names of many of the files in your new project will be based upon the name you supply for your project. For this example, type in "Jello" for the Project Name. Optionally, you can also fill in the company information at the top of the window.

Since the final three steps, called "Names, File Names, and Help Options" are not required for this example, press the "Finish" button on the bottom right of the AppExpress window.

You've now finished the *bulk* of the work needed to create "Jello World!" Are you tired?

The remaining development requires us to take a brief journey into Café's resource editor, *a.k.a.* Café Studio. Café Studio is described in detail in Chapter 11.

From Café's Resource menu select Edit. You're now taken into Café Studio. You'll initially see an almost empty dialog box with the word "Form" appearing in the upper-left-hand window. Click on the word "Form" and you should see an entry called "Jello.init" appear in the pane below it.

Now double-click on "Jello.init." You should see the following screen, pictured in Figure 2.2.

Notice that Café has supplied one single label to describe the applet that it generated for you. Double-click on the label, "A Jello Applet," and you'll see the Properties window come up. In the Caption field of the Properties window, type in "Jello World!"

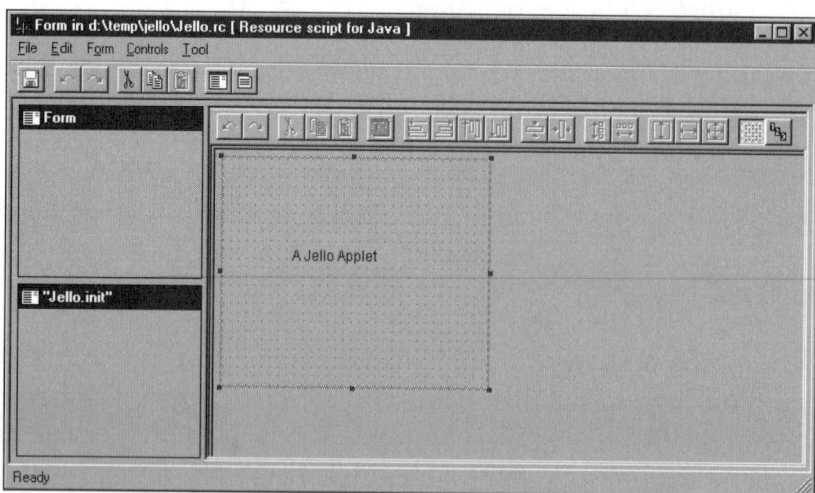

Figure 2.2   The Jello World! applet within Cafe Studio.

You're now ready to save your work and run the applet. From Café Studio's menu select "File | Save." Now go back to Café and from the Project menu select Rebuild All. After a few seconds, the output window should inform you that your build succeeded.

Next, choose "Project | Execute Program." Café starts up AppletViewer and displays a simple window containing the words "Jello World!" You can test that your new applet works in your favorite Java-enabled browser as well.

So that was it. You haven't written a line of code, but you've succeeded in creating your first Java applet!

Studying the Applet Code

Let's now take a quick look at some of the code that AppExpress generated. If you select the Edit tab within the Café IDDE you should see the Project window (if you do not see the Project Window you can bring it up by typing Ctrl-Shift-P or by selecting "Window | Goto View" and choosing Project).

You should see three files in the Project window: Jello.html, Jello.java, and Jello.rc. Double click on the file Jello.java. You'll see the following source, shown in Listing 2.1.

LISTING 2.1 THE JELLO.JAVA SOURCE CODE

```
/*
 This class is a basic extension of the Applet class. It would
 generally be used as the main class with a Java browser or the
 AppletViewer. But an instance can be added to a subclass of
 Container. To use this applet with a browser or the AppletViewer,
 create an html file with the following code:

    <HTML>
    <HEAD>
    <TITLE> A simple program </TITLE>
    </HEAD>
    <BODY>

    <APPLET CODE="Jello.class" WIDTH=332 HEIGHT=169></APPLET>

    </BODY>
```

```
        </HTML>

        You can add controls to Jello with Cafe Studio.
        (Menus can be added only to subclasses of Frame.)
     */

import java.awt.*;
import java.applet.*;

public class Jello extends Applet {

    public void init() {

        super.init();

        //{{INIT_CONTROLS
        setLayout(null);
        resize(229,189);
        label1=new Label("Jello World!");
        add(label1);
        label1.reshape(61,73,98,15);
        //}}
    }

    public boolean handleEvent(Event event) {
        return super.handleEvent(event);
    }

    //{{DECLARE_CONTROLS
    Label label1;
    //}}

}
```

As you can see, Café has created a new class called **Jello** that is a descendent
of an applet. The new class has also been furnished with an **init** method
and a method called **handleEvent**. Part of the **init** method's code was
created after you edited the project's resource file in Café Studio. In fact,
any code that resides between the special comment symbols *//{{* and *//}}*
is managed by Café Studio; so you should not put your *own* custom code
within these lines!

The sample HTML that is provided in the large comment at the top of the
source file is really not needed in this context, since the generated Java.html

file contains all of the HTML needed to make the applet appear and run. The line in the HTML file that is responsible for making this happen is shown here:

```
<APPLET CODE="Jello.class" WIDTH=230 HEIGHT=190></APPLET>
```

Note that when you change the size of your applet in Café Studio, the WIDTH and HEIGHT parameters in the HTML line above also get updated automatically.

Building an Application

Building "Jello World!" as a Java application is about as easy as building the applet version. Let's walk through the steps so you can become comfortable with this process.

From the Tools menu select "AppExpress." This time, select "Standalone Application" as your application type. Next, go to the "Select Directory" screen, which prompts you for a directory for your new application. Select an empty directory or create a new one.

Now select "Miscellaneous" and type in "JelloSDI" for your project name. SDI stands for Single Document Interface, and it is the type of Java application that Café will be generating for you.

Again, once you've finished the first three steps in AppExpress, you can select the "Finish" button to begin the code generation process. Press the "Finish" button now.

This time Café creates a Java source file and a resource file, but does not create an HTML file because you'll be running this application as a standalone program. The files that were generated by Café are called JavaSDI.java and JavaSDI.rc. As you'll see a little later, both of these files come *packed* with information about your new application.

Our task now is to get the "Jello World!" application up and running. We must first make another quick visit to Café Studio. To do this, select "Resource | Edit," and you will again be presented with a nearly empty dialog box, which this time contains the words "Form" and "Menu." In addition to several forms that were generated by Café, a simple menu for your standalone application was also supplied. We'll see this menu in action when we run the application.

For now, click on the word "Form" in the upper-left-hand pane. In the pane below you will see a number of other strings appear, all of which correspond to forms.

Double-click on "JelloSDI.JelloSDI." This will bring up the main form of the application and drop you into editing mode. This time, Café does not provide a dummy label for you. You'll need to create one from scratch.

The way to create a label from scratch is to find the label control on the toolbar (it has a "T" on it), click it once, and then click on an empty spot on your form. Once you've got a new label control on your form, double-click it to bring up the Properties window. As before, change the Caption field of the label to read "Jello World!"

This time, you'll also make the label a bit larger. In the Properties window, click on the tab called "Look." You'll see that you can select the type of font to use and the size of that font. Select "TimesRoman" with a size of 18. Now go back to the form and resize the label so that the text fits within it. Lastly, on the Café Studio toolbar, which is directly above the form, you will find two icons for vertically and horizontally centering components. Click on the label and then click on both of the centering icons, so that "Jello World!" will be centered inside the main window of the application.

You're now finished with your work in Café Studio. Choose "File | Save" to save your resource file and then return back to Café. You'll now want to rebuild your project by selecting "Project | Rebuild All."

Assuming you had no errors, run the application by selecting "Project | Execute Program" (you could also click on the running person icon off the toolbar to run the application). You should see the phrase, "Jello World!" appear right smack in the middle of the application's window. Click on "Help | About" or "File | Exit" to see an example of a window that was created for you by Café. We'll see some of the code for these windows a little later. The "Jello World!" application is shown in Figure 2.3.

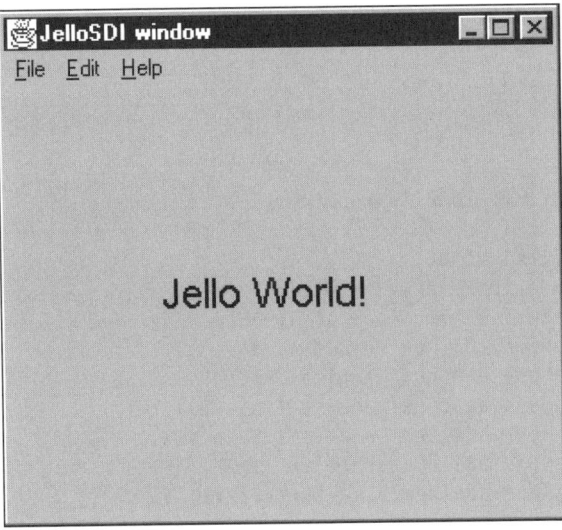

Figure 2.3   The Jello World! standalone application.

Again, with a few mouse clicks and a brief visit to Café Studio, you've created a standalone Java program. The generated resource file includes a default menu and some default forms. The idea is for you to take the skeleton of this default application and flush it out with some of your own real world code and resources.

The generated code is also a place to learn about how to write Java applications. Let's take a look at some of the code that was generated by Café for this project.

Studying the Application Code

You'll find the code listing for JelloSDI.java in Listing 2.2. Study this code for just a little while. When you're done, proceed to the section just after the code listing. There you will find a few techniques that will make your code studying sessions a *lot* more enjoyable.

LISTING 2.2   SOURCE CODE TO JELLOSDI.JAVA

```
/*
    This class is an extension of the Frame class for use as the
    main window of an application.

    You can add controls or menus to JelloSDI with Cafe Studio.
*/
```

```
import java.awt.*;

public class JelloSDI extends Frame {

    public JelloSDI() {

        super("JelloSDI window");

        //{{INIT_MENUS
        MenuBar mb = new MenuBar();
        fileMenu = new Menu("&File");
        fileMenu.add(new MenuItem("&New"));
        fileMenu.add(new MenuItem("&Open..."));
        fileMenu.add(new MenuItem("&Save"));
        fileMenu.add(new MenuItem("Save &As..."));
        fileMenu.addSeparator();
        fileMenu.add(new MenuItem("E&xit"));
        mb.add(fileMenu);
        editMenu = new Menu("&Edit");
        editMenu.add(new MenuItem("&Undo"));
        editMenu.addSeparator();
        editMenu.add(new MenuItem("Cu&t"));
        editMenu.add(new MenuItem("&Copy"));
        editMenu.add(new MenuItem("&Paste"));
        mb.add(editMenu);
        helpMenu = new Menu("&Help");
        helpMenu.add(new MenuItem("&About..."));
        mb.add(helpMenu);
        setMenuBar(mb);
        //}}

        //{{INIT_CONTROLS
        setLayout(null);
        addNotify();
        resize(insets().left + insets().right + 301, insets().top +
          insets().bottom + 250);
        label1=new Label("Jello World!");
        label1.setFont(new Font("TimesRoman",Font.PLAIN,22));
        add(label1);
        label1.reshape(insets().left + 72,insets().top + 99,134,26);
        //}}

        show();
    }

    public synchronized void show() {
      move(50, 50);
      super.show();
    }
```

```java
    public boolean handleEvent(Event event) {

      if (event.id == Event.WINDOW_DESTROY) {
          hide();          // hide the Frame
          dispose();       // tell windowing system to free
                           // resources
          System.exit(0); // exit
          return true;
}
return super.handleEvent(event);
    }

    public boolean action(Event event, Object arg) {
        if (event.target instanceof MenuItem) {
            String label = (String) arg;
            if (label.equalsIgnoreCase("&About...")) {
                selectedAbout();
                return true;
            } else if (label.equalsIgnoreCase("E&xit")) {
                selectedExit();
                return true;
            } else if (label.equalsIgnoreCase("&Open...")) {
                selectedOpen();
                return true;
            }
        }
        return super.action(event, arg);
    }

    public static void main(String args[]) {
        new JelloSDI();
    }

    //{{DECLARE_MENUS
    Menu fileMenu;
    Menu editMenu;
    Menu helpMenu;
    //}}

    //{{DECLARE_CONTROLS
    Label label1;
    //}}

    public void selectedOpen() {
        (new FileDialog(this, "Open...")).show();
    }
    public void selectedExit() {
        QuitBox theQuitBox;
        theQuitBox = new QuitBox(this);
```

```
            theQuitBox.show();
        }
    public void selectedAbout() {
        AboutBox theAboutBox;
        theAboutBox = new AboutBox(this);
        theAboutBox.show();
        }
    }


/*
    This class is a basic extension of the Dialog class.  It can be used
    by subclasses of Frame.  To use it, create a reference to the class,
    then instantiate an object of the class (pass 'this' in the
    constructor), and call the show() method.

        example:

        AboutBox theAboutBox;
        theAboutBox = new AboutBox(this);
        theAboutBox.show();

        You can add controls to AboutBox with Cafe Studio.
        (Menus can be added only to subclasses of Frame.)
    */

class AboutBox extends Dialog {

    public AboutBox(Frame parent) {

        super(parent, "About", true);
        setResizable(false);

//{{INIT_CONTROLS
        setLayout(null);
        addNotify();
        resize(insets().left + insets().right + 288, insets().top +
        insets().bottom + 84);
        label1=new Label("Simple Java SDI Application");
        add(label1);
        label1.reshape(insets().left + 15,insets().top + 18,161,16);
        OKButton=new Button("OK");
        add(OKButton);
        OKButton.reshape(insets().left + 194,insets().top +
        18,73,23);
        //}}
    }

    public synchronized void show() {
```

```
    Rectangle bounds = getParent().bounds();
    Rectangle abounds = bounds();

    move(bounds.x + (bounds.width - abounds.width)/ 2,
            bounds.y + (bounds.height - abounds.height)/2);

    super.show();
  }

  public synchronized void wakeUp() {
    notify();
  }

  public boolean handleEvent(Event event) {
    if (event.id == Event.ACTION_EVENT && event.target == OKButton)
{
      clickedOKButton();
      return true;
  }
else

if (event.id == Event.WINDOW_DESTROY) {
    hide();
    return true;
}
return super.handleEvent(event);
  }

  //{{DECLARE_CONTROLS
  Label label1;
  Button OKButton;
  //}}

  public void clickedOKButton() {
      handleEvent(new Event(this, Event.WINDOW_DESTROY, null));
  }
}


/*
    This class is a basic extension of the Dialog class.  It can be
used by subclasses of Frame.  To use it, create a reference to the
class, then instantiate an object of the class (pass 'this' in the
constructor), and call the show() method.

    example:

    QuitBox theQuitBox;
    theQuitBox = new QuitBox(this);
    theQuitBox.show();
```

```
     You can add controls, but not menus, to QuitBox with Cafe Studio.
     (Menus can be added only to subclasses of Frame.)
  */

class QuitBox extends Dialog {

    public QuitBox(Frame parent) {

      super(parent, "Quit Application?", true);
    setResizable(false);

 //{{INIT_CONTROLS
        setLayout(null);
        addNotify();
        resize(insets().left + insets().right + 257, insets().top +
          insets().bottom + 66);
        yesButton=new Button("Yes");
        add(yesButton);
        yesButton.reshape(insets().left + 68,insets().top +
          10,46,23);
        noButton=new Button("No");
        add(noButton);
        noButton.reshape(insets().left + 135,insets().top +
          10,47,23);
        //}}
    }

    public synchronized void show() {
      Rectangle bounds = getParent().bounds();
      Rectangle abounds = bounds();

      move(bounds.x + (bounds.width - abounds.width)/ 2,
            bounds.y + (bounds.height - abounds.height)/2);

super.show();
    }

    public synchronized void wakeUp() {
      notify();
    }

    public boolean handleEvent(Event event) {
      if (event.id == Event.ACTION_EVENT && event.target == noButton)
{
        clickedNoButton();
        return true;
}
    else
```

```
if (event.id == Event.ACTION_EVENT && event.target == yesButton) {
    clickedYesButton();
    return true;
}
else

if (event.id == Event.WINDOW_DESTROY) {
    hide();
    return true;
}
return super.handleEvent(event);
    }

    //{{DECLARE_CONTROLS
    Button yesButton;
    Button noButton;
    //}}

    public void clickedYesButton() {
        System.exit(0);
    }
    public void clickedNoButton() {
        handleEvent(new Event(this, Event.WINDOW_DESTROY, null));
    }
}
```

One of the best ways to study code in Café is to use the Class and Hierarchy Editors. Though we will look at the functionality of these utilities in detail in the next chapter, we can use them now to learn more about the code from JelloSDI.java.

Click on the "Browsing" tab within the Café IDDE to see the Class Editor. (You can also bring up the Class Editor by selecting "Window | Goto View | Class Editor".) Café's Class Editor shows you all of the classes within your project as well as the methods and data (i.e., variables) for each class. The classes from JelloSDI.java are shown in Figure 2.4.

If you click on "JelloSDI" in the classes pane of the Class Editor, you will see the methods and data for the JelloSDI class. Try clicking on some of the methods and variables; you will see code appear in the source code pane as you click on the various members of the JelloSDI class. In the constructor call to JelloSDI.java, you will see how the application's menu is constructed.

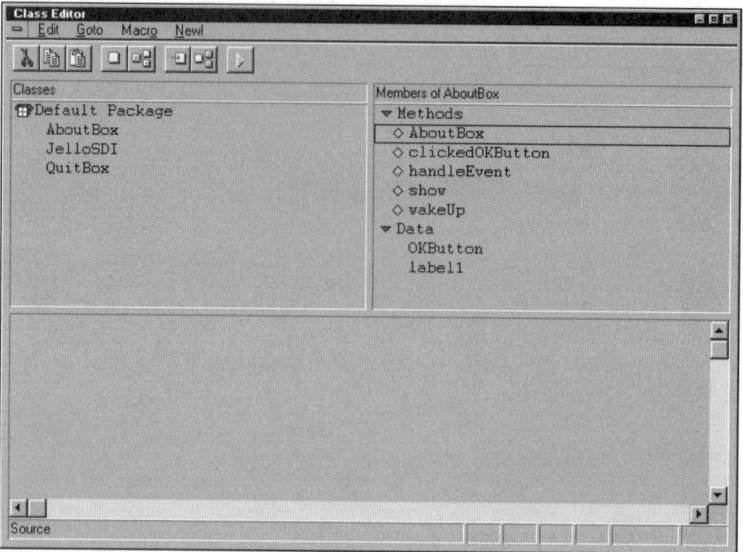

Figure 2.4   Class Editor showing classes from JelloSDI.java.

You might also have noticed the two classes, AboutBox and QuitBox in Class Editor's classes pane. These classes correspond to the "File | Quit" and "Help | About" dialog boxes that you might have visited earlier when you ran your application.

If you click on the **handleEvent**() method for classes **AboutBox** and **QuitBox**, you will see that Café has provided a substantial amount of code. You can learn a good deal from this generated code if you are new to Java or unsure about how the Abstract Window Toolkit (AWT) works.

Some project information that you will *not* be able to see in Class Editor about the classes that are the ancestors to **JelloSDI**, **AboutBox**, and **QuitBox**. You'll need to use the Hierarchy Editor to see this information.

Café's Hierarchy Editor is also a good tool for getting a high-level view of a project. Select "Window | Goto View | Hierarchy Editor" to bring up this utility. You should see your three classes showing, which are also pictured in Figure 2.5.

At this point you have still not seen the ancestors of these classes. To see that information, you'll need to change a setting on this project.

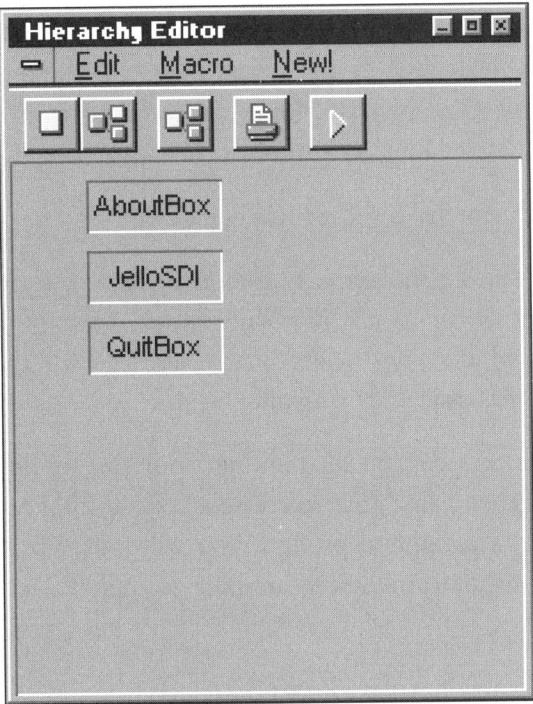

Figure 2.5   Hierarchy Editor showing classes from JelloSDI.java.

From the Project menu select Settings. Under the tab called "Target," there is a checkbox that says "Parse System Files." Click on this checkbox to turn on this feature. What you have just done is tell Café that you would like to have all the system files parsed so that you can see them in the navigation windows of Class Editor and Hierarchy Editor.

The next step is to go to the Project window. To do this, use the "Window | Goto View" menu and select "Project." There is a menu option in the Project window called "Parse." From the Parse menu select "Parse All." After a few moments of work, all of the system files will have been parsed. Next, return to the Hierarchy Editor.

You should now see many more classes in the Hierarchy Editor. Type the name "AboutBox" anywhere within the Hierarchy Editor window. You'll see that as you type, the Hierarchy Editor figures out where the class is that you are looking for. As you can see, the AboutBox is a descendent of

java.awt.Dialog. Now type in the name of the main class, "JelloSDI." The software will quickly find your class and show you that it is a descendent of **java.awt.Frame**. One of fastest and best ways to learn more about the contents of any large hierarchy of objects is to use the Hierarchy Editor.

The updated hierarchy is shown in Figure 2.6.

If you ever wish to remove the system files from your project, simply go back to Project settings, click off the option to "Parse System Files," return to the Project window, and select "Parse All." You will then see only your original three classes in the Hierarchy Editor.

That concludes our section on building your first applet and standalone application. You will find that to create a console application, or program that runs from a command prompt, you will follow practically the same directions as you did to create either an applet or application using AppExpress.

But what about ProjectExpress? We've seen very little of this utility so far. The next section will explain ProjectExpress.

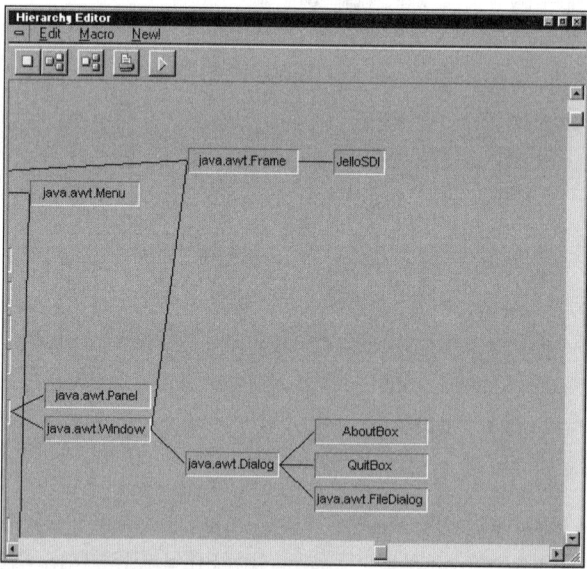

Figure 2.6   Hierarchy Editor showing JavaSDI classes and system classes.

ProjectExpress

As it was pointed out toward the beginning of this chapter, ProjectExpress is a tool for creating projects in Café. Although AppExpress also creates projects, the projects created by AppExpress always involve the creation of new source files. With ProjectExpress, typically you already have a source code file (or files) that you would like to bring in to a new Café project.

The source file could be an applet or application that you wrote or that someone else wrote. It could be a simple Java class defined in a file as well. To see the code in the Café environment, you'll need to add it to a Café project or create a new Café project. Without creating such a project, you can view source code files in Café's editor, but you will not be able to use the handy utilities of Café's Class or Hierarchy Editors. In addition, without having a Café project created, Café cannot automatically build all of the files in your project.

You are also not limited to adding just Java source code to your Café projects; ProjectExpress lets you add HTML files, project files (yes, you can have projects within projects, but we will cover that in the next chapter) as well as batch and resource files.

The ProjectExpress utility is very easy to use. Just like AppExpress, you navigate through a series of steps until you've completed enough of them to create your project.

We'll begin by writing a simple Java program that we will then integrate into a Café project using ProjectExpress.

Simple.java

The first step is to create a new directory for your work. Create one (using Windows Explorer or whatever method you prefer) called "simple" anywhere you like. I've created one in a directory called d:\temp\simple.

The second step is to create a source file named simple.java. At this point you should close all projects in Café (select "Project | Close" if you happen to have one open) and from Café's File menu select "New." You will be placed inside a fresh source code window.

Type in the following code, shown in Listing 2.3.

LISTING 2.3   SOURCE CODE TO SIMPLE.JAVA

```
// simple.java

class simple
{
  public static void main(String[] args)
  {
    System.out.println("It doesn't get simpler than this.");
  }
}
```

When you've finished typing this code, save the file under the name "simple.java" in the directory called "simple," which you created for this project.

Creating the Cafe Project

You're now ready to create a new Café project. From Café's Project menu select "New." You'll be presented with the first screen of ProjectExpress, pictured in Figure 2.7.

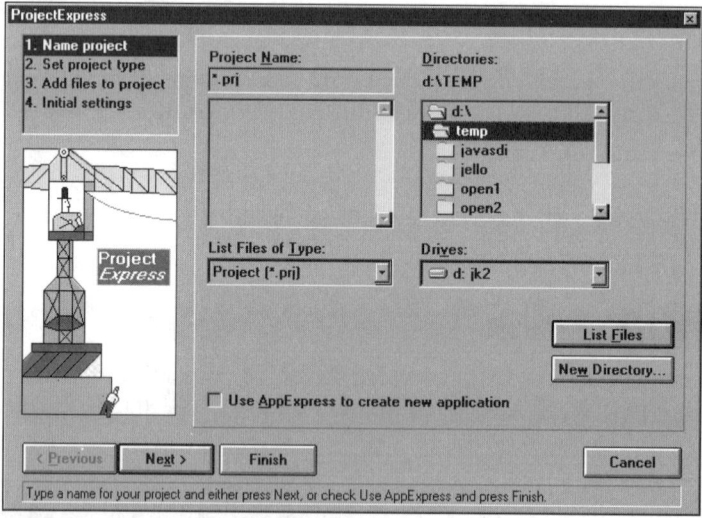

Figure 2.7   The first screen of ProjectExpress.

As you can see, ProjectExpress contains four steps. Just like AppExpress, you can click on any one of the four steps to navigate between them or just use the Next and Previous buttons to move between screens. Of the four steps, only the first one is actually required. Steps two, three, and four can be performed at any time using the "Project | Settings" dialog box.

For step one, select your newly created directory called "simple" and type in the name "simple.prj" for the Project Name.

You should take a moment to understand the checkbox at the bottom of this first screen. This checkbox, labeled "Use AppExpress to create new application," provides another way to invoke the AppExpress utility. If you click on this checkbox and then press the button "Finish," you will no longer be using ProjectExpress but will have switched over to using AppExpress. Don't do this now; we have more to learn about ProjectExpress.

Once you've finished setting your project name and selecting the directory called "simple," you're ready to move on to step two.

In this step you'll be setting various options for your project. As I mentioned above, you can either do this now or later; the screen you see in ProjectExpress corresponds exactly to the screen you'll find in "Project | Settings" under the tab called "Target." We'll set these values now.

For the "target type," select "application." For "Main Class," type in "simple" and leave all other controls with their default values. You're now ready to move on to step 3.

Now you'll tell ProjectExpress what files to include in your new project. Select the directory called "simple" and you should see the java source file, named "simple.java," that you created earlier. Double-click that file and you should see it get added to the "Project Files" list in the bottom part of the dialog box.

You've now completed all of the steps required to create a Café project. Since the fourth step merely prompts you for some optional information, you can bypass it altogether. Click on the "Finish" button now to let Café begin generating the various project files.

Building and Running the Application

You must now build your project in order to run the simple.java application. To do so, from the Project menu select Rebuild All. When the project is built, you'll need to run it from a command prompt (you can run it from Café, but the output message will flash by too quickly to be seen). To run your new application, open up a command prompt window, change to the directory where you created the project, and type:

```
java simple
```

You should see the message, "It doesn't get simpler than this." appear on the screen. And that's all there is to it! Simple enough?

We'll now look over just a few details of AppExpress and ProjectExpress, which we touched on earlier.

Some Details

As we've seen in both agents, certain steps can be skipped when creating new projects, applications, or applets. There are also a few things to watch out for when you are using these utilities. Let's now look at some of these details.

Class Path and Directories to Exclude

In ProjectExpress, the last step in the four-part project creation task is called "Initial Settings." This step prompts you to input a Class Path and something called "Browser Exclude Directories." In most situations, you'll not need to enter values for these two fields. But it you *do,* they are defined as follows:

Class Path: In Version 1.0 of Café, there is an environment variable called CLASSPATH, which Café uses to find classes. In Prerelease 1.2, Café writes and maintains this file in an .ini file (called sc.ini) so that it cannot easily be changed by other programs. You can add directory names to the Class Path, separating them with semicolons. The environment variable or sc.ini value, CLASSPATH, will be ignored if you supply a value for this field. Typically, you should have no reason to set this value if your CLASSPATH variable has been installed correctly.

Browser Exclude Directories: This option has a confusing name, but actually informs the Café parser of which directories to ignore.

Note that both Class Path and Browser Exclude Directories can be set from the Project Settings dialog box, under the tab "Directories."

Two Projects in the Same Directory

One limitation of Café as of Release 1.0 (as well as Prerelease 1.2), is the inability to have more than one project within the same directory. Although this is not an earth-shattering problem, it is something to be aware of, since it can cause some problems to an original project if a new project is created within the same directory.

For example, if you are working on an important project and happen to decide to create a quick test project in the same directory, your resource and resource constant files (having the extentions .rc and .k, respectively) from your original project will be overwritten by your new test project. The .rc file is especially important since it holds all of your user interface related information. So the general rule is to create a separate directory for every new Café project you create.

Adding Files from Other Directories

When you work with source code files and projects in Café, you might decide to add a source file to a project that happens to be in a *different* directory from that of your *current* project. While this makes sense and does work for other environments (like MSVC, for instance), it will *not* work under the current version of Café.

Let me clarify. You *can* work with Java packages that are in different directories provided that the Café environment is able to find these packages via the CLASSPATH variable. But you *cannot* do the same with simple source files containing Java classes that are not in packages.

This is consistent with the compiling behavior of the JDK. It is, however, a bit counterintuitive to those who have worked with some of the C++ IDEs. Your best bet for the moment will be to place all of your .java (nonpackage) files in the same directory as your project.

AppExpress Naming

The final three steps in AppExpress are called "Names, File Names and Help Options." You might remember that we skipped over these steps when creating your first Java app earlier in this chapter.

As of Release 1.0 and Prerelease 1.2, these three screens display only information about the file names that AppExpress will be generating for your new Café project. In later releases you might be able to influence the naming of these files.

Conclusion

Café not only offers an environment that is easy to work in, but also provides you with "express" agents to speed up your Java development efforts. Whether you're creating your first applet, or building a large project from a number of source files and packages, AppExpress and ProjectExpress are handy tools that can improve your productivity by automating frequently performed tasks.

Using Café to the Max!

Joshua Kerievsky

3

A simple text file, filled with Java source code, becomes a whole different animal inside Symantec Café. In this chapter, you'll learn how the Café development environment is optimized for the visual, object-oriented architect, how to configure and manage your Java projects, how to visually design and navigate the JDK and your own object hierarchies, and some secrets that will have you producing and managing Java code faster than you might have thought possible.

When the early betas of Java were first released by Sun, development environments for Java did not exist. If you wanted to work with Java, you needed to write source code in your editor of choice and compile your code from a command line. If you used a more sophisticated programmer's editor, you might have simulated a sort of crude development environment by configuring your editor to support the Java language and the Java compiler. Still, before a truly integrated development environment was commercially released, Java development consisted of writing your own code in a source window, performing multi-file searches to track down JDK classes and methods, compiling your code using the relatively slow Java compiler, and testing your work by writing or re-editing HTML files for viewing within AppletViewer or your Web browser.

The release of Symantec Café changed all of that. Café's IDDE, or Integrated Development and Debugging Environment, elevated Java development to the standards to which many programmers have now become accustomed. This standard is that of a visual development environment; a place to design, develop, debug, and document small or large projects.

As you'll see in this chapter, Café contains many different ways to accomplish development tasks. The product contains a rich array of graphical tools that are integrated with each other to facilitate rapid development. In addition, because these tools are so visual in nature, navigating and understanding other people's code—like the JDK itself—becomes a whole lot faster and easier. And if you've had experience doing some of this navigation by performing endless searches across files, you will quickly see how much more efficient you can become using Café.

In the previous chapters you've had a brief tour of Café Studio and have learned some of the basics of using the Café environment. Let's now get a more advanced view of Café and see how you can use it to gain control over your applet and application development.

The Café Desktop

The Café desktop is based on the idea of a main floating window at the top of the screen (much like that found in Visual Basic or Delphi) and various screens that you can show or hide based upon the context that you are in. The main window contains convenient "tabs" for switching between Editing, Browsing, Debugging, and Output. There are also three separate toolbars for controlling project builds, debugging, and window viewing.

One of the nicest features of the Café Desktop is that it is very customizable, as we'll see shortly.

Customizing Café

A feature that you might find quite useful is the ability to save and manage custom arrangements of windows in Café. Under the "Environment | Workspace" menu item, you can create and name a new workspace, delete one, clone one, or even rename one. Before we go through the steps of creating your own workspaces, let's first see how the "Save Workspace Set" option works. In Figure 3.1 you can see a customized workspace that was created using the "Workspace | Save Workspace Set" option in Café's Workspace menu.

Creation of this workspace simply involved selecting the appropriate tab for the work: In this case, it was Café's Editing tab. Next, the windows that were needed for the workspace were opened by clicking on the appropriate icons on the toolbar (this could also be done from the main menu's Window | Goto View option). The windows were then resized and moved to occupy different areas of the screen. And finally, when everything looked good, the workspace was saved by going to the Environment menu, selecting Workspace, and within the Workspace submenu selecting "Save Workspace Set."

The new saved workspace will now always look this way whenever you are in the Editing tab for *any* project. If you do not want this layout to be used for *all* projects, you can create your own tabs to appear alongside the four existing tabs, for Editing, Browsing, Debugging, and Output. These new

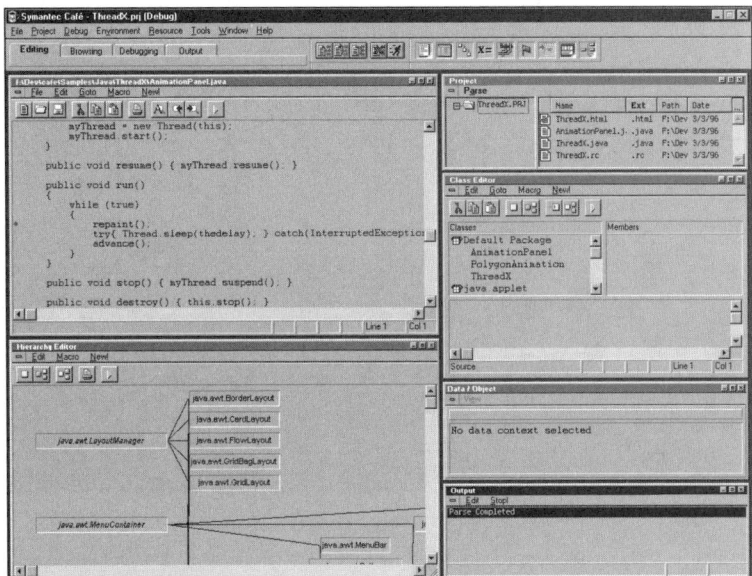

Figure 3.1   A customized setup of Café using "Environment | Workspace | Save Workspace Set".

tabs can be named whatever you like and display whatever Café windows you like. You'll learn how to create such workspaces next.

If you repeatedly open up certain windows, such as Café's Class Editor and Hierarchy Editor, and then close these windows to see your other windows, you might find that it is much more convenient to create a custom tab for the type of work you're doing. Custom tabs are created using the Workspace menu under the Environment main menu choice.

Let's now go ahead and create a new tab for our version of Café that will feature the Class Editor, Hierarchy Editor, and Project Window all in one view. We'll call the new tab "SkyView," since it will feature windows that give us an overview of a project.

To create the new tab, we select "Environment | Workspace | New..." and type in the name of our new tab. As you can see in Figure 3.2, we now only have four tabs.

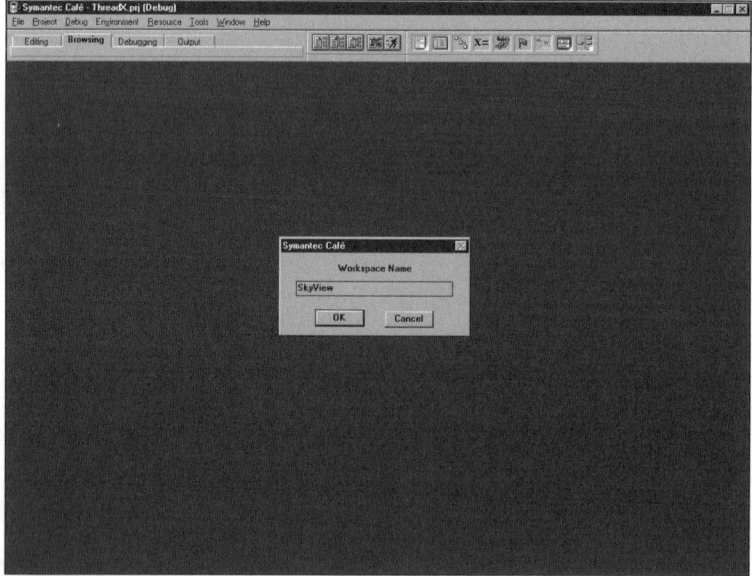

Figure 3.2   Creating a custom tab in Café.

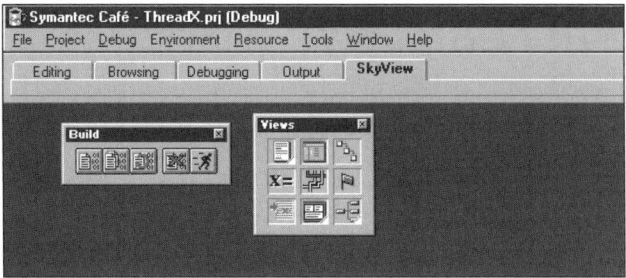

Figure 3.3   A new tab for a new workspace.

Once we've entered a name for our new workspace, a fifth, new tab will appear next to the other tabs as shown above in Figure 3.3.

The toolbars for the new SkyView workspace are initially within their own windows. You can drag them up and "dock" them beside the tabs, as they appear in the other workspaces. Next, you'll want to open up the three windows that this SkyView will support, which are Café's Class Editor, Hierarchy Editor, and Project Window. Once you've positioned and resized these windows to meet your needs, you can save the workspace by selecting "Save Workspace Set" from the Workspace menu.

You can later choose to rename the tab from "SkyView" something else. This can be done by selecting "Rename" from the Workspace menu. In addition, as was mentioned earlier, you can clone tabs or delete ones that you no longer use.

That concludes our discussion of customizing the Café development environment. You will find other ways to customize Café in the sections that follow.

The Programmer's Editor

If you've ever used a professional programmer's editor, you've certainly come to expect a lot from editors in general. Features like color syntax highlighting, delimiter matching, and control over key mapping have become common even in the editors that come with integrated development environments. Café's editor is no exception to this trend. As you'll see, the editor even contains some features that you might not find in today's standalone editors.

General Features

Like other good graphical editors, the Café editor supports a host of features that let you define the character of the editor. The following features are summarized:

◆ Undo and Redo: If you make mistakes, you can easily "undo" them, and if you undo too much you can quickly "redo" what you "undid." You can also control the number of "undo" operations that will be remembered by setting this value under "Edit | Text Settings…" within the "General" tab.

◆ Color syntax highlighting: This supports "custom" colors for Comments, Keywords and Custom Keywords, the Current Line, Preprocessor, and Error lines. You can select and configure color syntax support within the "Display" tab of the "Edit | Text Settings…" dialog box.

◆ Column and Line highlighting: By right-clicking within the source code editor and then selecting "Select," you can choose to toggle between highlighting lines of code or columns. Column highlighting can be quite useful if you have to copy a considerable amount text that occupies a column (like a series of numbers) to another area in your project.

◆ Automatic backup: This supports automatic saving of source code after a designated number of minutes or changes to a file. The product also lets you creates backups to .BAK files when you save your work and can even back up an entire project after a save. You'll find these features under the "Backup" tab of the "Edit | Text Settings…" dialog box.

◆ Keyboard emulation settings: You can choose to use "Brief-Compatible" text selection, control whether typing on highlighted text replaces or does not replace the highlighted text, enable or diable Menu accelerators, and so forth. The "Text" tab in the "Edit | Text Settings…" dialog box is where you'll control these features.

◆ Keyboard Mappings: Under the "Key" tab of the "Edit | Text Settings…" dialog box, you can make changes to the way keys are mapped to editor functions, create your own custom mappings, or choose from mappings like those found in the Microsoft Visual C++ environment, the Emacs editor, or the standard Norton editor.

◆ Buffer Settings: Under the "Buffer" tab of the "Edit | Text Settings..." dialog box, you can control how comments are aligned, whether or not autoindenting is on, whether or not to expand tabs with spaces, word-wrapping, and a host of other controls.

Searching

You can initiate searches from the "Edit" menu or from the source code window toolbar. The standard search dialog box allows you to ignore case and search for whole words only and supports regular expressions. You can perform repeat searches and initiate a replace from the "Edit" menu.

If you want to find some text across multiple files, you'll need to use the Global Find utility. You can select it from the "Edit" menu. The Global Find utility lets you search for text within all the files of your current project or within a criteria that you specify. You can even specify which files should be ignored in a multi-file search based on their date and/or time stamp.

Global Search and Replace

In Version 1.0 of Café, there is no support for a global search and replace. This feature has not been added to any of the updates to Café; however, customers on the newsgroup comp.lang.java have requested this type of replace capability and Symantec has added it to its list of requested features.

Finding Methods Fast

Although using the searching feature of the editor is a perfectly fine way to look for particular methods within your classes, there is an alternative that you might find is a little faster. When searching for methods in your code, the editor's GOTO facility can't be beat. If you often find yourself paging up and down and looking all around for methods within your code, you might find it easier simply to look at nice, short list of methods. By selecting "Goto | Function," you will be presented with a list of all methods (I use the word "method" to refer to functions within objects and functions to refer to functions that stand alone, and are not part of objects) within all of the classes in your current source file. This can be a great way to navigate large files that might contain Java packages or even small files with objects that have a large number of methods. Figure 3.4 shows the Goto Function list for the source file in the ThreadX project.

The Goto command also supports going to lines and bookmarks. From the Goto menu you can also access the Buffer window (pictured in Figure 3.5), which gives you control over a number of aspects of your editing windows.

From the Buffer window you can get a bird's eye view of *all* the source code you might be editing. All source code means not only the source code in the editor windows but also the bits of code you might be editing in the Class Editor source pane. The Context field lets you select either File Buffers or Member Buffers to switch between code in source code windows and code in the Class Editor.

In addition to letting you set Buffer properties, from the Buffer window you can also open new files, save all or particular files, close all or particular files, and initiate searches.

Navigating Errors

While you write code and run it through the Café compiler, you might find that you "rack up" more than one error. In Café's Output window you

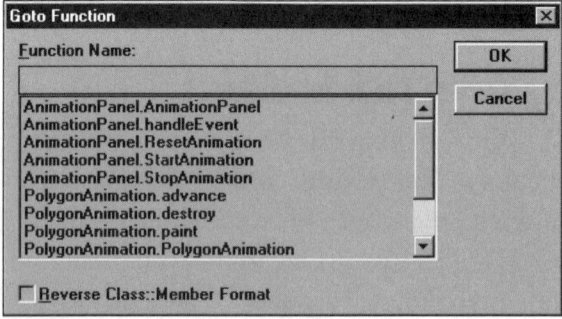

Figure 3.4   The Goto Function window.

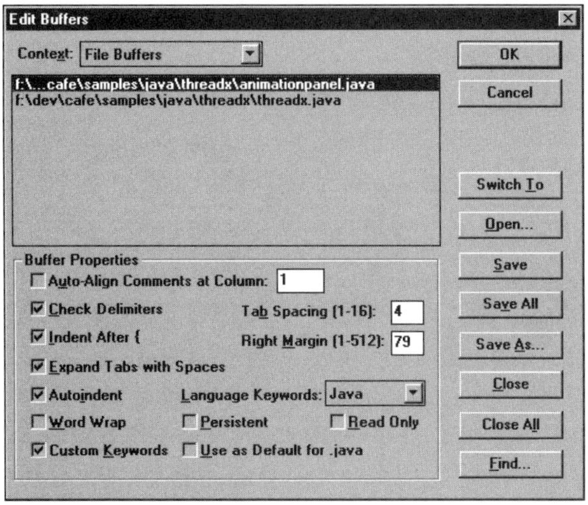

Figure 3.5   The Edit Buffers window.

will see a list of all the errors and warnings found in your code. By double-clicking on any of the errors or warnings you will be taken to the place in the source code where the offensive line resides.

You can go back and forth between the Output window and your source code windows to find and fix your error. But the Café editor also supplies a neat way of navigating error messages.

Although it does not appear as an option off the editor window, to navigate between your First, Next, Previous, and Current errors, right-click within a source code window and choose "Goto." You will be presented with a submenu that will let you select how you wish to navigate your error messages. This can be a more efficient way of finding error than always using the Output window.

Formatting Text

Another "buried" feature of the text editor is a menu that only appears off the the right-click menu and lets you format text.

Within any source code window, right-click and choose "Format Text." You will be given options to do the following tasks as shown in Table 3.1.

Table 3.1   Text Formatting functions.

Function	Note/Description
Indent Block	Will only be enabled when you've highlighed a block in the editor.
UnIndent Block	Will only be enabled when you've highlighed a block in the editor.
Upper Case	Converts to upper case whatever is highlighted.
Lower Case	Converts to lower case whatever is highlighted.
Tabs to Spaces	Converts your tabs to spaces. This feature can be automatically controlled via the Buffer window.
Spaces to Tabs	Convert your spaces to tabs. This feature can be automatically controlled via the Buffer window.

Macros

Using macros means saving time. Using macros in Café is *so* simple that if you do not use them, you will certainly be less productive than you could be. One of the nicest things about using macros in Café is that you do not have to learn the macro language in order to use them. As you'll see, macros can simply be recoded and played whenever you like. And should you choose to learn the macro language, you will be working with the very simple Symantec Basic, a language that closely resembles Microsoft's Visual Basic.

You'll find the "Macro" menu entry in many of the "tool windows" in Café, including the source code editor, Class Editor, and Hierarchy Editor. From the Macro menu, you can record a macro, play the default macro, edit and copy macros using Café's ScriptMaker, and select one of your custom macros to play.

To get familiar with Café's Macros, let's begin by learning about ScriptMaker. You will be using the default macro and ScriptMaker to create your own macros. ScriptMaker is pictured in Figure 3.6.

As you can see under "Existing Macros" in Figure 3.6, <Default> is the first and only entry in the list of existing macros. If you select <Default> and

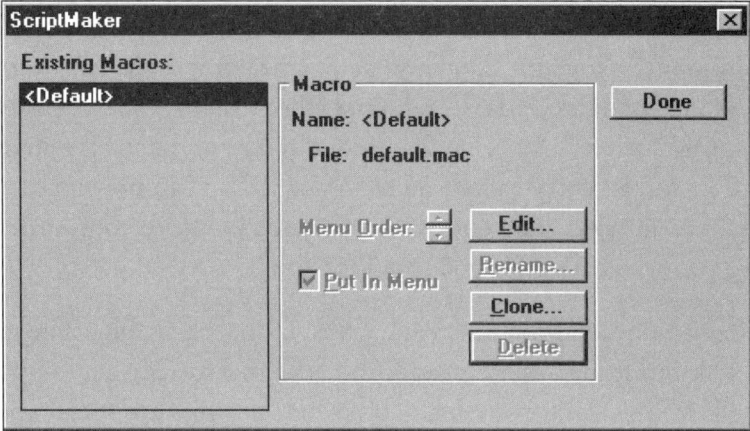

Figure 3.6   A typical help window for a Java API method.

then press the "Edit" button, you'll see the code for this macro, which initially looks like this:

```
sub main()
end sub
```

To create your own macros, you will record over the default macro and then clone the default macro in ScriptMaker to create a new macro with an appropriate name. Let's do that now to create a macro called "quickUpdate."

The quickUpdate macro will create an implementation for an **update**() method that will simply call a **paint**() method. (Such a method is typically used in Java to cut down on screen flicker.) In a source code editor window, find an open area of text, select "Macro | Record Macro," answer "OK" when you are prompted to record over the default macro, and type the following code:

```
public void update(Graphics g)
{
    paint(g);
}
```

When you are finished, select "Macro | Stop Recording" and then select "Macro | ScriptMaker." Inside ScriptMaker, you should select the default

macro and press the "Clone" button. This will bring up a dialog box that will prompt you to name the new macro and supply a file name for it. Call the new macro "quickUpdate" and supply the file name "quickUpdate.mac." Click "OK," select "Done," and you should now see as the last item in the Macro menu, an entry called "quickUpdate." You can now go to another empty area in your code and select the "quickUpdate" option from the Macro menu to have code generated for you.

Using this technique you can create a host of macros to automate much of your text-inputting tasks. In addition, the macro language is powerful enough to let you automate many tasks in Café. To learn more, check out the section called "Automating Tasks with the Symantec Basic Macro Editor" in the online help.

Integrated Help

For many early users of Java, especially Windows and Mac users, the lack of hypertext help resources for the Java language and API led to many hours of frustrating searches through the documentation that came with the JDK as well as many code "surfing" sessions.

Adding well-indexed hypertext Java API and Java Language references to Café made life a lot easier for developers. But the creators of Café went one step further by integrating their help resources with the Café editor windows. This means that inside both the buffer (or source code) editor as well as the source editor in Café's Class Editor, you can highlight a word or method name that you are not familiar with and press F1, and Café will search its help topics and display the results. This might be the fastest way to get up to speed on the many API methods available in Java.

Figure 3.7 shows the result after highlighting the word "handleEvent" and pressing F1.

In addition to API and Java language help, Café also provides a very useful discussion of some Java fundamentals in *Intro to Java Programming*, which can be found under the main Café Help menu.

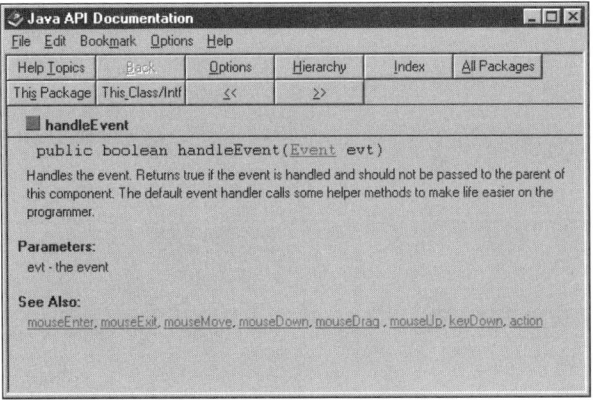

Figure 3.7   A typical help window for a Java API method.

The Class Editor

Complex classes can often contain dozens of methods and variables that might be public, private, protected, or private-protected. When you want to study such code, it often helps to work with tools that were designed to make object-oriented code easier to follow. The Café Class Editor is just such a tool.

The Class Editor can be started from Café's toolbar, or you can typically find it under the Café workspace tab called "Browsing." It is a three-paned window that shows classes in the upper-left pane, members of these classes in the upper-right pane (member are methods and variables), and source code for members in the lower pane. The Class Editor supports "undo," so if you make a mistake, don't worry too much.

Figure 3.8 shows the Class Editor with some code from the sample project, ThreadX.

In each of Class Editor's three panes, you will find that there is a popup menu (accessed by right-clicking), which allows you to do some very powerful things. Let's look at the capabilities of each of these popup menus.

Class Menu

By right-clicking within the "Class" pane of the Class Editor, you will see a popup menu that will let you manipulate classes in one of the following ways shown in Table 3.2.

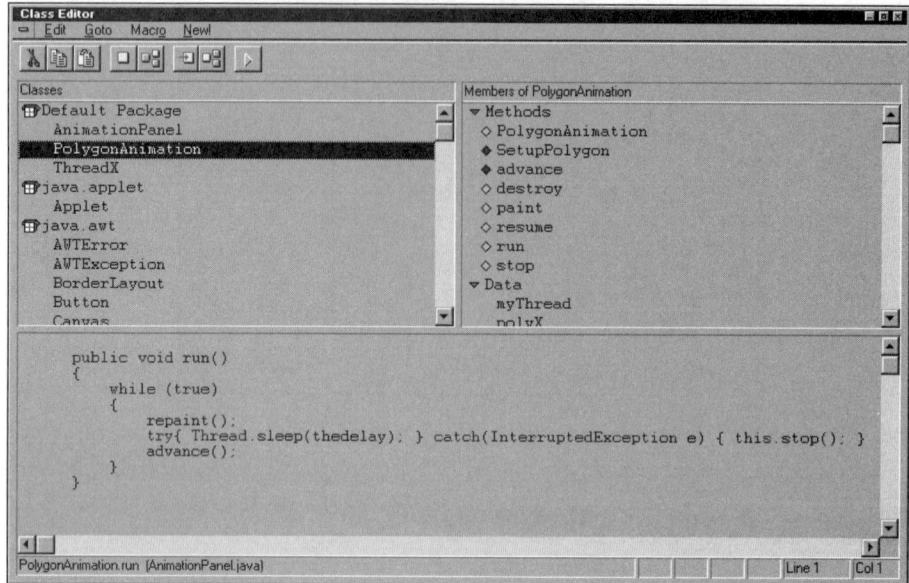

Figure 3.8   Café's Class Editor.

From the Class pane of the Class Editor you can also drag class names to your source code windows.

Members Menu

By right-clicking within the "Members" pane of the Class Editor, you will see a popup menu that will let you work with members in one of the following ways as shown in Table 3.3.

Note that by double-clicking any of the elements in the Members pane, you will be shown the source code for that member in the lower pane. You can then edit the code for that member in the source code pane.

Source Code Menu

The source code pane, or the lower pane, is where you see and can edit little snippits of code from your project. The editor in this pane is the same one you are used to using from the source code editor windows.

The source code popup menu allows you to copy, cut, paste, and delete text, navigate errors, select columns or lines of text, format text, and set breakpoints.

To search for text, use the main menu of the Class Editor.

Table 3.2 Options off the popup menu in the Class pane of Class Editor.

Function	Note/Description
Add Derived	Create a new class that extends the currently selected class. There is an icon on the toolbar to do this as well. You will be prompted in a dialog box to supply a new class name. As you type the name of the new class, the name of a source file containing the new class will be created for you.
Add Top	This will let you create a class that does not extend from any other class, sometimes called a base class. There is also an icon on the toolbar to perform this task and you'll be presented with the same dialog box as that from the Add Derived function.
Add Sibling	A sibling is a class that is at the same level on the hierarchy as the selected class; it extends from the same super class. This feature was not enabled in version 1.0 of Café but will be available in version 1.1
Go to Source	Brings up a new source code window containing the class that was selected.
Connect Base	Brings up a dialog box listing all classes that the currently selected class could become a descendent of.
Edit Base Attributes	Not available in version 1.0 of Café, this option lets you control access rights to a base class and will be available in version 1.1 of Café.
Delete Base Connection	Enabled when the connection between a base and derived class is highlighed (usually within the Hierarchy Editor), this option will delete the connection and bring the derived class to the top so that it does not extend from another class.
Settings	Choosing this option will bring up the "Class" tab in the browser settings dialog box and let you control how classes are listed. You can choose to have classes listed alphabetically, hierarchically or by package, which is the default.

Table 3.3   Options off the popup menu in the Members pane of Class Editor.

Function	Note/Description
Add	Lets you add a new member variable or method with your choice of access rights to the current class. See Figure 3.9 to see what this window looks like. Can also be invoked by pressing the INSERT key as well.
Delete	Lets you delete a member variable or method. This can be invoked by using the DELETE key.
Edit Attributes	Lets you change the access rights (public, private, protected, etc) for a given member variable or method.
Go to Source	Takes you to a source window and positions you on the current member variable or method.
Settings	The settings option takes you to the "Member" tab in the browser settings dialog box so that you can configure how members are grouped and sorted.

Searching For Classes, Methods or Variables

One of the slickest features of the Class Editor is the ability to easily find classes, methods, or variables in a hurry. This feature is one of the few that you will *not* find in the Class Editor menu or in any of the popup menus.

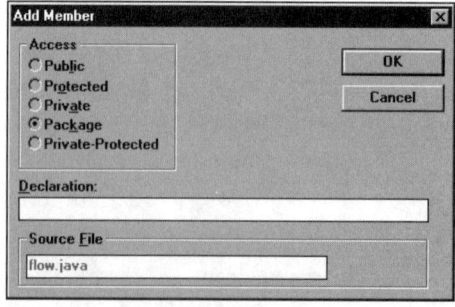

Figure 3.9   Configuring class member variables and methods.

Nevertheless, the search feature is powerful and might become one of your favorite features of the Class Editor.

The search feature is simple to use. To search for a class, click on the upper-left hand pane and then type the name of the class. The incremental search engine will take you to the class as you type its name!

To search for methods or variable, click on the upper-right hand pane and start typing. That's all there is to it.

Hierarchy Editor Connection

As you will soon learn, when you start using the Hierarchy editor you will be able to double-click on a class and be transferred directly to the Class Editor, whereupon you will be positioned on the same class you double-clicked on in the Hierachy editor. Using the two editors to visually navigate a project's classes can be a good way to understand a new project.

Café Studio Connection

As you will see in the chapter on using Café Studio, there is also a connection between the Class Editor and Café Studio. When you are designing your screens you will often specify the events to which components respond. When doing so, you can choose to edit code, and when you do, you will be dropped into the Class Editor and positioned on the appropriate event handler in the source code pane.

A Known Class Editor Problem

In Release 1.0 of Café, if you delete a member variable or method by removing the member's code in the source pane, this will cause an unexpected-end-of-file warning. Members should be deleted by right-clicking on the member name and selecting Delete, or by selecting the member to highlight it and pressing the Delete key. (Class Editor prompts for confirmation if Confirm Member Delete is set—this is the default—in the Editing/Browsing Settings dialog, under the "General" tab.)

The Hierarchy Editor

Once you start doing a good deal of object-oriented programming, you'll soon find that you'll have object hierarchy trees coming out of your ears. You will not only be working with existing hierarchies that might be very large, but you will most likely be creating your own. As your hierarchy trees grow, it will be become more and more difficult to manage and find what you are looking for.

The Café Hierarchy Editor was designed to make life easier. It is a graphical way of seeing all of the classes in your project. In addition, you can use this tool to visually change the inheritance hierarchies in your projects.

Figure 3.10 shows the Class Hierarchy for one of the sample project that comes with Café, called ThreadX. Notice the three classes, PolygonAnimation, AnimationPanel, and ThreadX, in the hierarchy.

By double-clicking any of the classes in the hierarchy you will be taken to the Class Editor and positioned on the appropriate class. If you right-click on any of the classes, you will get the same popup menu that you would see in the Classes Pane of the Class Editor (as described above).

The Hierarchy editor allows you to connect classes to visually build your project, as we'll see next.

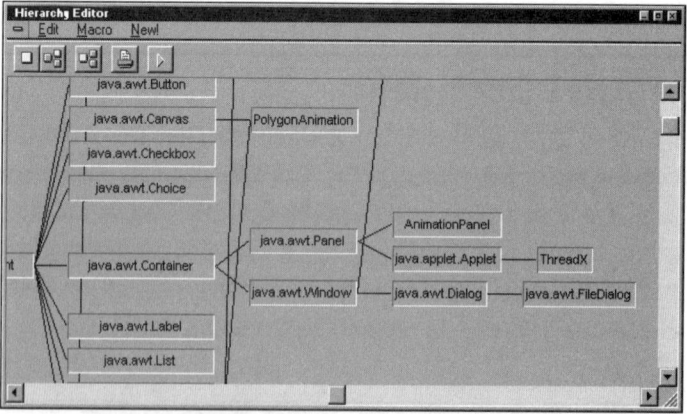

Figure 3.10   Class Hierarchy for ThreadX.

Visual Architecture

Being able to see class hierarchies visually is great for getting a sense of where things are in your project's food chain. But Café's Hierarchy editor goes one step further to allow you to actually build or reconfigure your project in a visual way.

The basic idea is a lot like linking up table fields in a visual database product like Paradox for Windows or Microsoft Access. In those products, you specify database links by drawing lines between columns in tables. In Café, you can specify which classes descend from which other classes by drawing lines to and from the appropriate classes. You can also create new classes in the hierarchy by creating a line that doesn't connect to another class.

Let's look at an example to see how this is done. We'll use the sample program, ThreadX, which was pictured above in Figure 3.10. Let see what we'd need to do if we wanted to change the parent class of the AnimationPanel class. In the project it is defined to be a descendent of java.awt.Canvas. We'll temporarily change it to be a descendent of java.awt.Panel.

The first step is to click on the line that connects AnimationPanel to java.awt.Canvas. Once you've clicked on the line you'll see a small black square appear next to java.awt.Canvas. You're now ready to move this line. Click on the black square, hold the left mouse button down, and move the mouse to java.awt.Panel. When you release the mouse button you'll be asked whether you'd like to replace the base connection, java.awt.Canvas. Answer "Yes." The result will be similar to what you see in Figure 3.11.

The source code will have been updated automatically for you after this change, and the Class Editor will know of the change as well. Now, since you might not actually want AnimationPanel to be a descendent of java.awt.Panel, you can select "Edit | Undo Replace Base Connection" to undo the changes.

To create a new class off of an existing class, simply click on the existing class and drag the mouse to an open area on in the Hierarchy editor. You'll be presented with a dialog box called "Create Derived Class," which you might remember seeing from the Class Editor.

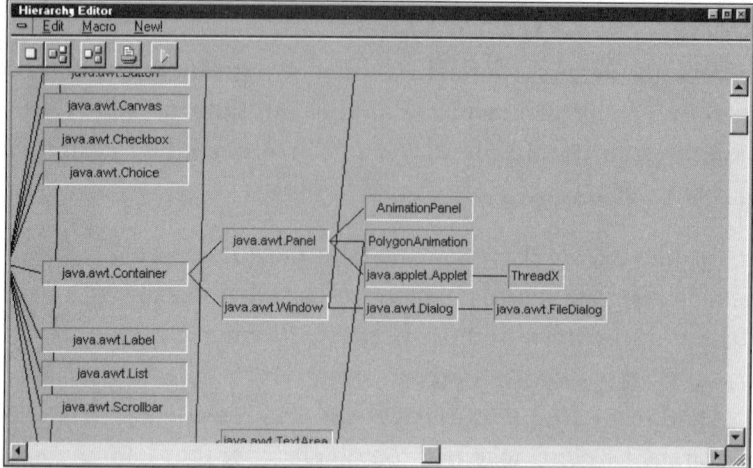

Figure 3.11 Visually changing the base class of AnimationPanel.

A Multiple Inheritance Problem

As you begin to use the Hierachy Editor to visually architect your projects be careful, if you are using Version 1.0, to not let classes have multiple parents. The Java language does not support multiple inheritance but uses interfaces to achieve much the same result. Currently, in Version 1.0, you can make connections between classes that will yield incorrect results and cause you to have a number of errors when you build your projects. This will most certainly be fixed in an update or new release of the product.

Application Navigation

A great and easy way to navigate your projects is to use the Hierarchy editor. You can see all of your classes in one place and easily jump to the source code for a class by either double-clicking the class to get into Class Editor or right-clicking on the class to obtain a popup menu from which you can select "Go to Source" to see the class in a source code window.

The Class hierarchy can also be a great place to decide where to create a new class or interface.

Visual Searching

Like the search engine in the Class Editor, the Hierarchy Editor also supports a powerful search feature that you wont find on any menu. The difference here is that when the engine finds your class, it will take you to its location within the class hierarchy! This can be a great way to find classes within the JDK.

To use the search feature, simply start typing the name of your class within the Hierarchy Editor. The incremental search engine will take you to any class that matches what you've typed. Try it!

Projects

The Café project management system provides an easy and sophisticated way to organize all of the diverse files that will become a part of many of your Java projects. Behind the scenes, the Café project management systems maintains a MAKE file (.mak) that keeps track of all of the files and settings you've added and selected for your project. To control these settings and to maintain your projects, you'll use a number of Café's integrated tools and windows, all of which are described below.

Customizing Project Settings

Under the Project menu off of Café's main menu, you'll find a choice called "Settings." If you select this choice you'll be taken to a Project Settings dialog box that will look like that shown in Figure 3.12.

The first tab, called "Target," lets you control some rather important switches for your project. It is here that you can ultimately specify that you'd like to create a release build of your applet or an application. (A release build doesn't have any debugging information built into it and cannot be debugged.) You can also specify the HTML file associated with your applet; in the case of a Java application, you would specify the main class from which your application runs.

There are also three checkboxes that let you control how your project is handled by Café during loading and building. These are:

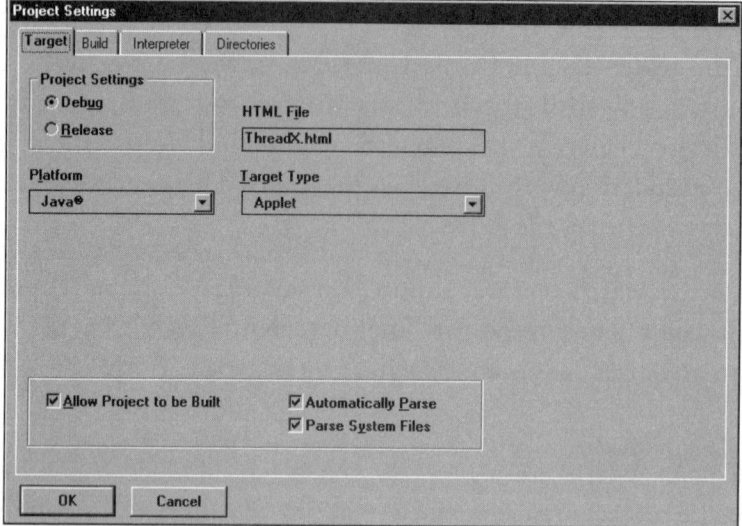

Figure 3.12   The Project Settings dialog.

◆ Allow Project to be Built: Defaults to being on; you will usually want to be able to build your project; however, this setting has more of an impact when you start dealing with subprojects, described in a section below.

◆ Automatically Parse: Café parses source files to gain information about them to assist in displaying their content in tools like Class Hierarchy, Class Editor, and Café Studio. This checkbox simply controls whether or not you will be prompted before parsings or reparsings take place. This is also on by default.

◆ Parse System files: Off by default; you will typically not need to parse the Java systems files. You can always manually parse these files if you need to look at them in Class Hierarchy or Class Editor.

The second tab in the Project Setting dialog, called "Build," lets you control which compiler is used during builds (Symantec's or Sun's) and lets you set the following options either on or off:

◆ Debug Information: The default for this is on.

◆ Disable Warnings: Warnings are not disabled by default.

◆ Enable Optimizations: Optimizations include inlining final or static methods and removing "useless" code such as (if (true)). Turning this option on is the equivalent of using the Java compiler option -O ("javac -o"). Optimizations are not enabled by default.

◆ Verbose Output: Verbose output from the Java compiler is not enabled by default.

The third tab, "Interpreter," gives you control over how the Java Interpreter functions at runtime. Four sections of this dialog box give you a fine degree of control over how the interpreter does its job. These four sections are:

◆ Garbage Collection: Java does not require you to handle the allocation and deallocation of memory, but does let you control memory allocation if you wish. Normally, a garbage collection thread runs while your applet or application is running. This garbage collection thread runs asynchronously with the other threads in your code. By turning the "Disable Asynchronous" option on, you basically tell the interpreter that you will handle memory allocations and deallocations. The verbose option tells the garbage collector to print out a message every time some memory is freed.

◆ Stack and Heap: Threads in Java actually have stacks for Java code and C code. You may specify the maximum sizes for both of these stacks in either kilobytes (use a "k") or megabytes (use an "m"). The initial heap is the size of the memory allocation pool at startup, while the maximum Java heap is the maximum size to which the pool can grow. You may also use "k" or "m" to specify heap sizes.

◆ Bytecode Verification: Bytecodes, or what is created when you "compile" your Java source code, are normally verified at runtime by the interpreter. You can specify whether you'd like bytecode verification to happen only when classes are loaded by the classloader, all the time, or not at all.

◆ Miscellaneous: To see how efficient your code is performing, you can turn on "Generate Profile Information." When enabled, profile information will automatically be sent to a file named java.prof. Turning on "Verbose Interpreter Output" will cause java to print a message each time a class is loaded.

The fourth and last tab, called "Directories," lets you control various directories for your project. These are:

◆ Class Path: This is the path that is used to look up classes and that you can set yourself, by separating directories with semicolons. The environment variable, CLASSPATH, will be ignored if you supply a value for this field. Typically, you should have no reason to set this value if your CLASSPATH variable has been installed correctly.

◆ Library Directories: This has been disabled in Version 1.0 of Café.

◆ Compiler Output Directories: This specifies the directory to which your class files will be placed. The default is to be blank, which represents the directory in which the project resides.

◆ Target Output Directories: This has been disabled in Version 1.0 of Café.

◆ Browser Exclude Directories: This specifies which directories should not be "seen" by Café's parser.

◆ Source Search Path: This specifies which directories should be searched when doing debugging.

The Project Window

The Café Project window has two panes: The left pane lists the name of the project or .prj file; the right pane lists the files associated with the project listed in the left pane. Each of the panes has its own popup menu that you can use to work with your project as a whole or with individual files.

From the left pane's popup menu, you can create a subproject, build, rebuild, or reparse your project, add new files to your project, or edit your project's settings.

From the right pane, you can sort your project's files by Name, Extension, Path, Date, Time, or Parse status. To sort, simply click on the heading of any one of the columns, and the files will be sorted by whichever column you selected. From the popup menu in the Project Window's right pane, you can compile individual files, remove files, make a file read-only or both readable and writeable, and control which of the parsed, dependency, or module files you see or don't see in the file listing.

Subprojects

The Café project management system supports something known as subprojects. This powerful feature allows you to group projects within projects.

But why would you want to do that?

Creating a project does not necessarily mean that you've created something that is an application or even an applet. A project could simply contain some Java source files that you use on a regular basis. Let's say that you have a project called "A" that contains some very useful code, perhaps some code in a Java package that you wrote. By making project "A" a subproject of project "B," you would have access to all of the code within project "A" and would be able to control whether or not the source from project "A" can be changed or whether project "A" should be "built" during a build of project "B."

In addition, you might wish to take all of the Java system files, put them into one Café project that contains a fully parsed source, and make this a subproject for your other projects.

To create a subproject, go to the left pane of the Project window, right-click to bring up the popup menu ,and select "Create Subproject." You will be presented with a dialog box that will prompt you to supply the name of another Café project (.prj) file.

Parsing Technology

Café's parser is responsible for creating something like an "internal database" that gets updates whenever a change is made in one of Café's many editor windows. This "internal database" holds information about your projects classes, variables, and methods. Parsing results may be seen in Café's output window, and parsing may be controlled from the Project window or specifically controlled via the Project settings screen as mentioned above.

You'll see in the source code, in many of your projects that Café generates, certain specialized comments. The parser uses these special comments when adding and removing code from your source files. It is important that you

not place your own code within the lines between these special comments. Two samples from some Café Studio generated code are shown below in Listing 3.1.

LISTING 3.1   EXAMPLES OF THE SPECIAL COMMENTS USED BY CAFÉ'S PARSER

```
//{{INIT_CONTROLS
setLayout(new BorderLayout());
buttonPanel=new Panel();
add("South",buttonPanel);
//}}

//{{DECLARE_CONTROLS
Panel buttonPanel;
Panel aPanel;
Button startButton;
Button stopButton;
//}}
```

Concluding Words

Symantec Café is an integrated development and debugging environment that goes a long way in making Java development more enjoyable and efficient. As a 1.0 product, Café is fairly robust; it supports an object-oriented language that is similar in many ways to C++, and as a result is built around a visual development environment that greatly resembles some of the mature visual development environments available for C++.

In this chapter, you've seen how to configure and manage projects, use the Hierarchy Editor to view and edit your classes, use the programmer's editor to quickly edit and navigate your code and compiler errors, and use the Class Editor to work with your classes, methods, and variables.

Hopefully, this chapter has helped you to learn ways in which you may maximize your productivity using Café. As we've seen in our journey around the many windows in the Café IDDE, popup menus turn up everywhere and support some rather diverse and powerful features. Use them as often as you can!

Java Language Fundamentals 4

Anthony Potts

The language building blocks of Java are similar to those found in C++, but keep a close eye out because there are some subtle differences.

You should now have a basic understanding of the Café development environment and how it works with the Java language. In this chapter and the ones that follow, we'll uncover the key Java language features that you'll need to know to write useful programs with Café. In particular, we'll explain the basic Java language components in this chapter—everything from comments to variable declarations. Then we'll move ahead and cover operators, expressions, and control structures in Chapter 5.

For those of you who are already familiar with programming, especially C or C++ programming, this chapter and Chapter 5 should serve as a good hands-on review. As we discuss Java, we'll point out the areas in which Java differs from other languages. If you don't have much experience using structured programming languages, this chapter will give you a good overview of the basic components required to make programming languages like Java come alive.

The actual language components featured in this chapter include:

- ◆ Comments
- ◆ Identifiers
- ◆ Keywords
- ◆ Data types
- ◆ Variable declarations

What Makes a Java Program?

Before we get into the details of each Java language component, let's stand back ten steps and look at how many of the key language components are used in the context of a Java program. Figure 4.1(shown later) presents a complete visual guide. Here we've highlighted components such as variable declarations, Java keywords, operators, literals, expressions, and control structures. As we work our way through the next two chapters, you'll learn how these components are defined and used.

In case you're wondering, the output for this program looks like this:

```
Hello John my name is Anthony
That's not my name!
Let's count to ten....
1 2 3 4 5 6 7 8 9 10
Now down to zero by two.
10 8 6 4 2 0
Finally, some arithmetic:
10 * 3.09 = 30.9
10 * 3.09 = 30 (integer cast)
10 / 3,09 = 3.23625
10 / 3,09 = 3 (integer cast)
```

Lexical Structure

The lexical structure of a language refers to the elements of code that make the code easy for us to understand, but have no effect on the compiled code. For example, all the comments you place in a program to help you understand how it works are ignored by the Java compiler. You could have a thousand lines of comments for a twenty line program and the compiled *bytecodes* for the program would be the same size if you took out all the comments. This does not mean that *all* lexical structures are optional. It simply means that they do not effect the bytecodes.

The lexical structures we will discuss include:

◆ Comments

◆ Identifiers

◆ Keywords

◆ Separators

Comments

Comments make your code easy to understand, modify, and use. But adding comments to an application only after it is finished is not a good practice. More often than not, you won't remember what the code you write actually does after you get away from it for a while. Unfortunately, many programmers follow this time-honored tradition. We suggest you try to get in the habit of adding comments as you write your code.

Java supports three different types of comment styles. The first two are taken directly from C and C++. The third type of comment is a new one that can be used to automatically create class and method documentation.

COMMENT STYLE #1

```
/* Comments here... */
```

This style of commenting comes to us directly from C. Everything between the initial slash-asterisk and ending asterisk-slash is ignored by the Java compiler. This style of commenting can be used anywhere in a program, even in the middle of code (not a good idea). This style of commenting is useful when you have multiple lines of comments because your comment lines can wrap from one line to the next, and you only need to use one set of the /* and */ symbols. Examples:

```
/*
 This program was written by Joe Smith.
```

```
   It is the greatest program ever written!
   */

while (i <= /* comments can be placed here */ maxnum)
{
   total += i;
   i++;
}
```

In the second example, the comment line is embedded within the program statement. The compiler skips over the comment text, and thus the actual line of code would be processed as:

```
while (i <= maxnum)
...
```

Programmers occasionally use this style of commenting while they are testing and debugging code. For example, you could comment out part of an equation or expression:

```
sum = i /* + (base - 10) */ + factor;
```

COMMENT STYLE #2

```
// Comment here...
```

This style of commenting is borrowed from C++. Everything after the double slash marks is ignored by the Java compiler. The comment is terminated by a line return, so you can't use multiple comment lines unless you start each line with the double-slash. Examples:

```
// This program was written by Joe Smith.
// It is the greatest program ever written!

  while (i <= // this won't work maxnum)
{
   total += i;
   i++;
}

base = 20;
// This comment example also won't work because the Java
   compiler will treat this second line as a line of code
value = 50;
```

The comment used in the second example won't work like you might intend because the remainder of the line of code would be commented out (everything after i <=). In the third example, the second comment line is missing the starting // symbols, and the Java compiler will get confused because it will try to process the comment line as if it were a line of code. Believe it or not, this type of commenting mistake occurs often—so watch out for it!

COMMENT STYLE #3

```
/** Doc Comment here... */
```

This comment structure may look very similar to the C style of commenting, but that extra asterisk at the beginning makes a huge difference. Of course, remember that only one asterisk must be used as the comment terminator. The Java compiler still ignores the comment; but another program called JAVADOC.EXE that ships with the Java Development Kit uses these comments to construct HTML documentation files that describe your packages, classes, and methods as well as all the variables they use.

Let's look at the third style of commenting in more detail. If implemented correctly and consistently, this style of commenting can provide you with numerous benefits. Figure 4.2 shows what the output of the JAVADOC program looks like when run on a typical Java source file.

If you have ever looked at the Java API documentation on Sun's Web site, Figure 4.2 should look familiar to you. In fact, the entire API documentation was created with JAVADOC.

JAVADOC will work if you have created comments or not. Figure 4.3 shows the output from this simple application:

```
class HelloWorld {
   public static void main(String args[]) {
      System.out.println("Hello World");
   }
}
```

```
/**                                    ─── unique Java style comment
 * Sample Java Application
 * @author Anthony Potts
 * @version 1.0              ─── superclass
 */                                            ─── standard C++ style comment
class Test extends Object { // Begin Test class
    // Define class variables
                                 ─── standard data type
    static int i = 10;
                              ─── variable
    static final double d = 3.09;
                                 ─── literal

    /*
    The main() method is automatically called when
    the program is run. Any words typed after the program
    name when it is run are placed in the args[] variable
    which is an array of strings.
    For this program to work properly, atleast one word must
    be typed after the program name or else an error will occur.
    */
    public static void main(String args[]) {
        Test thisTest = new Test(); // Create instance (object) of
class
                                 ─── declaration and assignment
        String myName = "Anthony";
                              ─── assignment operator
        boolean returnValue;
                                         ─── string data type
        System.out.println("Hello " + args[0] + " my name is " +
myName);


        if(thisTest.sameName(args[0], myName)) {
            System.out.println("Your name is the same as mine!");
        } else {
            System.out.println("That's not my name!");
        }
                                         ─── if-then-else
                                             control structure
        System.out.println("Let's count to ten....");
                                 ─── increment operator
        for (int x = 1; x < 11; x++) {
            System.out.print(x + " ");
        }                                ─── expression
```

variable declarations

Figure 4.1   A visual guide to the key Java language components.

Continued

```
                 System.out.println("\nNow down to zero by two.");
                                        ┌──────── logical expression
                 while ( i > -1) {
                     System.out.print(i + " ");
                     i -= 2;
                 }

                 System.out.println("\nFinally, some arithmetic:");

                 thisTest.doArithmetic();──── method call
             }

             // This method compares the two names sent to it and
             // returns true if they are the same and false if they are not
             public boolean sameName(String firstName, String secondName) {
                 if (firstName.equals(secondName)) {
                     return true;──────────┐
                 } else {                  ├── returns value to
                     return false;─────────┘   calling class
                 }
             }

             // This method performs a few computations and prints the result
             public void doArithmetic(){
                 i = 10;──────────────── assignment expression
                 System.out.println(i + " * " + d + " = " + (i * d));
                 System.out.println(i + " * " + d + " = " +
                                    (int)(i * d) + " (Integer)");
                 System.out.println(i + " / " + d + " = " + (i / d));
                 System.out.println(i + " / " + d + " = " +
                                    (int)(i / d) + " (Integer)");
             }
         } // End of class
```

while control statement (label for `while` block)

method modifier (label for `public`)

Figure 4.1   A visual guide to the key Java language components   (Continued).

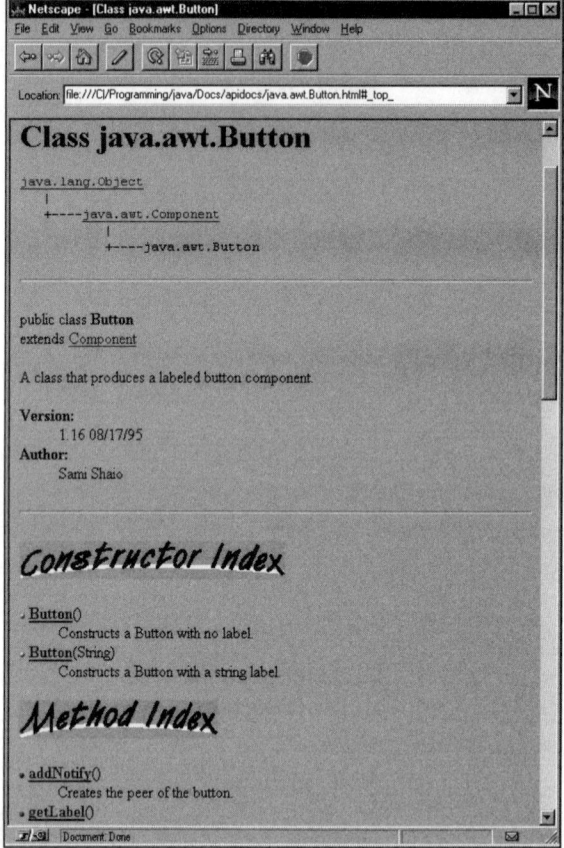

Figure 4.2   Sample output from the JavaDoc program.

To add a little more information to our documentation, all we have to do is add this third style of comments. If we change the little HelloWorld application and add a few key comments, the code will look like this:

```
/**
 * Welcome to HelloWorld
 * @author Anthony Potts
 * @version 1.1
 * @see java.lang.System
 */
class helloworld {
    /**
     * Main method of helloworld
     */
    public static void main(String args[]) {
```

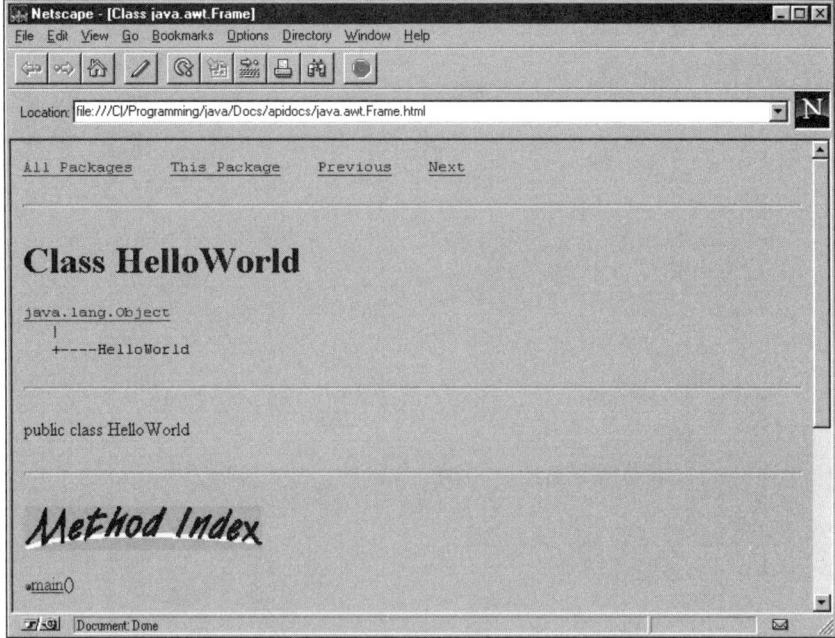

Figure 4.3   Simple output from the JavaDoc program.

```
        System.out.println("Hello World!");
    }
}
```

If you now run JAVADOC, the browser will display what you see in Figure 4.4. As you can see, this gives us much more information. This system is great for producing documentation for public distribution. Just like all comments though, it is up to you to make sure that the comments are accurate and plentiful enough to be helpful. Table 4.1 lists the tags you can use in your class comments.

Identifiers

Identifiers are the names used for variables, classes, methods, packages, and interfaces to distinguish them to the compiler. In the sample program from Chapter 2 the identifier for the applet's class was **TickerTape**. We also used identifiers like **fontHeight** and **fontWidth** to name some of the variables.

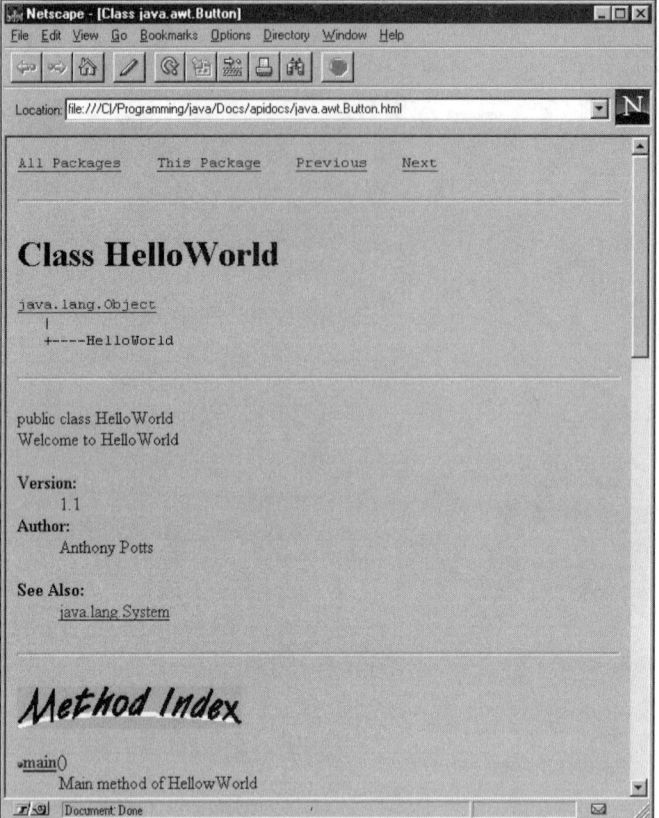

Figure 4.4   the new JavaDoc output.

Identifiers in the Java language should always begin with a letter of the alphabet, either upper or lower case. The only exceptions to this rule are the underscore symbol (_) and the dollar sign ($), which may also be used. If you try to use any other symbol or a numeral as the initial character, you will receive an error.

After the initial character you are allowed to use numbers, but not all symbols. You can also use almost all of the characters from the Unicode character set. If you are not familiar with the Unicode character set or you get errors, we suggest that you stick with the standard alphabetic characters.

The length of an identifier is basically unlimited. We managed to get up to a few thousand characters before we got bored. It's doubtful you will ever need nearly that many characters, but it is nice to know that the Java compiler

Table 4.1   Tags Used in Class Comments.

Tag	Description
@see classname	Adds a hyperlinked "See Also" to your class. The classname can be any other class.
@see fully-qualified-classname	Also adds a "See Also" to the class, but this time you need to use a fully qualified class name like "java.awt.window."
@see fully-qualified-classname #methodname	Also adds a "See Also" to the class, but now you are pointing to a specific method within that class.
@version version-text	Adds a version number that you provide. The version number can be numbers or text.
@author author-name -	Adds an author entry. You can use multiple author tags.
	The tags you can use in your method comments include all of the "@see" tags as well as the following:
@param paramter-name description...	Used to show which parameters the method accepts. Multiple "@param" tags are acceptable.
@return description...	Used to describe what the method returns.
@exception fully-qualified-classname description...	Used to add a "throw" entry that describes what type of exceptions this method can throw. Multiple "@exception" tags are acceptable. (Don't worry about exceptions and throws too much yet.)

won't limit you if you want to create long descriptive names. The only limit you may encounter involves creating class names. Since class names are also used as file names, you need to create names that will not cause problems with your operating system or anyone who will be using your program.

You must also be careful not to use any of the special Java keywords listed in the next section. The following are examples of valid identifiers:

```
HelloWorld          $Money      TickerTape
_ME2       Chapter3     ABC123
```

And here are some examples of invalid identifiers:

```
3rdChapter      #Hello     -Main
```

COMMON ERRORS WITH USING IDENTIFIERS

As you are defining and using identifiers in your Java programs, you are bound to encounter some errors from time-to-time. Let's look at some of the more common error messages that the Java compiler displays. Notice that we've included the part of the code that is responsible for generating the error, the error message, as well as a description of the message so that you can make sense of it.

Code Example:
```
public class 1test {
}
```

Error Message:
```
D:\java\lib\test.java:1: Identifier expected.
```

Description:
An invalid character has been used in the class identifier. You will see this error when the first character is invalid (especially when it is a number).

Code Example:
```
public class te?st {
}
```

Error Message:
```
D:\java\lib\test.java:1: '{' Expected
```

Description:
This is a common error that occurs when you have an invalid character in the middle of an identifier. In this case, the question mark is invalid, so the compiler gets confused where the class definition ends and its implementation begins.

Code Example:
```
public class #test {
}
```

Error Message:
```
D:\java\lib\test.java:1: Invalid character in input.
```

Description:
Here, the error stems from the fact that the initial character is invalid.

Code Example:
```
public class catch {
}
```

Error Message:
```
D:\java\lib\test.java:1: Identifier expected.
```

Description:
This error shows up when you use a protected keyword as an identifier.

Keywords

In Java, like other languages, there are certain *keywords* or "tokens" that are reserved for system use. These keywords can't be used as names for your classes, variables, packages, or anything else. The keywords are used for a number of tasks such as defining control structures (*if*, *while*, and *for*) and declaring data types (*int*, *char*, and *float*). Table 4.2 provides the complete list of the Java keywords.

The words marked with an asterisk (*) are not currently used in the Java language, but you still can't use them to create your own identifiers. More than likely they will be used as keywords in future versions of the Java language.

Literals

Literals are the values that you assign when entering explicit values. For example, in an assignment statement like this:

```
i = 10;
```

the value 10 is a literal. But do not get literals confused with types. Even though they usually go hand in hand, literals and types are not the same.

Table 4.2   Java Language Keywords.

Keyword	Description
abstract	Class modifier
boolean	Used to define a boolean data type
break	Used to break out of loops
byte	Used to define a byte data type
byvalue *	Not implemented yet
cast	Used to translate from type to type
catch	Used with error handling
char	Used to define a character data type (16-bit)
class	Used to define a class structure
const *	Not implemented yet
continue	Used to continue an operation
default	Used with the switch statement
do	Used to create a do loop control structure
Double	Used to define a floating-point data type (64-bit)
else	Used to create an else clause for an if statement
extends	Used to subclass
final	Used to tell Java that this class can not be subclassed
finally	Used with exceptions to determine the last option before exiting. It guarantees that code gets called if an exception does or does not happen.
float	Used to define a floating-point data type (32-bit)
for	Used to create a for loop control structure
future *	Not implemented yet
generic *	Not implemented yet
goto *	Not implemented yet
if	Used to create an if-then decision-making control structure
implements	Used to define which interfaces to use
import	Used to reference external Java packages
inner	Used to create control blocks
instanceof	Used to determine if an object is of a certain type
int	Used to define an integer data type (32-bit values)
interface	Used to tell Java that the code that follows is an interface
long	Used to define an integer data type (64-bit values)

Continued

Table 4.2   Java Language Keywords. (continued).

Keyword	Description
native	Used when calling external code
new	Operator used when creating an instance of a class (an object)
null	Reference to a non-existent value
operator *	Not implemented yet
outer	Used to create control blocks
package	Used to tell Java what package the following code belongs to
private	Modifier for classes, methods, and variables
protected	Modifier for classes, methods, and variables
public	Modifier for classes, methods, and variables
rest *	Not implemented yet
return	Used to set the return value of a class or method
short	Used to define an integer data type (16-bit values)
static	Modifier for classes, methods, and variables
super	Used to reference the current class' parent class
switch	Block statement used to pick from a group of choices
synchronized	Modifier that tells Java that only one instance of a method can be run at one time. It keeps Java from running the method a second time before the first is finished. It is especially useful when dealing with files to avoid conflicts.
this	Used to reference the current object
throw	Statement that tells Java what exception to pass on an error
transient	Modifier that can access future Java code
try	Operator that is used to test for exceptions in code
var *	Not implemented yet
void	Modifier for setting the return value of a class or method to nothing
volatile	Variable modifier
while	Used to create a while loop control structure.

Types are used to define what type of data a variable can hold, while literals are the values that are actually assigned to those variables.

Literals come in three flavors: numeric, character, and boolean. Boolean literals are simply True and False.

NUMERIC LITERALS

Numeric literals are just what they sound like—numbers. We can subdivide the numeric literals further into *integers* and *floating-point* literals.

Integer literals are usually represented in *decimal* format although you can use the *hexadecimal* and octal format in Java. If you want to use the hexadecimal format, your numbers need to begin with an 0x or 0X. Octal integers simply begin with a zero (0).

Integer literals are stored differently depending on their size. The **int** data type is used to store 32-bit integer values ranging from -2,147,483,648 to 2,147,483,648 (decimal). If you need to use even larger numbers, Java switches over to the **long** data type, which can store 64 bits of information for a range of - 9.223372036855e+18 to 9.223372036855e+18. This would give you a number a little larger than 9 million trillion—enough to take care of the national debt! To specify a **long** integer, you will need to place an "l" or "L" at the end of the number. Don't get confused by our use of the terms **int** and **long**. There are many other integer data types used by Java, but they all use **int** or **long**literals to assign values. Table 4.3 provides a summary of the two integer literals.

Here are some examples of how integer literals can be used to assign values in Java statements:

```
int i;
i = 1;  // All of these literals are of the integer type
i= -9;
i = 1203131;

i = 0xA11;  // Using a hexadecimal literal
i = 07543;  // Using an octal literal
```

Table 4.3   Summary of Integer Literals.

Integer Literals Ranges	Negative Minimum	Positive Maximum
int data type	-2,147,483,648	2,147,483,648
long data type	-9.223372036855e+18	9.223372036855e+18

```
i = 4.5;      // This would be illegal because a floating-point
              // literal can't be assigned to an integer type
long lg;
lg = 1L;      // All of these literals are of the long
              // integer type
lg = -9e15;
lg = 7e12;
```

The other type of numeric literal is the floating-point literal. Floating-point values are any numbers that have anything to the right of the decimal place. Similar to integers, floating-point values have 32-bit and 64-bit representations. Both data types conform to IEEE standards. Table 4.4 provides a summary of the two floating-point literals.

Here are some examples of how floating-point literals can be used to assign values in Java statements:

```
float f;
f = 1.3;  // All of these literals are of the floating-point
          // type float (32-bit)
f = -9.0;
f = 1203131.1241234;
double d;
d = 1.0D;  // All of these literals are of the floating-
           // point type double(32-bit)
d = -9.3645e235;
d = 7.0001e52D;
```

CHARACTER LITERALS

The second type of literal that you need to know about is the *character literal*. Character literals include single characters and strings. Single character literals are enclosed in single quotation marks while string literals are enclosed in double quotes.

Single characters can be any one character from the Unicode character set. There are also a few special two-character combinations that are non-

Table 4.4 Summary of Floating-Point Literals.		
Floating-Point Ranges	**Negative Minimum**	**Positive Maximum**
float data type	1.40239846e-45	3.40282347e38
double data type	4.94065645841246544e-324	1.79769313486231570e308

printing characters but perform important functions. Table 4.5 shows these special combinations.

The string character literal are any number of characters enclosed in The character combinations from Table 4.5 also apply to strings. Here are some examples of how character and string literals can be used in Java statements:

```
char ch;
ch = 'a';    // All of these literals are characters
ch = \n;     // Assign the newline character
ch = \';     // Assign a single quote
ch = \x30;   // Assign a hexadecimal character code

String str;
str = "Java string";
```

Operators

Operators are used to perform computations on one or more variables or objects. You use operators to add values, comparing the size of two numbers, assigning a value to a variable, incrementing the value of a variable, and so on. Table 4.6 lists the operators used in Java. Later in this chapter, we'll

Table 4.5   Special Character Combinations in Java.

Character Combination	Standard Designation	Description
\	\<newline\>	Continuation
\n	NL or LF	New Line
\b	BS	Backspace
\r	CR	Carriage Return
\f	FF	Form Feed
\t	HT	Horizontal Tab
\\	\	Backslash
\'	'	Single Quote
\"	"	Double Quote
\xdd	0xdd	Hex Bit Pattern
\ddd	0ddd	Octal Bit Pattern
\uddd	0xdddd	Unicode Character

Table 4.6   Operators Used in Java

Operator	Description
+	Addition
-	Subtraction
*	Multiplication
/	Division
%	Modulo
++	Increment
—	Decrement
>	Greater than
>=	Greater than or equal to
<	Less than
<=	Less than or equal to
==	Equal to
!=	Not equal to
!	Logical NOT
&&	Logical AND
||	Logical OR
&	Bitwise AND
^	Bitwise exclusive OR
|	Bitwise OR
~	Bitwise complement
<<	Left shift
>>	Right shift
>>>	Zero fill right shift
=	Assignment
+=	Assignment with addition
-=	Assignment with subtraction
*=	Assignment with multiplication
/=	Assignment with division
%=	Assignment with modulo
&=	Assignment with bitwise AND

Continued

Table 4.6 Operators Used in Java (continued).

Operator	Description
|=	Assignment with bitwise OR
^=	Assignment with bitwise exclusive OR
<<=	Assignment with left shift
>>=	Assignment with right shift
>>>=	Assignment with zero fill right shift

explain in detail how each operator works; and we'll also explain operator precedence.

Separators

Separators are used in Java to delineate blocks of code. For example, you use curly brackets to enclose a method's implementation, and you use parentheses to enclose arguments being sent to a method. Table 4.7 lists the separators used in Java.

Types and Variables

Many people confuse the terms *types* and *variables*, and use them synonymously. They are, however, not the same. Variables are basically buckets that *hold information*, while types *describe what type of information* is in the bucket.

A variable must have both a type and an identifier. Later in this chapter we will cover the process of declaring variables. For now, we just want to guide

Table 4.7 Separators Used in Java.

Separator	Description
( )	Used to define blocks of arguments
[ ]	Used to define arrays
{ }	Used to hold blocks of code
,	Used to separate arguments or variables in a declaration
;	Used to terminate lines of contiguous code

you through the details of how you decide which types to use and how to use them properly.

Similar to literals, types can be split into several different categories including the numeric types—**byte**, **short**, **int**, **long**, **float**, and **double**—and the **char** and **boolean** types. We will also discuss the string type. Technically, the string type is not a type—it is a class. However, it is used so commonly that we decided to include it here.

All of the integer numeric types use signed 2's-complement integers for storing data. Table 4.8 provides a summary of the ranges for each of the key Java data types.

byte

The **byte** type can be used for variables whose value falls between -256 and 255. **byte** types have an 8-bit length. Here are some examples of byte values:

```
-7 5        238
```

short

The **short** numeric type can store values ranging from -32768 to 32767. It has a 16-bit depth, as in the following examples:

```
-7 256     -29524
```

Table 4.8   Summary of the Java Data Types.

Data Type	Negative Minimal	Positive Maximal
byte	-256	255
short	-32768	32767
int	-2147483648	2147483647
long	-9223372036854775808	9223372036854775807
float	1.40239846e-45	3.40282347e38
double	4.94065645841246544e-324	1.79769313486231570e308
boolean	False	True

---

int

The **int** data type takes the **short** type to the next level. It uses a 32-bit signed integer value that takes our minimal and maximal value up to over 2 billion. Because of this tremendous range, it is one of the most often used data types for integers.

Often, unskilled programmers will use the **int** data type even though they don't need the full resolution that this data type provides. If you are using smaller integers, you should consider using the **short** data type. The rule of thumb to follow is *if you know exactly the range of values a certain variable will store, use the smallest data type possible*. This will let your program use less memory and therefore run faster, especially on slower machines or machines with limited RAM.

Here are some examples of **int** values:

```
-7 256     -29523234     1321412422
```

long

The **long** data type is the mother of all integer types. It uses a full 64-bit data path to store values that reach up to over 9 million trillion. But be extremely careful when using variables of the **long** type. If you start using many of them or God forbid, an array of **long**s, you can quickly eat up a ton of resources.

The Danger of Using long

Java provides useful garbage collection tools, so when you are done with these large data types, they will be disposed of and their resources reclaimed. But if you are creating large arrays of long integers you could really be asking for trouble. For example, if you created a two-dimensional array of long integers that had a 100x100 grid, you would be using up about 100 kilobytes of memory.

Here are some examples of **long** values:

```
-7 256     -29523234     1.835412e15     -3e18
```

float

The **float** data type is one of two types used to store floating-point values. The **float** type is compliant with the IEEE 754 conventions. The floating-point types of Java can store gargantuan numbers. We do not have enough room on the page to physically show you the minimal and maximal values the **float** data type can store, so we will use a little bit of tricky sounding lingo taken from the Java manual.

"The finite nonzero values of type **float** are of the form s * m * 2e , where s is +1 or -1, m is a positive integer less than 2^24 and e is an integer between -149 and 104, inclusive."

Whew, that's a mouthful. Here are a few examples to show you what the **float** type might look like in actual use:

```
-7F      256.0   -23e34      23e100
```

double

As if the **float** type could not hold enough, the **double** data type gives you even bigger storage space. Let's look again at Sun's definition of the possible values for a **double**.

"The finite nonzero values of type **float** are of the form s * m * 2e , where s is +1 or -1, m is a positive integer less than 2^53 and e is an integer between -1045 and 1000, inclusive."

Again, you can have some truly monstrous numbers here. But when you start dealing with hard core programming, this type of number becomes necessary from time to time, so it is wise to understand its ranges. Here are a few examples:

```
-7.0D   256.0D  -23e424 23e1000
```

boolean

In other languages, the **boolean** data type has been represented by an integer with a nonzero or zero value to represent True and False, respectively. This method works well because it gives the user the ability to check for all kinds of values and perform expression.

```
x=2;
if x then...
```

This can be handy when performing parsing operations or checking string lengths. In Java, however, the **boolean** data type has its own True and False literals that do not correspond to other values. In fact, as you will learn later in this chapter, Java does not even allow you to perform casts between the **boolean** data type and any others. There are ways around this limitation that we will discuss in a few pages when we talk about conversion methods.

char

The **char** data type is used to store single characters. Since Java uses the Unicode character set, the **char** type needs to be able to store the thousands of characters, so it uses a 16-bit signed integer. The **char** data type has the ability to be cast or converted to almost all of the others, as we will show you in the next section.

string

The **string** type is actually not a primitive data type; it is a class all its own. We decided to talk about it a little here because it is used so commonly that it might as well be considered a primitive. In C and C++, strings are stored in arrays of chars. Java does not use the **char** type for this but instead has created its own class that handles strings. In Chapter 5, when we get into the details of declaring variables within classes, you will see the difference between declaring a primitive variable and declaring an instance of a class type.

One big advantage to using a class instead of an array of **char** types is that we are more or less unlimited in the amount of information we want to place in a string variable. In C++, the array of chars was limited, but now that limitation is taken care of within the class, where we do not care how it is handled.

Variable Declarations

Declaring variables in Java is very similar to declaring variables in C/C++ as long as you are using the primitive data types. As we said before, almost everything in Java is a class—except the primitive data types. We will show you how to instantiate custom data types (including strings) in Chapter 5. For now, let's look at how primitive data types are declared.

Here is what a standard declaration for a primitive variable might look like:

```
int i;
```

We have just declared a variable "i" to be an integer. Here are a few more examples:

```
byte i, j;
int a=7, b = a;
float f = 1.06;
String name = "Tony";
```

These examples illustrate some of the things you can do while declaring variables. Let's look at each one individually.

```
int i;
```

This is the most basic declaration, with the data type followed by the variable you are declaring.

```
byte i, j;
```

In this example, we are declaring two byte variables at one time. There is no limit to the number of variables you can declare this way. All you have to do is add a comma between each variable you wish to declare of the given type, and Java takes care of it for you.

You also have the ability to assign values to variables as you declare them. You can even use a variable you are declaring as part of an expression for the declaration of another variable in the same line. Before we confuse you more, here is an example:

```
int i = 1;
int j = i, k= i + j;
```

Here we have first declared a variable **i** as **int** and assigned it a value of 1. In the next line, we start by declaring a variable **j** to be equal to **i**. This is perfectly legal. Next, on the same line, we declare a variable **k** to be equal to **i** plus **j**. Once again, Java handles this without a problem. We could even shorten these two statements to one line like this:

```
int i = 1, j = i, k= i + j;
```

One thing to watch out for is using variables *before* they have been declared. Here's an example:

```
int j = i, k= i + j;   // i is not defined yet
int i = 1;
```

This would cause an "undefined variable" error because Java does not know to look ahead for future declarations. Let's look at another example:

```
float f = 1.06;
```

Does this look correct? Yes, but it's not. This is a tricky one. By default, Java assumes that numbers with decimal points are of type **double**. So, when you try and declare a **float** to be equal to this number, you receive the following error:

```
Incompatible type for declaration. Explicit cast needed to convert
    double to float.
```

Sounds complicated, but all this error message means is that you need to explicitly tell Java that the literal value 1.06 is a **float** and not a **double**. There are two ways to accomplish this. First, you can *cast* the value to a **float** like this:

```
float f = (float)1.06;
```

This works fine, but can get confusing. Java also follows the convention used by other languages of placing an "f" at the end of the literal value to indicate explicitly that it is a float. This also works for the double data type, except that you would use a "d." (By the way, capitalization of the f and d does not make a difference.)

```
float f = 1.06f;
double d = 1.06d;
```

You should realize that the "d" is not needed in the **double** declaration because Java assumes it. However, it is better to label all of your variables when possible, especially if you are not sure.

We will cover variables and declarations in more detail in Chapter 5, but you should have enough knowledge now to be able to run a few basic programs and will delve deeper into the Java fundamentals and look at operators, expressions, and control statements.

Using Arrays

It's difficult to imagine creating any large application or applet without having an array or two. Java uses arrays in a much different manner than other languages. Instead of being a structure that holds variables, arrays in Java are actually objects that can be treated just like any other Java object.

The powerful thing to realize here is that because arrays are objects that are derived from a class, they have methods you can call to retrieve information about the array or to manipulate the array. The current version of the Java language only supports the **length** method, but you can expect that more methods will be added as the language evolves.

One of the drawbacks to the way Java implements arrays is that they are only one dimensional. In most other languages, you can create a two-dimensional array by just adding a comma and a second array size. In Java, this does not work. The way around this limitation is to create an array of arrays. Because this is easy to do, the lack of built-in support for multi-dimensional arrays shouldn't hold you back.

Declaring Arrays

Since arrays are actually instances of classes (objects), we need to use constructors to create our arrays much like we did with strings. First, we need to pick a variable name and declare it as an array object and also specify which data type the array will hold. Note that an array can only hold a single data type—you can't mix strings and integers within a single array. Here are a few examples of how array variables are declared:

```
int intArray[];
String Names[];
```

As you can see, these look very similar to standard variable declarations, except for the brackets after the variable name. You could also put the brackets after the data type if you think this approach makes your declarations more readable:

```
int[] intArray;
String[] Names;
```

Sizing Arrays

There are three ways to set the size of arrays. Two of them require the use of the **new** operator. Using the **new** operator initializes all of the array elements to a default value. The third method involves filling in the array elements with values as you declare.

The first method involves taking a previously declared variable and setting the size of the array. Here are a few examples:

```
int intArray[];            // Declare the arrays
String Names[];

intArray[] = new int[10];        // Size each array
Names[] = new String[100];
```

Or, you can size the array object when you declare it:

```
int intArray[] = new int[10];
String Names[] = new String[100];
```

Finally, you can fill in the array with values at declaration time:

```
String Names[] = {"Tony", "Dave", "Jon", "Ricardo"};
int[] intArray = {1, 2, 3, 4, 5};
```

Accessing Array Elements

Now that you know how to initialize arrays, you'll need to learn how to fill them with data and then access the array elements to retrieve the data. We showed you a very simple way to add data to arrays when you initialize them, but often this just is not flexible enough for real-world programming tasks. To access an array value, you simply need to know its location. The indexing system used to access array elements is zero-based, which means that the first value is always located at position 0. Let's look at a little program that first fills in an array then prints it out:

```java
public class powersOf2 {

    public static void main(String args[]) {
        int intArray[] = new int[20];
        for (int i = 0; i < intArray.length; i++) {
            intArray[i] = 1;
            for(int p = 0; p <  i; p++) intArray[i] *= 2 ;
        }
        for (int i = 0; i < intArray.length; i++)
            System.out.println("2 to the power of " + i + " is " +
                intArray[i]);
    }
}
```

The output of this program looks like this:

```
2 to the power of 0 is 1
2 to the power of 1 is 2
2 to the power of 2 is 4
2 to the power of 3 is 8
2 to the power of 4 is 16
2 to the power of 5 is 32
2 to the power of 6 is 64
2 to the power of 7 is 128
2 to the power of 8 is 256
2 to the power of 9 is 512
2 to the power of 10 is 1024
2 to the power of 11 is 2048
2 to the power of 12 is 4096
2 to the power of 13 is 8192
2 to the power of 14 is 16384
2 to the power of 15 is 32768
2 to the power of 16 is 65536
```

```
2 to the power of 17 is 131072
2 to the power of 18 is 262144
2 to the power of 19 is 524288
```

So, how does the program work? We first create our array of integer values and assign it to the **intArray** variable. Next, we begin a loop that goes from zero to **intArray.length**. By calling the **length** method of our array, we find the number of indexes in the array. Then, we start another loop that does the calculation and stores the result in the index specified by the **i** variable from our initial loop.

Now that we have filled in all the values for our array, we need to step back through them and print out the result. We could have just put the **print** statement in the initial loop, but the approach we used gives us a chance to use another loop that references our array.

Here is the structure of an index call:

```
arrayName[index];
```

Pretty simple. If you try and use an index that is outside the boundaries of the array, a run-time error occurs. If we change the program to count to an index of 21 instead of the actual array length of 20, we would end up getting an error message like this:

```
java.lang.ArrayIndexOutOfBoundsException: 20
        at powersOf2.main(powersOf2.java:10)
```

This is a pretty common error in any programming language. You need to use some form of exception handling to watch for this problem unless you are positive you can create code that never does this (in your dreams). See Chapter 7 for additional information on exception handling.

Multidimensional Arrays

Multidimensional arrays are created in Java in using arrays of arrays. Here are a few examples of how you can implement multidimensional arrays:

```
int intArray[][];
String Names[][];
```

We can even do the same things we did with a single dimension array. We can set the array sizes and even fill in values while we declare the arrays:

```
int intArray[][] = new int[10][5];
String Names[][] = new String[25][3];

int intArray[][] = {{2, 3, 4} {1, 2, 3}};
String Names[][] = {{"Jon", "Smith"}{"Tony", "Potts"}{"Dave",
 "Friedel"}};
```

We can also create arrays that are not "rectangular" in nature. That is, each array within the main array can have a different number of elements. Here are a few examples:

```
int intArray[][] = {{1, 2} {1, 2, 3} {1, 2, 3, 4}};
String Names[][] = {{"Jon", "Smith"} {"Tony","A", "Potts"} {"Dave",
 "H", "Friedel", "Jr."}};
```

Accessing the data in a multidimensional array is not much more difficult than accessing data in a single-dimensional array. You just need to track the values for each index. Be careful though, as you add dimensions, it becomes increasingly easy to create out of bounds errors. Here are a few examples of how you can declare multidimensional arrays, assign values, and access array elements:

```
int intArray[][] = new int[10][5];          // Declare the arrays
String Names[][] = new String[25][3];

intArray[0][0] = 5;        // Assign values
intArray[7][2] = 37;
intArray[7][9] = 37;       // This will cause an out of bounds error!
Names[0][0] = "Bill Gates";
// Access an array element in a Java statement
System.out.println(Names[0][0]);
```

We will cover variables and declarations in more detail in Chapter 5, but you should have enough knowledge now to be able to run a few basic programs and get the feel for Java programming.

Using Command-Line Arguments

Programming with command-line arguments is not a topic you'd typically expect to see in a chapter on basic data types and variable declarations. However, because we've been using command-line arguments with some of the sample programs we've been introducing, we thought it would be important to discuss how this feature works in a little more detail.

Command-line arguments are only used with Java applications. They provide a mechanism so that the user of an application can pass in information to be used by the program. Java applets, on the other hand, read in parameters using HTML tags. Command-line arguments are common with languages like C and C++, which were originally designed to work with command-line operating systems like UNIX.

The advantage of using command-line arguments is that they are passed to a program when the program *first* starts, which keeps the program from having to query the user for more information. Command-line arguments are great for passing custom initialization data.

Passing Arguments

To pass arguments to a Café application, you have two options. One, you can use DOS command line arguments, or two, you can use Café's Tool Settings dialog box to tell Café what arguments to pass.

If you want to use the Café option, just click on the **Tools|Settings** menu option. This will bring up the Tool Settings dialog box as shown in Figure 4.5. In this dialog box is an entry field called **Arguments** where you can enter arguments.

The Café option will only work when you are testing your application from within Café. When you compile your application for use outside of Café, you will need to use command-line options, so let's cover those in detail.

The syntax for passing arguments to a program is extremely simple. Just start your programs as you usually would and add any number of arguments to the end of the line with each one separated by a space. Here is a sample call to a program named "myApp":

```
Java myApp open 640 480
```

In this case, we are calling the Java run-time interpreter and telling it to run he class file "myApp." We then are passing in three arguments: "open," "640," and "480."

If you wanted to pass in a longer string with spaces as an argument, you could. In this case, you enclose the string in quotation marks and Java will treat it as a single argument. Here is an example:

```
Java myApp "Nice program!" "640x480"
```

Once again the name of the program is "myApp." However, this time we are only sending it two arguments: "Nice program!" and "640x480." Note that the quotes themselves are not passed, just the string between the quotes.

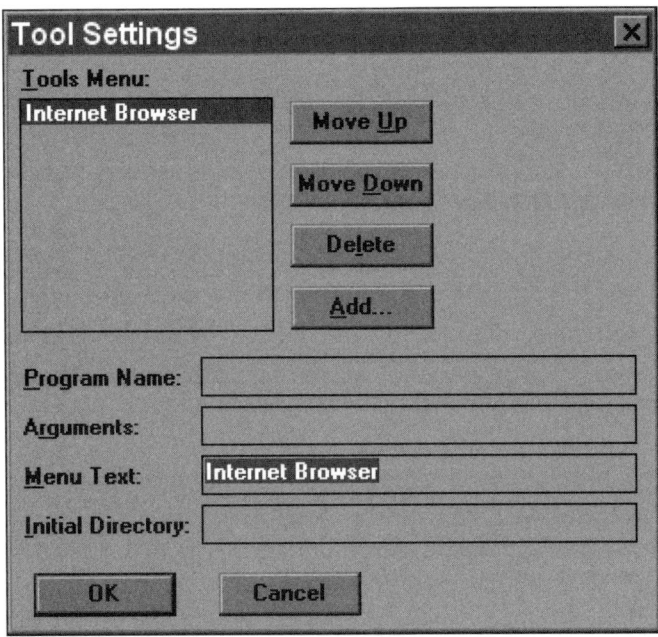

Figure 4.5   The Café Tool Settings dialog box.

Reading in Arguments

Now that we know how to pass arguments, where are they stored? How can we see them in our application? If you'll recall, all applications have a **main**() method. You should also notice that this method has an interesting argument structure:

```
public static void main(String args[]) {
   ...
}
```

Here, **main**() indicates that it takes an array named **args**[] of type **String**. Java takes any command-line arguments and puts them into the **args**[] string array. The array is dynamically resized to hold just the number of arguments passed, or zero if none are passed. Note that the use of the **args** identifier is completely arbitrary. You can use any word you want as long as it conforms to the Java naming rules. You can even get a little more descriptive, like this:

```
public static void main(String commandLineArgumentsArray[]) { ...
```

That may be a bit much, but you will never get confused as to what is in the array!

Accessing Arguments

Once we've passed in the arguments to an application and we know where they are stored, how do we get to them? Since the arguments are stored in an array, we can access them just like we would access strings in any other array. Let's look at a simple application that takes two arguments and prints them out:

```
class testArgs {
   public static void main(String args[]) {
      System.out.println(args[0]);
      System.out.println(args[1]);
   }
}
```

If we use this command line statement to run the application:

```
java testArgs hello world
```

we'd get this output:

```
hello
world
```

Now, try this command line:

```
java testArgs onearg
```

Here is the result:

```
onearg
java.lang.ArrayIndexOutOfBoundsException: 1
        at testArgs.main(testArgs.java:4)
```

What happened? Since we only were passing a single argument, the reference to **args**[1] is illegal and produces an error.

So, how do we stop from getting an error? Instead of calling each argument in line, we can use a **for** loop to step through each argument. We can check the **args.length** variable to see if we have reached the last item. Our new code will also recognize if no arguments have been passed and will not try and access the array at all. Enough talking, here is the code:

```
class testArgs {
    public static void main(String args[]) {
        for (int i = 0; i < args.length; i++) {
            System.out.println(args[i]);
        }
    }
}
```

Now, no matter how many arguments are passed (or none) the application can handle it.

Indexing Command-Line Arguments

Don't forget that Java arrays are zero based, so the first command-line argument is stored at position 0 not position 1. This is different than some other languages like C where the first argument would be at position 1. In C, position 0 would store the name of the program.

Dealing with Numeric Arguments

One more thing we should cover here is how to deal with numeric arguments. If you remember, all arguments are passed into an array of strings so we need to convert those values into numbers.

This is actually very simple. Each data type has an associated class that provides methods for dealing with that data type. Each of these classes has a method that creates a variable of that type from a string. Table 4.9 presents a list of those methods.

Make sure you understand the difference between the **parse*()** methods and the **valueOf()** methods. The parsing methods return just a value that can be plugged into a variable or used as part of an expression. The **valueOf()** methods return an *object* of the specified type that has an initial value equal to the value of the string.

Table 4.9   Classes and Their Associated Methods for Handling Data Types.

Class	Method	Return
Integer	parseInt(String)	An integer value
Integer	valueOf(String)	An Integer object initialized to the value represented by the specified String
Long	parseLong(String)	A long value
Long	valueOf(String)	A long object initialized to the value represented by the specified String
Double	valueOf(String)	A Double object initialized to the value represented by the specified String
Float	valueOf(String)	A Float object initialized to the value represented by the specified String

Operators, Expressions, and Control Structures

Anthony Potts

Operators, expressions, and control structures give you power to manipulate your data and steer your program.

*N*ow that you know about the types of data you can use in Java, you need to learn how to manipulate your data. The tools for manipulating data fall into three categories—operators, expressions, and control structures—each playing a more powerful role as you move up the ladder. In this chapter, we'll discuss each of the key Java operators—everything from assignment statements to bitwise operators. Although Java operators are very similar to C/C++ operators, there are a few subtle differences which we'll point out. Next, we'll show you the basics for creating expressions with Java. Finally, in the last part of the chapter, we'll investigate the world of Java control structures.

Using Java Operators

Operators allow you to perform tasks such as addition, subtraction, multiplication, and assignment. Operators can be divided into three main categories: *assignment*, *integer*, and *boolean* operators. We'll explore each Java operator in detail by examining each of the three categories. But first, let's cover operator precedence.

Operator Precedence

As you are writing your code, you need to keep in mind which operators have precedence over the others—the order in which operators take effect. If you are an experienced programmer or you can remember some of the stuff you learned in your high school algebra classes, you shouldn't have any problem with understanding the principles of operator precedence. The basic idea is that the outcome or result of an expression like this:

```
x = 5 * (7+4) - 3;
```

is determined by the *order in which the operators are evaluated* by the Java compiler. In general, all operators that have the same precedence are evaluated from left to right. If the above expression were handled in this manner, the result would be 36 (multiply 5 by 7, add 4, and then subtract 3). Because of precedence, we know that some operators, such as (), are evaluated before operators such as *. Therefore, the real value of this expression would be 52 (add 7 and 4, multiply by 5, and then subtract 3).

Table 5.1   Operator Precedence with Java.

Operators	Operator Type
() [] .	Expression
++ -- ! - ~	Unary
* / %	Multiplicative
+ -	Additive
<< >> >>>	Shift
< <= > >=	Relational (inequality)
== !=	Relational (equality)
&	Bitwise ADD
^	Bitwise XOR
|	Bitwise OR
&&	Logical AND
||	Logical OR
?:	Conditional
= *= /= %= += -= <<= >>= &= |= ^=	Assignment

The actual rules for operator precedence in Java are nearly identical to those found in C/C++. The only difference is that C/C++ includes a few operators, such as ->, that are not used in Java. Table 5.1 lists the major operators in order of precedence. Notice that some operator symbols such as (-) show up twice. The reason for this is because the operator has different meanings depending on how it is used in an expression. For example, in an expression like this

```
x = 7 + -3;
```

the (-) operator is used as a unary operator to negate the value 3. In this case, it would have a higher precedence than a standard additive operator (+ or -). In an expression like this, on the other hand,

```
x = 7 - 3 + 5;
```

the (-) operator is used as a binary additive operator, and it shares the same precedence with the (+) operator.

Which Operators Are Missing?

If you are an experienced C/C++ programmer, you're probably wondering what operators used in C/C++ are not available in Java. The ones missing are the four key data access and size operators shown in Table 5.2. These operators are not needed because Java does not support pointers and does not allow you to access memory dynamically. As we learned in Chapter 2, Java uses garbage collection techniques to provide its own internal system of memory management.

Table 5.2   C/C++ Operators Missing from Java.

Operator	Description
*	Performs pointer indirection
&	Calculates the memory address of a variable
->	Allows a pointer to select a data structure
sizeof	Determines the size of an allocated data structure

Assignment Operators

The most important and most often used operator is the assignment operator (=). This operator does just what it looks like it should do; it takes whatever variable is on the left and sets it equal to the expression on the right:

```
i = 35;
```

The expression on the right can be any valid Java expression—a literal, an equation with operands and operators, a method call, and so on. When using an assignment operator, you must be careful that the variable you are using to receive the expression is the correct size and type to receive the result of the expression on the right side. For example, statements like the following could cause you a lot of headaches:

```
short count;
// This number is way too big for a short type!
count = 500000000000;

char ch;
// Oops! We should be assigning a character here
ch = 100;
```

In the first example, the variable count is declared as a **short**, which means that the variable can only hold a number as large as 32767. Obviously, the number being assigned to the variable is way too large. In the second example, the variable ch expects to receive a character but in reality is assigned something else entirely.

If you look closely at the last line in Table 5.1, you'll see that Java offers a number of variations of the standard assignment statement. They are all borrowed from the C language. An assignment statement like this:

```
num *= 5;
```

would be equivalent to this expression:

```
num = num * 5;
```

The combination assignment operators turn out to be very useful for writing expressions inside loops that perform counting operations. Here's an example:

```
While (i <= count)
{
    i += 2;   // Increment the counting variable
    ...
}
```

In this case **i** is used as the loop "counting" control variable, and it is incremented by using a combination assignment statement.

Integer Operators

In the category of integer operators, there are two flavors to choose from: *unary* and *binary*. A unary operator performs a task on a single variable at a time. Binary operators, on the other hand, must work with two variables at a time. Let's start with the unary operators.

UNARY OPERATORS

There are four integer unary operators: negation, bitwise complement, increment, and decrement. They are used without an assignment operation. They simply perform their operation on a given variable, changing its value appropriately.

NEGATION (-)

Unary negation changes the sign of an integer. You must be careful when reaching the lower limits of integer variables because the negative limit is always one greater than the positive limit. So, if you had a variable of type **byte** with a value of -256 and you performed a unary negation on it, an error will occur because the **byte** data type has a maximum positive value of 255. Here are some examples of how this operator can be used:

```
- k;
-someInt;
x = -50 + 10;
```

As we learned earlier, the negation operator is at the top end of the precedence food chain; thus, you can count on operands that use it to be evaluated first.

BITWISE COMPLEMENT (~)

Performing a bitwise complement on a variable flips each bit of the variable—all 1s become 0s and all 0s become 1s. For strict decimal calculations, this operator is not used very often. But if you are working with values that represent bit settings, such as an index into a color palette, this type of operator is invaluable. Here is an example of the unary complement operator in action:

```
// input: byte type variable bitInt = 3 (00000011 in binary)
~bitInt;
// Output: bitInt = 252 (11111100 in binary)
```

INCREMENT (++) AND DECREMENT (- -)

The increment and decrement operators are very simple operators that simply increase or decrease an integer variable by 1 each time they are used. These operators were created as a shortcut to saying x=x+1. As we've already mentioned, they are often used in loops where you want a variable incremented or decremented by one each time a loop is completed. Here is an example of how each operator is used:

```
++intIncrement;
--intDecrement;
```

BINARY OPERATORS

When you need to perform operations that involve two variables, you will be dealing with binary operators. Simple addition and subtraction are prime examples of binary operators. These operators do not change the value of either of the operands, instead they perform a function between the two operands that is placed into a third. Table 5.3 lists the complete set of the binary integer operators. Let's look at each of these operators in detail.

ADDITION, SUBTRACTION, MULTIPLICATION, AND DIVISION

These operators are the standard binary operators that we have all used since we started programming. We won't explain the theory behind algebra because we assume you already know this stuff. We will, however, give you a few examples:

```
// X=12 and Y=4
Z = X + Y; // Answer = 16
Z = X - Y; // Answer = 8
Z = X * Y; // Answer = 48
Z = X / Y; // Answer = 3
```

MODULUS

The modulus operator divides the first operand by the second operand and returns the remainder:

```
// X=11 and Y=4
Z = X % Y; // Answer = 3
```

BITWISE OPERATORS

The bitwise binary operators perform operations at the binary level on integers. They act much like custom *if...then* statements. They compare

Table 5.3   The Binary Integer Operators.

Operator	Description
+	Addition
-	Subtraction
*	Multiplication
/	Division
%	Modulus
&	Bitwise AND
|	Bitwise OR
^	Bitwise XOR
<<	Left Shift
>>	Right Shift
>>>	Zero-Fill Right Shift

the respective bits from each of the operands and set the corresponding bit of the return variable to a 1 or 0 depending on which operator is used. The AND operator works as follows: "if both bits are 1 then return a 1, otherwise return a 0." The OR operators works like this: "if either bit is a 1 then return a 1, otherwise return a 0." Finally, the XOR operator works like this: "if the bits are different return a 1, if they are the same return a 0." Table 5.4 provides a set of examples that illustrate how each bitwise operator works.

And here are some code examples to show you how to incorporate bitwise operators into your Java statements:

```
// X=3 (00000011)
// Y=2 (00000010)
Z = X & Y; // Answer: Z = 2X 00000011
        //         Y 00000010
        //         Z 00000010

Z = X | Y; // Answer: Z = 3X 00000011
        //         Y 00000010
        //         Z 00000011

Z = X ^ Y; // Answer: Z = 1X 00000011
```

Table 5.4   Using the Java Bitwise Operators.

Operand 1	Operand 2	Bitwise Operator	Return
1	1	AND	True
1	0	AND	False
0	1	AND	False
0	0	AND	False
1	1	OR	True
1	0	OR	True
0	1	OR	True
0	0	OR	False
1	1	XOR	False
1	0	XOR	True
0	1	XOR	True
0	0	XOR	False

```
//          Y 00000010
//          Z 00000001
```

Boolean Operators

The boolean data type adds several new operators to the mix. All of the operators that can be used on boolean values are listed in Table 5.5.

BOOLEAN NEGATION (!)

Negation of a boolean variable simply returns the opposite of the boolean value. As you might have guessed, boolean negation is a unary operation. Here's an example:

```
// Bool1 = True
!Bool1; // Answer: Bool1 = False
```

LOGICAL AND (&), OR (|), & XOR (^)

The AND, OR, and XOR operators work identically to the way they do with integer values. However, they only have a single bit to worry about:

```
Bool2 = true;
Bool3 = true;
Bool4 = False;
Bool5 = False;
Bool1 = Bool2 & Bool3; // Answer: Bool1 = True
Bool1 = Bool2 & Bool4; // Answer: Bool1 = False
Bool1 = Bool2 | Bool3; // Answer: Bool1 = False
Bool1 = Bool2 | Bool4; // Answer: Bool1 = True
Bool1 = Bool3 ^ Bool4; // Answer: Bool1 = False
Bool1 = Bool4 ^ Bool5; // Answer: Bool1 = True
```

EVALUATION AND (&&) AND OR (||)

The evaluation AND and OR are a little different than the logical versions. Using these operators causes Java to avoid evaluation of the righthand operands if it is not needed. In other words, if the answer can be derived by only reading the first operand, Java will not bother to read the second. Here are some examples:

```
// op1 = True op2 = False
result = op1 && op2; // result=False-both ops are evaluated
result = op2 && op1; // result=False-only first op is evaluated
```

Table 5.5   Java Boolean Operators.

Operator	Operation
!	Negation
&	Logical AND
I	Logical OR
^	Logical XOR
&&	Evaluation AND
II	Evaluation OR
==	Equal to
!=	Not Equal to
&=	And Assignment
I=	OR Assignment
^=	XOR Assignment
?:	Ternary (Conditional)

```
result = op1 || op2; // result=True-only first op is evaluated
result = op2 || op1; // result=True-both ops are evaluated
```

EQUAL TO (==) AND NOT EQUAL TO (!=)

These operators are used to simply transfer a boolean value or transfer the opposite of a boolean value. Here are a few examples:

```
op1 = True;
if (result == op1); // Answer: result = true
if (result != op1); // Answer: result = false
```

ASSIGNMENT BOOLEAN OPERATORS (&=), (I=), (^=)

Boolean assignment operators are a lot like the assignment operators for integers. Here is an example of an assignment being used on both an integer and a boolean so that you can compare the two:

```
i    += 5;    // Same as int = int + 5
bool &= true; // Same as bool = bool & true
bool |= true; // Same as bool = bool | true
bool ^= false; // Same as bool = bool ^ false
```

TERNARY OPERATOR

This powerful little operator acts like an extremely condensed *if...then* statement. If you look at the example below you will see that if the operand is True, the expression before the colon is evaluated. If the operand is False, the expression after the colon is evaluated. This type of coding may look a little strange at first. But once you understand the logic, you'll begin to see just how useful this operator can be. In the following example, the parentheses are not actually needed, but when you use more complicated expressions they will make the code much easier to follow:

```
// op1 = True op2 = False
op1 ? (x=1):(x=2); // Answer: x=1
op2 ? (x=1):(x=2); // Answer: x=2
```

Floating-Point Number Operators

Almost all of the integer operators work on floating-point numbers as well, with a few minor changes. Of course, all the standard arithmetic operators (+, -, *, /) work as well as the assignment operators (+=, -=, *=, /=). Modulus (%) also works; however, it only evaluates the integer portion of the operands. The increment and decrement operators work identically by adding or subtracting 1.0 from the integer portion of the numbers. Be careful when using relational operators on floating-point numbers. Do not make assumptions about how the numbers will behave just because integers behave a certain way. For example, just because an expression like a==b may be true for two floating-point values, don't assume that an expression like a<b || a>b will be true. This is because floating-point values are not ordered like integers. You also have to deal with the possibility of a floating-point variable being equal to negative or positive infinity, **-Inf** and **Inf**, respectively. You can get a positive or negative **Inf** when you perform an operation that returns an overflow.

Using Casts

In some applications you may need to transfer one type of variable to another. Java provides us with *casting* methods to accomplish this. Casting refers to the process of transforming one variable of a certain type into another data type.

Casting is accomplished by placing the name of the data type you wish to cast a particular variable into in front of that variable in parentheses. Here is an example of how a cast can be set up to convert a **char** into an **int**:

```
int a;
char b;
b = 'z';
a = (int) b;
```

Since the variable **a** is declared as an **int**, it expects to be assigned an **int** value. The variable **b**, on the other hand, is declared as a **char**. To assign the contents of **b** to **a**, the cast is used on the right side of the assignment statement. The contents of **b**, the numeric value of the character 'z' is safely assigned to the variable **a** as an integer. If you wanted to, you could perform the cast in reverse:

```
short a;
char b;
a = 40;
b = (char) a;   // Convert value 40 into a character
```

Casting is extremely simple when you are using the primitive data types—**int, char, short, double**, and so on. You can also cast classes and interfaces in Java, which we'll show you how to do in Chapter 6.

The most important thing to remember when using casts is the space each variable has to work with. Java will let you cast a variable of one data type into a variable of a different data type if the size of the data type of the target variable is smaller than the other data type, but you may not like the result. Does this sound confusing? Let's explain this a little better. If you had a variable of type **long**, you should only cast it into another variable of type **float** or **double** because these data types are the only other two primitives with at least 64-bits of space to handle your number. On the other hand, if you had a variable of type **byte**, then you could cast it into any of the other primitives except boolean because they all have more space than the lowly **byte**. When you are dealing with **double** variables, you are stuck, since no other data type offers as much space as the **double**.

If you have to cast a variable into another variable having less space, Java will do it. However, any information in the extra space will be lost. On the plus side though, if the value of a larger variable is less than the maximum value of the variable you are casting into, no information will be lost.

Writing Expressions and Statements

So far we've been more or less looking at operators, literals, and data types in a vacuum. Although we've used these components to write expressions, we haven't formally defined what Java expressions are. Essentially, expressions are the Java statements that make your code work; they are the guts of your programs. A basic expressions contains *operands* and *operators*. For example, in this expression

```
i = x + 10;
```

the variable **x** and the literal 10 are the operands and + is the operator. The evaluation of an expression performs one or more operations that return a result. The data type of the result is always determined by the data types of the operand(s).

When multiple operands are combined, they are referred to as a *compound expression*. The order in which the operators are evaluated is determined by the precedence of the operators that act upon them. We discussed precedence earlier and showed you the relative precedence of each Java operator.

The simplest form of expression is used to calculate a value, which in turn is assigned to a variable in an assignment statement. Here are a couple assignment statements that use expressions that should look very familiar to you by now:

```
i = 2;
thisString = "Hello";
```

Here are a few assignment statements that are a little more involved:

```
Bool1 != Bool2;
i += 2;
d *= 1.9
Byte1 ^= Byte2;
```

An assignment expression involves a variable that will accept the result, followed by a single assignment operator, followed by the operand that the assignment operator is using.

The next step up the ladder is to create expressions that use operators like the arithmetic operators we have already discussed:

```
i = i + 2;
thisString = "Hello";
```

Expressions with multiple operands are probably the most common type of expressions. They still have a variable that is assigned the value of the result produced by evaluating the operands and operators to the right of the equal sign. You can also have expressions with many operators and operands like this:

```
i = i + 2 - 3 * 9 / 3;
thisString = "Hello" + "World, my name is " + myName;
```

The art of programming in Java—with Café or without it—involves using operators and operands to build expressions, which are in turn used to build *statements*. Of course, the assignment statement is just one type of statement that can be constructed. You can also create many types of control statements, such as while and for loops, if-then decision making statements, and so on. (We'll look at all of the control statements that can be written in Java in the last part of this chapter.)

There are essentially two types of statements you can write in Java: *simple* and *compound*. A simple statement performs a single operation. Here are some examples:

```
int i;      // Variable declaration
i = 10 * 5; // Assignment statement
if (i = 50) x = 200;  // if-then decision statement
```

The important thing to remember about simple statements in Java is that they are *always* completed with a semicolon (;). (Some of the others like class declarations and compound *if...else* statements don't need semicolons, but if you leave it off the end of an expression, you'll get an error.)

Compound statements involve the grouping of simple statements. In this case, the characters ({ }) are used to group the separate statements into one compound statement. Here are a few examples:

```
while (x < 10)
{
   ++x;
   if (sum < x) printline();
}

if (x < 10)
{
   i = 20;
   p = getvalue(i);
}
```

Notice that the (;) terminating character is not used after the final (}). The braces take care of this for us.

Control Flow Statements

Control flow is what programming is all about. What good are basic data types, variables, and casting if you don't have any code that can make use of them? Java provides several different types of control flow structures. These structures provide your application with direction. They take an input, decide what to do with it and how long to do it, and then let expressions handle the rest.

Let's look at each of these structures in detail. If you have done any programming before, all of these should look familiar. Make sure you study the syntax so that you understand exactly how they work in Java as compared to how they work in other languages.

Table 5.6 lists all of the standard control flow structures, and it shows you what the different parts of their structure represent.

Table 5.6   Control Flow Structures.

Structure	Expression
if...else	if (boolean = true) statement
	else statement;
while	while (boolean = true) statement;
do...while	do statement while (boolean = true);
switch	switch (expression) {
	case expression: statement;
	case expression: statement;
	...
	default: statement;
	}
for	for (expression1; expression2; expression3)
	statement;
label	label: statement
	break label;
	continue label;

if...else

The **if...else** control structure is probably used more than all the others combined. How many programs have you written that didn't include one? Not very many, we'll wager.

In its simplest terms, the **if...else** structure performs this operation: if *this* is true then do *that* otherwise do *something else*. Of course, the "otherwise" portion is optional. Since you probably already know what **if...else** statements are used for, we will just show you a few examples so you can see how they work in Java.

Here is the structure labeled with standard terms:

```
if (boolean) statement
else statement;
```

Here is a sample of what an **if...else** statement might look like with actual code:

```
if (isLunchtime) {
    Eat = true;
    Hour = 12;
}
else {
    Eat = False;
    Hour = 0;
}
```

You can also use nested **if...else** statements:

```
if (isLunchtime) {
    Eat = true;
    Hour = 12;
}
else if (isBreakfast) {
        Eat = true;
        Hour = 6;
    }
    else if (isDinner) {
            Eat = true;
            Hour = 18;
        }
        else {
            Eat = false;
            Hour = 0;
        }
```

The curly braces are used when multiple statements need to take place for each option. If we were only performing a single operation for each part of the **if...else** statement, we would not need the braces. Here is an example of an **if...else** statement that uses curly braces for one part but not the other:

```
if (isLunchtime) {
    Eat = true;
    Hour = 12;
}
else Eat = False;
```

while and do...while

The **while** and **do...while** loops perform the same function. The only difference is that the **while** loop verifies the expression *before* executing the statement, and the **do...while** loop verifies the expression *after* executing the statement. This is a major difference that can be extremely helpful if used properly.

Here are the structures labeled with standard terms:

```
while (boolean) {
    statement;
}

do {
    statement
} while(boolean);
```

while and **do...while** loops are used if you want to repeat a certain statement or block of statements until a certain expression becomes false. For example, assume you wanted to send e-mail to all of the people at a particular Web site. You could set up a **while** loop that stepped through all the people, one-by-one, sending them e-mail until you reached the last person. When the last person is reached, the loop is terminated and the program control flow moves on to the statement following the loop. Here is what that loop might look like in very simple terms:

```
boolean done = false;

while (!done){
    emailUser();
    goNextuser();
    if (noNewuser) done = true;
}
```

switch

The **switch** control flow structure is useful when you have a single expression with many possible options. The same thing can be done using recursed **if...else** statments, but that can get very confusing when you get past just a few options. The **if...else** structure is also difficult to change when it becomes highly nested.

The **switch** statement is executed by comparing the value of an initial expression or variable with other variables or expressions. Let's look at the labeled structure:

```
switch(expression) {
    case expression: statement;
    case expression: statement;
    case expression: statement;
    default: statement;
}
```

Now let's look at a real piece of code that uses the **switch** structure:

```
char age;

System.out.print("How many computers do you own? ");
age = System.in.read();
switch(age) {
    case '0':
        System.out.println("\nWhat are you waiting for?");
        break;
    case '1':
        System.out.println("\nIs that enough these days?");
        break;
    case '2':
        System.out.println("\nPerfect!");
        break;
    default:
        System.out.println("\nToo much free time on you hands!");
}
```

The **break** statement is extremely important when dealing with **switch** structures. If the **switch** finds a case that is true, it will execute the statements for that case. When it is finished with that case, it will move on to the next one. This process continues until a match is found or the **default** statement is reached. The **break** statement tells the **switch** "OK, we found a match, let's move on."

The **default** clause serves as the "catch-all" statement. If all of the other cases fail, the **default** clause will be executed.

for

for loops are another programming standard that would be tough to live without. The idea behind a **for** loop is that we want to step through a sequence of numbers until a limit is reached. The loop steps through our range in whatever step increment we want, checking at the beginning of each loop to see if we have caused our "quit" expression to become true.

Here is the labeled structure of a **for** loop:

```
for (variable ; expression1 ; expression2);
```

The variable we use can either be one we have previously created, or it can be declared from within the **for** structure. Expression1 from the above example is the expression we need to stay true until the loop is finished. More often than not, this expression is something like x<10 which means that we will step through the loop until x is equal to 10 at which time the expression (x<10) becomse false and drops us out of the loop.

Here is an example of a **for** loop that actually works:

```
for (int x = 0 ; x < 10 ; x++) {
  System.out.println(x);
}
```

If you put this code into an empty **main** method you should get the following output:

```
0
1
2
3
4
5
6
7
8
9
```

For loops are used for many different applications. They are a necessity when dealing with arrays and can really help when creating lookup tables or indexing a database.

labels

Java **labels** provide a means of controlling different kinds of loops. Sometimes, when you create a loop, you need to be able to break out of it before it finishes on its own and satisfies its completion expression. This is where **labels** come in very handy.

The key to **labels** is the **break** statement that you learned to use with the **switch** statement. You can also use the **break** statement to exit out of any loop. It is great for breaking out of **for** loops and **while** loops especially.

However, sometimes you have embedded loops and you need to be able to break out of a certain loop. A great example of this is two embedded **for** loops that are setting values in an array. If an error occurs or you get a strange value, you may want to be able to break out of one loop or another. It gets confusing if you have all these embedded loops and break statements all over with no apparent link to one loop or another. **labels** rectify this situation.

To use a label, you simply place an identifier followed by a colon at the beginning of the line that initiates a loop. Let's look at an example before we go further:

```
outer: for (int x = 0 ; x < 10 ; x++) {
   inner: for (int y = 0 ; y < 10 ; y++) {
  System.out.println(x + y);
      if (y=9) {
         break outer:
      } else {
         continue outer:
      }
   }
}
```

Labels are probably new to most of you, so you may not see a need for them right away. However, as your programs become more complicated you should think about using lables where appropriate to make your code simple and more readable.

Moving Ahead

We covered a lot of ground in this chapter and the previous one. If you are new to Java programming and have little C or C++ background, make sure you understand these concepts well so that you do not get confused in the upcoming chapters.

Let's now move on to another basic structure of Java programming. In fact, we would have to call it the basic structure of Java programming— the class.

Java Classes and Methods

David H. Freidel, Jr.

Classes are the key Java components that give the language its object-oriented personality.

If you have some experience programming in a language like C++, you are probably familiar with the power and flexibility that classes provide. They are ideal for plugging general information into a template-like structure for reusing over and over. For example, if you are developing an interactive drawing package, you could create standard classes for some of the fundamental drawing operations and then use those classes to create more sophisticated drawing tasks. If you are new to the world of object-oriented programming (OOP), you'll soon discover that classes are the essential building blocks for writing OOP applications. At first glance, Java classes look and operate like C++ classes; but there are some key differences which we'll address in this chapter.

We'll start by looking at the basics of classes. You'll quickly learn how classes are defined and used to derive other classes. The second half of the chapter covers *methods*—the components used to breathe life into classes.

Understanding Classes

In traditional structured programming languages like C or Pascal, everything revolves around the concepts of algorithms and data structures. The algorithms are kept separate from the data structures, and they operate on the data to perform actions and results. To help divide programming tasks into separate units, components like functions and procedures are defined. The problem with this programming paradigm is that it doesn't allow you to easily create code that can be reused and expanded to create other code.

To solve this problem, object-oriented programming languages like Smalltalk and C++ were created. These languages introduced powerful components called *classes* so that programmers could combine functions (operations) and data under one roof. This is a technique called *encapsulation* in the world of object-oriented programming. Every language that uses classes defines them in a slightly different way; however, the basics concepts for using them remain the same. The main advantages of classes are:

◆ They can be used to define abstract data types.

◆ Data is protected or hidden inside a class so other classes cannot access it.

◆ Classes can be used to derive other classes.

◆ New classes derived from existing classes can inherit the data and methods already defined—a concept called *inheritance*.

As you'll learn in this chapter, the techniques for defining and using Java classes are adapted from techniques found in the C++ language. In some cases, the Java syntax will look very similar to C++ syntax, but in other cases you'll find a number of differences, including new keywords that have been added to Java for declaring classes and methods; restrictions, such as the elimination of pointers; and different scoping rules that determine how classes can be used in an application.

Declaring a Class

Let's take look at the full declaration used to define classes in Java:

```
[Doc Comment] [Modifier] class Identifier
[extends Superclassname]
[implements Interfaces] {
    ClassBody;
}
```

Of course, keep in mind that you won't always use all of the clauses, such as *Doc Comment*, *Modifier*, **extends**, and so on. For example, here's an example of a very small class definition:

```
class Atom_ant {
    int a = 1;
}
```

This class has an identifier, **Atom_ant**, and a body, **int a = 1;**. Of course, don't try to compile this at home as is because it will only result in an error. Why? Well, even though it is a valid class, it is not capable of standing on its own. (You would need to set it up as an applet or a main program to make it work.)

A class declaration provides all of the information about a class including its internal data (*variables*) and functions (*methods*) to be interpreted by the Java compiler. In addition, class declarations provide:

◆ Programmer comments

◆ Specifications of the other classes that may reference the class

◆ Specifications of the superclass the class belongs to (the class' parent)

◆ Specifications of the methods the class can call

Using a Class

Before we move on and look at all of the other components used to declare classes, let's return to our simple class declaration to see how classes are used in Java programs. Once a class has been declared, you need to use it to create an object. This process is called making an "instance of" a class. In a Java program it requires two steps. First, you declare an object variable using a syntax that looks just like a variable declaration, except the class name is used instead of the name of a primitive data type. For example, this

statement would use the **Atom_ant** class we defined earlier to declare an object from the class definition:

```
Atom_ant crazyant;
```

Once the object has been declared, in this case **crazyant**, you then create an instance of it in a Java application by using the **new** operator:

```
crazyant = new Atom_ant();
```

Now the object **crazyant** can access all of the components in a **Atom_ant** class, thus making it an instance of an **Atom_ant** class. To see how this works in context, let's expand our example:

```
class Atom_ant {  // Simple class
    int a = 1;
}
public class Bug {
    int i = 10;
    Atom_ant crazyant;  // Declare an object

    public static void main (String args[]) {
        // Create an instance of Atom_ant called crazyant
        crazyant = new Atom_ant();
        System.out.println("There are " + bug.i + " bugs here but only "
            + crazyant.i + " atom ant.");
    }
}
```

The output produced by this example would be:

```
There are 10 bugs here but only 1 atom ant.
```

The main class, **Bug**, creates an instance of the **Atom_ant** class—the **crazyant** object. Then it uses the object to access the data member, **a**, which is assigned a value in the **Atom_ant** class. Notice that the dot operator (.) is used to access a member of a class.

Object Declaration Time Saver

In Java, you can both declare an object variable and create an instance all in one statement. Here's an example of how it is done:

```
Atom_ant crazyant = new Atom_ant();
```

Notice that the class Atom_ant is used to declare the object variable crazyant and then the new operator is used to create an instance of Atom_ant.

Components of a Class Declaration

Let's look at the components of the class declaration in a little more detail. As you recall from our first example, the only really necessary part of a class declaration is its name or *identifier*. However, whenever you need to reference your class in your program to reuse it, you'll need to reference it by its *fully qualified name*. This name is the package name, or group of classes from which it came, followed by the identifier. For example, if *Atom_ant* is the class name and it belongs to a package named *molecule*, its fully qualified name would be *molecule.Atom_ant*.

Documentation Comment

The *Doc Comment* clause of the class declaration is provided as an aid to help other programmers who might need to use your class. It allows you to write your documentation while you're writing the code. The comments you include as part of this clause can easily be converted into easy to read HTML pages. However, keep in mind that your HTML pages will only be as good as your comments. Let's look at an example to see how the *Doc Comment* feature works. The code snippet below:

```
/**
 * Atom ant is the world's smallest super hero,
    so we gave him a class by himself.
 * @author Dave Friedel
 */
class Atom_ant {
    int i = 1;
}
```

uses *Doc Comment* style comments to produce the HTML page shown in Figure 6.1. Notice how the comments are formatted and used to document the class. In this case, **Atom_ant** is a subclass under the **java.lang.Object** class—the default parent for all classes.

In case you're wondering, the **@author** notation is a special type of comment tag that allows you to personalize your class.

Class Modifiers

Modifiers define the rules for how classes are used in Java applications. They determine how other packages, or classes of other groups can interact

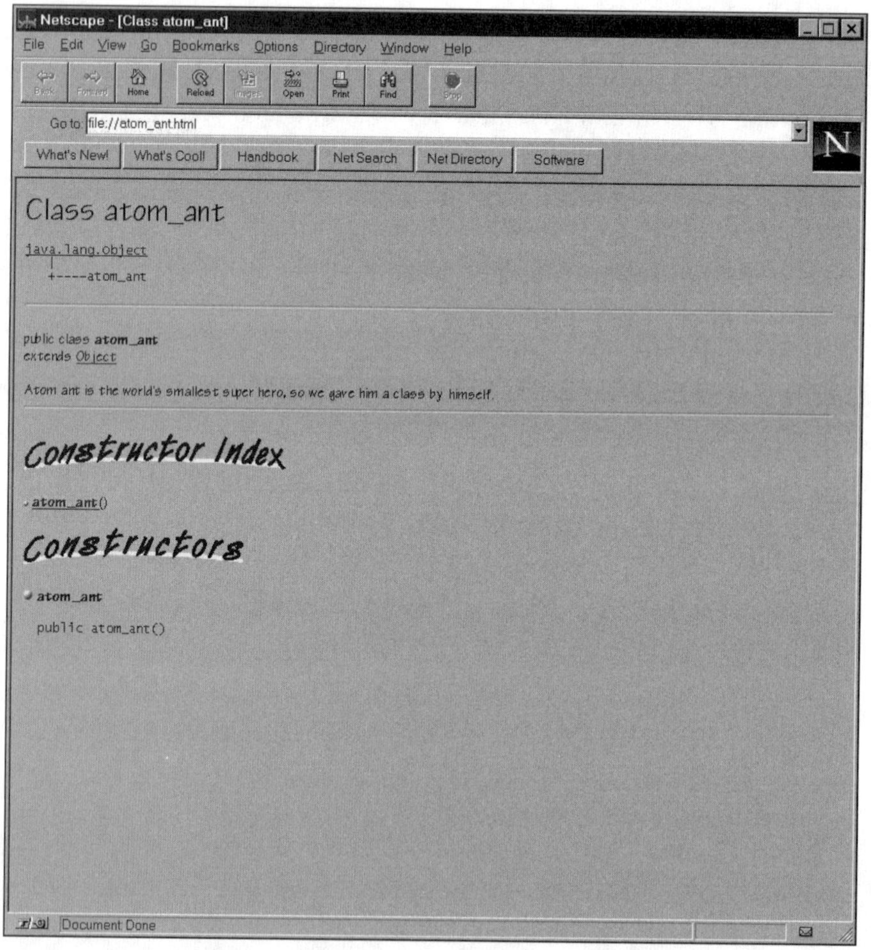

Figure 6.1 The HTML documentation created for the Atom_ant class.

with the current class. There are three kinds of modifiers that can be used in a class declaration:

◆ **public**

◆ **abstract**

◆ **final**

If you don't use one of these modifiers when declaring a class, Java will automatically decide that only other classes in the current package may access the class. Let's look at how each of these modifiers are used.

PUBLIC CLASS

The **public** modifier is used to define a class that can have the greatest amount of access by other classes. By declaring a class as **public**, you allow all other classes and packages to access its variables, methods, and subclasses. However, *only one public class is allowed in any single Java applet or a single source code file*. You can think of the one public class in an applet as serving the role that the **main()** function does in a C/C++ program.

The source code for an applet must be saved as *ClassName.java*, where *ClassName* is the name of the single public class defined in the applet. If we created a TickerTape applet, for example, the single public class might be defined as:

```
public class TickerTape extends Applet implements Runnable {...
```

and the name of the file would be TickerTape.java.

Let's look at another example of how the **public** modifier is used to define a Java class:

```
// Filename: Atom_ant.java
public class Atom_ant {
   public static void main (String args[]) {
      System.out.println("Hello World");
   }
}
```

In this case, **Atom_ant** is the name of the class and the filename for the applet is Atom_ant.java.

ABSTRACT CLASS

The **abstract** modifier is used to declare classes that serve as a shell or placeholder for implementing methods and variables. When you construct a hierarchy of classes, your top most class will contain the more general data definitions and method implementations that represent your program's features. As you work your way down the class hierarchy, your classes will start to implement more specific data components and operations. As you build your hierarchy, you may need to create more general classes and *defer* the actual implementation to later stages in the class hierarchy. This is where the abstract class comes in. This approach allows you to reference the operations that you need to include without having to restructure your entire hierarchy.

The technique of using abstract classes in Java is commonly referred to as *single inheritance* by C++ programmers. (By the way, limited multiple inheritance techniques can also be implemented in Java by using interfaces.)

Any class that is declared as an abstract class must follow certain rules:

◆ No objects can be instantiated from an abstract class.

◆ Abstract classes must contain at least one declaration of an abstract method or variable.

◆ All abstract methods that are declared in an abstract class must be implemented in one of the subclasses beneath it.

◆ Abstract classes cannot be declared as final or private classes.

Let's look at an example of how an abstract class is defined and used to help create other classes:

```
abstract class Quark extends Atom_ant {
    ...
    abstract void abstract_method1();
    abstract void abstract_method2();
```

```
    void normal_method();
    ...
}

public class Aparticles extends Quark {
    public void abstract_method1() {
        ... // Definition of the method
    }
}

public class Bparticles extends Quark {
    public void abstract_method2() {
 ... // Definition of the method
    }
}
```

Here, the class **Quark** is declared as an abstract class and it contains two methods that are declared as abstract methods. The subclasses **Aparticles** and **Bparticles** are located beneath the class **Quark** in the hierarchy of classes. Each one defines a method based on one of the abstract methods found in the **Quark** class. A compile-time error would occur if we had failed to define both of the abstract methods in the **Quark** class. All abstract methods must be defined in the subclasses that are derived from abstract classes.

Restrictions in Declaring Abstract Classes

An abstract class cannot be defined as a final class (using the final keyword) because the Java compiler will always assume that the abstract class will be used to derive other classes—other subclasses will follow it. (As you'll see in the next section, a final class defines the end of the line for a class hierarchy.) Furthermore, you cannot used a private modifier in an abstract class's method declarations because this modifier restricts methods from being used by any other classes except the class they are defined in.

FINAL CLASS

The **final** modifier is used to declare a class that will not be used to derive any other classes. The final class is like the last station on a railway line. By its position in a class hierarchy, a final class cannot have any subclasses beneath it. In **final** class declarations, you cannot use the **extends** clause because the Java compiler always assumes that a final class cannot be extended. Here's an example of what would happen if you tried to declare a final class and then use it in another class declaration:

```
final class Molecule extends Element {
    static String neutron = "molecule";
}

class Atom_ant extends Molecule {
    static String proton = "atom_ant";
}
```

```
Compiling...
E:\java\jm\element.java
E:\java\jm\element.java:12: Can't subclass final classes: class
  Moleculeclass Atom_ant extends Molecule {        ^1 errorsCompile
  Ended.
```

In this case, **Molecule** has been defined as a final class. But notice that the second class definition, **Atom_ant**, attempts to use **Molecule** as its parent. The Java compiler catches this illegal declaration and provides the appropriate warning.

Class Identifiers

Each class you define in a Java program must have its own unique identifier. The class's identifier or name directly follows the **class** keyword. The rules for naming classes are the same as those used to name variables. To refresh your memory, identifiers should always begin with a letter of the alphabet, either upper or lower case. The only exception to this rule is the underscore symbol (_) and the dollar sign ($), which may also be used. The rest of the name can be defined using characters, numbers, and some symbols.

Since class names are also used as file names, you need to create names that will not cause problems with your operating system or anyone who will be using your program.

Extending Classes

In most Java applets and programs you write, you will have a number of classes that need to interact each other—in many cases classes will be derived from other classes creating hierarchies. The keyword that handles the work of helping you extend classes and create hierarchies is named appropriately enough, **extends**.

In a class hierarchy, every class must have a parent—except the class that is at the top. The class that serves as a parent to another class is also called the superclass of the class it derives—the class that takes the position immediately above the class. Let's look at an example. As Figure 6.2 indicates, the classes *911*, *944*, and *928* all belong to the superclass *Porsche*. And *Porsche* belongs to the superclass *sportscar*, which in turn belongs to the superclass *automobile*.

When you derive a class from a superclass, it will inherit the superclass's data and methods. (For example, *911* has certain characteristics simply because it is derived from *Porsche*.) To derive a class from a superclass in a class declaration hierarchy, you'll use the **extend** clause followed by the name of the superclass. If no superclass is defined, the Java compiler assumes you are deriving a class using Java's top-level superclass named **Object**.

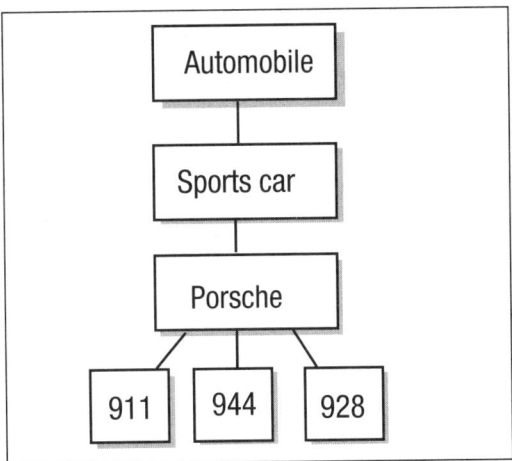

Figure 6.2   A sample class hierarchy.

```
public class Element extends Object {
   public static void main() {
      Atom_ant ATOMOBJ = new Atom_ant();
      Molecule MOLEOBJ = new Molecule();
      System.out.println(ATOMOBJ.proton);
   }
}

class Molecule extends Element {
   static String neutron = "molecule";
}

class Atom_ant extends Molecule {
   static String proton = "atom_ant";
}
```

In this class declaration section, the top-level class defined is **Element**. Notice that it is derived or "extended" from **Object**—the built-in Java class. The first line of the declaration of **Element** could have also been written as:

```
public class Element {
...
```

since the Java compiler will assume that a class is automatically derived from the **Object** class if the **extends** clause is omitted. The second class, **Molecule**, is derived from **Element** and the third class, **Atom_ant**, is derived from **Molecule**. As Figure 6.3 shows, both **Molecule** and **Atom_ant** inherit the components of the **Element** class.

Using the Implements Clause to Create Class Interfaces

When classes are used to derive other classes, the derived classes can access the data and methods of the classes higher up in the hierarchy chain. Fortunately, Java provides a mechanism called *interfaces* so that classes that are not part of a hierarchy can still access components of other classes. An interface is created for a class by using the **implements** clause. A class can implement as many interfaces as it wishes, but all the interfaces introduced must have all their methods defined in the body of the class implementing it. Thus, all the subclasses that follow from that point on will inherit the methods and variables defined.

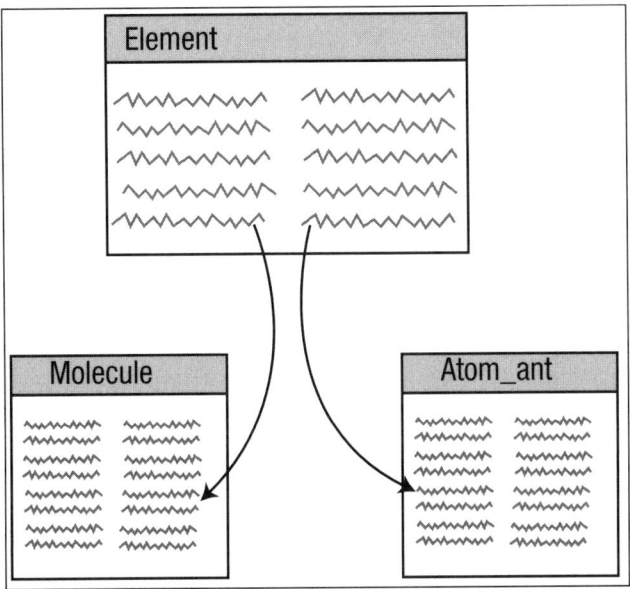

Figure 6.3 **Using the extends keyword to derive a series of classes.**

Let's develop the **Atom_ant** class we introduced in the previous section to see how an interface can be coded:

```
class Atom_ant extends Molecule implements Protons, Neutrons,
  Electrons {
    static int proton = 45378444;
    void Proton_function() {
       ... // definition of the Proton_function()
    }

    void Neutron_function() {
       ... // definition of the Neutron_function()
    }

    void Electron_function() {
       ... // definition of the Electron_function()
    }
}
```

Here we are making the assumption that the interfaces **Protons, Neutrons,** and **Electrons** only have one method declared in each of the interfaces. For example, **Protons** may be set up as follows:

```
Public interface Protons {

    void Proton_function(); // declares the method that will be used
}
```

As you can see, setting up the interface is a two step process. The class where the methods are defined uses the **implements** clause to indicate which interfaces can have access to the methods. Then, **interface** statements are used to declare the method that will be used.

In the source below, the **TickerTape** class implemented the interface **Runnable** from the package java.lang. The **Runnable** interface has only one method declared in it, which is **run()**. This method is then defined in the class that is implementing it. In this case, the applet TickerTape has defined **run()** to instruct the thread to sleep, call the **setcoord()** method, and rerun the **paint()** method every time the applet calls the **run()** method. This happens in situations where the screen is resized or, in this case, where the applet is instructed to move the text across the screen and the **run()** method is called.

```
// TickerTape Applet

import java.applet.*;
import java.awt.*;
// TickerTape Class
public class TickerTape extends Applet implements Runnable {
    ...
    public void run() {
        while(ttapeThread != null){ // verifies thread still active
            try {Thread.sleep(50);} catch (InterruptedException e){}
            setcoord();       // changes the placement of the text
            repaint();        // repaints the screen by activating the
    paint()
    // method
        }
    }
    ...

} // End TickerTape
```

This allows the ability to effectively encapsulate(hide) the classes and all its methods that actually support the **run()** method. Interfaces allow for distinct behaviors, defined by the programmer, to be used without exposing the class(es) to everyone.

Class Body

The class body contains the code that implements the class. This is where you provide the detail for the actions the class needs to perform (methods) and the data it needs to use (variables). The body can also contain constructors (special methods) and initializers. The basic format for a class body is:

```
{
   Variable-declarations;
   Method-declarations;
 }
```

The variable declarations can be any standard Java declaration. Later in this chapter we'll discuss how methods are declared and used. Here's an example of a class with a body:

```
public class TickerTape extends Applet implements Runnable {
// Beginning of class body
   String inputText;
   String animSpeedString;
   Color color = new Color(255, 255, 255);
   int xpos;
   ...
   // Methods
   public void paint(Graphics g) {
      paintText(osGraphics);
      g.drawImage(im, 0, 0, null);
   }
   ...
// End of Class Body

}
```

NAME SPACE

Every method and variable defined in a class is recorded into an area called a *name space*. This name space is then inherited by the other classes in a class hierarchy which are derived from the class. If a variable or method has been previously defined elsewhere in the structure with the same name, a *shadowing* effect occurs for that level. To access the value of a variable that supersedes the current value, you need to put the prefix clause **super** in front of the variable name. This clause instructs the expression to take the value of the superclass. To access the value of the current variable, you use the prefix **this**. Let's look at an example:

```
public class House extends Object {   static int tvamount = 8;    //
  Variable
    void main() {
       Room();
    }
}

public class Room extends House {   static int tvamount = 5;    //
  Variable
    int Child = this.tvamount;  // Child equals 5—same as saying
                               // tvamount
    int Parent = super.tvamount;     // Parent equals 8
}
```

In this example the **House** class is derived from the standard **Object** class. Then, the **Room** class is derived from **House**. Now notice that each class defines a variable named **tvamount** and assigns it a value. In the second assignment statement in **Room**, the variable **Child** is assigned the value 5 because **this** is used to access the class's local copy of the **tvamount** variable. In the next assignment statement, notice how **super** is used to access the value **tvamount** was assigned in **House**—the superclass.

Methods

As we've seen, the mechanisms used to implement operations in classes are called *methods*. This terminology is borrowed directly from object-oriented languages like Smalltalk and C++. Methods define the behavior of a class and the objects created from the class. A method can send, receive, and alter information to perform a task in an application. Java requires that every method be defined within a class or interface, unlike C++ where methods (functions) can be implemented outside of classes.

Let's refer to the car class hierarchy we presented earlier in this chapter to get a better understanding of the role methods play. All of the cars we introduced have doors and we could define two methods to operate on these doors: open and close. These same methods could be designed to perform operations on other car components such as windows, trunks, hoods, and so on. A component like a door can be viewed as an object. Of course, a car would be made up of many objects and many methods would be required to process all of the objects. As a programmer, it would be up to you to decide how to arrange the objects you need and what methods must be implemented.

Declaring a Method

Before moving on to the specifics of what Methods can consist of. Let's take a step back and look at the full declaration used to define a Java method:

```
[Modifier] ReturnType Identifier([ParameterList]) [Throws]
{
    MethodBody;
}
```

The *Modifier* and *Throws* clauses are optional. They are used to specify how the method needs to be accessed and which exceptions should be checked for.

Components of a Method Declaration

If you were to break down the method declaration, you would find it performs three main tasks:

◆ It determines who may call the method.

◆ It determines what the method can receive (the parameters).

◆ It determines how the method returns information.

Method Modifiers

Earlier in this chapter, you learned that a set of modifiers are available for defining how classes can be accessed. Methods also can be defined using modifiers, although the method modifiers only affect how methods are used, not the class they are defined in. Java provides eight modifiers for defining methods, but only one modifier from each of the groups listed next may be used in a method declaration. For example, you cannot use a

public and **private** modifier in the same declaration. Here is the complete set of method modifiers:

◆ **public, protected, private**

◆ **static**

◆ **abstract, final, native, synchronized**

Keep in mind that it doesn't make sense to use some modifiers in one group with modifiers from another group. For example, a method that is defined using the **private** and **abstract** modifiers contradicts itself. An abstract method is one that requires its actual code to be defined in the subclasses that follow, whereas a private method is one that can only be accessed in the class it is defined in. The rule of thumb when choosing and combining modifiers is that you need to make sure that they are complementary rather than contradictory. If a modifier is not used, the method may be accessed only by the classes that are in the current package.

PUBLIC METHOD

A method declared as public can be accessed by *any* class in the same package. It can also be accessed by other classes from other packages. This modifier gives a method the most freedom.

PROTECTED METHOD

A method declared as protected can only be used by other classes within the same package. All the subclasses beneath the class the method is defined in may access the method unless shadowing occurs. Shadowing involves naming a method using a name that already exists in a superclass above the class the method is defined in.

PRIVATE METHOD

A method declared as private is one that can only be accessed by the class it is defined in. This modifier gives a method the least amount of freedom.

STATIC METHOD

A method declared as static is one that cannot be changed. This type of method is also referred to as a *class method*, because it belongs explicitly to a particular class. When an *instance* of the class that defines the method is created, the static method cannot be altered. For this reason, a static method can refer to any other static methods or variables by name. Limitations of static methods to keep in mind are that they cannot be declared as final, and they cannot be overridden.

ABSTRACT METHOD

A method declared as abstract is one that must be defined in a subclass of the current class. However, an abstract method must be declared in the current class with a (;) semicolon in place of the method's block of code. Methods that are declared abstract are not required to be implemented in every subclass.

FINAL METHOD

A method declared as final is one that ends the hierarchical tree. No methods having the same name can be defined in subclasses that exist below the class that declares the method as final.

NATIVE METHOD

A method declared as native is one that will be implemented using outside code—code that is written in another language, to be used in conjunction with your current program. This limits you to a specific platform and restricts you from creating Java applets. Native methods are declared by leaving out the method body and placing a semicolon at the end of the method declaration.

SYNCHRONIZED METHOD

A method declared as synchronized limits it from being executed by multiple objects at the same time. This is useful when you are creating Java applets and you could have more than one thread running at the same time accessing one central piece of data. If the method is static (e.g., a class method), the whole class would be locked. If you just declare a particular method as synchronized, the object containing the method would only be locked until the method finishes executing.

Return Type of a Method

Any information that is returned from a method is declared as the *return type*. This assures that the information that is returned from a method call will be of the correct type; otherwise, a compile-time error will be generated. If no information will be returned by a method, the **void** keyword should be placed in front of the method name.

Parameter Lists for a Method

The parameter list consists of the ordered set of data elements passed to a method. You can pass zero, one, or multiple parameters by listing them between the parentheses, with each type and variable name being separated by a comma. If no parameters are passed, the parentheses should be empty. All variables that are passed become local for that instance of the method. Here's an example of how methods can be declared with and without parameters:

```
public static void MyFirstMethod(String Name, int Number) {
    ...
    // the String variable Name is assigned whatever is passed to it
    // the integer variable Number is assigned whatever is passed to
    // it
    ...
}

public static void MyFirstMethod() {
    ...
    // Nothing is passed  to it.
    ...
}
```

Method Throws

The **throws** clause is used to specify the type of error(s) that will be handled within a method. In effect, it is used to help you set up an automatic error-handler. In the event of an error, the error must be assignable to one of the exceptions in either the **Error**, **RunTimeException**, or **Exception** classes. (These are special classes that Java provides for catching compile-time and run-time errors.) Each method you declare does not need to use the **throws** clause in its declaration, but in the event of an error, the omission of this clause will leave the error handling up to the Java compiler or the Java interpreter. Let's look at an example of how the **throws** clause is used.

In the following method declaration, the Java exception named **ArrayOutOfBoundsException** is specified so that in the event an array range error occurs, the method will know how to handle the error:

```
public class Array_check() {
   String arr[5];

   public static void main(void) throws ArrayOutOfBoundsException {
      int i=0;
      char ch;

      // Specify which code should be tested
      try {
        while (i <= 5) ch = arr[i++];
      }
      // An error has occurred—display a message
      catch {
        System.out.println("Array out of bounds");
      }
   }
 }
```

At some point **main**() will try to access a location outside the legal range of the array **arr**[]. When this happens, an exception will be "thrown" and the **catch** clause will handle it. Also notice the use of the **try** clause which is needed to specify which code in the method should be tested. In our case, we want to check each iteration of the **while** loop.

Method Body

All executable code for Java classes is contained in the body of the methods. Unless a method is declared as abstract, native, or is declared in the body of an interface, the code for the method is placed between a pair of curly braces. This code can be any valid Java statements including variable declarations, assignment statements, method calls, control statements, and so on.

Here's an example of how a basic method is defined:

```
public int SimpleMethod(int Number) {

   // The integer variable Number is assigned whatever is passed to
   // it
```

```
int lowrange = 1;  // Local declarations for the method
int highrange = 10;

if (Number <= lowrange) return -1;
if (Number >= highrange) return 100
    else return 50;
}
```

In this case, the method's name is **SimpleMethod**(). Because it is declared as public, it can be used by any class in the package in which the method is defined. The return type for the method is **int** and it accepts one **int** parameter. The method body contains a few local declarations and a set of if-then decision-making statements.

For a method declared as abstract, native, or one that is declared in an interface, the body is left blank and the declaration is terminated with a semicolon. The bodies are then defined elsewhere depending on how they are declared. Here's an example:

```
abstract class Aparticles extends Quark {

    abstract int abstract_method();  // Defined in the subclasses of
  the class

    native void native_method ();  // Defined in an external process

    public String normal_method() {
        ... // Definition of the method
    }
}
```

Using the this and super Keywords

To access class variables and methods from within an object, you can reference them by using the keywords **this** and **super**. When the Java compiler encounters the **this** keyword in the body of a method, it knows that you are accessing other methods and variables defined within the scope of the class the method is defined in. On the other hand, variables and methods that are available for accessing in the parent class (superclass) to the current class are referenced using the **super** keyword. Here's an example of how each of these keywords can be used:

```
class Atom_ant extends Molecule {
   int Number;
   ...
}

class Quark extends Atom_ant {
   int Proton;
   int Neutron;
   String Electon = "Negative attraction";
   ...
   void Count() {
      System.out.println(this.Proton + " is the number of Protons");
      System.out.println(Neutron + " is the number of Neutrons");
      System.out.println(super.Number + " is the number of Atoms");
      System.out.println(Atom_ant.Number + " is the number of
        Atoms");
      ...
   }
}
```

In this example, this.Proton references the local variable Proton defined in the class Quark. But take a look at the second method call in the Count() method. Here, the variable Neutron, which is also declared in Quark, is referenced without the use of the **this** keyword. What gives? Actually, since both of these variables are defined within Quark, the **this** keyword is not really needed.

As for the two following lines of code, they each reference the **Number** variable declared in the **Atom_ant** class, which serves as the parent to the **Quark** class. Notice that the keyword **super** is placed in front of the variable **Number** to allow it to be accessed. This is the same as using the superclass name in the statement **Atom_ant.Number** to reference the value of **Number**. Superclass names can be referenced further up the hierarchical tree but the **super** keyword can only be used to access class members that reside one level above the current class. If the **Molecule** class contained a variable named **M1**, and we wanted to reference it from the **Quark** class, a statement like this would be required:

```
Proton = Molecule.M1;
```

Here the superclass named **Molecule** is included in the assignment statement. If it was omitted or the **super** keyword was used instead, as in the code line below:

```
Proton = super.M1;
```

the Java compiler would return an error because it would try to locate the **M1** variable in the class that is directly above the **Quark** class.

Overloading and Overriding Methods

A method may be declared with multiple declarations, each specifying different types and arguments that may be passed to the method. *The context in which the method is called will determine which actual method code is used.* The techniques of using a method's name more than once to define an operation in a class involves overloading and overriding methods. As long as you can define each method having the same name so that it can be distinguished from the others sharing the same name, the Java compiler will not give you an error. The technique for creating overridden methods involves using different parameters (types and numbers) and return types. Methods that are inherited from a superclass may be overridden but the overriding method must provide at least the same access.

Let's look at some examples of how we can override methods:

```
class Atom_ant extends Molecule {
    int Number;
    protected void Count(String Astring, int Number) {

        ...
    }
}

class Quark extends Atom_ant {
    int Proton;
    int Neutron;
    String Electon = "Negative attraction";
    ...
    public void Count(int Number, String Astring) { // Correct
        ...
    }
```

```
    protected void Count() {    // Correct
        ...
    }
}
```

Here we've declared two classes: **Atom_ant** and **Quark. Atom_ant** serves as the superclass. The method that is overridden is **Count**(). It is first introduced as a protected method in the **Atom_ant** class. Notice that it is declared here as taking two parameters: **Astring** and **Number**. Because **Atom_ant** is declared as a protected method, it is restricted from being called by other classes outside of the package **Atom_ant** is declared in.

The **Quark** class, which is derived from **Atom_ant**, provides two new variations of the **Count**() method, each one being overridden from the base method defined in **Atom_ant**. Notice that each of the overridden methods uses different parameters and/or return types than the original method.

To see how the different versions of the **Count**() method can be called, let's expand the **Quark** class a little:

```
class Atom_ant extends Molecule {
    int Number;
    protected void Count(String Astring, int Number) {
        ...
    }
}

class Quark extends Atom_ant {
    int Proton;
    ...
    public void Count(int Number, String Astring) { // Correct
  ...
    }

    void check() {
        Atom_ant.Count("Hello", 5); //Correct refer to superclass
                                    //method
        super.Count("GoodBye", 5);  //Correct same as previous
        Molecule.Count("Hello World"); //Correct as long as it exists
        Count(5, "World");          //Correct same as this.Count
    }
}
```

The first two calls to the **Count()** method result in calling the **Count()** method defined in **Atom_ant**. For the third call, we are making the assumption that the class **Molecule**, which **Atom_ant** is derived from, contains a **Count()** method. If it doesn't, a compiler error will occur. The last call to **Count()** accesses the method of the same name defined in **Quark**.

Constructors— The Special Methods

Although constructors are identified as special methods, it is important to distinguish between the two. Methods define an object's behavior in terms of what operations the object can perform. A constructor, on the other hand, determines how an object is initialized by creating a new instance of a class with specified parameters.

Methods and constructors actually differ in three ways. First, constructors do not have their own unique names; they must be assigned the same name as their class name. Second, constructors do not have a return type—Java assumes that the return type for a constructor is **void**. And third, constructors are not inherited by subclasses, as are methods.

To understand how constructors work conceptually, let's return to the car analogy we introduced earlier in this chapter. Each car in our hierarchy represents an object and the blueprint for each car is a class structure. Also recall that operations such as opening and closing car doors were considered to be our methods.

Now, imagine that we have a subclass, called *BodyShop*, which defines the body style for a car. This class could be inserted under the general *car* class in the class hierarchy. An object could be created from this class called *FrameCreation*, which is responsible for making body frames for cars. The process of building a frame could involve first calling a constructor to do the dirty work of "setting up the shop" for building a particular car frame. The manner in which the different classes are defined in the hierarchy will determine what frame a particular car gets at the *BodyShop* from the *FrameCreation* team. (The *FrameCreation* team is responsible for initializing an "object" depending on the information passed to a constructor.)

Now let's assume we have three choices for making body frames:

◆ 4 Door(*integer*) Falcon(*String*)

◆ 3 Door(*integer*) Pinto(*String*)

◆ 2 Door(*integer*) Mustang(*String*), which is the default.

We could just say 2, 3, or 4 doors, but the *FrameCreation* team insists on a certain format for each. The Falcon requires (*integer* Doors, *String* Name), the Pinto requires (*String* Name, *integer* Doors), and the Mustang doesn't require any values (). When you pass these values, known as **types** to the *FrameCreation* team, they immediately know which frame to create, or *initialize*, by the arrangement of the information passed to them (data types and number of parameters). By passing the information in a distinct pattern *FrameCreation(Doors, Name)*, *FrameCreation(Name, Doors)*, or *FrameCreation()* to create an object, we are using a *constructor*.

A constructor is a special method that determines how an object is initialized when created. The constructor is named the same as the class it follows. The code for our example could be written like this:

```
class FrameCreation extends BodyShop {
   // ** Initializing the object newcar **
   FrameCreation newcar = FrameCreation(4 , Falcon);

// ** The Beginning of the Constructor **
   FrameCreation {
   // ** An example of Overloading the Constructor **
     FrameCreation(int, String) {
       // Creates the FALCON
   }
// ** An example of Overloading the Constructor **
   FrameCreation(String, int) {
 // Creates the Pinto
   }

   FrameCreation() {    // ** An example of Overloading the
  Constructor **
 // Creates the Mustang
   }
// ** The End of the Constructor **
 }
```

FrameCreation is the constructor, which is declared multiple times—each taking different parameter configurations. When it is called with a configuration (a number, a word), the constructor with the matching configuration is used.

In calling a constructor, you need to disregard the rules for calling methods. Methods are called directly; constructors are called automatically by Java. When you create a new instance of a class, Java will automatically initialize the object's instance variables, and then call the class's constructors and methods. Defining constructors in a class can do several things, including:

◆ Setting initial values of the instance variables.

◆ Calling methods based on the initial variables.

◆ Calling methods from other objects.

◆ Calculating the initial properties of the object.

◆ Creating an object that has specific properties outlined in the new argument through overloading.

Components of a Constructor Declaration

The basic format for declaring a constructor is:

```
[ConstructorModifier] ConstructorIdentifier([ParameterList]) [Throws]
  {
    ConstructorBody;
}
```

As with the other declarations we've introduced in previous sections, only the identifier and body are necessary. Both the modifier and the throws clause are optional. The identifier is the name of the constructor; however, it is important to remember that the name of the constructor must be the same as the class name it initializes. You may have many constructors (of the same name) in a class, as long as each one takes a different set of parameters. (Because the different constructors in a class must have the same name, the type, number, and order of the parameters being passed are used as the distinguishing factors.) For example, all constructors for a class named **Atom_ant**, must be named **Atom_ant**, and each one must have different set of parameters.

In addition to having a unique declaration from that of a method, a special format is used for calling a constructor:

```
Typename([ParameterList]);
```

The only required element is *Typename*, which names the class containing the constructor declaration. Here's an example of a constructor, with the class **Atom_ant** and a constructor that uses the **new** operator to initialize instance variables:

```
class Atom_ant {
   String  superhero;
   int height;

   Atom_ant(String s, int h) {  // Declare a constructor
      superhero = s;
      height = h;
   }

   void printatom_ant() {
      System.out.print("Up and attam, " + superhero);
      System.out.println("!  The world's only " + height +
         " inch Superhero!");
    }

   public static void main(String args[])  {
      Atom_ant a;

      a =  new Atom_ant("Atom Ant" , 1); // Call the constructor
      a.printatom_ant();
      System.out.println("——");

      a = new Atom_ant("Grape Ape", 5000);
      a.printatom_ant();
      System.out.println("——");
   }
}
```

The output for this program looks like this:

```
Up and attam,  Atom Ant!  The world's only 1 inch Superhero!
───

Up and attam, Grape Ape!  The world's only 5000 inch Superhero!
───
```

Notice that each constructor call is combined with the **new** operator. This operator is responsible for making sure a new instance of a class is created and assigned to the object variable **a**.

USING JAVA'S DEFAULT CONSTRUCTOR

If you decide not to declare a constructor in a class, Java will automatically provide a default constructor that takes no arguments. The default constructor simply calls the superclass constructor **super**() with no arguments and initializes the instance variable. If the superclass does not have a constructor that takes no arguments, you will encounter a compile-time error. You can also set a class's instance variables or call other methods so that an object can be initialized.

Here is an example of a Java class that does not use a constructor but instead allows Java to initialize the class variables:

```java
class Atom_ant2 {
    String  superhero;
    int height;
    Boolean villain;
    void printatom_ant() {
      System.out.print("Up and attam, " + superhero);
      System.out.println("!  The world's only " + height +
            " inch Superhero!");
    }

    public static void main(String args[])  {
       Atom_ant2 a;

       a =  new Atom_ant2();
       a.printatom_ant();
       System.out.println("──") ;
    }
}
```

Because no constructor is defined for this example program, the Java compiler will initialize the class variables by assigning them default values. The variable **superhero** is set to null, **height** is initialized to zero, and **villain** is set to false. The variable **a**, in the **main()** method, could have been initialized at the time the constructor was called by substituting the code **a = new Atom_ant2();** for **Atom_ant2 a = new Atom_ant2();**. Either statement provides an acceptable means of creating an instance of a class— the object **a**. Once this object is in hand, the method **printatom_ant()** can be called.

The output for this program looks like this:

```
Up and attam, The world's only 0 inch Superhero!
```

CONSTRUCTOR MODIFIERS

Java provides three modifiers that can be used to define constructors:

◆ **public**

◆ **protected**

◆ **private**

These modifiers have the same restrictions as the modifiers used to declare standard methods. Here is a summary of the guidelines for using modifiers with constructor declarations:

◆ A constructor that is declared without the use of one of the modifiers may only be called by one of the classes defined in the same package as the constructor declaration.

◆ A constructor that is declared as public may be called from any class that has the ability to access the class containing the constructor declaration.

◆ A constructor that is declared as protected may only be called by the subclasses of the class that contains the constructor declaration.

◆ A constructor that is declared as private may only be called from within the class it is declared in.

Let's look at an example of how each of these modifiers can be used:

```
class Atom_ant2 {
   String  superhero;
   int height;
   String  villain;
   int numberofsuperheros;

   Atom_ant2() {
      this("Dudley Do Right", 60);
   }

   public Atom_ant2(String s, int h) {
      superhero = s;
      height = h;
   }

   protected Atom_ant2(int s, int h) {
      numberofsuperheros = s;
      height = h;
   }

   private Atom_ant2(String s, int h, String v) {
      superhero = s;
      height = h;
      villain = v;
      }

   void printatom_ant() {
      System.out.print("Up and attam, " + superhero);
      System.out.println("!  The world's only " + height +
         " inch Superhero!");
   }
   public static void main(String args[]) {
      Atom_ant2 a;

      a =  new Atom_ant2();
      a.printatom_ant();

      a = new Atom_ant2("Grape Ape", 5000);
      a.printatom_ant();
   }
}

class Molecule_mole extends Atom_ant2 {
   String  superhero;
   int height;
```

```
    public static void main(String args[]) {
        Atom_ant2 a;

        a = new Atom_ant2(); // Compile-time Error
        a.printatom_ant();

        a = new Atom_ant2("Atom Ant", 1);  // Correct
        a.printatom_ant();

        a = new Atom_ant2(5, 5); // Correct
        a.printatom_ant();

// Compile-time Error
        a = new Atom_ant2("Atom Ant", 1 , "Dudley Do Right");
        a.printatom_ant();
    }
}
```

In this example, the **Atom_ant2** class uses constructors with all three of the modifiers: **public, protected,** and **private.** In addition, a constructor is declared that does not use a modifier. Notice how the constructors are called from the **Molecule_mole** class. Each constructor type is both defined and called using a different parameter configuration. (This is how the Java compiler knows which constructor to use.)

The first constructor call, **Atom_ant2()**, produces a compiler error because of Java's scoping rules—the declaration of this constructor is outside of the range of the **Molecule_mole** class, and the constructor was not declared as public or protected. Also notice that the call to the fourth constructor produces a compiler error. In this case, the constructor was declared in the **Atom_ant** class as private, which limits the constructor from being called by the class it is declared in.

As this example illustrates, you need to make sure you understand the restrictions that modifiers can place on method declarations. For example, here is an example of a compile-time error you will encounter if you try to access a constructor from another class when its modifier has been declared as private:

```
Compiling...
E:\java\jm\Molecule_mole.java
E:\java\jm\Molecule_mole.java:8: No constructor matching _
```

```
    Atom_ant2(java.lang.String, int, java.lang.String) found in class
Atom_ant2.
                    a =  new Atom_ant2("Atom ant",5,"Dudley");
    ^1 error
Compile Ended.
```

Parameter List and Throws Clause

Both the parameter list and throws clause follow the same rules used for declaring and calling methods; after all, a constructor is just a special method. When calling a constructor, different parameter configurations (type of parameters and quantity) can be used as long as you have a matching declaration that uses the same parameter configuration.

Constructor Body

The body of the constructor is essentially the same as the body of a method. The only difference occurs in the first statement. If the constructor is going to call "itself" (an alternate constructor for the same class having the same name) or call the constructor of its superclass, it must do this in the first statement. To access its own class, the **this**() statement is used as a placeholder for the class's identifier. To refer to the class's superclass, the **super**() statement is used. Following each of the clauses are parentheses containing the parameter list to be passed to the constructor, identified by the keyword. Here is an example of how both the **this**() and **super**() statements are used within the constructors defined for **Atom_ant2**:

```
class Atom_ant2 extends Quark {
    String  superhero;
    int height;
    String  villain;
    int numberofsuperheros;

    Atom_ant2() {
    this("Atom Ant", 1);   // Call another Atom_ant2() constructor
    }

    public Atom_ant2(String s, int h) {
        superhero = s;
        height = h;
    }

    Atom_ant2(String s, int h, String v) {
```

```
    super(s, h);     // Call the superclass's constructor
  }

  protected Atom_ant2(int s, int h) {
    numberofsuperheros = s;
    height = h;
  }

  synchronized void printatom_ant() {
    System.out.print("Up and attam, " + superhero);
    System.out.println("!  The world's only " + height +
       " inch Superhero!");
System.out.print("\n—\n");
  }

  public static void main (String args[ ])  {
    Atom_ant2 a;

    a =  new Atom_ant2();
    a.printatom_ant();
    System.out.println ("——") ;
  }
}
```

When the program runs, the call to **Atom_ant2**() results in the first constructor defined in the **Atom_ant2** class being called. Then, the first constructor calls the second constructor defined in the class. This process is illustrated in Figure 6.4.

In the first constructor, **this**() is used so that the constructor can directly call one of **Atom_ant2**'s other constructors. How does the compiler know which one to use? It looks for a match between the parameters based on **this**("Atom Ant", 1) and one of the other **Atom_ant2**(...) constructors.

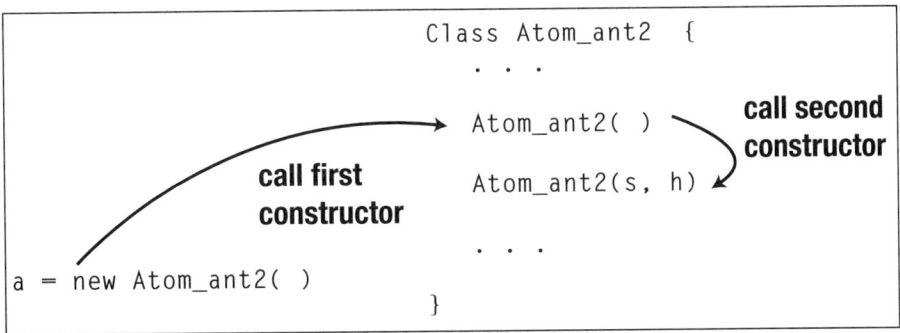

Figure 6.4   The chain of constructor calls in the Atom_ant2 example.

Since the **this**() statement passes a string and an integer, the actual constructor that is called is the second one defined in the **Atom_ant2** class.

In the third constructor declaration, the **super**() statement performs a similar operation except this time it searches the immediate superclass's constructor for a match. It is important to remember that when using either of these statements, you may not directly call instance variables of the object being created. Furthermore, an instance variable cannot be dependent upon another variable that has not yet been defined, or is defined after it.

Here's an example:

```
class Foo {
    int variableNow = variableLater + 10;
    int variableLater = 20;
}
```

As you can see, **variableNow** is trying to initialize itself before **variableLater** is assigned a value.

Object Creation

There are two ways to create an instance of a class: use a literal, specific to the **String** class or use the **new** operator. The **new** operator is placed in front of the constructor. The parameter list of the constructor determines what constructor is used to create an instance of an object.

```
...
public static void main(String args[])  {
    Atom_ant2 a;

    a =  new Atom_ant2();
    a.printatom_ant() ;
    System.out.println ("——");
}
...
```

Here, the **new** operator initializes **Atom_ant2** with an empty parameter list, initializes the variable to create an instance of the class **Atom_ant2**, and assigns it to **a**.

Variables for Classes

Before moving on, let's refresh your memory with some Java basics: A variable is a named storage location that can hold various values, depending on the data type of the variable. The basic format for declaring a variable is as follows:

```
VariableModifiers Type Indentifier = [VariableInitializer];
```

Only the *Type* and *Identifier* components are necessary. The modifiers are optional.

As with all the identifiers we've used throughout this chapter, the variable identifier simply names the variable. However, you can name any number of variables in the declaration by naming them in the identifier position and separating them with commas. If you decide to declare multiple variables, also realize that the modifiers and *Type* apply to all the variables that are named. For example, in these declarations

```
int paul, david, kelly;
static String henry, diana;
```

the variables **paul, david**, and **kelly** are declared as integers, and the variables **henry** and **diana** are declared as static strings.

VARIABLE MODIFIERS

Java provides seven different modifiers for declaring variables within classes. However, you can only use two of them—one from each group—in a declaration. Also, you can't use two modifiers that contradict each other in the same declaration. The two groups of modifiers are:

◆ **public, protected, private**

◆ **static, final, transient, volatile**

The **public, protected**, and **private** modifiers are discussed under the modifiers sections of class, method, and constructors.

STATIC MODIFIERS

A static variable is also known as a class variable. This is because there is only one variable of that name, no matter how many instances of the class are created. Here's an example of how the **static** modifier can be used:

```
Atom_ant2() {
    static int Doug = 9;
    this("Atom Ant", 1);
}

...
public static void main(String args[])  {
    Atom_ant2 a, b, c, d;

    a =  new Atom_ant2();
    b =  new Atom_ant2();
    c =  new Atom_ant2();
    d =  new Atom_ant2();
    a.printatom_ant() ;
    System.out.println("——") ;
}
...
```

Here, no matter how many objects we create, there is exactly one variable **Doug** for every instance of **Atom_ant()**.

FINAL MODIFIER

When a variable is assigned final, it acts as a constant throughout the instance of the class. They must be declared at time of initialization of the class or method.

TRANSIENT MODIFIER

This is a modifier that has been reserved by Java virtual machine language for low level segments that do not pertain to the persistent state of an object. Other implementations will follow for this modifier in future versions.

VOLATILE MODIFIER

These are modifiers that are processed through the multi-processor in an asynchronous manner. The variables are reloaded from and stored to memory every time the variables are used.

The Art of Casting with Classes

In previous chapters, we showed you how to use casting techniques to convert the values assigned to variables of predefined data types to other data types. For example, in a set of statements like this

```
int i;
short s;

s = 10;
i = (int) s;
```

the contents of the variable **s**—originally defined to be of the **short** type—is converted to an **int** type by using a cast in the assignment statement. When casting variable types from one to another, no information will be lost as long as the receiver is larger than the provider. Java also allows you to cast instances of a class, known as objects, to instances of other classes. The declaration for an explicit cast to a class is as follows:

```
(Classname)reference
```

The *Classname* is the name of the class you wish to cast to the receiving object. The reference specifies the object that is to receive the cast. When applying a narrowing effect to a class, as you will read about later, this type of cast is required by the Java compiler. Figure 6.5 illustrates this concept.

If a superclass attempts to cast an instance of itself to a subclass beneath it, a runtime error will occur even though this type of cast will be accepted by the Java compiler. The technique of passing object references down a class hierarchy is referred to as *widening*. As a class is located at lower levels in a hierarchy it becomes more specific and thus it contains more information than the classes above it in the hierarchy. Superclasses, on the other hand, are usually more general than the classes beneath them. Conversions that occur when you pass the references up the hierarchy are thus referred to a narrowing because not all the information is passed along to the receiving object. Furthermore, all instance variables of the same name in the receiving object are set to the class variables that are being cast.

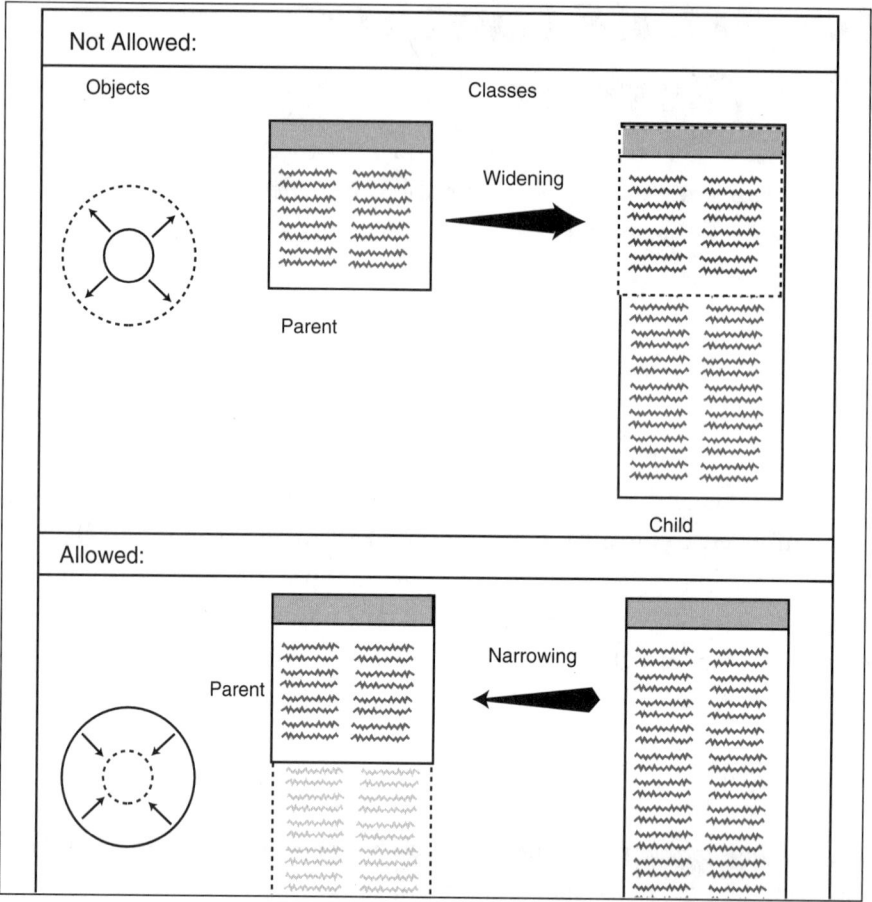

Figure 6.5 Widening and narrowing an instance of a class by using casts.

Casting an Object vs. Creating an Object

When casting between instances of a class, an object only assumes reference of the class. A new instance of the class is not created; the object merely points to the methods and variables of the casting class. It is important not to confuse the process of casting a object with the process of creating an object. Just as you pass the value of a variable through different types (e.g, int, float, double, and so on), you can pass an object through different classes, as long as the class is in the current hierarchy.

Here is an example of how you can cast references to objects between class types:

```java
public class atom_ant {
    String  superhero = "Atom Ant";
    int height = 10;

    atom_ant() {
    }

    void print() {
       System.out.print (superhero + " is " + height + "\n");
    }

    public static void main(String arg[]) {

        atom_ant a1;
        a1 = new atom_ant();
        a1.print();

        proton_pal p1, p2;
        p1 = (proton_pal) a1; // Runtime error due to casting error
        p1.print();  // Unable to execute because of the previous line

        electron_enemy e1;
        e1 = (electron_enemy) p2; // Compile-time error due to casting
                                  // to a sibling class
        e1.print();  // Unable to execute because of the previous line

        atom_ant a2;
        a2 = (atom_ant) p2;
        a2.print();
    }
}

class proton_pal extends atom_ant {

    String  superhero = "Proton Pal";
    int height = 1;

    proton_pal() {
    }

    void print() {
       System.out.print (superhero + " is " + height + "\n");
    }
}
```

```
class electron_enemy extends atom_ant{

    String  superhero = "Electron Enemy";
    int height = -1;

    electron_enemy() {
    }

    void print() {
        System.out.print (superhero + " is " + height + "\n");
    }
}
```

Here we've modified our previous **atom_ant** class to illustrate the basics of casting. Notice that two of the casts used will produce a runtime and compile-time error, respectively. (Thus, don't try to compile the code unless you remove the two illegal casts.) The first cast used in the **main**() method, **p1 = (proton_pal) a1**, produces a *widening* effect. Although this statement will compile, it produces a runtime error because the object **a1** cannot be expected to *grow* to accommodate the new variables and methods it references in **proton_pal**. The second casting statement used is a sibling cast: **e1 = (electron_enemy) p2**. It generates a compile-time error because an illegal reference to a *sibling* class, **electron_enemy** is used. This is due to the fact that the classes can have completely different variables and methods not related to each other. The last form of casting that is addressed in the **atom_ant** class produces a *narrowing* effect. In the statement, (**a2 = (atom_ant) p2**), the object **p2** references variables that are defined in the class, **atom_ant**, that is being cast. The reference is then past to the variable **a2**.

Interfaces and Packages

David H. Friedel, Jr.

You'll find that Java's flexible interfaces and packages provide a welcome boost to your programming productivity.

*A*fter writing a few applets and applications, you'll probably notice that the directory to which your classes are written will start to become obscenely large. This is the downside of the way Java processes classes; but the good news is that Java provides two key features called *interfaces* and *packages* to help you organize your code. We put these two topics in a chapter by themselves to emphasize how important they are. (Many Java books simply lump interfaces and packages in with classes, or they just skim over them—shameful!) As you start to work more with interfaces and packages, you'll discover a myriad of important program design issues that come into play which you'll need to master to use interfaces and packages effectively.

In this chapter you'll learn about:

◆ The basics of interfaces

◆ Techniques for implementing interfaces

◆ The hierarchical structure related to interfaces themselves

◆ Techniques for using casts with interfaces

◆ The basics of packages

◆ Techniques for creating packages

◆ Techniques for using Java's predefined packages

The underlying goal of this chapter is to help you transition from writing small standalone Java applications and applets to creating classes that can be used over and over. As you start to adopt this style of programming, you'll need the flexibility that interfaces and packages provide.

Understanding Interfaces

An *interface* is a collection of methods and variables that are declared as a unit but they are not implemented until a later stage. Basically this means that the code declarations placed in an interface serve as a shell so that you can create a truly *abstract class*. The goal behind an abstract class is to provide a mechanism so that you can define the *protocols* for a class—how a class should essentially communicate with other classes—early on in the development cycle. The upshot is that when you create your interfaces or abstract classes, you don't have to specify all of the details of how they will be implemented. This is saved for a later stage.

Before we jump in and start writing Java code for declaring interfaces, let's explore a few conceptual examples. The concept of abstract classes and interfaces is tricky to grasp at first. In fact, many experienced object-oriented programmers will tell you that they didn't quite master the concepts until they had written a number of programs. Fortunately, we can help you understand and use the techniques much quicker by providing the background information and conceptual models you'll need to apply them.

The simplest form of an interface involves adding methods and/or variables that are necessary to a particular class, but would disrupt the hierarchy of the class structure you are currently building for an application. If you chose to actually implement these elements in your class, they could limit how you planned to use the class to derive other classes. To make your classes more flexible, you can add interfaces to your classes in your hierarchy early on, so that the interfaces can be used in multiple ways to help construct the "behavior" of other classes that appear elsewhere in your class hierarchy. (If this discussion sounds like we are talking in circles—welcome to the world of interfaces! Hopefully these fine points will start to make sense to you in a moment when we look at a specific example.)

Let's assume that we need to develop an application that processes information about different forms of transportation. Figure 7.1 shows the hierarchy that could be used along with the list of components that could be implemented as interfaces.

As with typical class hierarchies, the classes shown in Figure 7.1 become more specific as they appear further down in the hierarchy tree. The interface components are advantageous when you have operations that are to be performed in one section of the hierarchy and not in the other areas. For example, the class *Car* has two subclasses: *Solar* and *Gas*. Let's assume you need to calculate the liters of gas that a gas car will use. You could include the methods and variables for performing this operation in the *Car*

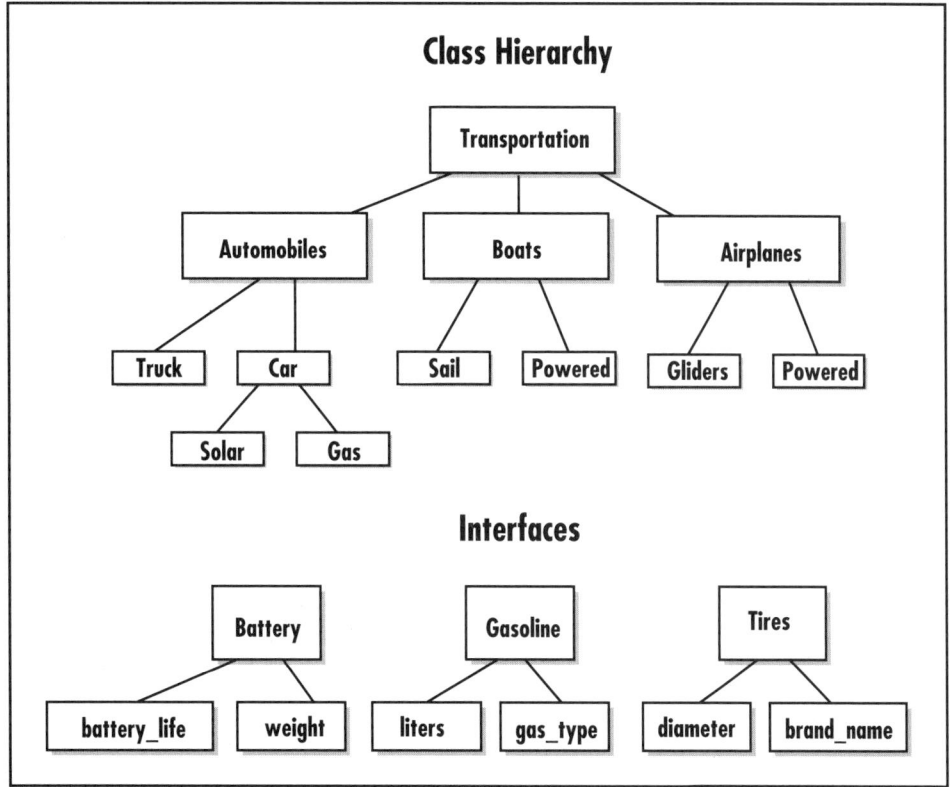

FIGURE 7.1   The hierarchy of classes for the transportation example.

superclass, or even better, up two levels in the *Transportation* class, so that the *Powered\Boats* and *Powered\Airplanes* classes could use this code also.

Unfortunately, when you consider the scope of the application and all of the subclasses that inherit this useless information, you'd probably agree that this design approach is flawed. After all, the *Solar\Car* class would never calculate the liters of gas used and neither would the *Sail\Boats* or *Gliders\Airplanes* classes. A class that handles the gas calculating operation would be an incredible pain to incorporate at the *Transportation* level so that it could be designed into the hierarchy, and thus forcing all the subclasses to inherit all of its methods. If we were creating a small application that only required a few classes, this approach could be used. But if you are building an application that uses lots of classes from the beginning or you are expecting to expand the application in the future, this approach could quickly become a programmer's nightmare because limitations could arise from placing such restrictions early on.

In applications that have class hierarchies like our transportation example, interfaces become priceless because they allow us to "mix-in" classes into the application, adding them only where they become absolutely necessary. Another feature that enhances the interface's capabilities is the use of multiple implementations of interfaces per class. For example, in our transportation application, theoretically the *Car* class would be interested in the *Gasoline* interface, but the *Tire* interface could also be of use. An abstract class could incorporate both of these interfaces (the methods and variables that define them) at the *Transportation* level, but the *Boat* class would also be forced to inherit them. The *Boat* class never would have any use for the *Tire*'s methods or variables.

Design Issues with Interfaces

Interfaces will usually fall into a class hierarchy without any problems when you are creating small scale applications. They also help separate the design process from the implementation process because they keep you from having to combine the more abstract design issues with implementation details in one component. They also allow you to derive classes without relying on the more limited technique of SINGLE INHERITANCE. A single inheritance model requires you to create class hierarchy trees by deriving one class from a single parent or superclass. Each class in the tree is created by using only data and operations that were defined in the levels above the current class.

Interfaces help you build class hierarchies that use more powerful object-oriented techniques like MULTIPLE INHERITANCE. With interfaces, you can define classes that have multiple parents. You can incorporate interfaces into a hierarchical class tree to include new methods and variables without having to worry about disrupting your current implementation tree.

Declaring an Interface

Let's look at the basic declaration for an interface and then we'll show you the syntax for implementing an interface. After that, we'll introduce some code to illustrate how the transportation example we presented in the previous section could be set up. The basic syntax for declaring an interface looks similar to the syntax used for defining a Java class:

```
public interface InterfaceName {
   StaticVariables;
   AbstractMethods;
}
```

In this case, however, the **class** keyword is not used; the keyword **interface** takes its place. The *InterfaceName* serves as the interface identifier name and the rules for specifying this name are the same as those used to name classes. The body of the interface declaration simply consists of the declaration of static variables and the names of one or more methods. Here's an example of an interface declaration:

```
public interface Gasoline {
// This variable is  defined as a constant
   public static final int Feet_in_Miles = 7245;

// A Method that is to be defined in a class
   void gas_type(String Name);
// Another method to be defined later
   void liters(int Amount);
}
```

Note that the variable **Feet_in_Miles** is declared as both static and final. This is required because all variables in interfaces *cannot* be changed. This type of declaration essentially turns the variable into a constant. If you leave out the **static** and **final** keywords, Java will force the variable to be declared as a constant. The two methods listed include both the method name and the method's parameter list. The actual code for the method will come when the interface is implemented.

Implementing an Interface

Declaring an interface is only half of the work. At some point, the interface must be implemented. This is accomplished by using the interface definition (or abstract class) to create a class. In a sense, a class can be "derived" using the interface shell. The syntax for implementing an interface is:

```
modifier class Identifier extends Superclass
implements InterfaceName [, InterfaceList ] {
    ClassBody;
}
```

In implementing an interface, you are essentially defining a special type of class. First, the class *modifier* is needed, followed by the **class** keyword. Then, the name of the class is provided. Next, the **extends** keyword is used followed by a superclass name to indicate that the class being defined is derived from a parent class. The **implements** keyword followed by the name of one or more interfaces, tells the Java compiler which interfaces will be used to implement the class. It is important to keep in mind that a class can implement more than one interface.

The class body consists of all of the variables and method definitions for the class. This is where all of the code must be placed for the methods that are listed in the interface declarations that are used. Using the **Gasoline** interface we declared earlier, here is a class called **Gas** that "implements" the **Gasoline** interface:

```
public class Gas extends Car implements Gasoline {
    int Miles;   // Variable declarations
    ...
    void gas_type(String Name) {
```

```
    ... // Add code  for this method
    }

    void liters(int Amount) {
    ... // Add code for this method
    }
}
```

Notice that this class is derived from a superclass named **Car**.

Now that we've covered the basics of declaring and implementing an interface, let's return to the transportation example we presented earlier. The first thing we need to do is declare the interfaces for the ones listed in Figure 7.1—**Gasoline**, **Battery**, and **Tire**:

```
public interface Gasoline {
// This variable is  now a constant
    public static final int Feet_in_Miles = 7245;

// A Method that is to be defined in a calling class
    void gas_type(String Name);
// Another method to be defined later
    void liters(int Amount);
}

public interface Batteries {
// A Method that is to be defined in a calling class
    void battery_life(int Time);
// Another method to be defined later
    void weight(int Amount);
}

public interface Tires {
// A Method that is to be defined in a calling class
    void diameter(int Distance);
// Another method to be defined later
    void brand_name(int Name);
}
```

With these interfaces in hand, we're ready to create the two classes—**Gas** and **Powered**—each one will implement some of the interfaces in different ways. They will also show you how multiple interfaces can be used in a class definition:

```java
public class Gas extends Car implements Gasoline, Batteries, Tires {

    int Feet_Traveled;
    int Miles_Traveled = 20;

    Feet_Traveled = Miles_Traveled * Feet_in_Miles;

    public static gas_type(String Name) {
        ... // Any functions that are to be performed with gas_type
        if(Name.equals("Diesel"))
           System.out.println("Ah, good power");
        if(Name.equals("Unleaded"))
           System.out.println("ok power");
        if(Name.equals("Leaded"))
           System.out.println("eh, clogged injectors");
    }

    public static liters(int Amount) {
        ... // Any functions that are to be performed with liters
    }

    public static battery_life(int Time) {
        ... // Any functions that are to be performed with battery_life
    }

    public static weight(int Amount) {
        ... // Any functions that are to be performed with weight
    }

    public static diameter(int Distance) {
        ... // Any functions that are to be performed with diameter
    }

    public static brand_name(int Name) {
        ... // Any functions that are to be performed with brand_name
    }
}

public class Powered extends Boat implements Gasoline, Batteries {

    int Feet_Traveled;
    int Miles_Traveled = 20;

    Feet_Traveled = Miles_Traveled * Feet_in_Miles;

    public static gas_type(String Name) {
        ... // Any functions that are to be performed with gas_type
        if(Name.equals("Diesel"))
```

```
      System.out.println("Required");
   if(Name.equals("Unleaded"))
      System.out.println("Not applicable");
   if(Name.equals("Leaded"))
      System.out.println("Not applicable");
}

public static liters(int Amount) {
   ... // Any functions that are to be performed with liters
}

public static battery_life(int Time) {
   ... // Any functions that are to be performed with battery_life
}

public static weight(int Amount) {
   ... // Any functions that are to be preformed with weight
}
}
```

Notice that the **Gas** class is extended from the superclass **Car** and implements the interfaces **Gasoline**, **Batteries**, and **Tires**. In the class body of **Gas**, the methods declared for these interfaces are coded as well as other variables that the class needs, such as **Feet_Traveled** and **Miles_Traveled**. The **Boat** class, on the other hand, only implements two interfaces: **Gasoline** and **Batteries**. Notice that the **Boat** class implementation for the **gas_type()** method (declared in the **Gasoline** interface) differs from the version implemented in the **Gas** class.

Tips on Using Interfaces

The implements clause lists all of the interfaces that are to be included in the class definition. By referencing the interface, the class implementing it must restate the methods and their definitions in the body of the class. Constructors—the special methods that initialize new objects—may not be included in the interface declaration because interfaces can not instantiate new objects. Interfaces reference an object that is an instance of a class. By doing this they state that the object being referenced includes all the methods in the class that created the object.

The Art of Casting with Interfaces

A cast can be used to change a reference to an object and not the actual object itself. Moreover, instance variables can be created and initialized to reflect the current reference to an object. This occurs when the names of the variable are the same in two classes—the one casting the object and the object the variable references.

Let's return to our **Gas** class example to see how we can use casts with interfaces. This time around **Gas** will reference the interfaces **Gasoline**, **Tires**, and **Batteries**; and **Gas** will create objects that reference the interfaces in different ways. Some of the references are correct and some of them will produce compile-time errors. We've included line numbers at the start of each line of code so that you can easily refer to the example in the discussion that follows:

```
1 public class Gas extends Car implements Gasoline, Tires, Batteries {
2
3 Gas       aCar    = makeGasCar();
4 Gasoline aGasCar = (Gasoline) makeGasCar();      // Use cast
5 Tires    aTireCar = (Tires) makeGasCar();       // Use cast
6
7 aGasCar.gas_type(Diesel);            // Valid
8 aGasCar.liters(5.8);                 // Valid
9
10                                     aTireCar.diameter(6.9);
                                       // Valid
11                                     aTireCar.gas_type(Unleaded);
                                       // Not Valid
12
13                                     aCar.gas_type(Diesel);// Valid
14                                     aCar.weight(12.7);  // Valid
15                                     aCar.diameter(6.9); // Valid
16                                     aCar.brand_name(Bridgestone);
                                       // Valid
17
18      . . .     // Any functions that you would perform on the Cars
                  // created
19 }
```

Let's break down what is going on here so that you can better understand some of the important and subtle Java programming techniques that are being used. Our example is only missing one thing that is not shown in the code—a method named **makeGasCar**() that creates and returns an object. Line 3 shows that an object is returned from the **makeGasCar**() method and is named **aCar** of type **Gas**. By assigning the returned value of **makeGasCar**() to an object variable of the type **Gas**, the object inherits all the methods pertaining to the **Gas** class. This means it acquires all the methods relating to the class, its superclass, and *the interfaces the class implements*. In line 4, we acquire an object from the **makeGasCar**() method, but this time we cast it as type **Gasoline** from the interface **Gasoline**. This means that the object, **aGasCar**, inherits all the methods that relate to the **Gas** class, its superclass, and *only the methods and variables declared in the interface Gasoline*. As we'll see in a second, this means no methods or variables from the other interfaces are available for the object to reference. The next line does the same as the previous line, but the **Tires** interface is used in place of **Gasoline**.

Lines 7 and 8 both have the object **aGasCar** call the methods **gas_type**() and **liters**(), which were originally declared in the **Gasoline** interface. These method calls are valid because the correct parameters are used and the object **aGasCar** has access to both of these methods because of the cast that was used. In line 10, the **aTireCar** object references the **diameter**() method which is also valid because this object was created using the (**Tires**) cast and the **diameter**() method is declared within the **Tires** interface. But in line 11, the **aTireCar** object tries to call a method that is declared in the **Gasoline** interface. This produces a compile-time error because the object does not implement the interface **Gasoline**. Only the methods declared in the **Tires** interface are available from the object.

In the last section of the **Gas** class, lines 13 through 16, the object **aCar** may call any of the methods available to the interfaces because this object is an instance of the class **Gas** and is not cast to any particular class. This shows you the versatility possible in creating objects using interfaces.

Tips on Implementing Interfaces

You'll notice that most applets that utilize the thread feature implement an interface named **Runnable** for the explicit function of moving (actually redrawing) text across the screen. When the applet is loaded into a browser, the browser checks to see if the object **ttapeThread**, which is an instance of the class **Thread** from a package that is imported into our class **TickerTape**, implements the **Runnable** interface. In this case, the browser detects the interface and uses the **run**() method declared in the class **Thread** during the operation of the applet:

```
// TickerTape Class
public class TickerTape extends Applet implements Runnable{
   ...
   // Change coordinates and repaint
   public void run(){
      while(ttapeThread != null){
         try {Thread.sleep(50);} catch (InterruptedException e){}
         setcoord();
         repaint();
      }
   }
   ...
}
```

This is a powerful feature for creating methods and variables in classes that can be set up with interfaces for future use, as long as the interface explains how information will be transferred to and from it. You don't need to allow others access to your original classes.

Using the instanceof Operator

To detect if an object implements an interface, you can use the INSTANCEOF operator. This operator allows you to look at a group of objects to pick out which ones can perform certain operations. Here's an example:

```
if (ttapeThread iinstanceof Runnable) {
((Runnable)ttapeThread).run(); // performs this function only
                               // if the object ttape implements
                               //   the Runnable interface
   }
```

In this case the IF statement checks to see if the object TTAPETHREAD is an instance of the RUNNABLE interface. If it is, the RUN() method defined in the RUNNABLE interface is called.

Creating and Using Packages

As you begin to design and code Java applications and applets that use multiple classes and interfaces, you'll need a way to organize your code so that you can easily update and reuse your growing library of classes and interfaces. Because the Java language is specifically designed to allow you to use classes and interfaces over and over, it's likely that you'll end up getting some of your class and interface names mixed up.

Furthermore, another programmer may design an excellent class that performs operations that you may want to use. Incorporating this class into one of your applications that already uses a number of classes could become difficult, especially if the class name conflicts with the name of a class you are already using. For example, you may have a custom print class named *Print* that performs certain functions for printing to the screen. After you've developed the class, another programmer might provide you with a class having the same name that prints a certain format to a printer that you need to support. You could actually use both of these classes even if they shared the name "Print"; however, they must be packaged in different groups so that the Java compiler can easily determine which one you want to use.

To help us combine classes into unique groups, Java supports the concept of *packages*. A package is essentially a device for grouping classes that you want to be labeled as a unit. You can actually combine any classes that you want into a single group. Usually, classes that share a common goal are combined in a class. For example, if you were creating a set of classes to handle drawing-related functions for a design application, you might create a package called *Draw* and place all of the related classes in this package.

One of the packages used for almost every applet that is created is the **Applet** package—a package that Java provides, which contains all the necessary classes for creating an applet. A package is introduced to a class by using the **import** keyword in the beginning of a source code file. This will be covered in more detail later in the chapter. As you will see, classes and packages are segregated according to the functions they perform. This reduces the risk of having methods that share the same name interfere with each other. Here is a simple example of how you can implement methods that belong to different packages into a common class:

```
// TickerTape Applet

import java.applet.*;
import java.awt.*;

// TickerTape Class
public class TickerTape extends Applet implements Runnable {
    ...
    public void init(){
        ...
    }
    public void start(){
        ...
    }
    public void run(){
...
    }
    public void graphics() {
...
    }
    public void stop(){
        ...
    }
    ...
} // End TickerTape
```

All of the methods declared in this example come from somewhere other than the current class. They have been *overridden* to perform a certain function specific to the operation of this applet. For example, the methods **init**(), **start**(), and **stop**() are defined in the **Applet** class that is contained in the java.applet package. The **run**() method is defined in the **Runnable** interface contained in the package java.lang.

Naming and Referencing Packages

Besides the fact that you may want to repeat a simple class name over and over, you'll want to create packages so that you can distribute your classes to other Java programmers. As with files on your computer, you list the directories in which they are contained to reference them. This creates a "path" for the Java compiler to follow so that it can locate designated classes and interfaces in your packages. Figure 7.2 shows an example of the directory hierarchy used to reference the package java.awt.image.

By convention, the first level of the hierarchy has been reserved for the name of the company that develops it. An example of this is **sun**.audio.AudioData—a package developed by Sun Microsystems. (Of course, as with every programming language, Java provides certain exceptions—one being the guideline for naming and referencing packages. For example, **java**.io.File was developed by Sun Microsystems, but this package is intended to be implemented by other companies as a foundation for building additional I/O packages.) The sections listed beneath the company name reference subdirectories that further specify where the class is located. For example java.**io**.File is a subdirectory that contains classes that relate to the input/output functions of Java. The extension **.class** has

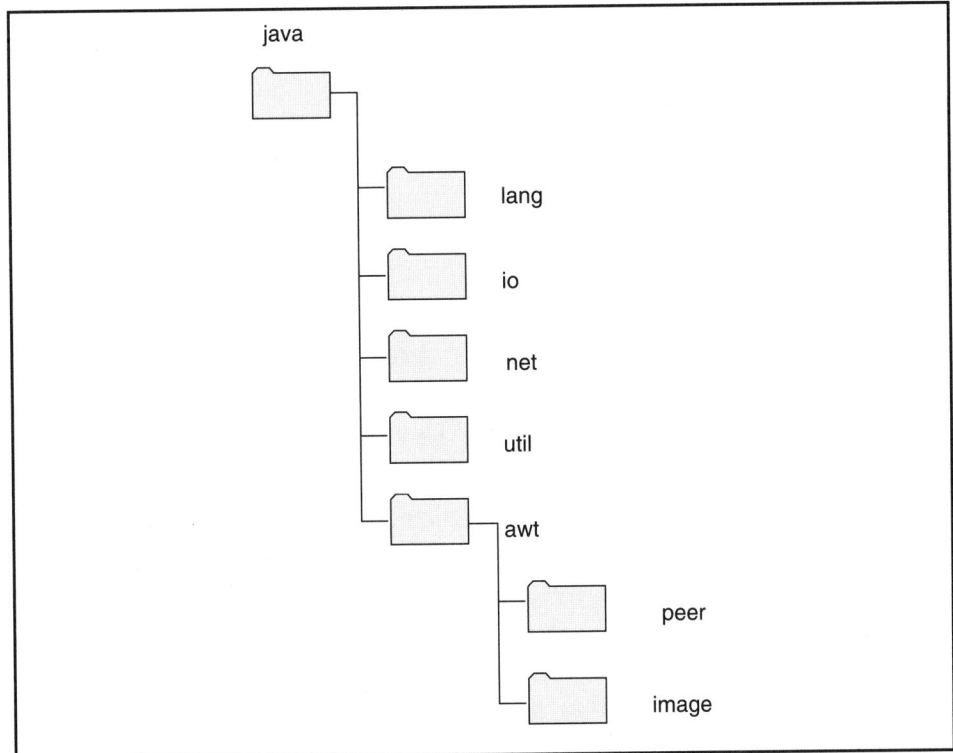

Figure 7.2   Graphical image of the hierarchy of java.awt.image and a call to the (import) java.awt.image on the other side.

been omitted from the reference to the **File** class because interfaces and classes are the only format contained in a package and both end in the **.class** extension.

Uppercase vs. Lowercase Package Names

A specific format should be followed for naming packages and the classes that are contained within them. All package names and the directories that follow them should be specified using lowercase letters. On the other hand, the class and interface names you wish to reference within a package should be specified using an uppercase letter as the first character. This allows other programmers who use your packages to easily determine which components are directory names and which ones are class and interface names.

Declaration for Creating Packages

To create a package, the following statement should be placed at the beginning of a source file that contains a set of class definitions:

```
package PackageName;
```

Each class defined in the source file will automatically be added to the package having the name specified by *PackageName*. The *PackageName* will be created under the subdirectory you have defined in the CLASSPATH variable set in your environment. (The instructions for setting this environment variable are presented in the sidebar, *Setting Your CLASSPATH Environment Variable*.) As an example, assume that you have a source file that contains a set of classes that implement different types of airplanes. These classes could be combined into a single package named **airplanes** by placing the package statement at the beginning of each source file that defines a public class:

```
package airplanes;  // This statement must come first

// Provide source code for Glider class

public class Glider {
```

```
    ...    // Class definition
}
// The end of this source file


package airplanes;  // This statement must come first

// Provide source code for Single_engine class

public class Single_engine {
    ...    // Class definition
}
// The end of this source file


package airplanes;  // This statement must come first

// Provide source code for Twin_engine class

public class Twin_engine {
    ...    // Class definition
}
// The end of this source file
```

The actual *PackageName* is extended by the Java compiler by preceding it with the *CLASSPATH*. (Each subdirectory included in the path name is separated by a period.) The nice part is that you don't need to create the path for the package you define yourself; it is generated by the compiler at compile-time automatically.

Interfaces and Public Classes

Only one public class can be declared in any one source file. Only classes defined as public may be referenced from outside the current package. Otherwise, the classes not defined as public are used to support the public classes in the package.

In another example, if the package CORIOLIS.BOOKS.PROGRAMMING.JAVA is declared, the directory structure will turn out like this:

```
c:\java\lib\coriolis\books\programming\java
```

Essentially, what the Java compiler does when it encounters a statement like PACKAGE CORIOLIS.BOOKS.PROGRAMMING.JAVA is create a new directory structure for

CORIOLIS.BOOKS.PROGRAMMING.JAVA using the directory path specified by the **CLASSPATH** environment variable. It then places all of the compiled class code defined in the source file in the JAVA directory. As the example above illustrates, the **CLASSPATH** would be:

```
c:\java\lib;
```

When the package is later referenced by a Java application, the compiler will know exactly where to look for each class that is referenced in the package.

Saving Java Source Code Files

It is wise to save your Java source code in the directories containing your compiled class. This will allow you to later edit your source code if you wish, but more importantly, you won't have to worry about your class definitions being overwritten with identical names in the default directory where you create and save your source code (.java extension). You'll want to save the different versions of your source files because as you create more and more classes, the chance for repeating a class name becomes more common. For example, assume you have a SPREADSHEET class that contains two classes; one that prints a graph and the other that prints a data sheet. Both classes perform very different operations, but both of them could be assigned the name PRINT.CLASS. In doing so, you must take two steps in generating source code with identical class names because the classes will share the same working directory in most instances. If you placed a statement like this in the beginning of your source code:

```
package acme.spreadsheet.graph;
```

The Java compiler would automatically place the PRINT.CLASS in the directory graph but the original source file (Print.java) would still be paced in the working directory. The next step would be to place the source file in the same directory. This is because the next Print.java source file created (for example, the class responsible for printing the data sheet) will be saved in the working directory, causing the old file to be overwritten. If you later need to modify the class file, you will still have the original source code. At the beginning, the next source file should provide the statement :

```
package acme.spreadsheet.datasheet;
```

Remember, you are required to manually move the source file to the appropriate directory.

Setting Your CLASSPATH Environment Variable

When your source code is compiled, the CLASSPATH environment variable specifies the default base directory for the packages you create. It also tells the compiler which directory path to search for the classes that are predefined. The order of directories defined by CLASSPATH determines the order in which the Java compiler will search for your classes. When a class is found that meets the requirements of the calling class, the compiler stops searching for a match. You should define the path of the default package that accompanies the Java Development Kit (JDK) and the temporary directory that you work from in this order. Here's an example:

```
CLASSPATH = c:\java\lib;.
```

The period sets the current directory you are compiling from. The first directory listed in the CLASSPATH also specifies where YOUR package structure will begin.

Using Packages

The one feature that makes the Java language very powerful is that it lets you use the same code (classes) over and over countless times. This is accomplished by referencing classes that are contained in packages. To use classes that have already been created by you or other Java programmers, you need to reference the package(s) the classes are grouped in. You can do this in one of three ways:

◆ Specify the full package reference each time a class is used that is defined in an outside package. This approach is the most cumbersome and least often used. Here's an example:

```
airplanes.Twin_engine twin = new airplanes.Twin_engine("Beach",
1100);
```

In this case, the object variable **twin** is declared and initialized as an instance of a **Twin_engine** class which is included in the **airplanes** package. With this approach, each time a *Twin_engine* class is accessed, its corresponding package name must also be included.

◆ Import the actual class needed from the package it is defined in. As an example, we could rewrite the previous example by using this code:

```
import airplanes.Twin_engine;
...
Twin_engine twin = new Twin_engine("Beach", 1100);
```

Notice that once the desired class is imported, the name of the **airplanes** package is not needed to reference the **Twin_engine** class.

◆ Import all of the classes defined in a package. The syntax for doing this is illustrated with this statement:

```
import airplanes.*;
```

In this case, all of the public classes combined in the airplanes class, such as **Glider, Single_engine**, and **Twin_engine**, would be included.

Importing Packages Is Like Including C/C++ Header Files

If you are an experienced C / C++ programmer, you can think of the technique of importing a package as you would the technique of using an include file. Typically, you would use an include file to specify the names of function prototypes you wish to call that are defined in external files.

Every class defined in an external package that you want to reference by a class in your Java application or applet must be called directly or with a wild card (*) in the immediate directory. For example, if you look at an example of a ticker tape applet, we called an instance of the class FONTMETRICS that is contained in the java.awt package (directory). The APPLET class imports the java.awt package with a wild card in the beginning of the code (e.g., IMPORT JAVA.AWT.*;). The wild card tells the Java compiler to import ALL of the public classes in the java.awt directory into the TICKERTAPE class. The compiler won't, however, import any of the classes that are contained

in the peer or image directories beneath java.awt. To include the classes in those directories, you must reference the directories directly (e.g., IMPORT JAVA.AWT.PEER.*; or IMPORT JAVA.AWT.IMAGE.*;).

```
// TickerTape Applet

import java.applet.*;
import java.awt.*;

// TickerTape Class
public class TickerTape extends Applet implements Runnable {

    // Draw background and text on buffer image
    public void paintText(Graphics g){
        ...
        FontMetrics fmetrics = g.getFontMetrics();
        ...
    }
}
```

Declaration for Importing Packages

When importing a package into a class, the declaration must appear before any class declarations. The format for declaring a package is as follows:

```
import PackageName;
```

The *PackageName* represents the hierarchy tree separating the directories of the package with decimals. The java.lang package is automatically imported into every class that is created. If you look at an example ticker tape applet, you will notice that it does not import the java.lang package but uses many of the classes that are contained in the package. The classes **String**, **Integer**, and **Thread** are just a few of the classes that are called from this package.

```
// TickerTape Class
public class TickerTape extends Applet implements Runnable {
    // Declare Variable
    String inputText;
    String animSpeedString;
    int xpos;
    int fontLength;
    int fontHeight;
```

```
    int animSpeed;
    boolean suspended = false;
      . . .
}
```

Standard Java Packages

Since we created our first applet, we have been using packages already defined by other developers including Sun Microsystems. These packages have been arranged by their category of usage. Table 7.1 shows the packages currently being distributed with the JDK.

Hiding Classes Using the Wild Card

We mentioned before that the Java wild card (*) will only allow you to bring in the public classes from an imported package. The benefit of this feature is that you can hide the bulk of your classes that perform support operations for your public classes. Users who use the public classes won't be able to look at the code or directly access the internal support classes.

Table 7.1   JDK packages included with Café.

Package	Description
java.lang	Contains essential Java classes for performing basic functions. This package is automatically imported into every class that is created in Java.
java.io	Contains classes used to perform input/output functions to different sources.
java.util	Contains utility classes for items such as tables and vectors.
java.net	Contains classes that aid in connecting over networks. These classes can be used in conjunction with java.io to read/write information to files over a network.
java.awt	Contains classes that let you write platform-independent graphics applications. It includes classes for creating buttons, panels, text boxes, and so on.
java.applet	Contains classes that let you create Java applets that will run within Java-enabled browsers.

Streams and File I/O

8

David H. Friedel, Jr.

It's now time to learn the ins and outs of how streams are used in Java to perform a variety of I/O operations.

*W*hat good is a program that has no means of communicating with the outside world? If you think about it, most programs you write follow a simple pattern of getting data from a user, processing the data, and presenting the user with the results in one format or another. Java arranges the world of input/output (I/O) into a system of byte *streams*. A byte stream is essentially an unformatted sequence of data which can come from or be sent to a number of different sources including the keyboard, screen, file, and so on. To help you process input and output streams in your programs, Java provides special streams in the **System** class as well as other custom classes including **InputStream** and **OutputStream**.

In this chapter we'll show you how to use the **System** class and the java.io package to perform different types of stream I/O from reading strings typed in at the keyboard to writing data to files. After we introduce the three streams supported by the **System** class we'll examine the other key stream processing classes including **InputStream**, **OutputStream**, **BufferedInputStream**, **BufferedOutputStream**, **ByteArrayInputStream**, **ByteArrayOutputStream**, **DataInputStream**, **DataOutputStream**, **FileInputStream**, **FileOutputStream**, and others.

Introducing the System Class

The **System** class is responsible for providing access to the three main streams: **System.in**, **System.out**, and **System.error**. All input streams are derived from **System.in**, which is responsible for reading data. All of the output streams are derived from **System.out**, which is responsible for sending out data in one form or another. The last stream is **System.error**, which is an output stream derived from **System.out**. As its name implies, **System.error** handles the errors that occur while I/O operations are performed.

To use the streams implemented by the **System** class, you must import the javio.io package:

```
import java.io.*;
```

Here's a simple program that uses **System.in** and **System.out** to read and write a string of text:

```
import java.io.*;

public class ProcessALine {
    public static void main(String arg[]) {
        // Bring in the stream from the keyboard and pipe it to
    DataInput
        DataInputStream aDataInput = new DataInputStream(System.in);
        String aString;

        try {
            // Continue to read lines from the keyboard until ^Z is
            // pressed
            while ((aString = aDataInput.readLine()) != null) {
                // Print the line out to the screen
                System.out.println(aString);
            }
        } catch (IOException e) { // Check for I/O errors
            System.out.println("An IOException has occurred");
        }
    }
}
```

The **System.in** stream is used to create an input stream object called **aDataInput**. This object is created as an instance of the **DataInputStream** class. The advantage of this class is that it contains methods like **readLine()** for processing input streams. In fact the work of reading a string is accomplishing using a single line of code:

```
while ((aString = aDataInput.readLine()) != null)  ...
```

The **readLine()** method will continue to read characters from the input stream until a Ctrl-Z character is encountered, which terminates the input stream. (Thus, when you run this program, make sure that you enter a Ctrl-Z at some point to tell the program to stop reading characters from the input stream.)

Checking for Errors

One important feature you'll find in our sample program is simple error handling code implemented with the try ... catch clause. When performing I/O stream operations, you must check for possible I/O errors. Notice that in our program, a try clause is used to check both the stages of reading and writing to a stream. If an error occurs, an IOException error is thrown and the catch clause will be executed.

Different Flavors of Streams

With the multitude of possible forms your data can come in and be sent out with, it's no wonder that Java offers a variety of stream handlers that can be implemented. Each stream type is capable of combining other stream types to handle unique situations. For example, if you want to buffer data that is being read from a file so that it may be read all at once, you could use a statement like this:

```
InputStream aStream =
    new BufferedInputStream(new FileInputStream("C:\foobar.txt"));
```

This line would bring in the data from a file, buffering it in a stream called **aStream**. Then, the data could be accessed all at once by using **aStream**. This technique could be very valuable in applications that need to read data all at once instead of having to read chunks and perform multiple read operations.

Understanding the Basics of Inputting and Outputting

All data that you manipulate in the form of strings and numbers, be it an integer or a double, must be transformed into a stream (bytes) in order for the information to be interpreted by the computer and the devices that use the data. This is considered outputting the data verses inputting the data. Likewise, if a user needs to understand the data, unless they read machine language, we need to convert it to a useful format by manipulating it with one of the input streams. Figure 8.1 shows the process of how data is converted and processed with both input and output streams.

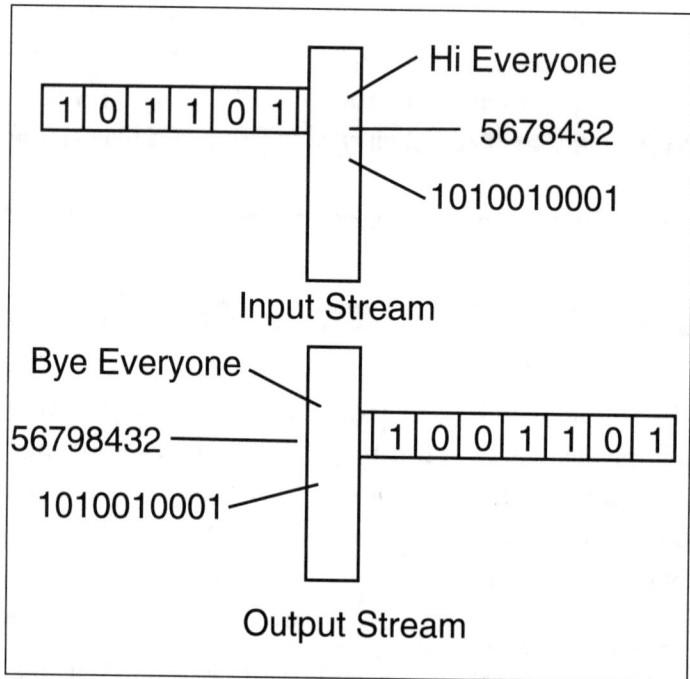

Figure 8.1 **A graphical example of converting data for input and output streams.**

InputStream and OutputStream Classes

In addition to the **System** class, Java provides other classes for handling stream input and output including **InputStream** and **OutputStream**, which are abstract classes responsible for the basic declarations of all the input and output streams that we'll be exploring next. All streams created from these classes are capable of throwing an **IOException** that must be dealt with by "re-throwing" it or handling it. To declare and create an object using **InputStream** or **OutputStream** you would use statements like the following:

```
InputStream aStream = getStreamFromASource();
OutputStream aStream = getStreamToASource();
```

In both declarations, the methods *getStreamFromSource()* and *getStreamToASource()* are any methods that return a stream. The stream returned by the method will be assigned to the object *aStream*. All information passed to and from the streams must be in the form of bytes. Table 8.1 presents the key methods defined in **InputStream** and Table 8.2 presents the methods defined in **OutputStream**.

Table 8.1 Key Methods Defined in the Input Stream Class.

Method	Description
available()	Returns the number of bytes available in the stream without invoking a block.
close()	Closes the stream.
mark(int)	Marks the current position in the stream.
markSupported()	Returns a true/false value to indicate if the stream supports marking capabilities.
read()	Reads bytes from the stream.
read(byte[])	Reads bytes from the stream and places them in an array.
read(byte[], int, int)	Reads a specified number of bytes from the stream and places them in an array starting at a specified index position.
reset()	Sets the stream to the last mark.
skip(long)	Skips a designated number of bytes in the stream.

Table 8.2 Key Methods Defined in the OutputStream Class.

Method	Description
close()	Closes the stream.
flush()	Clears the stream, forcing any buffered bytes to be written out.
write(int)	Writes n number of bytes to the stream.
write(byte[])	Writes an array of bytes to the stream.
write(byte[], int, int)	Writes an array of bytes of a specified size, starting at a specified index position.

Here's an example of an application that uses the **OutputStream** class to derive another class for performing a simple output operation:

```
import java.io.*;
import java.net.*;
import java.awt.*;

public class mrsServer extends Frame {
    TextArea serverScreen;

    mrsServer() {
        super("Server Application");
        serverScreen = new TextArea("mrsServer's Screen:\n", 10, 40);
        add("Center", serverScreen);
        pack();
        show();

        ServerSocket mrsServer = null;
        Socket socketReturn = null;
        // Assigns the variable rawDataOut to the class OutputStream
        OutputStream rawDataOut = null;

        try {
            mrsServer = new ServerSocket( 10, 2 );
            socketReturn = mrsServer.accept();
            serverScreen.appendText( "Connected to the mrsServer" );

            // Creates an instanceof the class OutputStream named
            // rawDataOut
            // rawDataOut receives the stream from the Socket
            socketReturn
```

```
                rawDataOut = socketReturn.getOutputStream();
                DataOutputStream DataOut = new
    DataOutputStream(rawDataOut);

                DataOut.write( 5 );
            } catch( UnknownHostException e ) {
            } catch( IOException e ) {
            }
        }
```

BufferedInputStream and BufferedOutputStream Classes

These classes are used to implement streams responsible for collecting data from a source that brings in data at a slower rate than the recipient. Then, the chunks of data collected may be delivered in larger, more manageable blocks than in the manner they were received. This proves beneficial for file systems and networks, where the connection depends on a device for transmission.

Here are the declarations for these classes:

```
InputStream aStream = new
 BufferedInputStream(getStreamFromASource());
OutputStream aStream = new BufferedInputStream(getStreamToASource());
```

In both declarations, a stream is returned to the parent class, **InputStream** or **OutputStream** depending if it is incoming or outgoing. The methods *getStreamFromSource()* and *getStreamToASource()* can be any methods that return a stream. The stream that the method returns will be buffered as the information comes in and is appended to the object **aStream**. All information passed to and from the streams must be in the form of bytes. Table 8.3 presents the key methods defined in **BufferedInputStream** and Table 8.4 presents the methods defined in **BufferedOutputStream**.

Here's an example of an application that uses the **BufferedInputStream** class to derive another class for performing a simple input operation:

```
import java.io.*;

// Reads from a file
```

Table 8.3   Key Methods Defined in the BufferedInputStream Class.

Method	Description
available()	Determines the number of bytes available in the stream without invoking a block.
mark(int)	Marks the current position in the stream.
markSupported()	Returns a true/false value to indicate if the stream supports marking capabilities.
read()	Reads bytes from the stream.
read(byte[], int, int)	Reads a specified number of bytes from the stream and places them in an array starting at a specified index position.
reset()	Sets the stream to the last mark.
skip(long)	Skips a designated number of bytes in the stream.

Table 8.4   Key Methods Defined in the BufferedOutputStream Class.

Method	Description
flush()	Clears the stream, forcing any buffered bytes to be written out.
write(int)	Writes n number of bytes to the stream.
write(byte[], int, int)	Writes an array of bytes of a specified size, starting at a specified index position.

```
public class  ReadAFile extends Object {
    ReadAFile(String s) {
        String line;
        FileInputStream fileName  = null;
        // Assigns the variable bufferedInput to the class
          // BufferedInputStream
        BufferedInputStream bufferedInput = null;
        DataInputStream dataIn = null;

        try {
            fileName = new FileInputStream(s);
            // Creates an instance of the class BufferedInputStream
            // named bufferedInput
```

```
        // bufferedInput receives the stream from the
FileInputStream
        // fileName as it is read
        bufferedInput = new BufferedInputStream(fileName);
        dataIn = new DataInputStream(bufferedInput);
    }
    catch(FileNotFoundException e) {
        System.out.println("File Not Found");
        return;
    }
    catch(Throwable e) {
        System.out.println("Error in opening file");
        return;
    }

    try {
        while ((line = dataIn.readLine()) != null) {
            System.out.println(line + "\n");
        }
        fileName .close();
    }
    catch(IOException e) {
        System.out.println("Error in reading file");
    }
}

// Where execution begins in a stand-alone executable
public static void main(String args[]) {
    new ReadAFile(args[0]);
}
}
```

ByteArrayInputStream and ByteArrayOutputStream Classes

These streams create a new stream from an array of bytes to be processed. They are used to perform the reverse operations of what most of the streams do. To declare and create an object from these classes you would use statements like the following:

```
InputStream aStream = new
 ByteArrayInputStream(getStreamFromASource());
OutputStream aStream = new
 ByteArrayInputStream(getStreamToASource());
```

The methods used above, *getByteArrayFromSource()* and *getByte ArrayToASource()* can be any methods that returns a byte array. The array is passed through the **ByteArrayInputStream** class and a stream is created from it. The stream that was converted from the class returns a value and is assigned to the object **aStream**. All information passed to and from the streams must be in the form of bytes. Table 8.5 presents the key methods defined in **ByteArrayInputStream** and Table 8.6 presents the methods defined in **ByteArrayOutputStream**.

Table 8.5   Key Methods Defined in the ByteArrayInputStream Class.

Method	Description
available()	Returns the number of bytes available in the stream without invoking a block.
read()	Reads bytes from the stream.
read(byte[], int, int)	Reads a specified number of bytes from the stream and places them in an array starting at a specified index position.
reset()	Sets the stream to the last mark.
skip(long)	Skips a designated number of bytes in the stream.

Table 8.6   Key Methods Defined in the ByteArrayOutputStream Class.

Method	Description
reset()	Resets the current buffer so that it may be used again.
size()	Returns the current size of the buffer.
toByteArray()	Returns a copy of the input data.
toString()	Converts input bytes to a string.
toString(int)	Converts input bytes to a string, sets the selected byte's first 8 bits of a 16 bit Unicode to hibyte.
write(int)	Writes n number of bytes to the buffer.
write(byte[], int, int)	Writes an array of bytes of a specified size, starting at a specified index position.
writeTo(OutputStream)	Writes the buffered information to another stream.

Here is a hypothetical example that uses a **ByteArrayInputStream** class. If you wanted to compile this program, you would need to supply a method to fill the array of bytes, **anArrayOBytes**:

```
import java.io.*;

// Reads from a file
public class  Byte2String extends Object {
   Byte2String(String s) {
      byte[] anArrayOBytes;

      …

      //fills the anArrayOBytes with data

      …

      try {
         // Creates an instanceof the class InputStream named
         // byteDataIn
         // byteDataIn receives the stream from the
 ByteArrayInputStream
         // anArrayOBytes
         InputStream byteDataIn = new
 ByteArrayInputStream(anArrayOBytes);
      }
      catch(IOException e) {
      }

      …

      // perform some process with the stream
   }

   // Where execution begins in a stand-alone executable
   public static void main(String args[]) {
       new Byte2String(args[0]);
   }
}
```

DataInputStream and DataOutputStream Classes

All methods defined in these classes are actually declared in an interface named **DataInput**. To declare and create a **DataInputStream** or **DataOutputStream** object you would use statements like the following:

```
DataInputStream aStream = new
 DataInputStream(getStreamFromASource());
DataOutputStream aStream = new
 DataOutputStream(getStreamToASource());
```

Notice in both declarations the need to declare the class type, **DataInputStream** or **DataOutputStream**, instead of type **InputStream** or **OutputStream**. The methods *getStreamFromSource()* and *getStreamToASource()* can be any methods that return a stream. Once the stream is passed to the **DataInputStream** or **DataOutputStream** object, the methods declared in the interface can be applied to the stream. Table 8.7 presents the key methods defined in **DataInputStream** and Table 8.8 presents the methods defined in **DataOutputStream**.

Let's revisit our example of the client application once more to demonstrate the use of a **DataInputStream**:

```
import java.io.*;
import java.net.*;
import java.awt.*;

public class mrClient extends Frame {
    mrClient() {
        super("Client Application");
        TextArea clientScreen = new TextArea("mrClient's Screen:\n",
            10, 40);
        add("Center", clientScreen);
        pack();
        show();
        Socket mrClient = null;
        InputStream rawDataIn = null;
```

Table 8.7   Key Methods Defined in the DataInputStream Class.

Method	Description
flush()	Clears the stream, forcing any buffered bytes to be written out.
size()	Returns the number of bytes in the stream.
write(int)	Writes n number of bytes to the stream.
write(byte[], int, int)	Writes an array of bytes of a specified size, starting at a specified index position.
writeBoolean(boolean)	Writes a boolean to the stream.
writeByte(int)	Writes an 8-bit byte to the stream.
writeBytes(String)	Writes a string of bytes to the stream.

Table 8.8   Key Methods Defined in the DataOutputStream Class.

Method	Description
read(byte[])	Reads an array of bytes from the stream.
read(byte[], int, int)	Reads a specified number of bytes from the stream and places them in an array starting at a specified index position.
readBoolean()	Reads a boolean from the stream.
readByte()	Reads a 8-bit byte from the stream.
readChar()	Reads a 16-bit character from the stream.
readDouble()	Reads a 64-bit double from the stream.
readFloat()	Reads a 32-bit float from the stream.
readFully(byte[])	Reads bytes from the stream, blocking until all bytes are read.
readFully(byte[], int, int)	Reads bytes from the stream, blocking until all bytes are read. The starting point to begin reading and the maximum number of bytes to read are passed as parameters.
readInt()	Reads a 32-bit integer from the stream.
readLine()	Reads a line from the stream until an \n,\r,\n\r \, or EOF is reached.
readLong()	Reads a 64-bit long from the stream.
readShort()	Reads a 16-bit short from the stream.
readUTF()	Reads a UTF formatted string from the stream.
readUTF(DataInput)	Reads a UTF formatted string from a specific stream.
readUnsignedByte()	Reads an unsigned 8-bit byte from the stream.
readUnsignedShort()	Reads an unsigned 8-bit short from the stream.
skipBytes(int)	Skips a designated number of bytes in the stream, blocking until finished.

```
        try {
            mrClient = new Socket( InetAddress.getLocalHost(), 10 );

            rawDataIn = mrClient.getInputStream();
            // reads in the stream for the InputStream rawDataIn and
            // pipes it to DataIn
            DataInputStream DataIn = new DataInputStream(rawDataIn);
            // the array of bytes is then read from the stream
            clientScreen.appendText( "mrClient receives -  " +
            DataIn.read() );
        } catch( UnknownHostException e ) {
        } catch( IOException e ) {
        }
    }
```

Here the stream used with the **Socket** object, **mrClient**, is piped from the **InputStream** to the **DataInputStream**. The bytes are then read from the stream, **DataIn**, and appended to the text box with this line:

```
clientScreen.appendText("mrClient receives -  " + DataIn.read());
```

By simply changing the method, we can read any type of data that resides in the stream. For example, if we wanted to read a stream of chars, we would use a statement like this:

```
clientScreen.appendText("mrClient receives -  " + DataIn.readChar());
```

FileInputStream and FileOutputStream Classes

The most common use for these streams is to apply them to a file to be read from and written to. Here are the declarations for these classes:

```
InputStream aStream = getStreamFromASource();
OutputStream aStream = getStreamToASource();
```

In both declarations, the methods *getStreamFromSource()* and *getStreamToASource()* can be any methods that return a stream. The stream that the method returns is assigned to the object **aStream**. All information passed to and from the streams must be in the form of bytes. Table 8.9 presents the key methods defined in **FileInputStream** and Table 8.10 presents the methods defined in **FileOutputStream**.

Table 8.9   Key Methods Defined in the FileInputStream Class.

Method	Description
available()	Returns the number of bytes available in the stream without invoking a block.
close()	Closes the stream.
finalize()	Closes the stream when the garbage collector is invoked.
getFD()	Returns the file descriptor of the file associated with the stream.
read()	Reads bytes from the stream.
read(byte[])	Reads into an array of bytes from the stream.
read(byte[], int, int)	Reads a specified number of bytes from the stream and places them in an array starting at a specified index position.
skip(long)	Skips a designated number of bytes in the stream.

Table 8.10   Key Methods Defined in the FileOutputStream Class.

Method	Description
close()	Closes the stream.
finalize()	Closes the stream when the garbage collector is invoked.
getFD()	Returns the file descriptor of the file associated with the stream.
write(int)	Writes n number of bytes to the stream.
write(byte[])	Writes an array of bytes to the stream.
write(byte[], int, int)	Writes an array of bytes of a specified size, starting at a specified index position.

Here is a practical example of how you can use the **FileOutputStream** and **FileInputStream** classes:

```java
import java.io.*;

public class WriteAFile {
    WriteAFile(String s) {
        write(s);
    }

    // Writes to a file
    public void write(String s) {
        // Assigns the variable writeOut to the class FileOutputStream
        FileOutputStream writeOut = null;
        DataOutputStream dataWrite = null;

        try {
            // Creates an instanceof the class FileOutputStream named
            // writeOut
            // writeOut receives the stream from the File designated in
            // the variables
            writeOut = new FileOutputStream(s);
            dataWrite = new DataOutputStream(writeOut);
            dataWrite.writeChars("This is a Test");
            dataWrite.close();
        }
        catch(IOException e)  {
            System.out.println("Error in writing to file");
        }
        catch(Throwable e)  {
            System.out.println("Error in writing to file");
        }
        finally {
            System.out.println("\n\n.....creating a backup file.");
            try {
                // Recreates an instanceof the class FileOutputStream
                // named writeOut
                // writeOut receives the stream from the File named
                // "MyBackup.sav"
                writeOut = new FileOutputStream("MyBackup.sav");
                dataWrite = new DataOutputStream(writeOut);
                dataWrite.writeChars("This is a Test");
                dataWrite.close();
            }
            catch (IOException e) {
                System.out.println("Error in writing backup file");
            }
        }
```

```
   }
   // Where execution begins in a stand-alone executable
   public static void main(String args[]) {
       new WriteAFile(args[0]);
   }
}
```

The variable **writeOut**, which is of type **DataOutputStream**, is actually used twice in this example: once to write the file specified by the user and again to write a file MyBackup.sav.

FilterInputStream and FilterOutputStream Classes

These are classes that act as channels for streams to be passed through. As a stream is passed through the shell, a hierarchy of stream containers are created to perform some processing of bytes as the methods are passed along with it. This structure allows for a chaining effect of shells to break up a complicated task into small steps. Here are the declarations for these classes:

```
FilterInputStream anotherStream = new FilterInputStream(aStream);
FilterOutputStream anotherStream = new FilterOutputStream(aStream);
```

In both declarations, the methods **FilterInputStream**() and **FilterOutputStream**() require that a stream be passed to each method. In return, a stream is assigned to the object named **anotherStream**. Table 8.11 presents the key methods defined in **FilterInputStream** and Table 8.12 presents the methods defined in **FilterOutputStream**.

Here is an example of how a **FilterOutputStream** class can be manipulated at different stages without actually changing the original stream from the **OutputStream**:

```
import java.io.*;
import java.net.*;
import java.awt.*;

public class mrsServer extends Frame {
   TextArea serverScreen;
```

Table 8.11   Key Methods Defined in the FilterInputStream Class.

Method	Description
available()	Returns the number of bytes available in the stream without invoking a block.
close()	Closes the stream.
finalize()	Closes the stream when the garbage collector is invoked.
getFD()	Returns the file descriptor of the file associated with the stream.
read()	Reads bytes from the stream.
read(byte[])	Reads an array of bytes from the stream.
read(byte[], int, int)	Reads a specified number of bytes from the stream and places them in an array starting at a specified index position.
skip(long)	Skips a designated number of bytes in the stream.

Table 8.12   Key Methods Defined in the FilterOutputStream Class.

Method	Description
close()	Closes the stream.
flush()	Clears the stream, forcing any bytes to be written out.
write(int)	Writes n number of bytes to the stream.
write(byte[])	Writes an array of bytes to the stream.
write(byte[], int, int)	Writes an array of bytes of a specified size, starting at a specified index position.

```
mrsServer() {
    ... // perform functions previous to opening the socket
    try {
        mrsServer = new ServerSocket( 10, 2 );
        socketReturn = mrsServer.accept();

        OutputStream stageOneDataOut =
socketReturn.getOutputStream();
        FilterOutputStream stageTwoDataOut = new
```

```
        FilterOutputStream(stageOneDataOut);
        // perform some operations on stageTwoDataOut stream
        ...
        FilterOutputStream stageThreeDataOut = new
        FilterOutputStream(stageTwoDataOut);
        // perform some operations on stageThreeDataOut stream
        ...
        FilterOutputStream stageFourDataOut = new
          FilterOutputStream(stageThreeDataOut);
        // write the data from stageFourDataOut
        ...

    } catch( UnknownHostException e ) {
    } catch( IOException e ) {
    }
    ...
}
```

LineNumberInputStream Class

This class allows for line numbering of each line processed through the stream. It is useful for determining which lines errors have occurred on. To declare and create an object from this class, you use a statement like the following:

```
LineNumberInputStream aStream =
  LineNumberInputStream(getStreamFromASource());
```

In the declaration above, the method **getStreamAFromSource**() retrieves a source stream that is assigned line numbers. The stream that the method **LineNumberInputStream**() returns is assigned to the object **aStream**. Table 8.13 presents the key methods defined in **LineNumberInputStream**.

Here is a real world example of how the **LineNumberInputStream** class can be used:

```
import java.io.*;

// Reads from a file
public class  ReadAFile extends Object {
   ReadAFile(String s) {
      String line;
      FileInputStream fileName  = null;
      // Assigns the variable bufferedInput to the class
```

Table 8.13   Key Methods Defined in the LineNumberInputStream Class.

Method	Description
available()	Returns the number of bytes available in the stream without invoking a block.
getLineNumber()	Returns the current line number of the stream.
mark(int)	Marks the current position in the stream.
read()	Reads bytes from the stream
read(byte[], int, int)	Reads a specified number of bytes from the stream and places them in an array starting at a specified index position.
reset()	Sets the stream to the last mark.
setLineNumber(int)	Sets the current line number.
skip(long)	Skips a designated number of bytes in the stream.

```
BufferedInputStream
    BufferedInputStream bufferedInput = null;
    DataInputStream dataIn = null;

    try {
        fileName = new FileInputStream(s);
        // Creates an instanceof the class LineNumberInputStream
        // named parsedData
        // parsedData receives the stream from the FileInputStream
        // fileName as it is read
        LineNumberInputStream parsedData = new
        LineNumberInputStream(fileName);
        dataIn = new DataInputStream(parsedData);
    }
    catch(FileNotFoundException e) {
        System.out.println("File Not Found");
        return;
    }
    catch(Throwable e) {
        System.out.println("Error in opening file");
        return;
    }

    try {
        while ((line = dataIn.readLine()) != null) {
            // adds the current line number to the beginning of
            // every line
```

```
                System.out.println(parsedData.getLineNumber() + ": " +
                    line +
                    "\n");
            }
        fileName .close();
        }
        catch(IOException e) {
            System.out.println("Error in reading file");
        }
    }

    // Where execution begins in a stand-alone executable
    public static void main(String args[]) {
        new ReadAFile(args[0]);
    }
}
}
```

As the stream is passed to the **parsedData** stream, a line number is assigned to each line in the stream. The line number is then added to the line before printing the line to the browser.

PipedInputStream and PipedOutputStream Classes

These classes allow for pipe-like connection between two threads to allow for safe communication between a shared queue. For this technique to be effective, both threads must implement the class. To declare and create objects from these class, you use statements like the following:

```
PipedInputStream aThreadStreamIn =
  PipedInputStream(getStreamFromASource());
PipedOutputStream aThreadStreamOut =
  PipedOutputStream(aThreadStreamIn);
```

In both declarations, they must be implemented in the threads to ensure a data stream is not being written to by the other thread. The stream that the method returns is assigned to an **aThreadStreamIn** or **aThreadStreamOut** object. Table 8.14 presents the key methods defined in **PipedInputStream** and Table 8.15 presents the methods defined in **PipedOutputStream**.

Table 8.14   Key Methods Defined in the PipedInputStream Class.

Method	Description
close()	Closes the stream.
connect(PipedOutputStream)	Connects the stream to a PipedOutputStream of the sender.
read()	Reads bytes from the stream.
read(byte[], int, int)	Reads a specified number of bytes from the stream and places them in an array starting at a specified index position.

Table 8.15   Key Methods Defined in the PipedOutputStream Class.

Method	Description
close()	Closes the stream.
connect(PipedInputStream)	Connects the stream to a PipedInputStream of the intended recipient.
write(int)	Writes n number of bytes to the stream.
write(byte[], int, int)	Writes an array of bytes of a specified size, starting at a specified index position.

PrintStream Class

This class is most commonly used to create an instance of the **System** class, where the methods **print()** and **println()** are referenced as class variables for use in the **System.out** and System.err calls. The most common output device for this class is the screen. The declaration for the **PrintStream** class is:

```
PrintStream aStream = new PrintStream( getStreamFromASource() );
```

Along with this class accepting the **write()**, **flush()**, and **close()** methods, it supports a slew of print methods that will handle just about every I/O operation you will need to perform. Most often, an object created from this class will be used like the following:

```
System.out.print(aStream);
System.out.println(aStream);
```

The only difference between the two calls is that the second call appends a return character to the end of the stream. Table 8.16 presents the key methods defined in **PrintStream**.

Table 8.16   Key Methods Defined in the PrintStream Class.

Method	Description
checkError()	Flushes the stream and returns a boolean in the event of an error.
close()	Closes the stream.
flush()	Clears the stream, forcing any bytes to be written out.
print(Object)	Prints an Object.
print(String)	Prints a String.
print(char[])	Prints an array of chars.
print(char)	Prints a char.
print(int)	Prints an Integer.
print(long)	Prints a long.
print(float)	Prints a float.
print(double)	Prints a double.
print(boolean)	Prints a boolean.
println()	Prints a newline chatacter.
println(Object)	Prints an Object with a newline appended to the end.
println(String)	Prints a String with a newline appended to the end.
println(char[])	Prints an array of chars with a newline appended to the end.
println(char)	Prints a char with a newline appended to the end.
println(int)	Prints an integer with a newline appended to the end.
println(long)	Prints a long with a newline appended to the end.
println(float)	Prints a float with a newline appended to the end.
println(double)	Prints a double with a newline appended to the end.
println(boolean)	Prints a boolean with a newline appended to the end.
write(int)	Writes n number of bytes to the stream.
write(byte[], int, int)	Writes an array of bytes, starting point to begin writing, number of bytes to write.

Here is a simple example of how the **PrintStream** class can be used to return a line that was typed in by the user:

```
import java.io.*;

public class ProcessALine {
   public static void main(String arg[]) {
      DataInputStream aDataInput = new DataInputStream(System.in);
      String aString;

      try {
      // A Control Z exits
        while ((aString = aDataInput.readLine()) != null) {
            System.out.println(aString);
        }
      } catch (IOException e) {
          System.out.println("An IOException has occurred");
      }
   }
}
```

PushbackInputStream Class

This class causes the stream to reaccept a byte that was passed to it by the **InputStream**. By forcing the byte back to the delivering **InputStream**, you can reread the byte as if it had never been read. To declare a stream as **PushbackInputStream** and instantiate it, you could type the following:

```
PushbackInputStream aStream =
   new PushbackInputStream (getStreamFromASource());
```

The **getStreamFromASource**() method can be any method that returns a stream. The stream that the method is assigned to the object **aStream**. All information passed to and from the streams must be in the form of bytes. Table 8.17 presents the key methods that are defined in **PushbackInputStream**.

SequenceInputStream Class

This class allows for two streams to be seamlessly joined. This is especially useful when creating an exception that would pick up where it left off last

Table 8.17   Key Methods Defined in the PushBackInputStream Class.

Method	Description
available()	Returns the number of bytes available in the stream without invoking a block.
markSupported()	Returns a true/false value to indicate if the stream supports marking capabilities.
read()	Reads bytes from the stream.
read(byte[], int, int)	Reads a specified number of bytes from the stream and places them in an array starting at a specified index position.
unread(int)	Returns a char to the stream as if it had not been read in the first place.

in a transfer. To declare a stream as type **SequenceInputStream** and instantiate it, you would type the following:

```
InputStream aStream = new SequenceInputStream(firstStream,
   secondStream);
```

In the declaration, **firstStream** is appended to the **secondStream** to create a single seamless stream, **aStream**. Table 8.18 presents the key methods defined in **SequenceInputStream**.

Table 8.18   Key Methods Defined in the SequenceInputStream Class.

Method	Description
close()	Closes the stream.
read()	Reads bytes from the stream.
read(byte[], int, int)	Reads a specified number of bytes from the stream and places them in an array starting at a specified index position.

StringBufferInputStream Class

This class is very similiar to the **ByteArrayInputStream** class. The difference is that it combines an array of char types into a stream. Note, an array of chars is actually a string. To declare and create an object from this class, you use a statement like the following:

```
InputStream aStream = new StringBufferInputStream(String);
```

The classes declared here passes a string through the **StringBufferInputStream** class and a stream is created from it. The stream that was converted from the class returns a value and is assigned to the object **aStream**. Table 8.19 presents the key methods defined in **StringBufferInputStream**.

Here is another hypothetical example, but this time a **StringBufferInputStream** class is used. (You may have recognized this example earlier when we introduced the **ByteArrayInputStream** class. We decided to reuse the sample program because of the similarity between the two classes.)

Table 8.19   Key Methods Defined in the StringBufferInputStream Class.

Method	Description
available()	Returns the number of bytes available in the stream without invoking a block.
read()	Reads bytes from the stream.
read(byte[], int, int)	Reads a specified number of bytes from the stream and places them in an array starting at a specified index position.
reset()	Sets the stream to the last mark.
skip(long)	Skips a designated number of bytes in the stream.

```
import java.io.*;

// Reads from a file
public class  Char2Stream extends Object {

  Char2Stream(String s) {
      String aCommonString = "The quick brown fox jumped over the
  lazy dog";
      try {
          // Creates an instanceof the class InputStream named
          // charDataIn
          // charDataIn receives the stream from the
          // StringBufferInputStream aCommonString
          InputStream charDataIn = new
          StringBufferInputStream(aCommonString);
      }
      catch(IOException e) {
      }
      ...
      // perform some process with the stream
  }

  // Where execution begins in a stand-alone executable
  public static void main(String args[]) {
      new Char2Stream(args[0]);
  }
}
```

The stream is piped through the **StringBufferInputStream** class before being sent to the **InputStream** object, **charDataIn**. This technique converts the string of characters into a sequence of bytes so that they can be used in a stream. The stream then can be passed to any of the **InputStreams** to be manipulated later in the program.

A Look into the Applet Class

John Rodley

The Applet Class is your applet's doorway into the browser. Check here as we cross the threshold.

Applets are the sizzle in the Java steak, allowing you to put exciting user interfaces on WWW applications. We've already written a number of applets, so we have an idea of what an applet is. Now, it's time to get into more of the details.

In this chapter we'll write some applets and talk about where they appear, what they look like, when they run, and how they interact with their environment. When we're done, we should have a good idea of just what happens when a browser plows into that **<applet>** tag in an HTML document.

Positioning Applets on the Screen

As we've seen, the only way to get an applet to appear on the browser screen is by embedding an **<applet>** tag in an HTML document and then viewing that document. Like every other HTML element, the placement of the **<applet>** tag determines where on the screen the applet appears. Consider the simple example in Listing 9.1. Listing 9.2, which provides the HTML code to run the applet, contains a number of HTML elements, including text paragraphs and images, our simple applet, then more HTML elements. Figure 9.1 shows how this applet appears running in Netscape.

LISTING 9.1   POSITIONING AN APPLET

```
package chap4;

import java.awt.Graphics;
import java.applet.Applet;

/** An applet that prints the string "Hello world" at absolute
applet-relative coordinates x=20, y=50.
@author John Rodley
@version 1.0
*/
public class ch4_fig1 extends Applet {

/** Actually paint the string on the screen
*/
  public void paint(Graphics g) {
    g.drawString( "Hello world", 20, 50 );
  }
}
```

LISTING 9.2   HTML PAGE REFERENCING CODE

```
<!DOCTYPE HTML PUBLIC
"-//SQ//DTD HTML 2.0 HoTMetaL + extensions//EN">
<HTML><HEAD><TITLE>An Applet in the HTML Milieu</TITLE></HEAD>
<BODY><H1>Some Text</H1>
<P>When you want to place an applet, you simply place it
within the page at the spot you want it to appear.  The
problem of placing applets is the same problem all HTML
elements have - the fact that HTML tags are 'suggestions', not
directives, which browsers are free to interpret
differently.  Now, a pair of goodogs, for your amusement:
```

```
<IMG SRC="chap4/ch4_fig1a.jpg" ALIGN="BOTTOM">
<IMG SRC="chap4/ch4_fig1b.jpg" ALIGN="BOTTOM">
<P>Below is the applet.  Can you tell the difference between
the applet text, and the HTML?</P>
<applet code=chap4/ch4_fig1.class width=100 height=100>
</applet>
The applet is above us.  Notice that as long as you don't
use non-default backgrounds, it's impossible to tell the
applet from the HTML.</P></BODY></HTML>
```

The two **import** statements used in Listing 9.1 are for the **Applet** class, which all applets subclass, and for the **Graphics** class, which we use in the **paint** method. The code line **extends Applet** tells the compiler that this class should get all the functionality of the **Applet** class. The **paint** method overrides a do-nothing method that is part of the **Applet** class (via its inheritance of **Component**). The line **g.drawString** tells the **Graphics** object to draw a **String** at 20 on the X-axis and 50 on the Y. If you think about it, six lines of code (three of which are boilerplate stuff) have gotten us a functional and useful applet. We'll talk more about the **paint** method later in this chapter. For now, what we're mainly interested in is how the applet fits into the host HTML document.

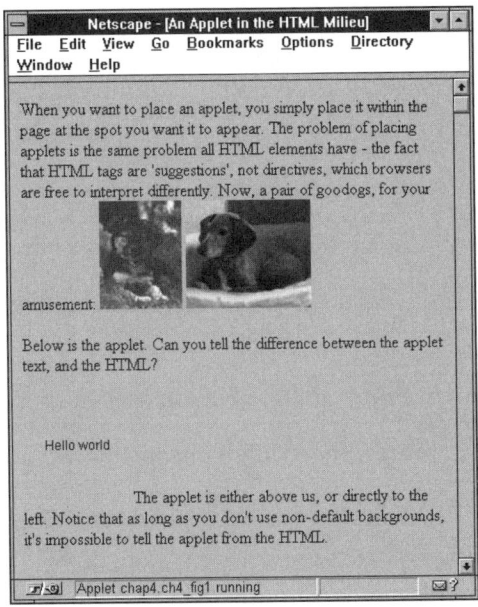

FIGURE 9.1   An applet running in Netscape.

The rule browsers use when formatting a document is to stretch or compress the document vertically such that a line of text never rolls off the horizontal edge of the screen. If you resize the screen, Netscape will reformat the text *and* reposition the applet. As we resize the document in Figure 9.1 to make it narrower (smaller horizontally), our applet will eventually be pushed out the bottom of the window and we'll have to scroll vertically to get it back on the screen.

If you've played with browsers much, you've probably seen that browsers treat text and images differently. For instance, if you shrink the document in Figure 9.1 to make the window smaller horizontally than the width of our images, you'll see the browser add a horizontal scrollbar for scrolling the entire image. Browsers treat applets the same as images—as lumps that always get a rectangular area whose shape can't be changed by the browser.

Breaking Down the Applet Class

So far, we've talked about applets in general terms—as small applications. But in Java, **Applet** is an actual class of its own, with very specific capabilities. In fact, the **Applet** class is at the end of a fairly long chain of inheritance consisting of the **Object**, **Component**, **Container**, **Panel**, and **Applet**. In simplistic terms, the first four superclasses give **Applet** the following capabilities:

◆ **Object** provides the ability to behave as a Java entity.

◆ **Component** provides the ability to appear as a visual entity on-screen.

◆ **Container** provides the ability to *encapsulate* other visual entities.

◆ **Panel** provides the ability to align encapsulated visual entities.

We've already talked a little about the basic Java **Object**. The remaining three classes are part of the windowing system, AWT, which we'll discuss briefly here, and will look at in more detail later. From these superclasses, we can easily infer a lot about what an applet is—it's a space on the screen, a window if you wish, that is a child of the window in which the browser is displaying the HTML text.

Component is the key class in this inheritance chain. Subclassing **Component** makes **Applet** a child window. Visually, a child window is a space on the screen that has the same background color as its parent, the browser main window. It has no border, and no menu, and nothing appears in that window unless we put it there. It can be drawn on at the pixel level (via **Graphics**) and it has the ability to capture events, like mouse clicks and key presses.

However, the **Applet** class is not just the sum of its superclasses. It implements many methods of its own, as shown in Table 9.1.

Over the course of this chapter, we'll use each of these methods, except for **getImage** and the URL grabbing methods, **getDocumentBase** and **getCodeBase**. If you're psyched to start displaying images via **getImage**,

TABLE 9.1   The Applet Class.

Operators	Operator Type
() [].	Expression
++ — ! - ~	Unary
* / %	Multiplicative
+ -	Additive
<< >> >>>	Shift
< <= > >=	Relational (inequality)
== !=	Relational (equality)
&	Bitwise ADD
^	Bitwise XOR
|	Bitwise OR
&&	Logical AND
||	Logical OR
?:	Conditional
= *= /= %= += -=	Assignment
<<= >>= &= |= ^=	

you'll have to wait until Chapter 11. **getDocumentBase** and **getCodeBase** are both used extensively in Chapter 13.

Resizing an Applet

The size of an applet is set through the **<applet>** tag in the HTML document. In Listing 9.1, we specified a height of 100 pixels and a width of 100 pixels, so the browser made a hole of that size in the document and flowed the text around it.

Unfortunately, some of the current crop of browsers don't deal well with reformatting the HTML document if the applet changes size. Suppose you use **Applet.resize** to make your applet smaller than the size set from the **<applet>** tag with **height** and **width** parameters. The HTML document should reflow to fit exactly around the new, smaller size. If the browser doesn't reflow the HTML document, there'll be an embarrassing strip of default background in the spaces around the applet. Listing 9.3 changes our applet to downsize itself, uses a background color other than the default for the applet, and adds a background image to the HTML document. Figure 9.2 shows the improved applet running in Netscape.

LISTING 9.3   A SHRIVELED APPLET

```
package chap4;

import java.awt.Graphics;
import java.applet.Applet;
import java.awt.Color;

/** An applet that prints the string "Hello world, again" at
absolute applet-relative coordinates x=20, y=50 after clearing
the applet workspace to yellow.
@author John Rodley
@version 1.0
*/
public class ch4_fig2 extends Applet {

/** Resize the applet to slightly smaller than the applet
tag sizes us.
*/
  public void init() {
    resize( 90, 90 );
  }
```

```
/** Actually paint the string on the screen, first clearing the
workspace to yellow.
*/
  public void paint(Graphics g) {
    g.setColor(Color.yellow);
    g.fillRect(0,0,size().height, size().width);
    g.setColor(Color.black);
    g.drawString( "Hello world, again", 20, 50 );
  }
}
```

LISTING 9.4   HTML CODE THAT RUNS THE SHRIVELED APPLET

```
<!DOCTYPE HTML PUBLIC
"-//SQ//DTD HTML 2.0 HoTMetaL + extensions//EN">
<HTML><HEAD><TITLE>The Shrivelling Applet</TITLE></HEAD>
<BODY BACKGROUND="background.jpg">
<P>A pair of goodogs, to watch your incredible shrinking
applet:
<IMG SRC="chap4/ch4_fig1a.jpg" ALIGN="BOTTOM">
<IMG SRC="chap4/ch4_fig1b.jpg" ALIGN="BOTTOM">
Below is the applet, started with an initial size of 100 by
100 pixels:
<applet code=chap4/ch4_fig2.class width=100 height=100>
</applet>
The first word of this sentence should butt right up against
the applets right hand edge even though the applet has shrunk
to 90 by 90 pixels, assuming the browser re-flowed correctly.
</P></BODY></HTML>
```

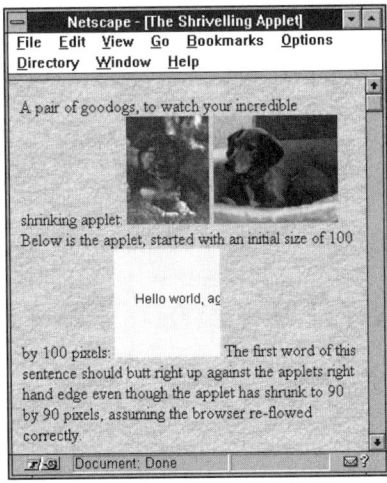

FIGURE 9.2   The improved applet in Netscape.

So that's what happens if you shrink an applet within its allotted browser space. But what if you want to grow the applet beyond its browser space? It's the same issue in reverse: the HTML document has to be reflowed to provide more space for the growing applet. Listing 9.5 changes the applet in Listing 9.3 to burst out of its allotted space, and Figure 9.3 shows the results.

LISTING 9.5 GROWING AN APPLET

```
package chap4;

import java.awt.Graphics;
import java.applet.Applet;
import java.awt.Color;

/** An applet that prints the string "Hello world, again" at
absolute applet-relative coordinates x=20, y=50 on a red
background.
@author John Rodley
@version 1.0
*/
public class ch4_fig3 extends Applet {

/** Resize the applet to slightly larger than the applet
tag sizes us.
*/
  public void init() {
    resize( 120, 120 );
  }


/** Actually paint the string on the screen, after clearing the
applet to red first.
*/
  public void paint(Graphics g) {
    g.setColor(Color.red);
    g.fillRect(0,0,size().height, size().width);
    g.setColor(Color.black);
    g.drawString( "Hello world, again", 20, 50 );
  }
}
```

LISTING 9.6 HTML CODE THAT RUNS THE GROWING APPLET

```
<!DOCTYPE HTML PUBLIC
"-//SQ//DTD HTML 2.0 HoTMetaL + extensions//EN">
<HTML><HEAD><TITLE>The Growing Applet</TITLE></HEAD>
<BODY BACKGROUND="background.jpg">
<P>A pair of goodogs, to watch over your growing applet:
```

```
<IMG SRC="chap4/ch4_fig1a.jpg" ALIGN="BOTTOM">
<IMG SRC="chap4/ch4_fig1b.jpg" ALIGN="BOTTOM">
Below is the applet, started with an initial size of 100 by
100 pixels:
<applet code=chap4/ch4_fig3.class width=100 height=100>
</applet>
The first word of this sentence should butt right up against
the applets right hand edge even though the applet has grown to
120 by 120 pixels, assuming the browser re-flowed correctly.
</P></BODY></HTML>
```

The growing applet running in Netscape. As you can see, Netscape correctly reflows the document to accommodate whatever applet resizing you might do. Notice also that our text string doesn't completely print out. This is the fate of graphics operations that try to exceed the bounds of the applet: they simply don't happen.

When Does an Applet Run?

For traditional computer programs the answer to the question "when does the program run?" is obvious. When the user runs the program, it runs, and when the user closes it, it stops running. The user doesn't have that kind of control over an applet. It is the browser, not the user, that loads, runs, stops, and unloads applets, so the answer becomes a lot more involved.

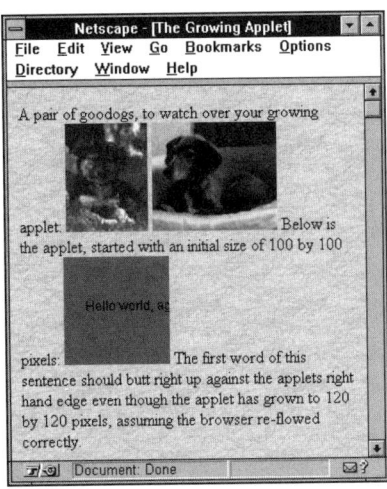

FIGURE 9.3   An applet bursts out of its allotted space.

The simplistic answer to the question is this: An applet runs when its space in the HTML document is visible, and stops running when, for whatever reason, that space in the HTML document is not visible.

Unless an applet creates and runs in its own thread, the simple answer holds true. This is because an applet like the simple one shown in Listing 9.1 is running in a thread that the browser has created and controls. When Java applets create their own threads, the answer becomes more complicated. Technically, because these threads are beyond the control of the browser, there is no written-in-stone rule on when an applet runs. In theory, browsers expect well-behaved applets to adhere to the basic rule of run when you're on-screen, and stop running when you're off-screen, but whether or not an applet implements that theory is completely up to the applet writer. We'll discuss threads in more detail in Chapter 12, and eventually write our own multi-threaded and ill-behaved, but wickedly useful, applets.

Whether the applet itself is single or multi-thread, ill or well-behaved, the browser obeys a certain set of rules when trying to run it. In this sense, the browser treats the applet as a peer, where, no matter how the applet behaves, it can expect certain behaviors from the browser. These behaviors, the browser invoking one of four applet methods, are clues as to what is going on in the browser.

Here's a brief rundown of the methods: When the browser first encounters the <applet> tag in the HTML doc, it calls **Applet.init**. When a user visits the applet's page, the browser calls **Applet.start**. When the user leaves the applet's page, the browser calls **Applet.stop**, and whenever it decides the applet is not needed anymore and should be expunged from memory, it calls **Applet.destroy**. Thus, **Applet.init** and **Applet.destroy** get called once in the life of an applet, while **Applet.start** and **Applet.stop** can be called any number of times. An applet that cares about whether or not it's loaded or on-screen can override **init**, **start**, **stop** and **destroy**, as shown in Figure 9.4.

Adding Sound to an Applet

Let's improve our simple applet to sing us a little song. Listing 9.7 shows these modifications. Play with the applet. See what happens if you scroll the applet off screen, or if you hyperlink to another page.

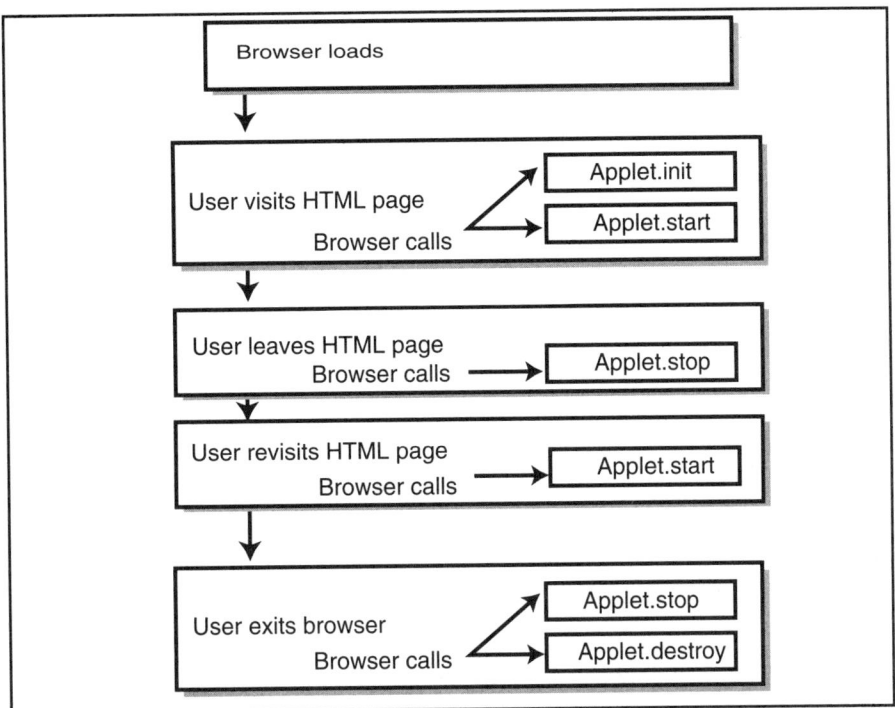

FIGURE 9.4   An applet that cares. It feels your pain.

LISTING 9.7   THE DO-NOTHING APPLET, WITH SOUND

```
package chap4;

import java.awt.Graphics;
import java.applet.Applet;
import java.applet.AudioClip;
import java.net.*;

/** A simple app that plays a tune, supplied by the applet tag
via the name "StartClip" every time Applet.start is called, and
plays another tune, paramter name "EndClip" every time
Applet.stop is called. Plays the RunningClip in a loop between
start and stop.
@version 1.0 12/20/1995
@author John Rodley
*/
public class ch4_fig4 extends Applet {
   String sAppletInfo;
   URL StartClipURL;
   URL EndClipURL;
   AudioClip RunningClip;
```

```
        String pinfo[][] = {
            {"StartClip", "URL", "The URL of an audio clip played at
            startup" },
            {"RunningClip", "URL",
             "The URL of an audio clip played between start and stop" },
            {"EndClip", "URL", "The URL of an audio clip played at stop" }
            };

    /** Whenever a user visits our page, the browser calls this.
    This is an override of an Applet method.. */
      public void start() {
        if( RunningClip == null || StartClipURL == null )
          return;
        play( StartClipURL );
        RunningClip.loop();
        System.out.println( "after loop" );
      }

    /** Whenever the user leaves our page, this gets called.
    Another override of an Applet method.
    */
      public void stop() {
        if( RunningClip == null || EndClipURL == null )
          return;
        RunningClip.stop();
      play( EndClipURL );
      }

    /** Tell anyone who might inquire what we are.
    @return A string describing this applet.
    */
      public String getAppletInfo() {
      return("JRodley - Java Applets Book - Chapter 4 figure 4");
        }

    /** Tell anyone who might inquire how to use this applet.
    @return A 2d string array describing the arguments to this
    applet.
    */
      public String[][] getParameterInfo() {
        return pinfo;
      }

    /** Connect to the URLs specified by the StartClip and EndClip
    parameters in the applet tag.
    */
      public void init() {
      try {
            StartClipURL = new URL(getParameter("StartClip"));
```

```
       RunningClip = getAudioClip(new
 URL(getParameter("RunningClip")));
       EndClipURL = new URL(getParameter("EndClip"));
       } catch( MalformedURLException e )
         { System.out.println("exception"+e );}
   }
}
```

Listing 9.8   HTML That Runs the Do-Nothing Applet

```
<!DOCTYPE HTML PUBLIC
"-//SQ//DTD HTML 2.0 HoTMetaL + extensions//EN">
<HTML><HEAD><TITLE>The Singing Applet</TITLE></HEAD>
<BODY>
<applet code=chap4/ch4_fig4.class width=100 height=100>
<param name=StartClip value="http://www.coriolis.com/japp/chap4/
  charge.au">
<param name=RunningClip value="http://www.coriolis.com/japp/chap4/
  charge.au">
<param name=EndClip value="http://www.coriolis.com/japp/chap4/
  retreat.au">
</applet>
</P></BODY></HTML>
```

Audio and Parameters

The basis of Java's audio capability is the **AudioClip** class. In order to do any audio, you need to get the actual audio data from a file somewhere on the Net. Where is that file? We could hardwire the filename into the class file, as in the following code snippet:

```
public final static string startClipFile =
new String( "http://www.channel1.com/users/ajrodley/start.au" );
```

However, a more flexible way of dealing with data like this is to pass it in as an argument via the **<param name=value=>** construct within the HTML source. In Listing 9.8, we've defined three arguments—**StartClip**, **RunningClip**, and **EndClip**—each of which is the URL of an audio file somewhere out on the Net. In the **init** method, which as we've said is the first override method invoked by the browser, we query these arguments via **Applet.getParameter**. When, in our HTML page, we say

```
<param name=StartClip value="http://www.channel1.com/users/ajrodley/
  start.au">
```

the call

```
String s = getParameter("StartClip");
```

returns the **String** http://www.channel1.com/users/ajrodley/start.au.

Applets, as we'll discuss later, operate in a multi-applet environment. This is a good thing, but it imposes some responsibilities on well-behaved applets. The first of these is the responsibility to document the arguments the applet accepts via the **getParameterInfo** method. Listing 9.4 implements both this and the **getAppletInfo** method, which allows users of our applet to find information about the applet's author, its version, and whatever else we want to put in the returned string. These methods are not required, but are courtesies we extend to other applets that may want to know something about us, or to HTML and/or applet writers who may want to use our applet in their own code.

The singing applet uses two different methods for playing audio clips. The start and end clips only need to play one time through, whenever their method (**start** or **stop**) is invoked, so we can play them simply by passing their URLs to **Applet.play**. We want the running clip to play continuously, though. For that, we need explicitly to create an **AudioClip** object. Thus, in our **init** method, we create three objects: a **URL** for the start clip, a **URL** for the end clip, and an **AudioClip** for the running clip.

The **init** method also contains a new wrinkle for us, an exception handling clause. We deal with exceptions in more detail in Chapter 14. What you need to remember here is that if a method is defined as "throwing" an exception, any method that calls it has to either define itself as *also* throwing that exception, or it has to handle that exception with a **try-catch** statement. Here, we use the latter method. The **URL** constructor throws **MalformedURLException**, so we catch it, and simply make a note of it on standard output. The **URL** constructor throws an exception if the specified URL is not accessible. Thus, if our **init** method runs without throwing an exception, we can be sure that there are accessible files at the URLs we specified.

When **init** is done, we have three objects: two **URLs** and one **AudioClip**. The **URL** constructors only made sure there was a file at the URL but the **AudioClip** constructor actually fetched the data from the URL. To play the start and end clips within the **start** and **stop** methods, we simply invoke the **play** method with the proper audio file's **URL** as the argument. To keep the running clip playing continuously while the applet is on-screen, we simply invoke **AudioClip.loop** in the **start** method. **AudioClip.loop** returns immediately, even though the clip continues to play until **AudioClip.stop** in our applet's **stop** method. Listing 9.9 presents a slightly different version of our do-nothing applet.

LISTING 9.9 THE DO-NOTHING APPLET IN ITS OWN THREAD

```
package chap4;

import java.util.*;
import java.applet.*;
import java.awt.*;

/* A do-nothing applet that runs in its own thread.

@version x.xx 1.10, 1 August, 1995 xxx
@author John Rodley
*/

public class ch4_fig5 extends Applet implements Runnable {
/** The main thread. */
Thread myThread;
String TheString;
int iteration = 0;

/** Start the main thread for this game. */
  public void start() {
    TheString = new String( "Applet is on screen now in " );
    if( myThread == null )
        {
        myThread = new Thread( this );
        myThread.start();
        }
  }

/** Stop this thread. */
  public void stop() {
    TheString =
      new String("Applet is off screen but still running in ");
  }
/** The main loop for the main thread. */
  public void run() {
        while( myThread != null )
```

```
            {
            try {
            Thread.sleep( 300 );
              } catch( InterruptedException e )
            { System.out.println("exception" ); }
            showStatus( TheString+iteration+"th iteration ");
            iteration++;
            }
        myThread = null;
    }
}
```

In this example, we run the applet in its own thread. The key things to note here are the **start** and **run** methods, and the fact that our applet implements the **Runnable** interface. In the **start** method, we push the applet into its own thread by creating a new **Thread** object and passing the applet itself as the only argument to the constructor. This is only possible because our applet implements **Runnable**.

The only requirement of the **Runnable** interface is that you implement a **run** method, as we have here. Sometime after the call to **myThread.start** returns, the **run** method will begin executing asynchronously. Within this **run** method, we simply sit in a loop, sleeping for 300 milliseconds, then incrementing a counter and displaying it in the browser status line. Note that because we only want *one* of these independent threads to run, we check **myThread** within **start**. Otherwise, every visit to this page would create a new thread with the predictable effect on system performance.

Run this applet under Netscape. You'll see the status string changing regularly. Now, hyperlink away to some other HTML page. Notice that the status string keeps changing. We have violated one of the rules of well-behaved applets. Our host HTML document has disappeared, but our applet is still running!

Our new do-nothing applet will continue to run for as long as the browser is up. To kill it, you have to close Netscape. This persistence presents ominous possibilities. In Listing 9.10, a simple change turns the do-nothing applet into a malicious do-nothing applet.

Note: Do not run the applet shown in Listing 9.10 or you will have to kill your browser to get rid of it.

LISTING 9.10   EATING CPU CYCLES

```
package chap4;

import java.util.*;
import java.applet.*;
import java.awt.*;

/* A malicious do-nothing applet that runs in its own thread,
eating up CPU cycles because it neither sleeps nor exits.

@version x.xx 1.10, 1 August, 1995 xxx
@author John Rodley
*/

public class ch4_fig6 extends Applet implements Runnable {

/** The main thread. */
Thread myThread;
String TheString;
int iteration = 0;

/** Start the main thread for this game. */
  public void start() {
    TheString = new String( "Applet is on screen now in " );
   if( myThread == null )
        {
      myThread = new Thread( this );
      myThread.start();
        }
 }

/** Stop this thread. */
  public void stop() {
    TheString =
      new String("Applet is off screen but still running in ");
  }

/** The main loop for the main thread. */
  public void run() {
      while( myThread != null )
        {
        showStatus( TheString+iteration+"th iteration ");
        iteration++;
        }
      myThread = null;
  }
}
```

The malicious applet eats up a lot of CPU cycles when it is run. Let's take a close look at the code changes in this listing to see why. We removed the **sleep** call from the **run** method, which results in us simply sit in a loop incrementing a variable. We also removed the call to **showStatus** which alerts the user that we are still running. If you were to run this applet in Netscape and then hyperlink to another page, you would notice how unresponsive the browser becomes. The key features of this malicious applet are actually omissions, the fact that our **run** method never blocks, and that we didn't implement an **Applet.stop** method that stops our thread. All applets that run in their own thread must take special care to run only when, and only as much as necessary.

By this point, you've seen the light and want to write well-behaved, threaded applets. But how? Listing 9.11 modifies the threaded do-nothing applet to stop running whenever the user leaves the page, and then re-start whenever the user returns.

LISTING 9.11 A WELL-BEHAVED DO-NOTHING APPLET

```
package chap4;

import java.util.*;
import java.applet.*;
import java.awt.*;

/* A do-nothing applet that runs in its own thread.

@version x.xx 1.10, 1 August, 1995 xxx
@author John Rodley
*/

public class ch4_fig7 extends Applet implements Runnable {

/** The main thread. */
Thread myThread;
String TheString;
int iteration = 0;
/** Start the main thread for this game. */
  public void start() {
    TheString = new String( "Applet is on screen now in " );
    if( myThread == null )
        {
      myThread = new Thread( this );
      myThread.start();
        }
  }
```

```
/** Stop this thread. */
  public void stop() {
    TheString =
      new String("Applet is off screen but still running in ");
// This line is the key. If myThread is null, the run method
// returns and the thread disappears.
    myThread = null;
  }

/** The main loop for the main thread. */
  public void run() {
      while( myThread != null )
        {
        try {
        Thread.sleep( 300 );
          } catch( InterruptedException e )
        { System.out.println("exception" ); }
        showStatus( TheString+iteration+"th iteration ");
        iteration++;
        }
  }
}
```

With a threaded applet, the thread the applet runs in only exists for as long as the **run** method is running. What we need is code in our **stop** method (which the browser calls whenever the user leaves the page) that will cause the **run** method to break out of its loop. This is what setting **myThread** to **null** does. Then in the **start** method (called whenever the user visits our page) we re-create the thread and set it running. We'll talk more about threads in Chapter 12. In the meantime, the well-behaved, threaded do-nothing applet will serve as a good template for any threaded applets we might need.

Making Our Applets Interact with the Browser

Prior to the beta version of Java, applets existed in a vacuum. They had no way of knowing anything about any other applets. Now, applets can call **Applet.getAppletContext**. This call returns an object that implements the **AppletContext** interface. Usually, this object will be the browser itself, but it might not be. In fact, browsers that wish to protect themselves from rogue applets may create a separate class just to contain the applet context for this call. In any case, it doesn't matter to us because, as with any interface, the definition of the interface is all that you can rely on.

The **AppletContext** class, shown in Table 9.2, provides six methods, which allow an applet to get images and audio clips, learn about other applets active in the browser, and show new HTML documents.

Using **getAppletContext**, we can modify our well-behaved, threaded do-nothing applet to get information about all the other running applets. Listing 9.12 shows our new applet, while Listing 9.13 shows the HTML code used to create four of these applets on one Web page. Figure 9.5 shows the output of our new applet.

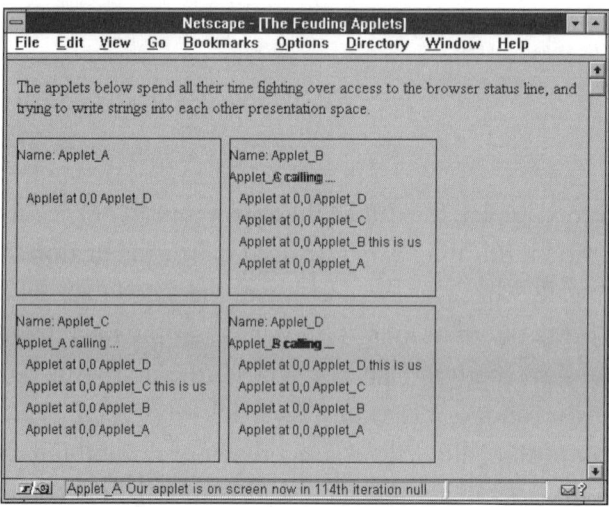

FIGURE 9.5   **The output of our new applet.**

TABLE 9.2   **The AppletContext Interface.**

Operator	Description
*	Performs pointer indirection
&	Calculates the memory address of a variable
->	Allows a pointer to select a data structure
sizeof	Determines the size of an allocated data structure

LISTING 9.12 FINDING OTHER APPLETS

```
package chap4;

import java.util.*;
import java.io.*;
import java.net.*;
import java.applet.*;
import java.awt.*;
/** An applet that finds the other applets that exist within
this AppletContext, fights with them to write a string to the
browser status line, and writes a string directly into the
other applet windows.

@version 1.10, 11/20/95
@author John Rodley
*/

public class ch4_fig8 extends Applet implements Runnable {


/** The main thread. */
Thread myThread = null;
String TheString = null;
String myName;
String paintString = null;
int iteration = 0;
int paintIteration = 0;

/** Start the main thread for this game. */
  public void start() {
    TheString = new String( "Our applet is on screen now in " );
  if( myThread == null )
        {
          myThread = new Thread( this );
        myThread.start();
        }
  }
/** Stop this thread. */
  public void stop() {
    myThread = null;
  }

/** The main loop for the main thread. */
  public void run() {
        while( myThread != null )
          {
          try {
          Thread.sleep( 300 );
```

```
                } catch( InterruptedException e )
                { System.out.println("exception" ); }
            showStatus( myName+'"'+TheString+iteration+
                    "th iteration "+paintString );
            repaint();
            iteration++;
            }
    }

/** Paint our window.  Display a string in this window for
each applet we find, then display a string in each of the other
applets windows.
*/
public void paint( Graphics g ) {
  String gString;
  int i = 0;

  // Label this applet with its name
  g.drawString( "Name: "+myName, 0, 20 );

  AppletContext ac = getAppletContext();
  Enumeration e = ac.getApplets();
  Dimension d = size();
  g.drawRect( 0, 0, d.width-5, d.height-5 );
  while( e.hasMoreElements()) {
        Applet a = (Applet)(e.nextElement());
        // If this applet is a ch4_fig8 then it has a name parameter
set
        String s = a.getParameter("Name");
        if( s == null )
          s = new String( "not a ch4_fig8 applet" );
        Point p = a.location();
        gString = new String( "Applet at "+p.x+","+p.y+" "+s );
        // The list will always include "this", so check it
        if( a == this )
          gString = new String( gString+" this is us" );
        else {
          // Now draw a string into the other applets window
          Graphics g1 = a.getGraphics();
          g1.drawString( myName+" calling ...", 0, 40 );
          }
        // Draw the string describing the other applet in our window
        g.drawString( gString, 10, 20*(i+3) );

        i++;
        }
    }

/** If the user clicks on the applet, stop it.
```

```
@return false
*/
  public boolean mouseDown(Event e, int x, int y) {
  stop();
    return( false );
  }

/** Initialize the applet. Resize it and give it a name.  Make
sure that the applet is "named" via the applet tag.
*/
  public void init() {
  myName = getParameter( "Name" );
    if( myName == null )
        myName = new String( "Set the Name= parameter please!" );
  resize( 210, 210 );
  }
}
```

The **AppletContext** interface provides the method **getApplets**, which returns an **Enumeration** (basically a vector) containing all the applets running in this **AppletContext**. We retrieve each individual applet via **Enumeration. nextElement**.

The applet returned by **getApplets** is completely capable. We can call any method available in the **Applet** class against that applet. Thus, in our **paint** method, we call **drawString** against our own applet, and against each of the other applets we find. As this page runs, you can see the four applets dueling over the status line and drawing over each other as they draw the intrusive string into each other's graphics context.

In Listing 9.12, we introduce a new class, **Point** and a new interface, **Enumeration**. **Point** simply encapsulates two **int**s, the X and Y coordinates of the point. In C or C++, this would undoubtedly have been implemented as a simple **struct**. **Enumeration** is a far more interesting concept. What does it mean to enumerate something? Here, enumeration means "to walk through a list, using up the elements as you go." Essentially, an **Enumeration** is a list that you can go through once and only once. The interface requires only two methods, **hasMoreElements** and **nextElement**, which force you to use the same flow-control whenever you're dealing with an **Enumeration**. The technique is illustrated in the following code snippet:

```
// assume e is an object that implements the Enumeration interface
while( e.hasMoreElements()) {
 Object o = e.nextElement();
 ...
 }
// At this point e has been "used up."  It cannot be walked through
 again.
```

In Listing 9.12's **paint** method, we get an **Enumeration** of **Applets** from the **AppletContext** interface method **getApplets**, then walk through it, dueling with each of the applets it returns. The following code line illustrates one of the powers of Java's object orientation that might not be obvious:

```
Applet a = (Applet )(e.nextElement());
```

This power works like this: **Enumeration.nextElement** always returns an **Object**, but a simple cast of that **Object** to **Applet**, gives us access to the much wider range of capabilities of the **Applet** class. That **Object** was always an **Applet**. It's just that the **Enumeration** doesn't *care* what class its elements are, so it stores them as **Object** and lets the user of the **Enumeration** deal with casting them back to the proper type. What would happen if, by some chance, the call to **e.nextElement** returned an **Object** that was *not* of the **Applet** class? The Java interpreter would throw an **IllegalCastException**. This is something you have to consider very carefully whenever you cast from a base class to a superclass, especially when you're using **Vectors** or **Enumerations** you get from someone else's objects.

With that bit of type-casting wisdom in mind, consider the following code snippet from Listing 9.12:

```
Applet a = (Applet)(e.nextElement());
// If this applet is a ch4_fig8, then it has a name parameter set
String s = a.getParameter("Name");
if( s == null )
 s = new String( "not a ch4_fig8 applet");
```

This code simply determines whether we're dealing with the proper class of object, a ch4_fig8. However, there's a much better way to deal with this, as shown in the following code snippet:

```
Applet a = (Applet)(e.nextElement());
// If a is not a ch4_fig8, move on to the next applet
if( a instanceof ch4_fig8 )
  ...
else
  continue;
```

The **instanceof** operator tells us whether **Object a** is an instance of class **ch4_fig8**. Checking objects with the **instanceof** operator is usually a good idea *before* you try a type cast. In this particular instance, **AppletContext.getApplets** guarantees that it will return an **Enumeration** of **Applets**, so the cast to **Applet** should be safe, but beyond that, we can't be sure, so we use **instanceof**.

AppletContext.getApplets gives us an inter-applet communication mechanism for which there are any number of uses. As another brutally simple example, let's modify the dueling applet of Listing 9.12 so that it kills off all the other applets on a page via **Applet.stop**, ensuring that it's the only running applet on a page.

LISTING 9.13   A KILLER APPLET

```
package chap4;

import java.util.*;
import java.applet.*;
import java.awt.*;

/** An applet that finds the other applets that exist within
this AppletContext, and stops them.

@version 1.10, 11/20/95
@author John Rodley
*/

public class ch4_fig9 extends Applet implements Runnable {

/** The main thread. */
Thread myThread = null;
String TheString = null;
int iteration = 0;
int paintIteration = 0;

/** Start the main thread for this game. */
  public void start() {
```

```
      TheString = new String( "Our applet is on screen now in " );
  if( myThread == null )
        {
          myThread = new Thread( this );
        myThread.start();
        }
  }

/** Resize us to be wide enough for the status string. */
  public void init() {
    resize( 300, 100 );
  }

/** Stop this thread. */
  public void stop() {
    myThread = null;
  }

/** The main loop for the main thread. */
  public void run() {
        while( myThread != null )
           {
           try {
           Thread.sleep( 300 );
             } catch( InterruptedException e )
             { System.out.println("exception" ); }
           showStatus( iteration+"th iteration " );
           repaint();
           iteration++;
           }
  }
/** Paint our window.  Destroy each applet we find,
then display a string boasting of this achievement.
*/
  public void paint( Graphics g ) {
    String gString;
  int i = 0;

    AppletContext ac = getAppletContext();
  Enumeration e = ac.getApplets();
    while( e.hasMoreElements()) {
         Applet a = (Applet)(e.nextElement());
        Point p = a.location();
        // The list will always include "this", so check it
         if( a instanceof ch4_fig9 )
         gString = new String( "this is us" );
        else {
         Container c = a.getParent();
         if( c == null ) // this applet was already removed
```

```
          continue;
          // Now destroy the other applet
       a.stop();
       c.remove(a);
         gString = new String( "Stopped applet at "+p.x+","+p.y+"
           "+iteration);
         }
     g.drawString( gString, 10, 20*(i+3) );

         i++;
 }


   }
}
```

LISTING *9.14* HTML CODE THAT RUNS THE KILLER APPLET

```
<!DOCTYPE HTML PUBLIC
"-//SQ//DTD HTML 2.0 HoTMetaL + extensions//EN">
<HTML><HEAD><TITLE>The Killer Applet</TITLE>
</HEAD>
<BODY>
<P>
The applets below spend all their time fighting over access to
the browser status line, and trying to write strings into each
other presentation space.
</P>
<applet code=chap4/ch4_fig8a.class width=100 height=100>
<param name=Name value=Applet_A>
</applet>
<applet code=chap4/ch4_fig8a.class width=200 height=100>
<param name=Name value=Applet_B>
</applet>
<applet code=chap4/ch4_fig8a.class width=300 height=100>
<param name=Name value=Applet_C>
</applet>
<applet code=chap4/ch4_fig9.class width=400 height=100>
</applet>
</BODY></HTML>
```

Try running this applet and you'll see that only the killer applet remains running. Notice also that, not only do the applets stop running, but their screen output disappears. While we'll talk more about removing **Components** in the next section, it's important to note that even though we've stopped the other applets via the **stop** method, those applets continue to exist, and the **AppletContext** still returns them every time we call

getApplets. That's why we check the return from **getParent.** Calling **Container.remove** on a **Component** means that the next call to **getParent** will return a null. That's how we know that the **Component** is no longer displayed.

Controlling Stopped Applets

What to do with stopped applets is a more interesting question than it might seem. In Listing 9.12, we added a method, **mouseDown,** that stops the applet if the user clicks on it. This method is shown in the following code snippet:

```
public boolean mouseDown( Event e, int x, int y ) {
      stop();
      return( false );
}
```

Run Listing 9.12 once again and try clicking on one of the applets. What you see is that the applet does stop running, but that its last "state" remains on the screen. In the **AppletContext**'s (browser's) view of the world, the stopped applet still exists, and the allocated section of the browser window should remain uncleared and unused. Try stopping one of the applets, then moving the browser window around. What you'll see is that the applet hasn't really gone away at all. All that's happened is that the **run** method has returned. When the applet window gets covered and then uncovered, Java decides that all the applets need to be repainted and it calls **Applet.paint** for all the applets on the screen. What we need to do is remove the applet from the list of things that get repainted. To do this, we add a single line to **Applet.stop,** as shown in Listing 9.15.

LISTING 9.15 CLEARING THE APPLETS WINDOW

```
package chap4;

import java.util.*;
import java.io.*;
import java.net.*;
import java.applet.*;
import java.awt.*;

/** An applet that finds the other applets that exist within
this AppletContext, fights with them to write a string to the
```

browser status line, and writes a string directly into the
other applet windows. Modified to stop and 'disappear' from
the screen if the user clicks on the applet.

```
@version 1.10, 11/20/95
@author John Rodley
*/


public class ch4_fig11 extends Applet implements Runnable {


/** The main thread. */
Thread myThread = null;
String TheString = null;
String myName;
String paintString = null;
int iteration = 0;
int paintIteration = 0;

/** Start the main thread for this game. */
  public void start() {
    TheString = new String( "Our applet is on screen now in " );
 if( myThread == null )
        {
          myThread = new Thread( this );
        myThread.start();
        }
  }


/** Stop this thread. */
  public void stop() {
    myThread = null;
  }

/** The main loop for the main thread. */
  public void run() {
        while( myThread != null )
          {
          try {
          Thread.sleep( 300 );
            } catch( InterruptedException e )
            { System.out.println("exception" ); }
          showStatus( myName+" "+TheString+iteration+
                  "th iteration "+paintString );
          repaint();
          iteration++;
          }
  }
```

```
/** Paint our window.  Display a string in this window for
each applet we find, then display a string in each of the other
applets windows.
*/
public void paint( Graphics g ) {
 String gString;
 int i = 0;

 // Label this applet with its name
 g.drawString( "Name: "+myName, 0, 20 );

 AppletContext ac = getAppletContext();
 Enumeration e = ac.getApplets();
 Dimension d = size();
 g.drawRect( 0, 0, d.width-5, d.height-5 );
 while( e.hasMoreElements()) {
        Applet a = (Applet)(e.nextElement());
        // If this applet is a ch4_fig8 then it has a name parameter
set
        String s = a.getParameter("Name");
        if( s == null )
          s = new String( "not a ch4_fig8 applet" );
        Point p = a.location();
        gString = new String( "Applet at "+p.x+","+p.y+" "+s );
        // The list will always include "this", so check it
        if( a == this )
          gString = new String( gString+" this is us" );
        else {
          // Now draw a string into the other applets window
          Graphics g1 = a.getGraphics();
      // If this applet's already stopped, g1 will be null
      if( g1 != null )
          g1.drawString( myName+" calling ...", 0, 40 );
          }
        // draw the string describing the other applet in our window
        g.drawString( gString, 10, 20*(i+3) );

        i++;
        }
 }

/** If the user clicks on the applet, stop it.
@return false
*/
  public boolean mouseDown(Event e, int x, int y) {
 stop();
   getParent().remove(this);
   return( false );
  }
```

```
/** Initialize the applet. Resize it and give it a name.  Make
sure that the applet is "named" via the applet tag.
*/
  public void init() {
 myName = getParameter( "Name" );
   if( myName == null )
        myName = new String( "Set the Name= parameter please!" );
 resize( 210, 210 );
 }
}
```

Our addition to **Applet.stop** clears the space that our **Applet** once occupied, and removes it from the list of **Components**, ensuring that it never gets repainted. Removing the applet **Component** from the **Container** it resides in results in an applet that has no screen representation. This means that *any* call to that applet's **Component** superclass, such as the **paint** method's call to **a.getGraphics**, will probably fail. We take this into account in **paint** by adding a **null** return check to **a.getGraphics**.

In truth, you can't really get rid of an applet. There's no **delete** operator in Java, so you can't just destroy it, and the garbage collector won't get rid of it automatically until there are no more references to it. The applet was created (via the **new** operation) by the browser, and the applet itself doesn't have write access to the browser's list of applets, so there will always be that one reference to the applet. For now, the best we can do is to remove the applet **Component** from the browser's list of **Components**, and hope that the browser (whichever one it is) will reuse the now-available screen space. We'll talk more about **Components** and **Containers** in Chapter 5.

Applets and Hyperlinks

We can combine our persistent applet with the **AppletContext** to implement a rudimentary Web trolling applet. This applet takes a list of URLs and instructs the **AppletContext** to visit those URLs, in sequence, with a delay of 30 seconds at each document.

LISTING 9.16   A WEB-CRAWLING APPLET

```
package chap4;

import java.util.*;
import java.io.*;
```

```
import java.net.*;
import java.applet.*;
import java.awt.*;

/* A threaded applet that takes a list of URLs as an argument,
then visits each of those URLs, delaying for delay milliseconds
between URL switches.

@version 1.0 12/23/95
@author John Rodley
 */


public class ch4_fig12 extends Applet implements Runnable {

/** The main thread. */
Thread myThread = null;
int iteration = 0;
Vector docURL;
int delay = 10000;

/** Start the main thread for this game. */
public void start() {
 if( myThread == null )
       {
       myThread = new Thread( this );
 myThread.start();
       }
 }


/** Stop this thread. */
public void stop() {
 myThread = null;
 }

/** The main loop for the main thread. */
public void run() {
 System.out.println( "Runnable.run" );
 iteration = 0;
      while( myThread != null )
        {
        AppletContext ac = getAppletContext();
        showStatus( "Switching to "+docURL.elementAt(iteration));
        ac.showDocument((URL) docURL.elementAt(iteration ));
        try {
        Thread.sleep( delay );
          } catch( InterruptedException e ) {
          System.out.println("exception" ); }
        iteration++;
```

```
            if( iteration >= docURL.size() )
               iteration = 0;
            }
         myThread = null;
  }

/** Initialize the applet. Resize and load images.
*/
public void init() {
  docURL = new Vector(1);
  int i = 1;
  String sDelay = getParameter("Delay");
  if( sDelay != null )
         delay = new Integer( sDelay ).intValue();
  while( true ) {
         String s = getParameter("Document"+i);
         if( s == null ) break;
         i++;
         try {
         docURL.addElement( new URL(s));
           } catch( Exception e) { break; }
         }
  resize( 210, 210 );
  }
}
```

The showDocument method is optional

One serious caveat about this applet: The documentation for APPLETCONTEXT describes SHOWDOCUMENT as an optional method; browsers are NOT required to implement it. Different browsers implement in different ways, and some don't implement it at all.

The browser makers' reasoning is easy to divine. If you could jump around to various links via Java applets, using the browser simply as a base, then the usefulness of the browser's fancy interface is called into question. In fact, the whole design of SHOWDOCUMENT smells of the kind of corporate politics that often makes programming an exercise in nonsense-control. Why, if SHOWDOCUMENT's behavior is undefined, doesn't it at least return a value (instead of a void) or throw an exception to tell you whether it's going to do what you requested?

In Chapter 13, we'll take a more hands-on approach to Web trolling by recursively fetching HTML documents ourselves and searching them for patterns.

Reloading Applets

Most browsers support the notion of "reloading" an HTML page—clearing the browser window, rereading the HTML source from the http server, and redisplaying it in the browser window. This is useful, for example, where pages have cgi scripts embedded (for hit counting, for example) and the page needs to be downloaded for the script to run or when a page currently in local cache is known to have changed back on the server. Unfortunately, there is no hard and fast rule as to just what it means to reload an applet.

Going strictly by the HTML example, what you might expect is that the applet gets stopped, unloaded (whatever that means), reread from the Web server, reloaded, and restarted. The simple applet in Listing 9.17, a modification of the singing applet shown in Listing 9.7, plays a different audio clip whenever **init**, **start**, **stop**, or **destroy** get called. Try it under your favorite browser and see what happens.

LISTING 9.17 TESTING THE RELOAD BUTTON

```
package chap4;

import java.awt.Graphics;
import java.applet.Applet;
import java.applet.AudioClip;
import java.net.*;

/** A simple app that plays tunes at the four different stops
along the applet execution trail - init, start, stop, and
destroy.  The parameters?
  StartClip
  StopClip
  DestroyClip
  InitClip

@version 1.0 12/20/1995
@author John Rodley
*/
public class ch4_fig13 extends Applet {
```

```
   String sAppletInfo;
   URL StartClipURL;
   URL StopClipURL;
   URL InitClipURL;
   URL DestroyClipURL;

   String pinfo[][] = {
     {"InitClip", "URL",
          "The URL of an audio clip played at init" },
     {"StartClip", "URL",
          "The URL of an audio clip played at start" },
     {"StopClip", "URL",
          "The URL of an audio clip played at stop" },
     {"DestroyClip", "URL",
          "The URL of an audio clip played at destroy" }
      };

/** Whenever a user visits our page, the browser calls this.
This is an override of an Applet method.. */
   public void start() {
     if( StartClipURL == null )
       return;
     play( StartClipURL );
   }

/** Whenever the user leaves our page, this gets called.
Another override of an Applet method.
*/
   public void stop() {
     if( StopClipURL == null )
       return;
     play( StopClipURL );
   }

/** Tell anyone who might inquire what we are.
@return A string describing this applet.
*/
   public String getAppletInfo() {
     return("JRodley - Java Applets Book - Chapter 4 figure 13");
     }

/** Tell anyone who might inquire how to use this applet.
@return A 2d string array describing the arguments to this
applet.
*/
   public String[][] getParameterInfo() {
     return pinfo;
     }
```

```
/** Play the destroy clip. */
  public void destroy() {
    if( DestroyClipURL != null )
      play( DestroyClipURL );
  }

/** Connect to the URLs specified by the StartClip and EndClip
parameters in the applet tag.
*/
  public void init() {
    try {
      InitClipURL = new URL(getParameter("InitClip"));
      StartClipURL = new URL(getParameter("StartClip"));
      StopClipURL = new URL(getParameter("StopClip"));
      DestroyClipURL = new URL(getParameter("DestroyClip"));
      } catch( MalformedURLException e )
          { System.out.println("exception"+e );}
    if( InitClipURL != null )
      play( InitClipURL );
  }
}
```

For single-threaded applets, this is all very simple, but it gets much more complicated when applets start creating their own threads. It is very difficult, perhaps impossible, for a browser to shut down independent applet threads in an orderly fashion, mostly because there's no way to know what those threads are doing: only the applet that created the threads knows that. Thus, it is incumbent upon the applet to shut down its own threads in **stop** and/or **destroy**.

Conclusion

Here, we've seen what applets look like, where they appear, and how they behave. We've shown how the interaction between the browser and its applets is strictly defined by the **Applet** class and the **AppletContext** interface. We've also discussed the methods available to an applet, the flow of execution, applet persistence, and the environment in which applets execute. And finally, with the Web-trolling applet, we've seen a little glimpse of how applets can enhance the functionality of browsers to the point of turning them into little more than Java platforms.

Debugging with Café

Joshua Kerievsky

In this chapter, you'll examine objects and variables, set and remove breakpoints, inspect a call chain, do drag-and-drop debugging, debug multithreaded code, and learn some advanced debugging features.

Although it's nice to never have to use them, debuggers can be your best friend on those rare occasions when things don't go *exactly as you planned*. Whether you call them "bugs" or "unexpected features," when certain errors emerge that simply can't be fixed by staring at your code, a good debugger can often save the day. To track down and terminate difficult, subtle, or even "nasty" Java bugs, the very visual and integrated Café debugger is ready to do your bidding.

At an early stage in your development cycle you may debug your code by simply writing strings to an output window, typically using Java's flexible **System.out.println()** method. The makers of Café have made it very easy for you to debug this way. They designed Café to route all output from calls to **System.out.println()** to Café's output window. This window is similar to the Java Console window under Netscape Navigator 2.0. Café's output window will work for apps or applets and will gather all text that is output from your code, including any exceptions that get raised while your code is running.

But although Café's output window and **System.out.println**() work fine for simple debugging, you might find that to track down subtle bugs, you need more control. The debugger built into Café was designed to give you a great deal of this kind of control. Using it, you'll find that you can quickly move between your source code, breakpoints, data, objects, and your project's threads.

Although many people are used to working with IDEs that come with separate debuggers (sometimes text-based, sometimes Windows-based), Café's debugger is thoroughly integrated and is part of what Symantec calls an IDDE, or Integrated Development and *Debugging* Environment. The added "D" for the debugger *does* merit its name here; as you'll see below, Café's debugger is fully integrated with the rest of the development environment and supports just about all debugging functions with a few clicks of the mouse.

Finally, before we dive into the Café debugger, it may be interesting to note that compared to the rather slow, but functional Java-based debugger that Sun shipped with the JDK, the integrated debugger in Café is a speed demon. (If you ever used Sun's debugger you'll understand). The Café debugger is written in C++ for very fast performance. The fact that it is not written in Java also helps to ensure that it does not conflict with your executing Java apps or applets.

Installation Check

Before we begin learning how to use the Café debugger, it is important to make certain of a few things so that the Café Debugger will function correctly. Although some of these issues have been resolved as of the 1.2 release of Café, in version 1.0 of Café you must ensure that the Café installer succeeded in setting up some important environment variables, that TCP/IP is configured correctly on your machine, and that other versions of the JDK are not interfering with your Café version. These issues are covered below.

Historical note on version numbers of Symantec Cafe

You may be wondering why we've talked about version 1.0 of Cafe along with version 1.2, without mentioning version 1.1. The reason is that version 1.1 never existed! Symantec released a minor patch to Cafe, which was called version 1.0.1, and this minor update later was misinterpreted by some to be version 1.1. To not add to the confusion, the latest version was dubbed 1.2. Still confused?

Environment Variables

In your autoexec.bat file, or if you are using Windows NT, in your "System" settings, you must make sure that the following environment variables were set up similar to the following (substitute your drive letter for "D"):

```
CLASSPATH=.;D:\Cafe\JAVA\LIB\CLASSES.ZIP
HOMEDRIVE=D:
HOMEPATH=\Cafe\JAVA
JAVA_HOME=D:\Cafe\JAVA
PATH=D:\CAFE\BIN;D:\CAFE\JAVA\BIN;C:\WIN95;C:\WIN95\COMMAND
```

Release 1.2 of Café removed this requirement (putting all entries above—except for PATH—in a file called sc.ini).

TCP/IP

If you're working with Version 1.0 of Café, you must ensure that TCP/IP software is installed and configured on your computer before you'll be able to use the debugger. This does not mean that you have to be online while you debug; it simply means that you have to have a TCP/IP stack configured on your machine. The reason you need this software installed is that the Café 1.0 debugger communicates with the Java Virtual Machine using Sun's debug interface, which operates via TCP/IP.

If you start the Java debugger without having TCP/IP correctly installed and configured, you'll see an **unknownHostException** raised in the Output window.

If you do not have TCP/IP software loaded and configured on your machine, you can install it using the helpful guide provided by Symantec in the Café

Help system. Under index, type "debugging" and then select "Debugging with Café." You can then follow the steps for installing TCP/IP software for either Windows 95 or Windows NT 3.5x.

TCP/IP not required for Local Debugging in version 1.2

Unlike version 1.0, one of the most significant enhancements to Cafe 1.2 was the dropping of the TCP/IP requirement for local debugging. This eliminated many complications involving dial-up and network connection configurations. TCP/IP is STILL required in Cafe 1.2 for doing REMOTE debugging.

Previous Versions of the JDK

If you have other installations of the JDK on your machine, prior to installing Café, you may experience problems using the Café debugger.

Often the problem arises because the debugger isn't finding the correct versions of classes.zip or javai.dll. To fix this, make sure that no other version of the JDK is being referenced in your path or classpath before Café.

If you continue to have problems, you can find that by simply removing previous versions of the JDK, the Café Debugger will run without a hitch.

Café Debugger Basics

Debugging in Café can be initiated from the main menu, from hot keys, or from the convenient debug toolbar.

Note for Experienced Debuggers

For those of you who are well-versed with visual debuggers, you may wish to skip ahead to the section below on drag and drop debugging. Drag and drop debugging is an aspect of the Café debugger that may not be obvious to you and could certainly help you be more productive.

When you begin to debug in Café, always make sure you have a project open (if you do not have one open, the debug menu will be completely disabled and the toolbar will not respond). Figure 10.1 shows what can be done from Café's debugging toolbar.

Using the Debug Toolbar

Like other panes within Café's main toolbar, the debugging toolbar may be dragged into its own window, which can be resized and/or relocated to suit your needs.

Once the toolbar becomes its own window, you may work with it that way for a while and later drag it back up to "dock" it on the main toolbar.

Debugging NervousText

To get a basic feel for using the Café debugger, let's open one of the example projects that comes with Café and step through a few lines of code. The NervousText project is a good starting point for seeing the effects of stepping through Java code. Figure 10.2 shows three separate screen shots of NervousText in action.

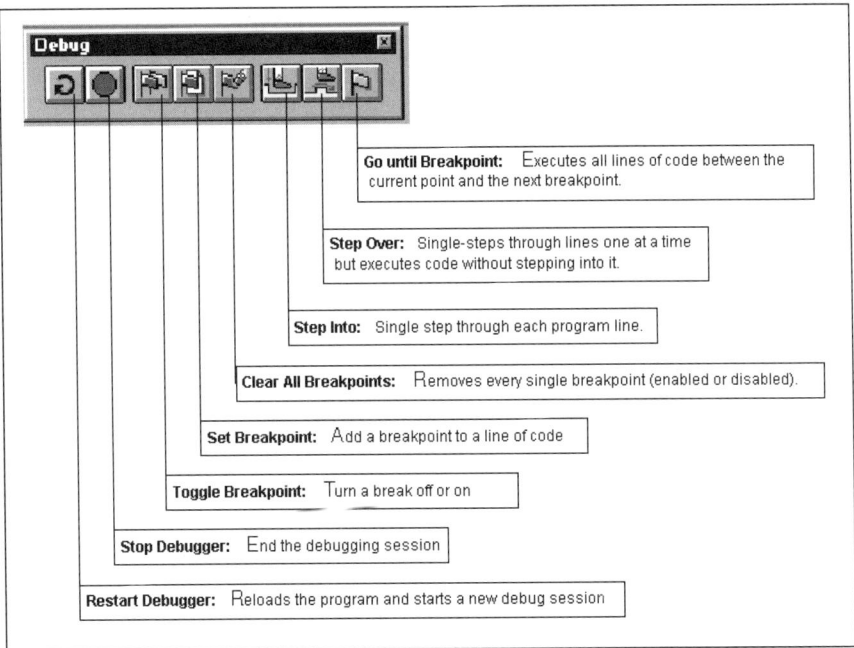

Figure 10.1   The Debug Toolbar and its functionality.

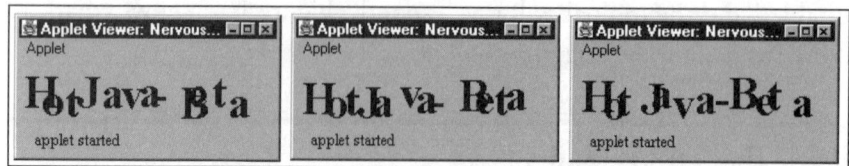

Figure 10.2   Three separate views of the NervousText applet in action.

We'll now step through some lines of code in the NervousText applet. Open the NervousText project (it is under \Café\Samples\Java\NervousText) and get into debug mode by pressing F4 or picking the "Start/Restart Debugging" option under the Debug menu.

Next, go to the NervousText **run**() method so that we can set a breakpoint on the **repaint**() method. The **run**() method is shown below in listing 10.1.

LISTING 10.1   SETTING A BREAKPOINT IN THE NERVOUSTEXT RUN() METHOD

```
public void run() {
 while (killme != null) {
 try {Thread.sleep(100);} catch (InterruptedException e){}
 repaint();
 }
 killme = null;
 }
```

To set the breakpoint on the **repaint**() method, position the cursor on that line, right-click once, and then select "Set/Clear Breakpoint." Once you see the red dot appear to the left of the line you know that the break has been set.

Now you will run the applet until it hits the breakpoint. To do this, go to the debug menu and press "Go until breakpoint" (or just press F4). You should see the applet flash by very quickly and then the debugger will highlight the **repaint**() line. You are now ready to start stepping through some lines of code.

Stepping Into and Over Java Code

The "Step Into" command will take you into the code behind a statement or method call while the "Step Over" command will execute the statement or method currently highlighted and then move you on to the next line of code. You can press **F8** to step into code and **F10** to step over code or choose these commands from the debug menu or debug toolbar.

Stepping Out

Although you will not find this feature in release 1.0 of Cafe, the ability to "step out" of a function or method you've stepped "in to" has been added to the Café 1.2 prerelease. You "step out" of the current method you're in by using the Step Out menu selection off the debug menu. This will execute the current method until its return address is reached or a breakpoint is reached.

Choose the "Step Over" command right now. The debugger will take you to the beginning of the while loop. Keep selecting "step over" and you will see the applet's text change (nervously). When you've had enough of that, keep selecting step over until you get back to the **repaint**() method. Now select "step into."

The debugger now takes you to the **repaint**() method of one of this applet's ancestors (or superclass), called "component." Select "step over" and you will be back at the top of the while loop. This is the basic idea of stepping through Java code.

To conclude, let's clear the breakpoint and tell the debugger to let the applet continue executing. To clear all breakpoints we again select this option from the debug menu. Do that now and you should see the red dot next to the repaint line disappear. Now let the applet continue running. You will select "Go until end" from the debug menu and you'll then see text gyrating (nervously) all over the place.

So much for your first session with the integrated debugger. Let's now learn more about the functionality and integrated nature of the Café debugger.

Drag-and-Drop Debugging

Besides what the debug menu and toolbar provide, there's quite a bit more under the hood of Café's integrated debugger. When you press the "Debug" tab on an already open project, you'll see a number of windows that are used for debugging. There are five such windows, and you will be working with them closely during your debug sessions. These windows support a high degree of interwindow communication, or what I like to call "Drag-and-Drop Debugging."

As you'll see later in this chapter, by simply dragging things like variables or threads to different windows, you can easily ascertain the information you need during a debug session. In fact, the degree to which you can use right-mouse clicks to display sub-menus and drag elements like code, methods, and threads all over the Café environment is a sure sign that the developers of Café succeeded in fully integrating the debugger with the rest of the IDE. They've also pretty much ensured that your won't have to spend your time typing variable names or methods in order to see values or code during your debug sessions.

The five debugger windows and their basic functions are listed in Table 10.1.

Since the Café debug windows support a high degree of dragging and dropping, you can find it helpful to review the following table that lists all of the paths by which you can drag and drop while debugging. Table 10.2 summarizes these paths.

Table 10.1   Cafe's five debug windows.

Window	Function
Breakpoint	set, delete, clear all breakpoints.
Call	examine the call chain, or the list of methods that have been executed for a given process like an applet or a thread.
Data/Object	view the values of variables and objects and provide a navigation mechanism for descending and ascending into data structures.
Output	see the output from your code.
Thread	see which threads are running, which are suspended, which are disabled and which are currently at a breakpoint. Freeze (stop) and Thaw (restart) individual or groups of threads.

Table 10.2   What you can drag from and where you can drop it to while debugging in Cafe.

Drag From Window	Drop To Window(s)
Breakpoint	Source code
Call	Data/Object and Source code
Thread	Call, Data/Object and Source code
Data/Object	None

Managing Debug Windows

You may find during your debug sessions that having all five debug windows up can occupy too much screen real estate. If this is the case, close the windows that you are not using and later, when you need them, go to "Window I Window List..." and select the windows that you wish to redisplay.

If you ever close one of your source windows and need to view the source, you can go to the project window and double-click the source file or drag it onto an open space on your screen.

Finally, once you've arranged the windows to your preference, you may save the layout by selecting "Environment" from Cafe's main menu, picking "Workspace," and choosing "Save Workspace Set."

Watching Data and Objects

If you've worked with other visual debuggers you might be wondering where the "watch" window is. The watch window is actually what is called the Data/Object window in Café. As its name implies, this window lets you view the values of data elements as well as the value of variables and constants within objects.

However, having the ability to view *objects* means a little more in Café. When you inspect an object you can also navigate upward to the object's parent or down to one of its children. This can be quite useful when you're looking for a variable that an object inherits from a parent or when you just want to inspect an object that is a member variable of your current object.

So now that you've had a brief tour of Café's integrated debugger, let's jump right in and begin debugging a simple program using some of the resources in this visual debugging environment.

Debugging Your Second Java Applet

Let's continue by debugging a very simple Java applet named DebugFun. We use Café's AppExpress to generate a project called FunWithDebugging and AppStudio to add some simple UI elements to the form (or applet window). The source code for this project resides in a file called DebugFun.java, which is shown in listing 10.2.

LISTING 10.2 DEBUGFUN APPLET

```
/*
    This class is a basic extension of the applet class.  It would
generally be used as the main class with a Java browser or the
AppletViewer.  But an instance can be added to a subclass of
Container. To use this applet with a browser or the AppletViewer,
create an html file with the following code:

    <HTML>
    <HEAD>
    <TITLE>DebugFun window</TITLE>
    </HEAD>
    <BODY>

    <APPLET CODE="DebugFun.class" WIDTH=332 HEIGHT=169></APPLET>

    </BODY>

    </HTML>

    You can add controls to Simple with Cafe Studio.
    (Menus can be added only to subclasses of Frame.)
 */

import java.awt.*;

public class DebugFun extends java.applet.Applet {

    public void init() {
```

```
    //{{INIT_CONTROLS
    setLayout(null);
    addNotify();
    resize(insets().left + insets().right + 299, insets().top +
    insets().bottom + 122);
    label2=new Label("Are We Having Fun Yet?");
    label2.setFont(new Font("Dialog",Font.PLAIN,18));
    add(label2);
    label2.reshape(insets().left + 41,insets().top + 15,210,30);
    button1=new Button("Yes :-)");
    add(button1);
    button1.reshape(insets().left + 7,insets().top + 53,56,30);
    button2=new Button("No :-(");
    add(button2);
    button2.reshape(insets().left + 70,insets().top + 53,63,30);
    button3=new Button("What was the Question?");
    add(button3);
    button3.reshape(insets().left + 140,insets().top +
    53,147,30);
    //}}

    super.init();
}

public boolean handleEvent(Event event) {
    if (event.id == Event.ACTION_EVENT && event.target ==
    button1) {
            clickedButton1();
            return true;
    }
    else
    if (event.id == Event.ACTION_EVENT && event.target ==
    button2) {
            clickedButton2();
            return true;
    }
    else
    if (event.id == Event.ACTION_EVENT && event.target ==
    button3) {
            clickedButton3();
            return true;
    }

    return super.handleEvent(event);
}

//{{DECLARE_CONTROLS
Label label2;
Button button1;
```

```
Button button2;
Button button3;
//}}

public void clickedButton3() {
    label2.setText("Are We Having Fun Yet?");
}
public void clickedButton2() {
    label2.setText("Well, I'm sorry to hear that.");
}
public void clickedButton1() {
    label2.setText("I thought so!");
}
}
```

Before Debugging Your Code

Although it is the default setting, always remember to check the project settings to see that the code you wish to debug the default setting.

For an existing project, go to "Project | Settings" and make sure that under the tab called "Target," Project Settings is again set to "debug."

Finally, as of Version 1.0 of the Cafe debugger, if you want to be able to debug your own classes, do not specify a compiler output directory in "Project Settings | Directories."

Using Breakpoints And the Data/ Object Window

Our first debug mission will be to set some breakpoints, run an applet until we hit those breakpoints, inspect certain fields and objects when we come to our breakpoints, and finally, continue running the applet.

First, we start a debug session by pressing "Debug | Start/Restart Debugging." Next, we must set some breakpoints. For this example, we will go to the seventh line within DebugFun's **init**() method, which looks like this:

```
label2.reshape(insets().left + 41,insets().top + 15,210,30);
```

Once positioned on that line, right-click the mouse to obtain a debug submenu. Note that the sub-menu you see now is specifically designed for debugging: You won't see this menu if you have not entered debug mode by clicking "Start/Restart Debugging" off the debug menu.

In this debug submenu, select "Set/Clear Breakpoint." As before, you will see a small red dot appear on the far-left side of the code, which indicates that the breakpoint was set. If you inspect the Breakpoint window at this point, you will also see that the class, filename, and line number of the breakpoint have been registered. In fact, if you choose to quit Café right now and save the project, when you return, your breakpoint will be remembered.

Now let's set another breakpoint. Go to one of the last lines in the code, which is in a method called clickedButton1. The line reads:

```
label2.setText("I thought so!");
```

Okay, we are now ready to dive into our second debug session. Under the Debug menu, press "Go until breakpoint" (or press F5). You will now hear some disk activity, see the applet's window flash for a moment, and then see the line containing your first breakpoint highlighted. The screen should look something like it does in Figure 10.3.

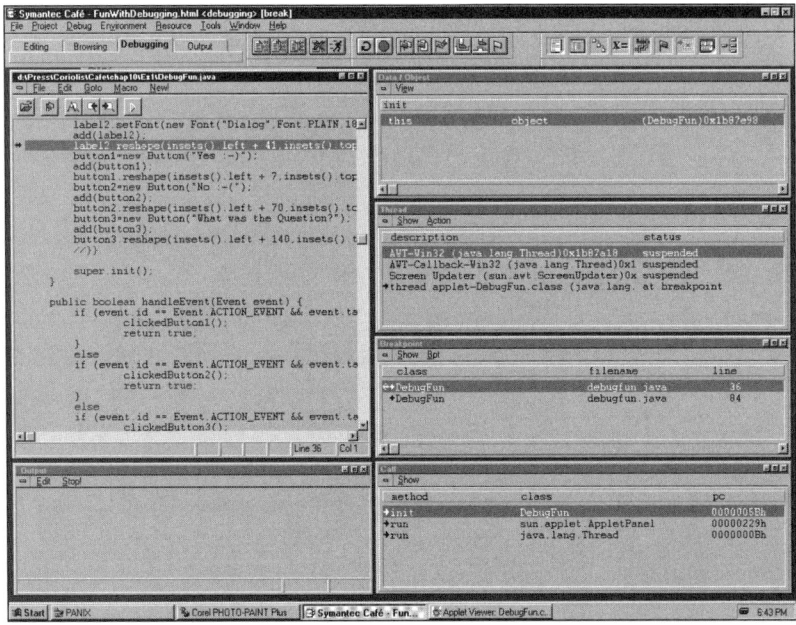

Figure 10.3   Halted at a breakpoint while debugging the applet, DebugFun.

In the Data/Object window you should now see one line that displays an object called "this" and tells us the name of this object, which is DebugFun. Right-click on this line. You will see a submenu appear that lets you choose "Parent," "Child/Contents," or "Variable Level." Table 10.3 lists the functions of the Data/Object window.

If you click on "Child/Contents" you will see all of the member variables and their values from the DebugFun applet. (Note: Clicking on "Parent" after clicking on "Child/Contents" takes you back up to the "DebugFun" object.). Figure 10.4 shows you some values contained by the "DebugFun" applet object.

You may click on some of the variables within this list in order to see more. For instance, since the variable called "label2" was instantiated before we hit out first breakpoint, you can click on it to see its contents. Since a label is an object in Java, the member variables of the label2 object are displayed. The "label" variable of the label2 object correctly shows the value "Are We Having Fun Yet?" When you've finished inspecting all of the object's values, click the right-mouse button and select "Parent." This will send you back up to label2's parent, also known as "this."

Table 10.3   Function within the Data/Object window.

Function	Description
Parent	Lets you move up a level in a data structure that you moved down into with the Child/Contents command.
Child/Contents	Displays the next level of data structures beneath the current data structure.
Variable Level	Returns you to the top nesting level (or variable level) of the data display. You would use this command if you repeatedly selected the Child/Contents command to descend into some data structures and then wanted to return to the top variable level without repeatedly using the Parent command.

```
Data / Object                                                    ▄□▨
 □ | View
 init.this
   peer                 java.awt.peer.Compon  (sun.awt.win32.MPanelPeer)0x1b87fd8
   parent               java.awt.Container    (sun.applet.AppletViewerPanel)0x1b877a0
   x                    int                   208
   y                    int                   172
   width                int                   299
   height               int                   122
   foreground           java.awt.Color        null
   background           java.awt.Color        null
   font                 java.awt.Font         null
   visible              boolean               false
   enabled              boolean               true
   valid                boolean               false
   ncomponents          int                   1
   component            java.awt.Component[]  0x1b87f38 Object[4] = { java.awt.Label[0
   layoutMgr            java.awt.LayoutManag  null
   stub                 java.applet.AppletSt  (sun.applet.AppletViewerPanel)0x1b877a0
   label2               java.awt.Label        (java.awt.Label)0x1b88068
   button1              java.awt.Button       null
   button2              java.awt.Button       null
   button3              java.awt.Button       null
 ◄□                                                                              ►
```

Figure 10.4   Data/Object window displaying DebugFun variables.

Within object "this," you might notice the field's components and component. These fields tell you how many components are in the current container and what these components are. If you click on the "component" array and scroll to the far right you will see a Label object containing the value "Are We Having Fun Yet." Later on, when all the components have been instantiated, you will be able to see all of the components that were added to DebugFun.

If you now go to the Breakpoint window, you will see the two breakpoints that we had set earlier. The Breakpoint window shows you all of your breakpoints broken down by class name, source file, and line number within source file. This one window makes it very convenient for removing breakpoints or changing locations of breakpoints while debugging. The window also contains its own menu (which will let you clear all breakpoints) and supports the right-mouse button. Inside the Breakpoint window you can position the highlight on a breakpoint and right-click it to do one of the following tasks shown in Table 10.4.

Table 10.4   Functionality within the Breakpoint window.

Task	Hot-Key	Function
Show Source	Ctrl-S	Go to the line in the source code at which the breakpoint was set.
Clear breakpoint	Ctrl-C	Remove the highlighted breakpoint
Enable breakpoint	Ctrl-E	Enable the highlighted breakpoint
Disable breakpoint	Ctrl-D	Disable the highlighted breakpoint

Some Notes about Browsing Data and Setting Breakpoints

In Version 1.0 of the Cafe debugger, you will not be able to browse data arrays, since the debug interface for these arrays was not defined by Sun. In release 1.2, this problem was resolved; to view the contents of an array, simply double-click it in the Data/Object window.

Another bug in the Cafe debugger prevents you from setting breakpoints in classes you define that have the same name as classes already defined in other packages.

Now let's use one of the functions from the Breakpoint window. After highlighting the second breakpoint that we set, right-click and press "Show Source." You have now been sent back to your source code and positioned on the line at which the break was set. Next, on the debug toolbar, press the green flag button to the far right (it has the tool-tip "Go Until Breakpoint"). This will bring up the AppletViewer window and show you DebugFun in action.

Press the "Yes" button (you are having fun, right?). Since we set a breakpoint in the code that executes when the "Yes" button is pressed, we are placed back into the debugger and positioned on the breakpoint line.

Now notice the "Call" window (see Figure 10.5). It shows us the complete call chain (or complete list of all methods called) since we started running the applet. The list is in reverse order: The entry on the top of the window was the last method called; the entry on the bottom was the first.

```
Call                                                      _ □ ✕
 ▫  Show
   method              class                    pc
 ➨clickedButton1       DebugFun                 00000000h
 ➨handleEvent          DebugFun                 00000016h
 ➨postEvent            java.awt.Component       00000007h
 ➨postEvent            java.awt.Component       00000026h
 ➨action               sun.awt.win32.MButtonPeer 0000001Ch
 ➨run                  sun.awt.win32.MToolkit   00000019h
 ➨run                  java.lang.Thread         0000000Bh
```

Figure 10.5   Call window displaying all methods called while running DebugFun.

Some of the methods in the Call window may look mysterious if you haven't spent hours plumbing the depths of Java's class libraries. Not to worry. This window is a good launching point for learning more about Java methods. First, let's look at the functionality supported by the Call window, as summarized in Table 10.5.

Now if you want to see some source code, select the method called "run" from the class **java.lang.Thread** and either double-click it or "drag" it to the Editor window. When you do this, Café gets the source file associated with the method you selected, and then positions you on the line in the source code where the method was executed.

You can do this for *most* of the methods in the call chain; some methods belong to source files that have not been made public by Sun or Symantec. The reason these files are not available is that Café ships with the general license to Java, and certain Java system files are shipped only in .class bytecode form for the general release. If you are ever presented with an Open File dialog box during your debugging, chances are you are trying to see the contents of some source file that is not shipped with the general license copy of Java. Simply click cancel and continue debugging. Alternatively, you could obtain a different license from Sun if you *really* needed to see the source.

In the next section we'll look at some of more advanced "break" features that were added to Café 1.2.

Table 10.5   Functionality within the Call window.

Task	Function
SHOW SOURCE	WHEN POSITIONED ON A METHOD, THIS COMMAND WILL TAKE YOU TO THE SOURCE CODE WHERE THE GIVEN METHOD LIVES. (IF THE SOURCE FOR THE METHOD IS NOT AVAILABLE, YOU WILL BE PRESENTED WITH A DIALOG BOX PROMPTING YOU FOR THE SOURCE FILE.)
SHOW DATA	THIS COMMAND WILL UPDATE THE DATA/OBJECT WINDOW WITH WHATEVER OBJECTS OR VARIABLES ARE ASSOCIATED WITH THE GIVEN METHOD.
SHOW ALL	SHOWS THE SOURCE IN A SOURCE WINDOW AND DATA IN THE DATA/OBJECT WINDOW.
Code Address	Shows the code address where the selected method resides (this is also displayed on the far right of Call window).

Breaking During Running

One of the most convenient additions made to the 1.2 release of Café is the ability to break execution of your code at will. This means that while your applet or application is running, you may stop execution and be positioned on the line of source at which the break occurred.

This feature of the debugger is very simple to use. Simply start the debugger, clear all breakpoints in your project, select "Go until breakpoint," and then, when you are ready, select "break" from the Debug menu. The Café debugger will pause execution of your code and position you on the line in a source code window where the break occurred. As usual, to continue debugging select either "Go until breakpoint" or "Go until End".

Live Control of Breakpoints

Another handy enhancement made to the 1.2 release of Café was the ability to set and remove breakpoints while your applet or application is running.

To use this feature, simply start up the debugger, set some breakpoints, select "Go until breakpoint," and then, perhaps before your first breakpoint is hit, remove it from the breakpoint window and add a new breakpoint at another location in your project.

Conditional Breakpoints

By now one question you might be asking is, "How do I set conditional breakpoints?" For the uninitiated, a conditional breakpoint is a breakpoint that is set based upon some condition, like when a variable takes on a certain value. Sadly, both Versions 1.0 and 1.2 of Café's debugger do not support conditional breakpoints.

For now, you will have to check the Data/Object window for the values of variables. Remember that you can always watch the call-chain, and when you need to, drag a method from the Call window to the Data/Object window to view the data and objects associated with that method.

That concludes our look at Breakpoints and the Data/Object window. We are now going to inspect ways of debug multithreaded code.

Debugging Multithreaded Code

Because nobody likes to wait on the Web, many Java programmers (or multithreaded programmers) choose to relegate certain activities to threads so that other activities may proceed at their own pace. Multithreaded programming often plays an essential role in the creation of high-performance applets and applications. However, with the addition of threads comes a certain additional complexity, and again, a good debugger can go a long way toward helping resolve conflicts.

If you've been writing Java applets or applications that do not spawn their own threads, you might not have much use for the Thread window provided in the Café debugger. If, on the other hand, your code creates more than one thread, you will certainly find the Thread window to be indispensable. This Thread window, like many of the other debug windows, allows you to drag threads to neighboring windows in order to learn more about the thread's current location in your source code, the methods that have been called during the life of the thread, and the data and objects with which the thread is associated.

Are We Freezing or Thawing?

Java threads can be started, stopped, paused, resumed, suspended, given priorities, joined with other threads, and in general, behave in complex ways. Often during your multithreaded debugging sessions, you will need to hone in on a particular thread, stop it from executing, and see what is going on. In Café, the terms *freeze* and *thaw* are used to mean "suspend execution" and "resume execution," respectively. You can manage thread execution using the Thread window. This window supports the following functionality (as shown in Table 10.6).

In the next section you'll see how the Thread window is integrated with the other debug windows to support drag-and-drop debugging. You'll also see how an applet's threads may be suspended and resumed.

Debugging ThreadX

There's nothing like a good example to make a new concept clear, and the ThreadX applet, which is one of the sample applets that comes with Café, may be as good a place as any to begin learning about debugging multithreaded code. ThreadX creates three polygons in three panels and has a dial that spins around in each panel. Figure 10.6 shows this applet in action.

Each one of ThreadX's three panels is an instance of AnimationPanel, and each contains a PolygonAnimation object (AnimationPanel and PolygonAnimation are defined in the source file AnimationPanel.java). The PolygonAnimation class is a descendent of the Canvas class and implements the Runnable interface. Within the constructor to PolygonAnimation, a thread called "myThread" is instantiated and started as shown in Figure 10.6.

```
public PolygonAnimation(int delay)
    {
        resize(130, 130);
        SetupPolygon();
        thePolygon = new Polygon(polyX, polyY, 9);
        position = 0;

        if(delay < 0 || delay > 300) delay = 100;
        else thedelay = delay;
```

Table 10.6   Functionality within the Thread window.

Task	Hot-Key	Function
SHOW ALL	CTRL-L	TYPICALLY UPDATES THREE SEPARATE WINDOWS: DATA/OBJECT, CALL, AND SOURCE. IN THE DATA/OBJECT WINDOW YOU WILL SEE THE DATA AND OBJECTS ASSOCIATED WITH THE HIGHLIGHTED THREAD. IN THE CALL WINDOW, YOU WILL SEE THE CALL-CHAIN FOR THE HIGHLIGHTED THREAD, AND IN THE SOURCE CODE WINDOW YOU WILL SEE THE LOCATION IN THE CODE WHERE THE THREAD IN CURRENTLY POSITIONED.
FREEZE	CTRL-F	SUSPENDS THE HIGHLIGHTED THREAD.
FREEZE OTHERS	CTRL-O	SUSPENDS ALL THREADS BUT THE HIGHLIGHTED THREAD.
THAW	CTRL-T	TURNS UP THE HEAT ON A THREAD: I.E. MAKES A THREAD RESUME EXECUTION.
Thaw Others	**Ctrl-M**	**Thaws all threads but the highlighted thread.**

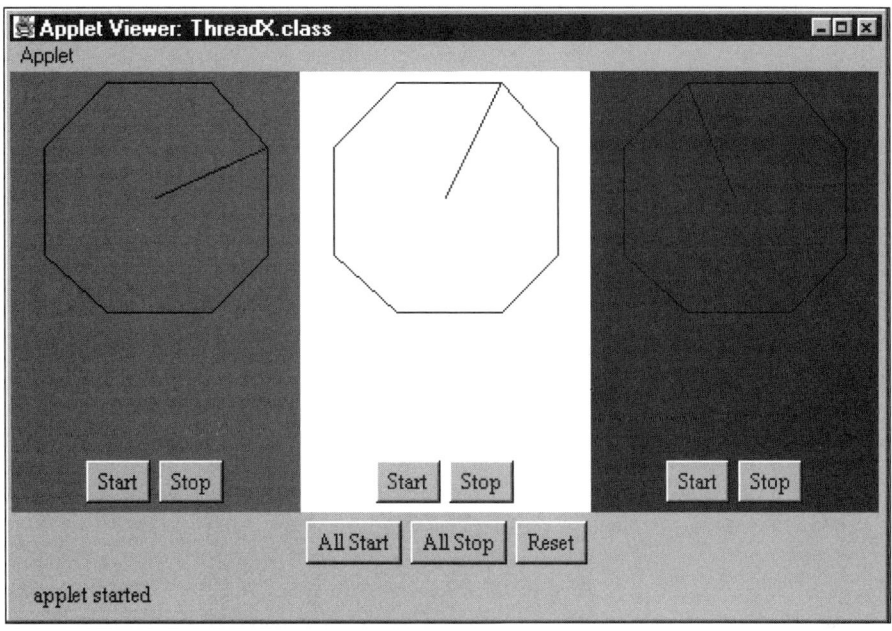

Figure 10.6   The multithreaded ThreadX applet.

```
myThread = new Thread(this);
  myThread.start();
}
```

The class also implements start and resume methods that tell the thread to either suspend running or resume running, and these methods get called by methods in the AnimationPanel class. PolygonAnimation's stop() and resume() methods looks like the code snippet below.

```
public void stop() { myThread.suspend(); }
public void resume() { myThread.resume(); }
```

The class that sets everything in motion is called ThreadX. ThreadX creates the three AnimationPanels and handles requests to start, stop, or reset all threads at once.

Let's begin debugging ThreadX to see how we can work with threads. As before, open the ThreadX project (it is located in the \Café\Samples\Java\ThreadX directory) and get into debug mode. If you look for a moment at the Call window you will see that the **run**() method was called from the MainThread class and that main() was called from the AppletViewer. In addition, if you look at the Data/Object window you will see one line that shows "this" and tells us that "this" is an object called ThreadX.

Now set a breakpoint in the first line of the AllStop() method where the code says "**panelOne.StopAnimation**();" From the debug menu select "Go until breakpoint" (or press F5). You should see the ThreadX applet come up in the AppletViewer, and it should be running. Inside the applet, press the "All Stop" button. You will now see a number of methods appear in the Call window, with the latest method—"AllStop"—on top. We are now in a position to examine one of many threads in this applet.

The Threads window will show you the current state of all the threads in ThreadX. As you can see in Figure 10.7, most of these threads are suspended.

Let's now see what the call-chain looks like for one of the Animation threads. Go to the Threads window, grab the thread named Thread-2 and drag it onto the Call window. What you just did caused two windows to be updated:

```
Thread                                                          ▣□▣
  ▫ | Show  Action
  ┌──────────────────────────────────────────────┬──────────────┐
  │ description                                   │ status       │
  ├──────────────────────────────────────────────┴──────────────┤
  │ AWT-Win32 (java.lang.Thread)0x1b87418     suspended          │
  │▸AWT-Callback-Win32 (java.lang.Thread)0x1 at breakpoint       │
  │ Screen Updater (sun.awt.ScreenUpdater)0x  suspended          │
  │ thread applet-ThreadX.class (java.lang.T  suspended          │
  │ Thread-2 (java.lang.Thread)0x1b87ce8      suspended          │
  │ Thread-3 (java.lang.Thread)0x1b87e58      suspended          │
  │ Thread-4 (java.lang.Thread)0x1b87fd0      suspended          │
  └──────────────────────────────────────────────────────────────┘
```

Figure 10.7   State of threads at a breakpoint in the ThreadX applet.

the Call window and the Data/Object window. The Call window now shows you all methods that have been called thus far within the thread named Thread-2. You can see that method **run**() from **java.lang.Thread** was called first, followed by a call to PolygonAnimation's **run**() method. To see the source for PolygonAnimation's run method, right-click on that line and then click on "show source." Alternatively, if you ever want to see where in the source a thread is without looking at the call-chain, you can simply grab the thread and drag it to the Source window.

Now look at the Data/Object window. It too was updated when you dragged the thread from the Thread window to the Call window. The Data/Object window will be showing the object "this"— though now it is no longer the ThreadX object but one of the PolygonAnimation objects. To inspect the properties of this object, simply double-click on it. Another path you could take to inspect Thread2 in the Data/Object window would be to drag Thread2 directly from the Thread window onto the Data/Object window.

Now it's time to see how to freeze and thaw threads in the multithreaded ThreadX applet.

First, if you would like to follow along with the rest of this example, you'll need to have the latest update to Café, which at this point is release 1.2. (Café 1.0 does not support freezing or thawing of threads even though the Threads menu and popup menu contain entries for these functions.)

In the example we've been following, we are currently stopped within the first line of ThreadX's AllStop() method. Lets now return to the threads window (which again is pictured above in Figure 10.7) and freeze one of ThreadX's threads.

We'll choose Thread-4 to freeze. Select the row in the Threads window containing Thread-4. This thread controls the right-most animation panel (colored blue); right-click to bring up the popup menu and select "Freeze". Although the screen still says "suspended" for Thread-4 (at least, as of prerelease 1.2) this thread is actually now stopped. If you choose "Go until breakpoint" you will see that dial for the right-most panel is not moving while the two are continue to rotate. Pretty simple, huh?

Let's now "thaw" or restart Thread-4. You can do this while ThreadX is running in the AppletViewer. Simply go back to the Threads window, select Thread-4, right-click, and choose "Thaw." If you go back to the AppletViewer you'll see the third dial turning again.

From the Threads window you can also choose to "Freeze Others" or "Thaw Others." This means that if you highlight a certain thread, and then choose "Freeze Others," for instance, *all* other threads within the Threads window will get halted. Using these functions is generally not a good idea (at present) since the command will freeze not only your applet's threads but all the system threads as well. In the future you might have a command to freeze "all" of your applet's threads, leaving the system threads alone.

That concludes our look at debugging with threads.

Advanced Debugging

In the next section, we will look at some of the advances features of the Café debugger. We will be looking at features that are mostly available only in version 1.2 of Café.

Remote Debugging

Remote debugging in Java can mean a few things. For one, it can mean debugging an applet while it's running within a Web page within a browser (either on a local machine or on a remote machine). It can also mean debugging a Java application from your box while the application is running under a Java interpreter on another box.

Although the debugger that comes with Sun JDK Version 1.0, called JDB, supports remote debugging, Version 1.0 of the Café debugger does not.

However, like many of the debugger enhancements found in version 1.2 of Café, support for some forms of remote debugging is now possible. Although this enhancement will not let you debug your applets while they run within a local browser, you will be able to debug applets and applications running on remote machines.

There are a few requirements you'll need to have met before remote debugging with Café will work. These are:

◆ Cafe needs to be installed on the remote machine.

◆ Your class files and HTML files need to be located on the remote machine.

◆ Both the local and the remote machine need to have TCP/IP installed and working properly.

Remote debugging happens by using a program called caferemote.exe. This program will be found in your Café/bin directory (for Café 1.2).

During a remote debug session, you'll need to have caferemote.exe up and running on the remote machine where your Java applet or application will be running. To start caferemote, simple open up a console window and change to the directory where you classes and HTML files are located. Start caferemote.exe and you will see some important information that you'll need to begin debugging back on your local debug machine.

When it starts up, Caféremote.exe shows version information about itself and then displays an agent password along with the current machine's IP address. Note down the agent password and current machine's IP address. You'll need these values back on your local debug machine.

Now on your local machine, load the project corresponding to those classes and HTML files that are currently on your remote machine. From Café's menu, select "Debug | Settings | General tab." You'll see a window that will look similar to Figure 10.8.

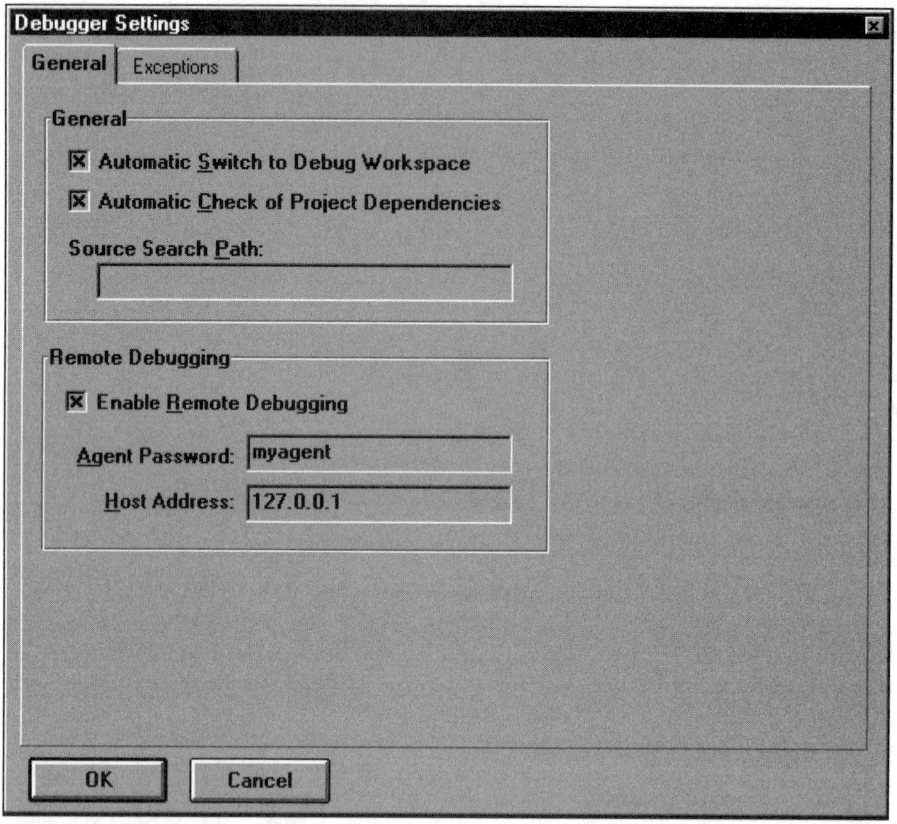

Figure 10.8   Enabling Remote Debugging in the Debug Setting dialog box.

Check the box with the label "enable remote debugging" and enter the Agent Password and IP Address that you obtained when you ran Caféremote.exe on the remote machine.

You can now begin a remote debugging session by simply selecting "Debug | Start/Restart debugging". To finish your remote debugging session, exit Caféremote.exe on the remote machine by typing "Ctrl-C".

Debugging with Packages or Native Libraries

And as of release 1.0, you may debug code within your own packages but there are a few problems to be aware of.

First, you can *not* set breakpoints in your code that resides in Java packages. The debugger will not show the small red dot to the left of your code when you try to do this.

And second, although you can step through the code within your packages, another small bug means that the highlighted bar which normally appears while stepping through your code will *not* appear inside a package. You can continue to step and code will get executed but you will not be able to see where in the code you are.

1.2 Update Fixes Package Debugging Bug

As of the 1.2 update to Cafe, full support for debugging within your own or someone else's Java packages has been added.

Debugging Exceptions

Support for controlling how the debugger handles exceptions was added to release 1.2 of Café. Essentially, you may specify within the Debug Settings dialog box, how the debugger should respond to exceptions, both system and your own.

You can have the debugger "Always Stop" when a particular exception is raised or specify that the debugger should only stop if the exception is "Not handled' by any code (system or otherwise).

Native Libraries

In Café release 1.0 if you are loading native libraries (such as a dynamic link library) with a call to **System.load**(), you must follow a particular naming convention which is set forth by Sun in their JDK. That is, if you have a .DLL named foo.dll, and you wish to debug a program in Café, you must (in versions 1.0) have a version of your .dll called foo_g.dll. Note that Symantec has fixed this issue in version 1.2 so your .DLLs may now be called whatever you like.

Coming Attractions

What's next for Café? In this section we detail just a few of the enhancements that we'd hope to see in later editions of the product.

Browser Debugging

Wouldn't it be nice if you could debug one of your applets while it is running within your browser? An issue surrounding the ability to do this is the information which the browser itself will supply to the debugger. At present, Café's debugger cannot get enough of this information from a browser such as Netscape Navigator. But stay tuned...

Conditional Breakpoints

At some point in the near future this important feature of a debugger will be added to the Café debugger. Symantec has not disclosed when this enhancement will be made available but it will likely accompany a major new release of the debugger.

Go Until End

As you surely know by now, "Go until end" is the command in the Café debugger which takes you to the end of an applet or application. Well, you've now reached the end of your journey into the heart of the Café debugger. You've come a long way! You've learned the ins and outs of the debugging environment, how to do drag and drop debugging, follow call-chains, view source code, and you've seen ways of viewing and managing threads. You've also learned about features of the debugger that are not currently supported in release 1.0, and what the future holds for Café's integrated debugging environment.

Finally, as Symantec races to make Café more robust, remember to keep current on the latest developments by visiting http://cafe.symantec.com/ cafe/index.html on a regular basis. There is even a mailing list to which you might subscribe to receive the latest news about Café — you can subscribe from the Symantec web site.

Good luck with all your Café debugging!

Working with Café Studio

11

Joshua Kerievsky

In this chapter, you'll develop user interfaces, control code generation, use Layout managers, build menus, work with events, and learn about Café Studio features you can code on your own.

Back in the days before many PC operating systems sported graphical user interfaces, programmers used to spend a good deal of time writing code to handle the appearance of custom screens and dialog boxes. Much of the coding involved positioning items at particular locations on the screen, a very time-consuming process involving a continuous cycle of coding and viewing until all items on a screen were placed in just the right positions.

Then Microsoft's Windows came into widespread use, and new Windows development tools changed everything. Programs like Visual Basic and resource editors, as well as studios bundled with various compilers began to support drag-and-drop screen creation. Suddenly, even nonprogrammers could snap together user interfaces with relative ease. The days of manual, "hand-coded" screen creation were fading fast.

But the Windows products that supported screen creation did so only for the Windows operating system. For Java, the requirements at the start were a lot bigger and much more ambitious. That is, Java code was designed so that it could run on any machine that could run the Java Virtual Machine.

That would mean that whatever screen components were supported by Java on one platform would need to be supported on all platforms.

Thus, the developers of the language built into Java what they called the AWT, or Abstract Windowing Toolkit. The AWT ensured that Java would remain platform-independent. This meant that you could write code with a Java component named "button" that would have the same appearance whether it was a button on Windows, a button on Unix, a button on the Mac, and so on.

The authors of Java also built into the AWT the notion of "layout managers." These classes or managers facilitate the consistent positioning of components on Java screens. Layout managers range from simple **Border** and **Card** layouts to the quite sophisticated **GridBag** layout. With such tools, developers could design screens that could look "similar" when running on different platforms.

The only problem was that developers still had no IDE (integrated development environment), and therefore they had to program screens manually. Anyone who was used to designing screens visually, and who began to work with Sun's JDK when the betas first came out, soon realized that although they hadn't gone as far back as the pre-GUI programming days, they were still quite far from the new world of drag-and-drop screen design.

Enter Café Studio

Symantec saw the need for a Visual Basic-like screen creation environment for Java and answered that need with Café Studio. Using Café Studio, developers can, with relative ease, create sophisticated screens and menu resources and easily "hook up" their components to their project code.

The amount of work this saves will be clear to you if you've already worked solely with Sun's JDK. And if you've tried to build Windows-like user interfaces using just the JDK, get ready for your job to become a whole lot easier. By using Café Studio, much of the tedious work has been eliminated so that you can build user interfaces quickly and have more time for developing the guts of your project.

What Café Studio will *not* do is eliminate *all* of your user interface programming responsibilities. As you get further into Java, perhaps you will begin to develop your own custom components, work with Graphic Contexts, paint canvases, or develop panels with more sophisticated layout managers like the **GridBag**. These activities go beyond the scope of what Version 1.0 of Café was designed to do.

There are some features of the Abstract Windowing Toolkit that Symantec did not support in the Café Studio environment (in Version 1.0); Those will be summarized near the end of the chapter. For now, let's get our hands dirty seeing everything that Café Studio has simplified and automated for us.

Look Ma, No Hands

We'll begin by creating a Java applet containing some standard UI components and do it all without writing a line of code! The applet we will create will be a Cousin manager, a simple program responsible for getting and setting information about cousins. Figure 11.1 is a screen shot of the finished result, all of which did not involve writing a single line of code.

Now, lest you be deceived, this applet is not completely functional as it stands. AppExpress and Café Studio have eliminated much of the work here, but some of the basic applet logic still remains to be coded. The point is, however, that you can get pretty far without writing code, and that is why it is important to use tools like Café Studio.

Let's now create the Cousin manager applet, step by step.

As step one, open Café's Tools menu and select AppExpress to create a new project. We'll call the project "nocode" and pick up all the default options supplied by AppExpress. Hit the "finish" button in AppExpress. Now, you're ready to begin working with your new applet and your project's resources.

From Café's main menu, select "Resource" and then select "Edit." You're now taken into Café Studio. If you take a quick glance back at the Project window in Café, you'll see that a file named "nocode.rc" has been added to your project. This file maintains a list of all resource components added to your project using Café Studio. This file is also the source from which much of your project's Java source code will be automatically generated later.

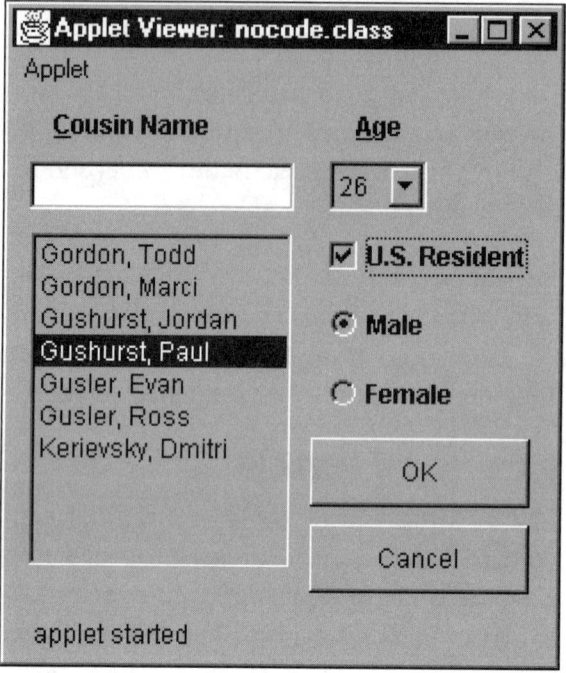

Figure 11.1   An applet composed with Café Studio without writing code.

After selecting "Edit" from the Resource menu, you are placed inside Café Studio's main dialog box. You will initially see the words "Form" in the upper-left pane of this window. This represents a placeholder for all of your forms: later, you'll see a similar one for all of your menus. Our applet, nocode, currently has one form. To see it, click on the word "Form." In the pane below (or the lower-left-corner pane), you will see something called "nocode.init." This name reflects the name of your applet followed by the name of the class method in which a resource (in this case, a form) exists. Had we been working with our applet's constructor, the name supplied would have been nocode.nocode.

If you now double-click on your nocode.init, you'll see, as is shown in Figure 11.2, your applet with one label inside of it that reads "A nocode Applet."

We'll start building the form in a moment. Let's first get a little more familiar with the environment.

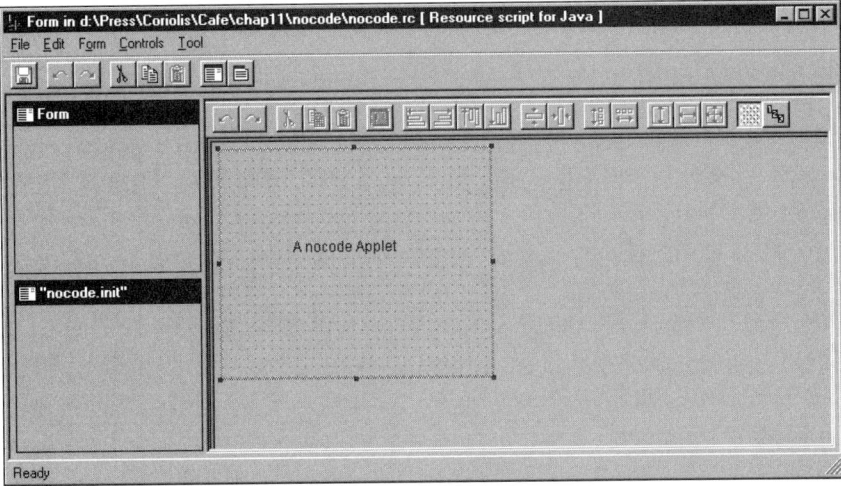

Figure 11.2   Café Studio's Main Dialog Box with the nocode applet loaded.

The Property Sheet and Toolbar

On the sides of the main Café Studio dialog box, you'll find two floating windows: a property sheet and a toolbar.

The property sheet is a dynamic window that will change depending on the component you're working with. From the property sheet, you typically specify the name of a component as it will appear within one of your classes, as well as its look (*i.e.*, caption, color, font, and so forth) and any events that the component may handle or initiate.

The toolbar supports most of the Java user interface components; the single exception is listed in Table 11.3, near the end of this chapter. You can drag components from the toolbar onto your form or just click on a toolbar component and then click on your form to create the component.

Adding Components to Forms

As you add components to panels (in this case, the main panel of our applet) you will be adding them in a particular order. Café Studio calls this the Creation Order. From the main menu of Café Studio, you can select Form | Creation Order to see the order in which components will be created on your panels. At times, you may want to change this order and Café

Studio makes this quite easy to do. Simply select a component, right-click on it, select Creation Order, and choose First, Forward, Back, or Last.

To continue building your applet, click on the "button" component in the toolbar (the button component says "OK" on it) and drag the new button to your form. You can see that the properties sheet changes when you click on the button, as it will when you click on the label or on the applet's panel itself.

Under the "General" tab of the properties sheet, you can see some of the default properties assigned to the button. Set the "Member" field to "OkBtn" and the caption to "OK." Now make a clone of this button and call it "Cancel."

Making clones of your UI components

If you often make copies or clones of user interface elements on your forms, a quick way to create a copy of one of these components is to hold down the Control key, click on the component you wish to copy, and then drag to an open area of the form.

This will work on groups of components as well. To select a number of elements within a form, hold down the Shift key and click on each element. When you're done, drag the entire group to an open area on the form, and a new batch of components will be created.

Finally, you can also use the cut, copy and paste functions from the Edit menu or from the editing window's toolbar.

Now that we've got OK and Cancel buttons, let's create some labels. First, let's take our existing label, drag it up to the upper-left portion of the form, and rename it (using the properties window) to read "Cousin Name." To make the label stand out, go to the "Look" tab on the properties window, specify the font "TimesRoman" and check the box marked "Bold."

Next, drag a new label (the label component has a "T" on it) from the toolbar to the form, rename it to "Age," and again change its look so that it uses a "Bold," "TimesRoman" font.

Now, we'll create a textfield to hold the "Cousin" name. The "TextArea/

TextField" component is located directly under the arrow on the toolbar. As its name implies, this component can either be a TextArea, which is typically a multiline component, or a TextField, which is normally one line in height. Since the default is a TextField, we'll leave it that way and change only the look of our TextField to use the "TimesRoman" font as well.

Identifying components on the Toolbar

If you don't know which Toolbar component is which, just position the mouse pointer on top of a component in the Toolbar and leave it there for a moment. A "tip box" will appear that tells you the name of the component under the mouse pointer.

Now we'll create a list box for a list of cousins. Go to the toolbar and drag a list component (it is directly to the right of the radio button component) to the form. After changing the component's font like the others, go to the "Init" tab on the properties toolbar. The "init" tab allows you to specify initial values for a component. Not all components have this feature, but list boxes and choices do. In this list box's initial values, I've supplied the names of some of my cousins (if you have 'em, you can supply the names of your own cousins). Keep in mind while adding values that pressing the "Enter" key after each addition will take you back to the form; to stay within the properties dialog, use the arrow keys to move up and down in the rows.

Now create a choice component to hold your cousins' ages. As with the list component, you can specify the correct font and supply values within the "Init" tab.

Finally, create one checkbox for the U.S. resident status, two radio buttons for the male and female genders, and set the fonts of each. The last steps are to position the components wherever you like and save your work in Café Studio by pressing File | Save, and you are ready to test your work.

The End Result

Back in Café, you can look at nocode.java to see all of the Java source code that was generated when you saved your work in Café Studio: (the code is shown in Listing 11.1). You should have something on the order of 115 lines of Java code that was generated for you. To test this code, simply build the project and select Project | Execute Program.

How's that for no coding at all? To make this a fully functional applet, you'd need to add only a small amount of code, which we will omit here for the sake of brevity.

LISTING 11.1   GENERATED SOURCE CODE FROM NOCODE.JAVA

```
/*
    This class is a basic extension of the Applet class.  It would
generally be used as the main class with a Java browser or the
AppletViewer.  But an instance can be added to a subclass of
Container.  To use this applet with a browser or the AppletViewer,
create an html file with the following code:

    <HTML>
    <HEAD>
    <TITLE> A simple program </TITLE>
    </HEAD>
    <BODY>

    <APPLET CODE="nocode.class" WIDTH=332 HEIGHT=169></APPLET>

    </BODY>

    </HTML>

    You can add controls to nocode with Café Studio.
    (Menus can be added only to subclasses of Frame.)
 */

import java.awt.*;
import java.applet.*;

public class nocode extends Applet {

    public void init() {

        super.init();

        //{{INIT_CONTROLS
        setLayout(null);
        resize(259,240);
        group1= new CheckboxGroup();
        Cancelbtn=new Button("Cancel");
```

```
add(Cancelbtn);
Cancelbtn.reshape(144,200,104,32);
OKbtn=new Button("OK");
add(OKbtn);
OKbtn.reshape(144,160,104,32);
label1=new Label("Cousin Name");
label1.setFont(new Font("TimesRoman",Font.BOLD,12));
add(label1);
label1.reshape(8,8,112,16);
edit1=new TextField(15);
edit1.setFont(new Font("TimesRoman",Font.PLAIN,12));
add(edit1);
edit1.reshape(8,32,128,24);
Age= new Choice();
Age.setFont(new Font("TimesRoman",Font.PLAIN,12));
add(Age);
Age.reshape(152,32,48,80);
Age.addItem("18");
Age.addItem("19");
Age.addItem("20");
Age.addItem("21");
Age.addItem("22");
Age.addItem("23");
Age.addItem("24");
Age.addItem("25");
Age.addItem("26");
Age.addItem("27");
Age.addItem("28");
Age.addItem("29");
list1=new List();
list1.setFont(new Font("TimesRoman",Font.PLAIN,12));
add(list1);
list1.reshape(9,65,126,167);
list1.addItem("Gordon, Todd");
list1.addItem("Gordon, Marci");
list1.addItem("Gushurst, Jordan");
list1.addItem("Gushurst, Paul");
list1.addItem("Gusler, Evan");
list1.addItem("Gusler, Ross");
list1.addItem("Kerievsky, Dmitri");
label2=new Label("Age");
label2.setFont(new Font("TimesRoman",Font.BOLD,12));
add(label2);
label2.reshape(152,8,48,16);
USResident=new Checkbox("U.S. Resident");
USResident.setFont(new Font("TimesRoman",Font.BOLD,12));
add(USResident);
USResident.reshape(152,64,104,24);
```

```
        Male=new Checkbox("Male",group1, true);
        Male.setFont(new Font("TimesRoman",Font.BOLD,12));
        add(Male);
        Male.reshape(152,96,72,24);
        Female=new Checkbox("Female",group1, false);
        Female.setFont(new Font("TimesRoman",Font.BOLD,12));
        add(Female);
        Female.reshape(152,128,72,24);
        //}}
    }

    public boolean handleEvent(Event event) {
        return super.handleEvent(event);
    }

    //{{DECLARE_CONTROLS
    CheckboxGroup group1;
    Button Cancelbtn;
    Button OKbtn;
    Label label1;
    TextField edit1;
    Choice Age;
    List list1;
    Label label2;
    Checkbox USResident;
    Checkbox Male;
    Checkbox Female;
    //}}

}
```

Layout Managers in Café Studio

The above example, nocode.java, required no coding but did not make use of Java's powerful layout managers. Instead, in one of the first few lines of nocode's init() method, the layout manager is set to null and all components are positioned (using hardcoded numbers and the **reshape**() method) to approximately where they were in Café Studio. While this approach works fine, it does not function well when your windows are resizable. Applets can be resized simply by using the width and height parameters you can pass in to them. Standalone applications can also contain resizeable windows. In these cases, only a layout manager would know how and where to position your components after a resizing occurs.

In addition, layout managers make it easier for you to add components to a form without having to position these components perfectly within your form. By selecting the appropriate layout manager and setting components to use the layout manager's directions, you can achieve just the look you want with a minimum of effort.

Finally, layout managers let you do things that would be much more difficult without them, as we'll see shortly.

BorderLayout

BorderLayout is based on the notion that when you add components to a panel, they will be placed in some geographical location that will remain consistent throughout the life of the panel. Consistent means that if the panel is resized, the components will also be resized but will retain location and relative proportion.

The geographical directions supported by **BorderLayout** are North, East, South, West, and Center.

Let's use **BorderLayout** to build a screen quickly in Café Studio. Create a new applet project using AppExpress in Café, give the project the name "border" (project names are specified under Miscellaneous in AppExpress), accept all defaults for the project, and then get back into Café Studio by selecting Resource | Edit. Click on "Form" and you should see the words "border.init." Double-click on "border.init" and you should see a simple form with one label on it called "A border Applet."

The first step is to tell this form to use the **BorderLayout**. Double-click on the main form, and in the Properties window, under the Tab called "Layout," select the **BorderLayout**.

Now add a list component to the form and, in the Properties window, under the "Init" tab, fill the list box with some initial values—say, two or three entries. When you're done adding some entries, go to the "General" tab and, in the drop-down list box next to the field called "Place," select "South." This means that we want this list box to be placed at the bottom of our form.

Double-click on the label, "A border Applet" and in the properties window (again, under the "General Tab") set its Place to "North."

You are now ready to see what you've done. Save your work by pressing File | Save in the Café Studio (not the Café) main menu. Then go back to Café, select "Project | Rebuild All," and execute your applet. You should see something like Figure 11.3.

Not pretty, right? Let's make some changes and add some more components. Quit the applet and go back to Café Studio.

This time, click on the list box and change its "Place" value from "South" to "Center." Now add a button to the form and set its place value to "South." Save and test the applet again. You should now see components at the North, Center, and South positions, resembling Figure 11.4.

You can continue adding components for the East and West locations. Keep in mind that you may not specify the same "Place" for two components. (Actually, you *can* specify the same place, but you probably wont be happy with the results).

Remember when working with the **BorderLayout** that the "Center" component will take all the room that is left after the other components have been drawn.

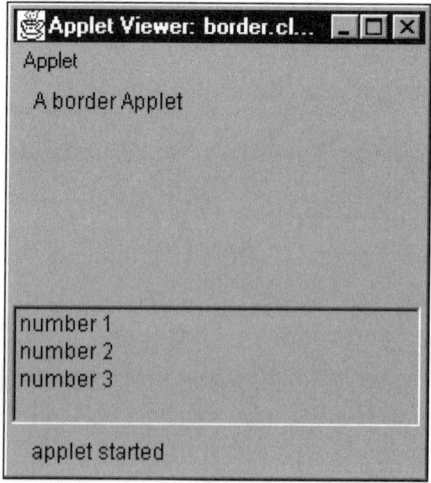

Figure 11.3   A simple applet using the BorderLayout.

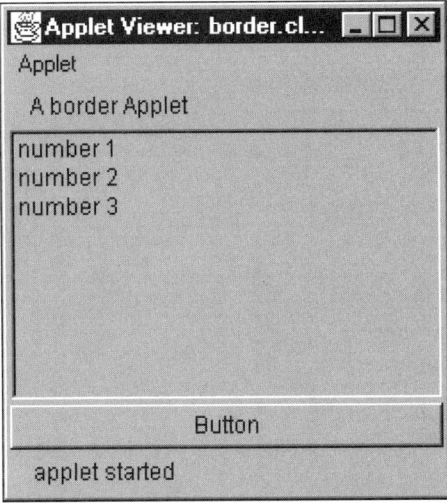

Figure 11.4   Components at North, Center, and South position using BorderLayout.

You may see the **BorderLayout** in action in some of the sample applets that come with Café. Check out the ThreadX sample applet, which is under Café\Samples\Java, as well as the BorderLayoutTest, which you will find under Café\Samples\Java\Intro\BorderLayoutTest.

FlowLayout

FlowLayout lets you group your components on a row-by-row basis. The rows start from the left, right, or center, and each component is added, using the minimal amount of space the component requires, until the process is repeated on the next row.

Let's look at an example. Create a new project using AppExpress, repeating the steps we performed in the above section on **BorderLayout**, but naming the project "flow." Then in Café Studio, double-click on "flow.init" to start editing the applet's panel.

Begin by widening the panel to twice its original size. Now add the following components to the panel: a Choice control, one button, another button (widened to about twice the size of the first button), and a horizontal scroll control. Don't worry about where you've added the components. They may appear anywhere on the panel, as you can see in Figure 11.5 (Note: I've shown the creation order of these components to make it easier to identify them).

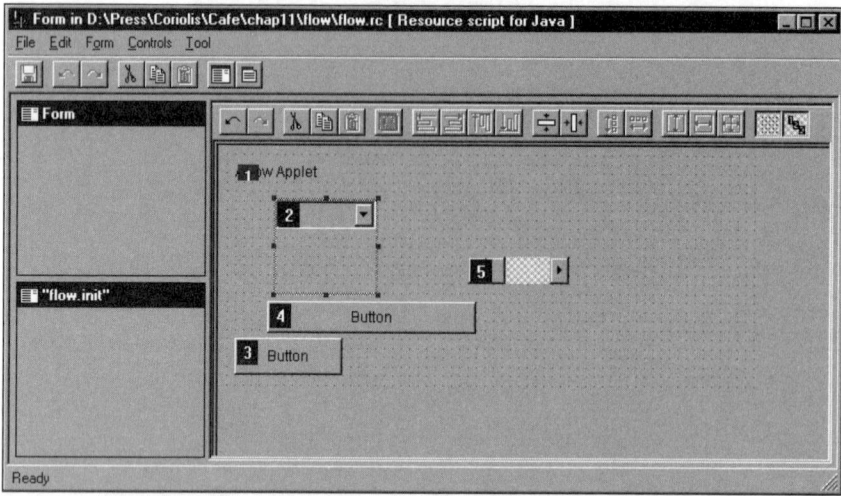

Figure 11.5   Building a form in Café Studio using FlowLayout (creation order is shown).

Save your work, go back to Café, rebuild the project, and execute it. You should see something like what is shown in Figure 11.6.

As you can see, the components are all laid out on the first row of the applet, in the center of the panel. You can also see that the minimum amount of space has been used for each component. Notice that although you widened one of the buttons in Café Studio, the **FlowLayout** manager has forced the button to use its minimal size.

Let's understand what happened. The reason the components were centered is because the **FlowLayout** manager defaults to centering components. Café

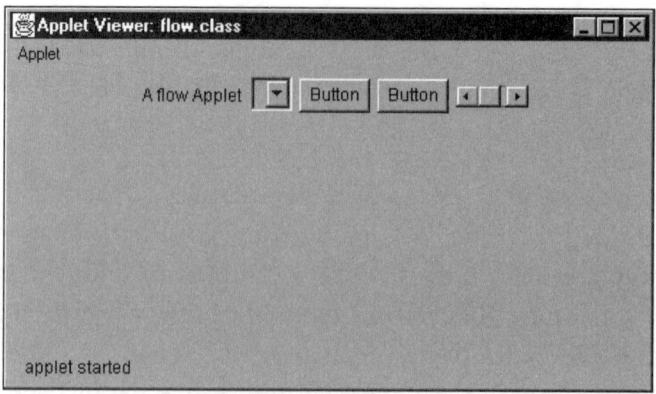

Figure 11.6   Result of building applet with FlowLayout.

Studio 1.0 does not currently allow you to specify that you would like a left or right alignment for your components. You may specify this within your code as shown below:

```
In your applet's init() method, change
    setLayout(new FlowLayout());
to
    setLayout(new FlowLayout(FlowLayout.LEFT));
```

Be advised, however, that if you change this in your code, go back to Café Studio, and redesign and save your applet, Café Studio's code generation will overwrite what you've changed. Support for left and right **FlowLayout**s will most likely come in a new version or upgrade of the product.

The shrinkage of your second button is part of the behavior of the **FlowLayout**. The idea is to get as much on a row as possible. This means that if a component on the row does not need all of the space that it initially occupied in Café Studio, it will be shrunk to a minimum size. For the case of the button, it is the button's caption that determines its size. Since the caption for the second, larger button is actually the same as the first, when the **FlowLayout** gets through with it, the button becomes the same size as the first button. To get a feel for this, try changing the caption of the second button so that it is very large. Then see how the **FlowLayout** treats it.

WORKING AROUND FLOWLAYOUT'S LIMITATIONS

At this point in the evolution of Café Studio, **FlowLayout** is supported, but missing some important functionality. If you must use this layout manager, you would do well to let Café Studio generate the initial code for you and then modify the generated code to suit your needs. Remember that when you modify code in Café Studio and save your work, you will overwrite your changes. Any code between the following comments is subject to change by the Café environment, particularly Café Studio:

```
//{{INIT_CONTROLS
//}}
```

Should you need to modify code within these comments, you may wish to write the new code outside of the comments, store it somewhere safe (like in another file), let the Café environment do its thing, and then restore your "custom" code after you've saved your work and code generation has completed.

CardLayout

CardLayout support in Café Studio is not very robust. In fact, about all Café Studio will help you do with a **CardLayout** is assign it to the layout manager with the standard call to **setLayout**(). You will need to add "cards" to any panel that uses **CardLayout** by writing your own code. You would probably want to add such code to your **init**() method, but beneath the generated code supplied by Café Studio.

GridLayout And GridBagLayout

In Release 1.0 of Café Studio, two useful layout managers, **GridLayout** and **GridBagLayout**, are not yet supported. To use these layouts, you'll need to write your own code.

The **GridLayout** lets you create components and position them in rows and columns that are all the same size. A good example may be found in the Café samples directory at \Café\Samples\Java\Intro\GridLayoutTest.

The **GridBagLayout** manager is one of the most complex layout managers and also one of the most useful. It allows you to create extremely flexible user interfaces. Components may be of many sizes and shapes, may reside next to each other and grow when resized. For doing sophisticated dialog boxes, no other layout manager comes close to this one in what it can deliver. But you will most certainly face a bit of a learning curve in getting to know it. In fact, it is not unreasonable to guess that this layout manager was not supported in Café Studio 1.0 because of its complexity. Nevertheless, it is well worth knowing and you may wish to study the code supplied in three Sample applets that use GridBag, which may be found at \Café\Samples\Java\Intro\GridBagTest1, \Café\Samples\Java\Intro\ GridBagTest2, and \Café\Samples\Java\Intro\GridBagTest3.

In the next section, you will learn more about some of Café Studio's most useful utilities.

FormExpress

When you work with Café Studio, you'll be creating resources that will be saved within an .rc resource file. Café Studio takes a project's resource file and generates Java source code from it. Before this code generation process takes place, however, Café Studio lets you specify where you would like generated code to be placed within your project.

You can control where generated code gets placed by using tools like FormExpress. This simple utility allows you to specify whether you would like to place generated code within a method of an existing class in your project or within a newly created class. In addition, FormExpress has some extra features that give you even more control over the types of classes that get generated in your project.

To start FormExpress from the main Café Studio window, right-click on the lower-left-hand pane and select "New Form" or simply press the icon associated with new forms off the toolbar. A picture of what FormExpress looks like is shown in Figure 11.7.

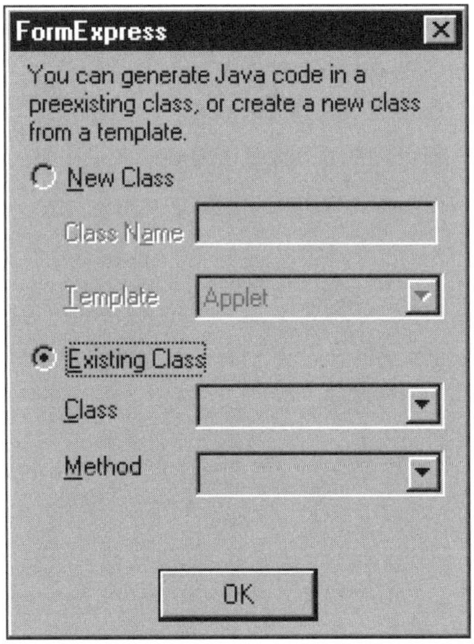

Figure 11.7   Café Studio's FormExpress.

Templates and an Undocumented Café Studio Secret

Now for some real inside information about Café Studio. Below, you will be shown a way of working with an undocumented feature of Café Studio that will make it possible for you to generate the kinds of forms you like, faster than you ever thought possible.

When you create a new form in Café Studio, you use FormExpress. In the FormExpress dialog, you are given an opportunity to select where you want new Java source code from your newest form to be placed. You may choose to have the new code placed within an existing class or within a brand-new class. Should you elect to have the new code placed into a brand-new class, you are asked to choose two things: a name for the new class and a template.

The name may be anything you like (as well as any length) provided the name is not the same as an existing class. The template must be selected from a list. But what is a template? I'm glad you asked.

Your new class may be based upon an existing Java class and may therefore "extend" that existing class. The existing classes are referred to here as templates. You may choose from one of the following as shown in Table 11.1. Depending upon the template you select, different code will be generated. If you select an application template, your code will contain a number of methods, one of which will have the following signature:

```
public static void main(String args[])
```

Table 11.1   Templates in FormExpress.

Template Name
Applet
Application
Dialog
Frame
Panel
Window

If you select a panel template, your new class will not have a **main**() method but, instead, will have a constructor method.

But what if you have a class named RunnableApplet from which you often create descendants? This would mean that every time you wanted to create a new descendent of RunnableApplet, you'd have to type in the same code over and over again. In addition, you might have to remember which methods need to be overridden. This will surely waste your time as you repeatedly go back to the RunnableApplet source file, study its contents, and then decide what you need to type.

Or what if someone else wants to "extend" one of your custom classes? Again, they would need to go study your parent class just to find out what to override and when.

Luckily, there is an undocumented feature of Café Studio that we can exploit; it lets us have our own custom entries in the template listbox.

In the Café\Bin directory, you will find a text file named Javacex.txt. This file is the template file for Café Studio. It can be modified to suit your own needs, but before you start fiddling around with it, you'd be wise to make a backup copy of the file.

The Javacex.txt file contains a minilanguage that is used to specify a new template name and how code is to be generated from the template. Let's take a look at an example of this language and then we'll review the symbols of the minilanguage.

The code from Javacex.txt that makes up the Applet template is listed below in Listing 11.2:

LISTING 11.2   JAVACEX.TXT CODE FOR APPLET TEMPLATE

```
..
.. Café Studio template file. Version 3.5
..
.template Applet
.nomenu
.default init
.classname __applet
.code
```

```
/*
     This class is a basic extension of the Applet class.  It would
generally be used as the main class with a Java browser or the
AppletViewer.  But an instance can be added to a subclass of
Container.  To use this applet with a browser or the AppletViewer,
create an html file with the following code:

     <HTML>
     <HEAD>
     <TITLE>__applet window</TITLE>
     </HEAD>
     <BODY>

     <APPLET CODE="__applet.class" WIDTH=332 HEIGHT=169></APPLET>

     </BODY>

     </HTML>

     You can add controls to Simple with Café Studio.
     (Menus can be added only to subclasses of Frame.)
 */

import java.awt.*;

public class __applet extends java.applet.Applet {
    public void init() {
        //{{INIT_CONTROLS
        resize(332, 169);
        //}}
        super.init();
    }
    public boolean handleEvent(Event event) {
        return super.handleEvent(event);
    }
    //{{DECLARE_CONTROLS
    //}}
}
```

The simple language used to specify the above "Applet" template is composed of six symbols, which are summarized below in Table 11.2.

We'll conclude this section by adding our own template to the Javacex.txt file. We'll call the new template RunnableApplet, which will be a version of an Applet that implements Java's Runnable interface. We'll define our new

Table 11.2   Symbols and their meaning in the Javacex.txt.

Symbol	Meaning
..	comment: anything after the dot dot will be ignored.
.template X	where X is the name of the template.
.nomenu	tells Café Studio to now include this template in the new Menu dialog box.
.default foo	normally, code goes into a class constructor; using this symbol plus a method name, foo, code will be generated and placed inside method foo.
.classname Y	a macro equal to the name entered by the user during new class creation.
.code	begin including whatever follows into the generated .java file — go until next .template or end-of-file (EOF) is encountered.

template as follows (and we'll add it to the end of the Javacex.txt file) in Listing 11.3:

LISTING 11.3   TEMPLATE CODE FOR THE RUNNABLEAPPLET TEMPLATE

```
.template RunnableApplet
.nomenu
.default init
.classname __runApplet
.code
/*
    This class is a basic extension of the Applet class.  It would
 generally be
    used as the main class with a Java browser or the AppletViewer.
 But an instance
    can be added to a subclass of Container.  To use this applet with
 a browser or
    the AppletViewer, create an html file with the following code:

    <HTML>
    <HEAD>
    <TITLE>__runApplet window</TITLE>
    </HEAD>
    <BODY>
```

```
    <APPLET CODE="__runApplet.class" WIDTH=332 HEIGHT=169></APPLET>

    </BODY>

    </HTML>

    You can add controls to Simple with Café Studio.
    (Menus can be added only to subclasses of Frame.)
 */

import java.awt.*;

public class __runApplet extends java.applet.Applet implements
 Runnable {

    public void init() {

        //{{INIT_CONTROLS
        resize(332, 169);
        //}}

        super.init();
    }

    void pause(int time) {
      try { Thread.sleep(time); }
      catch (InterruptedException e) {}
    }

    public void run() {
      // add your run code here
    }

    public boolean handleEvent(Event event) {
        return super.handleEvent(event);
    }

    //{{DECLARE_CONTROLS
    //}}
}
```

You can see in the above code that we've included a pause method and a run method and have made the new class implement the Runnable interface. The additions we've made to this template class are relatively simple; you could create more complex templates that would enable you or others to produce sophisticated descendents with but a few simple mouse clicks in Café Studio. One note of caution: At this point, if you add UI components to one of your template classes, these components will be ignored by Café Studio. For now, add as much non-UI code as you like and leave the UI stuff to the Café Studio environment.

MenuEXPRESS

Like FormExpress, MenuExpress makes it easy for you to create and place Java menu code wherever you want it in your project. You use the same steps to invoke this utility as you do with FormExpress: by right-clicking in the bottom-left corner of the main Café Studio screen or by clicking the "New menu" icon on the toolbar.

Whenever you create your first menu, you'll see a new entry named "Menu" added to the listbox in the upper-left portion of Café Studio. When you click on this entry, you'll see all of the menus you design in the lower-left listbox.

Editing Menus (or Forms) in Separate Windows

Note that when you're working with either Forms or Menus, you can do so in a window separate from the main Café Studio window. Just select the form or menu you'd like to work with in the lower-left corner of Café Studio, right-click, and select "Edit in Separate Window."

Menus can be added to either Java Applications or Frames (if you want to create a menu in an applet, you'll need to create one on a Frame and then create, show, hide, and destroy the Frame within the applet). If you select "New Class" in MenuExpress and choose a template, you'll see that only entries for Application and Frame are present. As before, you may add new entries to the Javacex.txt file to provide new template entrics. Just remember *not* to include the "nomenu" symbol when you create new entries.

Let's now get some hands-on experience working with Java menus in Café Studio. We'll first use AppExpress to create a standalone application, which we'll call FontMan. In this example, we will not create a menu from scratch, but instead allow AppExpress to do much of the initial work of setting up the application menu.

After creating the project with AppExpress, select "Resource" from the main menu and then choose "Edit." Once inside Café Studio, you'll see that AppExpress created some forms for you as well as a fairly substantial menu. Click on "Menu" and you should see something like you do in Figure 11.8.

As you can see, you've already got File, Edit, and Help items on the main menu. If you look back at the project in Café and examine the file FontMan.java, you'll see a significant amount of code that creates the menu structure and that handles events, such as when the "About" or "Exit" commands are selected.

We will now add some more items to this menu. Click on the top entry in the menu, the one that says "MenuBar." Now right-click on this entry and you will see the selection, "New Menu." Choose "New Menu" and you will see two new entries added to the menu (one says Menu: New Menu and the other says "End of Menu"). You are now ready to customize these new entries. Simply click on the first one, Menu: New Menu, and you will see the properties window display the values for this menu item. In the properties window, under the "General" tab, type in "Format" for the text field. When you're done, click back on the original menu item and you will see its name change.

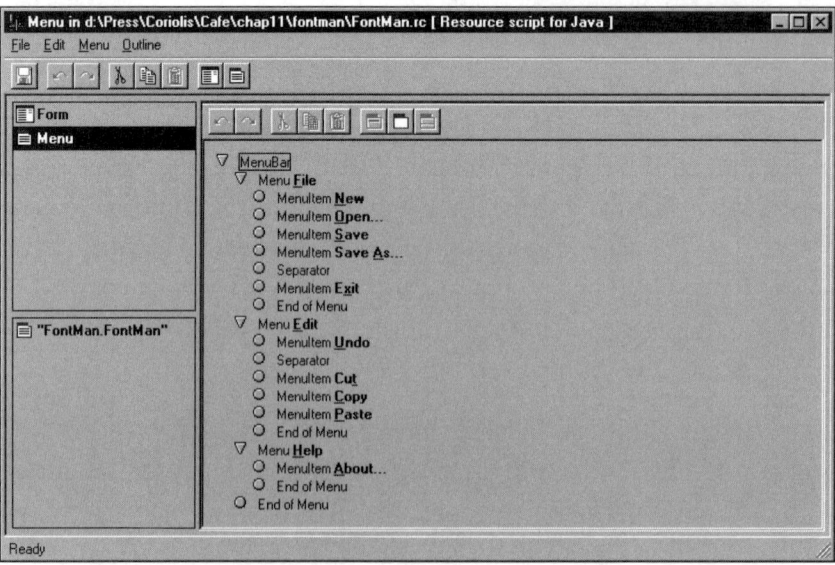

Figure 11.8   A Menu created by AppExpress.

At this point let's position the "Format" portion of the menu where we would like it. Right-click on it and select "Move Down." You will see that it is moved past the File menu and before the Edit menu. Do the same thing again to position the "Format" menu after the "Edit" menu.

Now position your mouse on the Format menu, right-click, and press "New Menu Item." (Alternatively, you could use the toolbar instead of right-clicking.) When you add a new item to the menu you are positioned on the new item and the properties window is updated. In the properties window, shown in Figure 11.9, you can see that there are tabs for general information about the menu item as well as event information. As you'll see shortly, it is quite easy to hook up an event to a menu item using MenuExpress.

We'll now change the text of the new menu item to say "Font" and give the menu item a member class name, such as itemFont. Testing the new menu requires almost no work. Café Studio keeps a window open called "Test Menu" that contains a working version of the menu we've just created. Click on the Format item and you should see the "Font" item. In addition, you may click on the main panel of the Test Menu window to work with a pop-up menu version of your menu.

Working With Menu Events

We're now ready to hook up our new menu item, Font, to a handler. Again, Café Studio makes this a very simple task so you don't have to search to find the right signature of the correct handler.

To add a handler to the Font item, select the Font item in the menu, go to the properties sheet, select the "Events" tab, choose "selected" (it should

Figure 11.9   The properties sheet after adding a new menu item.

already be highlighted), and then press the "Edit" button. You're now prompted to give a name to your handler, which we will leave as the default, selectedItemFont. When you press "Yes," some code will be generated, you'll be taken to the Café Class Editor, and positioned on the member function, selectedItemFont() as shown in Figure 11.10.

If you look in the upper-right portion of the Class Editor (where it says "Members of FontMan"), you'll see the other handlers that have been added to the project. Click on "selectedAbout" and you will see the code behind this menu item in the lower portion of the Class Editor window.

That concludes our section on Menus in Café Studio. By now, you should have a very good feel for creating your own menus, making them look the way you want them to and specifying which events they respond to. In the next section, we'll learn more about events.

Working with Events

One of hardest things about programming in object-oriented languages is the constant need to see which "services" are supported for a given object. You must often go back to an ancestor (or superclass) to see what

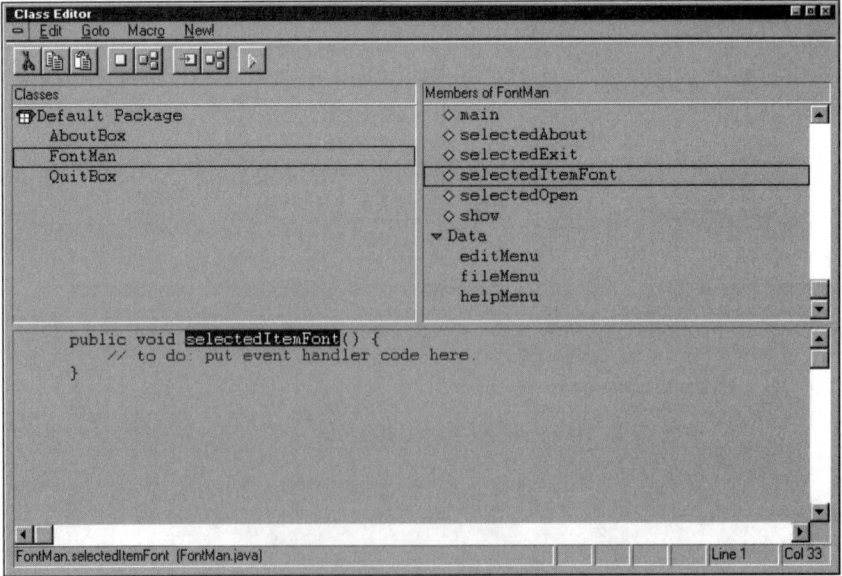

Figure 11.10   Café Class Editor after adding a new Event handler.

functionality is supported. "This class inherits that method, but not that one, this member variable, but not that one, etc." When it comes to AWT events, this can be a very time consuming process, because every component in Java responds to different events.

The designers of Café knew this and decided to make your life a whole lot easier.

We briefly looked at events in the section above on Menus. We saw that the generated menu responded to certain events. In Café Studio, when you design your forms, you may also specify the events to which the form or components on the form respond.

If you simply add a button to a form, double-click the button to bring up the Properties window, and then look at the "Events" tab you will see the list of events shown in Figure 11.11.

If you double-click on any of the events in this list, you'll be prompted to supply a handler method. (In the dialog box this is labeled a "member name" but it actually translates to a new method in your class that handles the particular event you selected). When you supply or accept the given name, you'll see a small red dot appear next to the event in the list and you'll be dropped into the Café Class Editor. Your new handler method will appear in the lower pane of the Class Editor window, ready for you to add code. Pretty simple, huh?

Back in Café Studio, if you ever need to see the code defined in a handler you've written for a particular component, just go to the "Events" tab on the Properties window, select the event associated with the handler (you'll

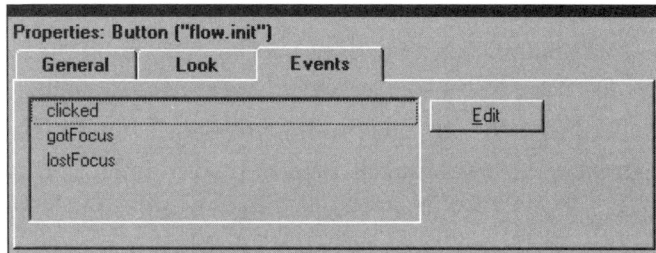

Figure 11.11   Events to which the button component responds.

see actual name of this handler in addition to the red dot) and press the "Edit" button. You'll be placed back inside the Class Editor.

Of all the components that you can place on a panel, the panel component itself has the longest list of events to which it responds. Remember that you can place panels within panels to get even greater control over what part of your form handles an event.

Maintaining Your HandleEvent Method

When you add event handlers to your classes, Café Studio updates a method called handleEvent in your project's source code. In the code snippet below, you can see the result of supplying a handler for the GotFocus event of a button named Button2:

```
public boolean handleEvent(Event event) {
        if (event.id == Event.GOT_FOCUS && event.target == button2) {
                gotFocusButton2(event);
                return true;
        }
        return super.handleEvent(event);
    }

(code excerped for the sake of brevity)

public void gotFocusButton2(Event ev) {
        // to do: put event handler code here.
    }
```

The handleEvent method contains the call to the handler name you specified in the Properties window. It is important to remember that although Café Studio creates the code for your handleEvent method, it does not fully control this generated code with respect to everything that you may do in Café Studio. That is, should you decide to change the name of Button2 to btnCalcExposure within Café Studio, your gotFocusButton2 handler will remain in the code as will the call to gotFocusButton2 inside the handleEvent method. If you later choose to add a new handler for btnCalcExposure, your new handleEvent method will keep *both* handlers in the code, as shown in the code snippet below:

```
public boolean handleEvent(Event event) {
        if (event.id == Event.ACTION_EVENT && event.target ==
  btnCalcExposure) {
                clickedBtnCalcExposure();
                return true;
        }
        else
        if (event.id == Event.GOT_FOCUS && event.target == button2) {
                gotFocusButton2(event);
                return true;
        }

        return super.handleEvent(event);
    }
```

It is your responsibility to maintain both the handleEvent method and the handlers that you create via the "Events" tab in the Café Studio Properties window.

That concludes out look at working with Events in Café Studio. Next, we'll see what was left out of release 1.0 of Café Studio and give you an idea of what may be coming in future releases.

What Café Studio Doesn't Support

As we've seen in this chapter, Café Studio is a tool that lets you do some pretty powerful development without having to write code. Symantec Café was the first commercially available integrated development (and debugging) environment for Java, and for a version 1.0 product, it is quite good. But being first to market also sometimes means that some features are put on hold for later release. In this section, we'll explore what Café Studio does not support so that you know what you will need to write yourself.

Custom Components

The major missing feature right now is the lack of support for custom components. What are custom components? They are components that you or other developers write, which are often descendents of existing components (like labels), and which you may prefer to use in your applets because of their extra functionality. Unfortunately, in Version 1.0 of Café

Studio, you cannot add these custom components to the toolbox that contains all of the "native" components like the button, label, and scrollbar. According to Symantec, support for custom components has been the number-one requested new feature for Café Studio, and chances are this request will be fullfilled by Symantec.

WYSIWYG Screen Testing

When you design a menu in Café Studio, you can see exactly what it is going to look like by simply checking out the "Test Menu" window. This window keeps track of any changes you make in the Menu Editor and immediatly reflects them in its window.

Unfortunately, this same feature is not currently supported for forms. The developers of Café have been asked for this feature as well, so we will see if support for it is added to a later version. For now, to see the results of your work on forms, you'll need to save your work in Café Studio, go back to Café, rebuild your project, and finally test it to see that appearance of your form.

Canvas Components

Of the "native" Java components, the only one that is not supported is the Canvas component as you can see in Table 11.3 below.

Combo Boxes, Grids, and More

If you're a Windows or Mac developer looking at the list of components above, you may be scratching your head wondering "where's the combo box, where's the grid or the guage component?" The answer is that Symantec Café supports the native components within the JDK (with the exception of Canvas) and the more sophisticated ones, like combo boxes and grids, will most certainly be supplied by third-party vendors in the near future.

Color

Support for Color has also not been added to Café Studio. This is an important point to keep in mind if you have only been programming using Symantec's Café. Remember that Java components like the Label support the setting of background and foreground colors. There is simply no way of setting these colors in the Café Studio properties window at present.

Table 11.3   UI Components Supported by Café Studio 1.0.

UI Component	Support by Café Studio 1.0
Button	Yes
Canvas	No
Checkbox	Yes
Choice	Yes
Label	Yes
List	Yes
Scrollbar	Yes
Text Area	Yes
TextField	Yes

Insets

Insets are like frames that you can put around panels, like the main panel of a Java applet. Support for insets has also not been worked into the Café Studio, yet. Insets also provide a flexible way of pushing your components down, up, to the left or right, or for just framing them all for aesthetic reasons.

All Layout Managers

Three of the five Layout managers defined in the JDK are supported by Café. One of the three, the **CardLayout** is really only partially supported by the product. Table 11.4 presents a complete list.

Table 11.4   Layout Managers supported by Café Studio 1.0.

Layout Manager in JDK 1.0	Support by Café Studio 1.0
BorderLayout	Yes
CardLayout	Yes
FlowLayout	Yes
GridLayout	No
GridBagLayout	No

Some Known Problems

There are a few known problems in Café Studio that may be fixed in an update but exist as of Version 1.0. These problems were compiled by Symantec and are listed below for your edification:

◆ Creating new classes in Café Studio when it is running as a stand-alone application requires that the RC be saved before a new resource (Form or Menu) can be added. Once the RC has been saved, Café Studio will generate the appropriate .java files in the same directory as the .rc file.

◆ When renaming controls or menus, Café Studio will update the init and declaration areas within the corresponding Java file accordingly. We are able to do this because of the tags used by Café Studio. However, it is the responsibility of the developer to manually update all other methods that may be affected by this change. For example, the handleEvent method.

◆ There are currently bugs in AWT font-mapping that may prevent the fonts in your controls from exactly matching the edited version. If the fonts look different in your browser, you might try using "Helvetica" instead of "Dialog" for your font.

◆ It is not possible to back out of Form or Menu Express. Instead enter a value into the existing class and member fields and then delete the resource.

◆ When editing method names in the property sheet, you must enter an existing class and method name (class.method). A new class and method name cannot be created from the property sheet.

◆ When panels are embedded, it is important to pay attention to the creation order of the panels (this is not a problem with controls). The outermost panels need to be created before the inner ones: otherwise, a runtime error will occur (a NullPointerException will be thrown).

Our Journey Ends

We've come a long way! Our journey into the very heart of Café Studio has taken us through many aspects of this very powerful piece of the Symantec Café product. I hope it has been an eye opener for you!

Before working with Café Studio, you may not realize just how much work you've been doing manually. But as soon as you start working with a tool like Café Studio, you may quickly see just how much more productive you may become. While it is not a replacement for everything involving user interface design, Café Studio is certainly a powerful addition to have in your arsenal of Java development tools. Good luck with your future interface designs!

Managing Multitasking

John Rodley

12

A powerful aspect of the Java language is its robust support of Threads. In this chapter you'll learn the basic concepts behind using threads to manage multitasking.

*F*or years, multiprocessing systems have allowed you to run multiple processes (programs) simultaneously. More recently, many operating systems have begun to support multithreading, allowing programmers to spawn multiple subprocesses, or *threads*, within each process.

Threads differ significantly from processes. In a non-multithreaded system, there are only processes and related processes. Related processes share only open file handles. In a multithreaded system, each process is made up of from *1 to n* threads and all the threads in the process generally share global variables as well as open file handles. This sharing of global variables makes it very easy for threads to share work product, while remaining single-mindedly dedicated to their assigned task.

To get a better handle on the shift from single-threaded to multithreaded programming, picture a company where every employee has his own building (complete with telephone system, bathroom, cafeteria, office supplies, and parking lot). Each employee can do his job as long as everything he needs is in his building, a condition the company goes to great expense to try to ensure. Any job that requires access to another employee's work product is immensely complicated and requires a considerable amount of communication. If the boss wants something done, he has to pick up the phone. This is the single-process/single-thread model. Now, put all those employees into a single building. You immediately get less cumbersome communication and more efficient resource utilization. This is the single-process/multithread model.

Java is an inherently multithreaded language. As such, it depends on operating system support for threads and multitasking. This is one of the reasons that, as of this writing, Java has not been ported to and Cafe has not been written for the immensely popular Windows 3.1 operating system. In fact, to see just how multithreaded Java is, we need only look at **Object**, the base class for all Java classes. Six of **Object's** twelve public methods involve thread control and inter-thread communication.

Creating Threads

Java encapsulates the notion of a thread in a class named, appropriately enough, **Thread**. Figure 12.1 shows you where the **Thread** class fits into the system class hierarchy while Table 12.1 lists the methods for the **Thread** class. This class incorporates most of the thread attributes and control methods available to programmers who write to the native operating system thread control API.

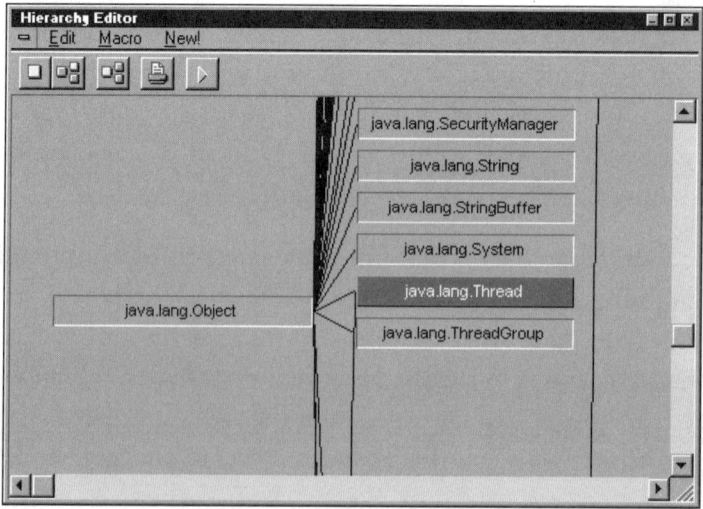

Figure 12.1   The Thread Class in the Java Class Hierarchy.

Table 12.1   Methods of the Thread Class.

Method	Description
public Thread()	Creates a new thread. Underlying operating system thread is not created until Thread.start is called. This applies to all Thread constructors.
public Thread(String NAME)	Creates a new thread with the specified name.
public Thread(ThreadGroup GROUP, String NAME)	Creates a new thread with the specified name and adds it to the specified ThreadGroup.
public Thread(Runnable TARGET)	Creates a new thread from an object implementing the Runnable interface.
public Thread(ThreadGroup GROUP, Runnable TARGET)	Creates a new thread from an object implementing the Runnable interface and adds it to the specified ThreadGroup.
public Thread(Runnable TARGET, String NAME)	Constructs a new thread from an object implementing the Runnable interface and sets its name to NAME.
public Thread(ThreadGroup GROUP, Runnable TARGET, String NAME)	Same as previous, but adds the thread to the specified ThreadGroup.
public static int activeCount()	Returns the number of active threads in this thread group; does not include subterannean threads.
public int countStackFrames()	Returns the number of stack frames in this thread. The thread must be suspended for this to work. Throws IllegalStateException if thread is not suspended.
public static Thread currentThread()	Returns the currently executing Thread object.
public void destroy()	Kills the thread without cleanup. The equivalent of Unix's "kill -9" for Java threads.
public static void dumpStack()	Dumps the stack for the current thread.
public static int enumerate (Thread tarray[])	Copies references to every active thread into the supplied Thread array. Returns the number of threads in the array.

Continued

Table 12.1   Methods of the Thread Class (continued).

public String getName()	Returns the thread's name; that is, whatever name was assigned by setName. If no name has been set using setName, Java assigns a name of the form "Thread-N" where N indicates that this is the Nth thread to be created in this thread group.
public int getPriority()	Returns the thread's priority. This will be a value between Thread.MIN_PRIORITY and Thread.MAX_PRIORITY.
public boolean isAlive()	Returns true if the underlying operating system thread is executing; that is, if start has been called successfully and stop has not been called yet. Also returns true if a running thread has been suspended. Equivalent to asking if Thread.run is still executing.
public boolean isDaemon()	Returns true if this is a daemon thread, that is, if a successful call to setDaemon(true) has been made.
public synchronized void join	Waits for NUM_MILLISECS milliseconds for this thread to die. Waits forever(int num_millisecs) if NUM_MILLISECS is 0.
public synchronized void join()	Waits forever for this thread to die. Do not call join on your own thread. Always use in a construction such as: Thread x = new Thread(); x.start(); x.join().
public void resume()	Resumes execution of a suspended thread. Throws IllegalStateException if thread was not suspended.
public void run()	Overrides this method with the main loop for the new thread. This is the method that runs in the new operating system thread.

Table 12.1   Methods of the Thread Class (continued).

public void setDaemon	Sets the threads daemon status to ʙDᴀᴇᴍᴏɴ. If true, Thread becomes a (boolean ʙDᴀᴇᴍᴏɴ) daemon thread. Must be called before the thread becomes active; that is, before any call to Thread.start.
public void setName	Sets the thread's name to newName. Can be called at any point in the (String newName) thread's life.
public void setPriority(int	Sets the threads priority to ɴᴇᴡPʀɪᴏʀɪᴛʏ. Throws Thread.MIN_PRIORITY to Thread.MAX_PRIORITY.
public static void sleep(int ᴍɪʟʟɪs)	Tells the current thread to pause for ᴍɪʟʟɪs milliseconds.
public synchronized void start()	Causes Java to create a new operating system thread and begin running the run method in the new thread. Returns immediately, usually before the thread has begun execution.
public synchronized void stop()	Stops a thread by throwing a ThreadDeath object. If the thread has not started, it will be killed immediately rather than waiting for it to start.
public void suspend()	Suspends the thread. Calls resume to restart the thread.
public String toString()	Returns a String that includes the thread name, priority, and thread group.
public static void yield()	Yields this thread's time slice to the next thread waiting to execute. Has no effect if there are no threads available to execute.

There are two types of **Thread** constructors that correspond with the two different ways of getting an object to run in its own thread. The first, most obvious, is to subclass the **Thread** class. This is entirely reasonable and is the method most often used. The other way to do it is to subclass **Socket**, thereby also creating a thread.

Thread Groups

You may have noticed in Table 12.1 that some of the **Thread** constructors take a **ThreadGroup** argument. As you have studied the JDK, you may remember how **Component**s are grouped into **Container**s to facilitate operations on collections of **Component** objects. **ThreadGroup** performs a similar function in thread control—to group threads into one lump where they can be operated on as a group, and to protect threads from each other.

The Runnable Interface

In a multiple-inheritance situation, the subclassing constructor would be all you'd need because all runnable objects could simply inherit **Thread** with all their other superclasses. But Java doesn't allow multiple inheritance, and it doesn't seem reasonable to create a long inheritance branch (with **Thread** up near the root) simply to make something runnable.

Fortunately, there's a second style of **Thread** constructor. This one takes an object that implements the **Runnable** interface as one of its parameters.

The **Runnable** interface has only a single method: **run**. The **run** method contains the main loop of a **Runnable** object.

The start and run Methods

When I think of a **Thread** object, what immediately comes to mind is a thread that begins execution with the constructor of the object, and terminates after the destructor returns. This is most emphatically *not* the case with Java **Thread** objects (or almost any objectified threads). The **Thread** constructor and the **start** method both execute in the thread *from* which they were invoked. Only the **run** method executes in the new thread. Of course, this means that any method invoked from within the **run** method will also execute in the new thread.

But no matter which type of **Thread** you create, it's important to realize just what methods execute in which thread.

Though we call the whole class **Thread**, you should really think of the **run** method and the underlying operating system thread as one and the same. The first line of the **run** method is the first line of Java code executed by the new thread, and the return from the **run** method is the last line of Java code executed by the new thread. This is why every **run** method you see will be some sort of loop. In essence, the **run** method is the equivalent of **main**() in a single-threaded C program. Everything that happens in the new thread starts within the **run** method. (Conversely, if you can't trace an instruction back to somewhere within the **run** method, it didn't happen in that thread!) When the **run** method returns, the thread disappears from the system. In fact, **run** never really returns. Because it executes independently, it has nowhere to return to.

The **run** method is never explicitly called. Instead, we invoke the **start** method which causes Java to create a new operating system thread that executes the **run** method. One of the most frustrating mistakes you can make in Java is to create a **Thread**, then forget to invoke **Thread.start**(). Another mistake (and yes, I've made it) is to invoke **run** rather than **start**. In that case, **run** executes in the invoking thread, and the code you thought would execute in the invoking thread never does, because **run** is running and doesn't return immediately the way **start** would.

Another thing to keep in mind is that **Applet.start** and **Thread.start** are fundamentally different things. **Applet.start** is designed to be overridden to do whatever needs doing when the user leaves a page. **Thread.start** should never be overridden, because it contains the functionality that actually creates the new operating system thread.

Thread Control

We've seen that the **Thread** object and the underlying operating system thread are not the same thing. You can actually have a **Thread** object without an underlying operating system thread. There are two points in a **Thread**'s life when this is the case: before the **start** method is invoked (the thread hasn't been created yet) and after the **run** method returns (the thread has already disappeared).

Thus, the **Thread** class is actually made up of the underlying operating system thread (the **run** method) and a set of thread monitoring and control methods. Some methods can be invoked from outside the thread (outside the **run** method) and some can't. Table 12.2 shows which **Thread** methods can be invoked on the current thread, and which need to be invoked against an external thread.

start and **stop** are used to create and destroy the underlying operating system thread. You must invoke **start** to create the thread, but you don't need to use **stop** to get rid of it. Most applets rely on the return from the **run** method to destroy the thread.

Table 12.2   Current and External Thread Invocation.

Method Name	Applies to Current Thread	Applies to Other Thread	Applies to All Threads
activeCount			X
checkAccess	X	X	
countStackFrames	X		
currentThread	X		
destroy	X	X	
dumpStack	X		
enumerate			X
getName	X	X	
getPriority	X	X	
getThreadGroup	X	X	
interrupt		X	
interrupted	X		
isAlive	X	X	
isDaemon	X	X	
isInterrupted		X	
join		X	
resume		X	
run	-	-	-
setDaemon	X		
setName	X		
setPriority	X	X	
sleep	X		
start		X	
stop		X	X
suspend	X	X	
toString	X	X	
yield	X		

We can also pause a thread with the **suspend** method. This method halts thread execution but leaves the thread in memory, allowing us to **resume** execution right where we left off when **suspend** was invoked. Later on, with animation, we create a series of threads, and **suspend** or **resume** them according to the activity of the remote agents.

join is another important thread-control mechanism. The point of calling **join** is to simply wait for the thread you're calling **join** against to die. For Unix types, it's the equivalent of **wait**ing for a child process. **join** is actually an easy concept, made difficult by a stupid label. In real life, if I join you, we both continue to exist. In threads, when one thread **join**s another, the one **join**ed must die before the **join**er can continue. By all rights, this method should have been named "waitForTheDeathOf."

Thread Attributes

Each thread has three attributes that can be set and queried: *name, priority,* and *daemon status.* The thread name is just that, an identifier we can attach to the **Thread**. Java itself doesn't use thread names for anything and there's no requirement for thread names to be unique. Internally to Java, threads are identified by the unique handle the operating system gives them.

Thread priority is also a straightforward concept, exactly analogous to process priority under Unix. Higher priority threads are scheduled (by the operating system) to run more frequently than lower priority threads. Priority can be changed on the fly via **Thread.setPriority**. Different operating systems use different ranges for priority values. Some even flip the precedence, with lower values getting higher priority. Thus, Java defines three constants, **MIN_PRIORITY**, **NORM_PRIORITY**, and **MAX_PRIORITY**. Any time you set the priority of a Java **Thread**, use a number based on these constants.

The concept of daemon status, though common to most multithreaded systems, is a little more difficult to explain. The Java interpreter also will not exit until all non-daemon threads have terminated. In essence, the interpreter **join**s all non-daemon threads before exiting. Giving a thread daemon status essentially frees it from that control, allowing the interpreter to exit without waiting for the thread to terminate. A thread should be made daemon unless it absolutely *must* do some cleanup (other than memory management), like closing open files, before the system exits.

Daemon status is set via **Thread.setDaemon**, which must be invoked *before* the **Thread**'s **start** method gets invoked (that is, before the underlying system thread actually starts executing). I generally put it in the constructor.

When Do Applet Threads Run?

One of the first questions that arises when you start spawning multiple threads is determining when each of these threads will be running. Consider the following scenario: a user enters a page that contains an applet and a single link to another HTML page. The browser reads the <applet> tag, loads the applet, and sets it running. The user then clicks on the hyperlink, taking him to another page. The page with your applet in it disappears, but what happens to the thread running on the user's machine that contains your applet code? The short answer, as you might expect, is that it stops running. No surprise there.

But what if you want this applet, or at least some threads within it, to keep running even after the user is no longer viewing the page on which the applet resides?

To create this behavior, you must break one of the cardinal rules of applet writing, which says that when the browser invokes **Applet.stop** against your applet, you should stop running. When the browser invokes **Applet.stop** against this applet, the only thread we would terminate would be the one that updates the display window, which of course we don't need when the user is looking at another page. All the other threads remain running.

Shared Resources and Synchronization

One issue that single-threaded programmers never have to deal with is coordinating access to shared resources. By shared resources, we mean anything that more than one thread needs to use. In most cases, this means a file or a block of memory. We need to coordinate access because we're doing a series of operations on the resource that need to happen in one lump so that other threads don't see partial changes.

One of the ways we coordinate access to shared resources is via synchronized methods/blocks. There are many places in an application where synchronized methods/blocks might be useful. Suppose you are writing strings to a results file and many different threads can be responsible for populating this shared results file.

The key feature of scenario could be a method that uses the **synchronized** keyword in its declaration. The situation we want to avoid is one where two threads invoke the method at the same time and calls to **println** get interlaced. The **synchronized** keyword in the method declaration guarantees that only one copy of the method can be running at one time.

Efficient Serialization

One must be careful when using the **synchronized** keyword, however, because it can prevent code from running that does not need to be synchronized. That is, synchronizing a method locks the entire method when all you may really need to do is lock a part of the method. In the example above of writing to a results file, you would want to ensure, for the purpose of efficient serialization, that synchronization only occurs during your invocations to **println**.

So your method itself must no longer be synchronized. Multiple threads can invoke the method without blocking waiting for another thread to finish with it. What you'll add, however, is a synchronized block within the method, which creates the smallest possible window of time where one thread might be waiting for another to finish working.

Each object in the system has a lock associated with it. In most cases, the lock is not used. Various threads can use the object without restriction. However, when thread A invokes a **synchronized** method (or block), it "acquires" the lock for the object associated with that **synchronized** method (or block). If thread B has already acquired the lock, thread A waits until thread B releases the lock before it executes the **synchronized** method.

This locking mechanism is exactly analogous to the more familiar record, table, and file locking that current operating systems and DBMSs provide. In DBMS record and table locking, we try never to lock more code than is absolutely necessary. Each time a thread fails to acquire a lock, it (and possibly the user) waits until the lock is released. This is wasted time that should be kept to an absolute minimum.

As you begin to use synchronized methods and block, *be careful.* Remember that many synchronization issues have already been addressed by the Java language. The method, **println,** is itself **synchronized.** Considerable care has been taken with the multithreading issues in Java, so it's often the case that the level of synchronization you need is already implemented. Don't go around synchronizing blocks and methods until you're sure the synchronization you need isn't already there.

It's often hard for people to grasp the pervasiveness of synchronization situations, especially if they're new to the multithreading world. For a quick indication, flip through the class documentation and see just how many of the methods are synchronized.

Subterranean Threads

You now have the wherewithal to go out and create billions and billions of threads of your very own, but even if your applet never explicitly creates a single thread of its own, there are already multiple threads in any Java applet. These are the four subterranean threads that always exist in a running Java program: the main interpreter thread, the finalizer thread, the idle thread, and the garbage collector.

Interpreter Thread

The interpreter thread is the easiest to understand because its sole purpose is to execute the compiled Java byte codes from the .class file. You can think of a traditional, single-threaded interpreter as one in which all the functionality is stuffed into the interpreter thread.

Idle Thread

The idle thread, the garbage collector, and the finalizer work together. The idle thread, running at a very low priority, simply maintains a flag that tells whether or not it has run. The idle thread's priority is chosen so that it almost never runs unless all other threads in the Java runtime are blocked.

Garbage Collector

The garbage collector, running at an even lower priority than the idle thread, checks whether the idle thread has run. If the idle thread has been running, that probably means that it's a good time to run a garbage collection.

Finalizer Thread

The finalizer thread is a low-priority thread that helps with garbage collection. After the garbage collector identifies an object as inaccessible, the finalizer calls the object's **finalize** method (if it exists) to do any cleanup that might be necessary. The system tries to run garbage collection and finalization only when there is CPU time to spare. This design provides good performance for event-driven applications where the majority of realtime is spent waiting for events.

Other Threads

The subterranean threads exist in any Java program—applet or application. Applets have another whole class of peer threads—the browser threads. Web browsers are all multithreaded by design. When you see a browser changing the status line, updating the screen, and responding to user input all while downloading a graphics file, that's a result of conscious multithreaded design. In most browsers, applets will not have access to any threads other than those the applet itself creates, but you should be aware that in any browser, threads are coming and going all the time.

Inter-Process Communication

Java does not really support the notion of inter-process communication (IPC), not much of a surprise since it doesn't really believe in processes either. This has important implications for coders who've written multithreaded or multiprocess applications in C. As language features, DDE, semaphores, mailboxes, queues, OLE, system-wide shared memory, and most other traditional forms of IPC are absent at present.

There is only one form of IPC that is provided for Java programs—anonymous pipes via the **Process** and **Runtime** classes. In brief, **Runtime.exec** gets you a **Process** object, from which you can get **Stream** objects connected to the process standard in, standard out, and standard error. For security reasons, **Runtime.exec** is usually unavailable to applets. Thus, it's use is beyond the scope of this book.

Inter-Thread Communication

Java provides anonymous pipes for inter-thread communication via the **PipedInputStream** and **PipedOutputStream** classes. These are classic anonymous pipes that function just like the ones we're all familiar with from Unix. The basic theory of PipedStreams is that you create one end, then create the other end, passing it the handle to the first end in the constructor.

Inter-Applet Communication

Using the **AppletContext** interface we talked about in Chapter 9, it is relatively easy to get applets to communicate. In fact, once an applet retrieves an **Applet** object from the **AppletContext**, communication is as easy as invoking a method or setting a public variable. There is no need to use extraordinary mechanisms like sockets or anonymous pipes.

When to Thread

We've learned how useful and necessary threads are, so by now you should be bursting to turn every Integer into its own thread. Hold on and take a deep breath. Threads *are* useful and necessary, but they have limitations that you need to consider too.

For one thing, context switching involves some amount of overhead, so every thread you create adds some drag to the overall system—the operating system spends cycles switching among threads, and the more threads, the more cycles the OS spends context switching.

Threads are also a system resource and most operating systems have a hard limit on both the total number of threads in the system and the number of threads that one user can create. Think of it this way: if you spend 500 threads making "active" integers for your rotisserie baseball league scoring application, then your DBMS may run out of transaction processing threads—a bad tradeoff. For total threads, a number somewhere around one thousand is typical. Per-user threads will be something less than that.

When deciding whether or not to thread an object, I tend to concentrate first on the difference between active and passive objects. A network socket is an active object, an integer is not, keyboard is active, file is not. Most objects that respond to events generated outside the application deserve their own threads.

A final reason to get with the program when it comes to threads: Java provides weak to non-existent support for polling I/O. There is no analogy to the Unix select system call which so many Unix programmers rely on for polling I/O. If you intend to do network I/O you will probably want to write it by blocking I/O in a separate thread.

Native Methods

The first thing I always look at when reviewing a new language like Java is how to get out of it. This is only natural, as most programmers are already productive in one language and most projects need some of the functionality of last year's language in the new product they're writing in next year's language. Windows GUI development languages, like Easel or Toolbook, usually provide the ability to make DLL calls and Java provides an analogous escape hatch—native methods.

Native methods allow you to link dynamic libraries written in C, C++, or some other language via a method "wrapper." Basically, if your DLL call obeys certain rules about parameter passing, memory management, and such, you can write a method that simply calls out to that external DLL. Native methods are crucial for shrink-wrapped, standalone Java applications where your program is competing against code written to the native operating system API. Native methods, however, are not useful for the purposes of many applications for two reasons. First and most important, by definition a native method is not portable and often a base requirement for an applet is that it run in any Java-capable browser. Second, and perhaps not so obvious, is the whole question of how you would get your native method onto a user's machine. The Java classloader is designed for moving java .class files, not Windows .DLL files. Thus, you could write the world's coolest native method, but any Java-capable browser trying to run your applet over the Net would throw an exception when it tried to (locally) load your native method.

Conclusion

Java makes threading simple and worthwhile. You can write Java applets the same way you used to write single-threaded applications in C or C++, but you'd be wasting much of the power of the language. The current generation of browsers are all multithreaded, and threading will only become more prevalent as a method of increasing the real and apparent efficiency of applications.

Network Communication 13

John Rodley

Network I/O is one of the keys to writing useful Java applets. Here, we present a potpourri of applets that use Java's network I/O in interesting ways.

*E*very programming tool has a dirty little secret that makes using it less pleasant than the walk in the park promised by the marketing brochures. Basic has its spaghetti code and C has its wild pointers. Java, even embodied in the friendly package of Café, is no different.

The dirty little secret of Java applet writing is that browser security mechanisms make it nearly impossible to write a useful Java applet that doesn't connect back via sockets to a daemon on the server. Specifically, browsers can, and do, prevent applets from doing any file I/O. This means that any persistence that an applet requires has to be implemented in a server application (not an applet) to which the applet talks over the Net.

Java provides network communication through the package java.net. This package contains a number of useful classes. The basic ones that we're going to use and talk about are **URL**, **Socket**, **ServerSocket**, and **InetAddress**. The class hierarchy for the java.net package is shown in Figure 13.1.

Another package that is inextricably bound up with network I/O and I/O in general is the aptly named java.io package. As the various examples will show, whenever you do any kind of I/O, you will have to use one of the Stream classes provided in the java.io package. Figure 13.2 shows the java.io class hierarchy.

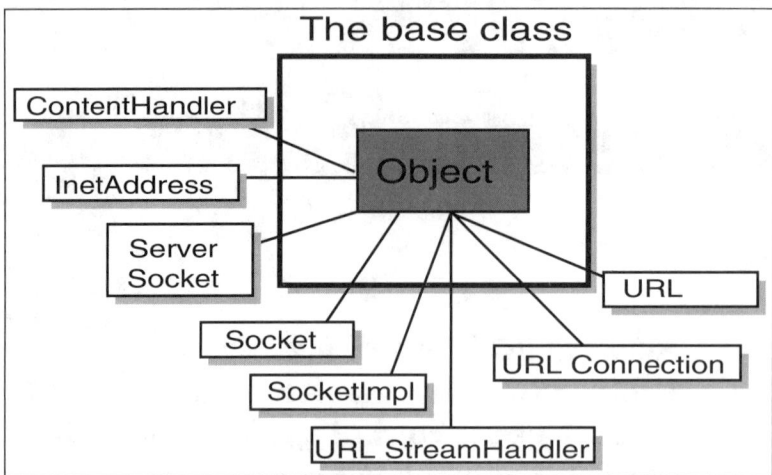

Figure 13.1   The java.net class hierarchy.

Using URLs

A URL, or *Uniform Resource Locator*, is basically just a network location. It tells you not only where something is, but *what* it is. For example, consider my home page URL:

```
http://www.channel1.com/users/ajrodley/index.html
```

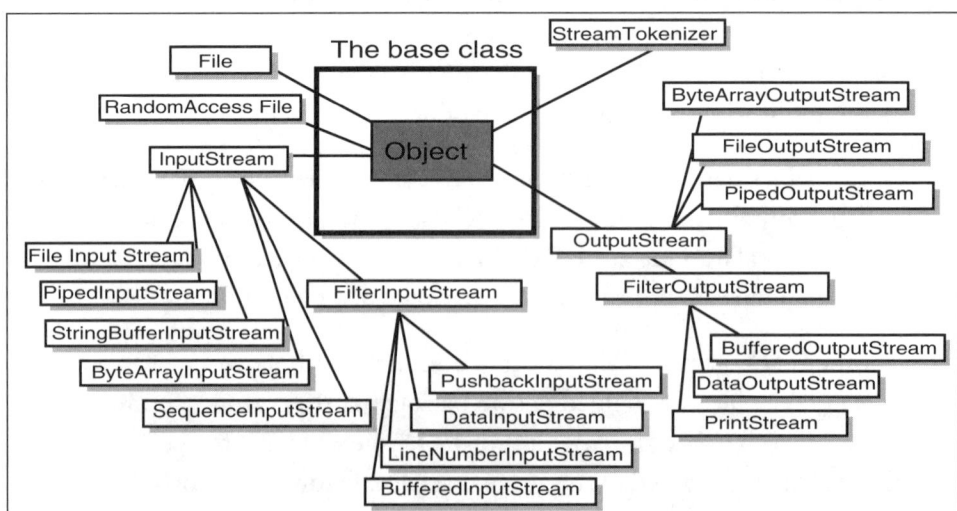

Figure 13.2   The java.io class hierarchy.

Briefly, the URL says that to use this "document," you connect to the http server on the machine named www.channel1.com, then tell it to send a stream of data made out of the file "/users/ajrodley/index.html."

Java's **URL** class takes this concept of an Internet location one step beyond. After all, a URL by itself can be easily represented by a **String**. A Java **URL** object, on the other hand, encompasses not just the address, but also the object at that address. Let's investigate URLs in more detail.

Word-Searching an URL

Many organizations are sitting on huge piles of information that they want to make available via the Web. After all, it's a perfect application of the technology, freeing information consumers from the time-consuming task of hauling themselves physically to the location (library, town hall ...) where the hard-copy information resides. For most companies in this situation, the easiest approach is to just dump the information out on the Web virtually unmodified from the hard-copy version. Although this is a valid approach, Java makes it easy to go one step beyond.

As a first step in adding value to a huge, raw document, you might want to add a word-search applet like the one shown in Listing 13.1, which scans a document for a particular word. Listing 13.2 shows the HTML code to load this applet.

LISTING 13.1 SEARCHING A DOCUMENT FOR A WORD

```
package chap7;

import java.awt.Graphics;
import java.awt.*;
import java.applet.Applet;
import java.net.*;
import java.lang.*;
import java.io.*;
import java.util.*;

/** A class to search for a word in a text document using only
URL.getContent to retrieve the document into a String.
@author John Rodley
@version 1.0 1/1/1996
*/
public class ch7_fig1 extends Applet {
```

```
    String stringURL;
    String desiredWord;
    public final static String buttonLabel =
                        new String("Start Search");
    TextField wordField;
    Panel controlPanel;
    Button searchButton;

    /** Get the parameter "URL" from the applet tag, create a
    panel with a text field for entering the word to search for,
    and a button for starting the search.
    */
      public void init() {
        stringURL = new String( getParameter( "URL" ));
        if( stringURL == null ) {
          System.out.println( "URL parameter not set" );
          return;
          }
        controlPanel = new Panel();
        searchButton = new Button( buttonLabel );
        controlPanel.add( searchButton );
        wordField = new TextField( 25 );
        controlPanel.add( wordField);
        add( controlPanel );
      }

    /** Do the search, using the URL provided in the URL parameter
    and the search phrase set previously in the text field. Skip
    the search if either of these variables is not set.
    */
    void dosearch() {
      if( desiredWord == null ) {
        System.out.println( "find parameter not set" );
        return;
        }
      try {
        URL u = new URL(stringURL);
        try {
          Object o = u.getContent();
          if( o instanceof String ) {
            FindTheWord( desiredWord, (String)o );
            }
          }
        catch( IOException e ) {System.out.println( "ioex "+e);}
      }
      catch( MalformedURLException ue ) {System.out.println( "urlex
    "+ue);}
    }
```

```
/** Search the supplied string for the specified sub-string.
Find by character position in the doc, as well as line
position. Report results to standard output.
@param  String  the phrase to search for
@param  String  a string that contains the ENTIRE document
*/
void FindTheWord( String find, String doc ) {
  int ret = doc.indexOf( find );
  if( ret != -1 ) {
    showStatus( "Found "+find+" at char offset "+ret );
    System.out.println( "found "+find+" at char offset "+ret );
    }

  // Split the doc into lines using a tokenizer with only \r
  // and \n as the delimiters.
  StringTokenizer lines = new StringTokenizer( doc, "\r\n" );
  int lineNo = 1;
  while( lines.hasMoreElements()) {
    String line = (String)lines.nextElement();
    // Create a second tokenizer, with space as the delimiter
    StringTokenizer words = new StringTokenizer( line );
    while( words.hasMoreElements()) {
      String word = (String)words.nextElement();
      if( word.toUpperCase().compareTo( find.toUpperCase())==0)
        {
        showStatus("found "+find+" on line "+lineNo );
        System.out.println( "found "+find+" on line "+ lineNo);
        }
      }
    lineNo++;
    }
  }


/** Handle the search button, starting a new search
if the start button is pushed.
*/
public boolean handleEvent(Event e) {
  if (e.id == Event.ACTION_EVENT) {
    if( e.target instanceof Button )
      {
      Button b = (Button )e.target;
      if( b.getLabel().compareTo( buttonLabel ) == 0 )
        {
        desiredWord = new String( wordField.getText());
        dosearch();
        }
      }
    }
```

```
    return( false );
  }
}
```

LISTING 13.2   THE HTML CODE THAT LOADS THE WORD
FINDER APPLET

```
<!DOCTYPE HTML PUBLIC "-//SQ//DTD HTML 2.0 HoTMetaL + extensions//
  EN">
<HTML><HEAD><TITLE>Chapter 7 - figure 1 - Finding a word in a
simple network text file.</TITLE>
</HEAD>
<BODY>
<applet code="chap7/ch7_fig1.class" width=600 height=600>
<param name=URL value="http://www.mymachine.com/temp/index.txt">
</applet>
</P>
</BODY></HTML>
```

The <applet> tag on the HTML page provides both the URL of a document to scan while a **TextField** gets the word to search for, and a Button starts the search.

One thing you need to note from Listing 13.2: the document we're scanning isn't an HTML document. We'll talk about that later.

Setting up the search requires getting the URL of the document we're scanning, and getting a word to scan for. In the **init** method, we get the URL via the **getParameter** method. We also setup a text field for entering the search word, and a button for starting the search. The text field and button arrangement require us to implement a **handleEvent** method. As you can see, the event handler deals with a single event (among the many that can occur)—the user pressing the button labeled "Start Search."

Once we have a word to search for, and a string URL of a document to search, the next logical step is to retrieve the document. This is the purpose of the first part of the **dosearch** method, specifically the calls to the **URL** constructor and **URL.getContent**. The **URL** constructor actually connects to the document specified by our string URL. If the document doesn't exist, or we can't make a connection to it, the **URL** constructor throws a **MalformedURLException**, which we are required to catch. Having connected to the document, we then retrieve it via the call to **getContext**, where most of the functionality of this applet is actually embedded. When the file we're pointing at is simple text, what we get back from the call to **getContent** is a **String** that holds the entire text of that file.

Having read our whole file into a **String**, we simply pass that **String** into the method **FindTheWord** that searches for a word occurrence. Within **FindTheWord**, we use two different ways to find our word within the String. The first way is an exact match via **String.indexOf**:

```
int ret = doc.indexOf(find);
if( ret != -1 ) {
  showStatus( ... );
```

This approach searches the whole **String**, whitespace included, for the word, returning the character offset of the word within the string. Unfortunately, knowing the character offset of a word within a file is rarely useful.

What's usually called for in word searches is a line number within the document. Thus, within **FindTheWord**, we also implement a second, more useful search algorithm. This one uses **StringTokenizer** to turn the **String** representing our whole file into a Vector of lines. Then it turns each line into a Vector of words and compares each member of that Vector to the desired word.

The two search algorithms, **indexOf** and **compareTo** will often find different things. **indexOf** will find the word within another word, while **compareTo** won't. **compareTo** combined with **toUpperCase** matches the words regardless of case.

The final thing to notice about our word-search applet is that we haven't talked at all about sockets, protocols, or daemons. All of the grunt work of connecting over the network and retrieving the file is handled entirely within **URL.getContent**.

Expanding the Search Beyond Simple Text

If you point the word search applet at a file with an .htm, or .html extension, something very disturbing happens: **getContent** throws a

ClassNotFoundException. This is because there is no content handler for content of type HTML. The steps **URL.getContent** goes through to deliver our **String** in Listing 13.1 are:

1. Make a connection over the Net via sockets.

2. Create a stream of characters flowing from the server to the applet.

3. Figure out that the stream is simple text and turn that stream of characters into a **String** object.

The problem with using this applet on HTML content is that Java figures out that the stream is HTML (not simple text), but it doesn't know how to create a sensible object from a stream of HTML text. This is unfortunate, but not insurmountable. Of the three steps, the first two are still available to us, regardless of the type of the URL's content. We just have to deal with the stream ourselves, rather than having **getContent** turn it into a **String**.

To do the same search and have it work whatever the content type, we have to modify the applet. Listing 13.3 shows those modifications.

LISTING 13.3 SEARCHING HTML DOCUMENTS FOR A WORD

```
package chap7;

import java.awt.Graphics;
import java.awt.*;
import java.applet.Applet;
import java.net.*;
import java.lang.*;
import java.io.*;
import java.util.*;

/** A class that searches the document specified in the URL
parameter for the word specified in the find parameter.
@author John Rodley
@version 1.0 1/1/1996
@see URL
@see InputStream
*/
public class ch7_fig3 extends Applet {
String stringURL;
String desiredWord;
public final static String buttonLabel =
                  new String("Start Search");
TextField wordField;
```

```
Panel controlPanel;
Button searchButton;

/** Get the parameter "URL" from the applet tag, create a
panel with a text field for entering the word to search for,
and a button for starting the search.
*/
  public void init() {
    stringURL = new String( getParameter( "URL" ));
    if( stringURL == null ) {
      System.out.println( "URL parameter not set" );
      return;
      }
    controlPanel = new Panel();
    searchButton = new Button( buttonLabel );
    controlPanel.add( searchButton );
    wordField = new TextField( 25 );
    controlPanel.add( wordField);
    add( controlPanel );
  }

/** Handle the search button, starting a new search
if the start button is pushed.
*/
public boolean handleEvent(Event e) {
  if (e.id == Event.ACTION_EVENT) {
    if( e.target instanceof Button )
      {
      Button b = (Button )e.target;
      if( b.getLabel().compareTo( buttonLabel ) == 0 )
        {
        desiredWord = new String( wordField.getText());
        dosearch();
        }
      }
    }
  return( false );
  }

/** Override of Applet.start. Gets the URL and search word
parameters, then opens a stream connection to the document at
that URL and passes the stream and the search word to the
FindWord method.
@see FindTheWord
@see URL
@see InputStream
*/
public void dosearch() {
  try {
```

```
    URL u = new URL(stringURL);
    System.out.println( "u="+u );
      try {
        InputStream is = u.openStream();
        FindTheWord( desiredWord, is );
      }
      catch( IOException e ) {System.out.println( "ioex "+e);}
    }
  catch( MalformedURLException e1 )
    {System.out.println( "mfuex "+e1);}
}


/** Find a word in an input stream, reporting the line number
to the standard output.
@arg  find  The word we're scanning the input stream for
@arg  is  An input stream
@see DataInputStream
@see StringTokenizer
@see String
*/
void FindTheWord( String find, InputStream is ) {
  int lineNo = 1;

  DataInputStream dis = new DataInputStream( is );
  while( true ) {
    try {
      String line = dis.readLine();
      if( line == null )
        break;
      StringTokenizer words = new StringTokenizer( line );
      while( words.hasMoreElements()) {
        String word = (String)words.nextElement();
        if( word.toUpperCase().compareTo( find.toUpperCase())
                              == 0)
          {
          showStatus("found "+find+" on line "+lineNo );
          System.out.println("found "+find+" on line "+lineNo);
          }
        }
      lineNo++;
      } catch( IOException e ) {break;}
    }
  }
}
```

We use the same basic structure as in Listing 13.1, getting the search word from a text field, and the URL from the **<applet>** tag. The real changes are to our content handling mechanisms—**dosearch** and

FindTheWord. Within **dosearch**, we get rid of the call to **getContent** using the lower level call **URL.open Stream** instead:

```
URL u = new URL(stringURL);
    System.out.println( "u="+u );
      try {
        InputStream is = u.openStream();
```

This approach gets us the **InputStream** that **getContent** uses in Listing 13.1 to create an object appropriate to the URL's content. You can see now, how high-level the **URL.getContent** method really is. We could easily write our own version of it using the skeleton of **FindTheWord**, as shown in Listing 13.4.

LISTING 13.4 OUR OWN VERSION OF URL.GETCONTENT

```
String ourGetContent( InputStream is ) {
 String content = new String("");

  DataInputStream dis = new DataInputStream( is );
  while( true ) {
    try {
      String line = dis.readLine();
        if( line == null )
        break;
        content = new String(content+line);
} catch( IOException e ) {break;}
    }
return( content );
  }
```

The main difference between **URL.getContent** and our **FindTheWord**, is that we embed a word search algorithm in **FindTheWord**. Within **FindTheWord** we turn the **InputStream** that **dosearch** got from our URL into a **DataInputStream**. This allows us to read the stream line by line rather than in byte or byte arrays, which are all the bare **InputStream** gives us. This technique is a common theme in Java I/O. The basic I/O object gives you an **Input/OutputStream** which you then turn into a more specialized stream, like **DataInputStream**, by passing the bare **Input/OutputStream** to the specialized stream constructor, as we do here in **FindTheWord**:

```
DataInputStream dis = new DataInputStream( is );
  while( true ) {
    try {
      String line = dis.readLine();
```

From this point, we use the same word search techniques as in Listing 13.1 to turn each line into a Vector of words and eventually compare the search word to each word in the document.

A Link-Checking Applet

Once you have access to the text of HTML documents on the Net, there are an endless number of interesting tasks you can take on. Because of the complex nature of my Web site, one of the most odious tasks I've had to deal with is checking all the links in my pages to make sure there aren't any dead ones. It's easy to get dead links in a page. A simple typo in the HREF tag will do it.

With a multi-level Web site containing many internal links, you really need an applet that will go through all the links top-to-bottom making sure the documents pointed to actually exist. We can develop an applet like this by combining the applets in Listing 13.1 and 13.3, as shown in Listing 13.5. Figure 13.3 shows the link-checking applet in action.

LISTING 13.5

A LINK-CHECKING APPLET

```
package chap7;

import java.awt.Graphics;
import java.awt.*;
import java.applet.Applet;
import java.net.*;
import java.lang.*;
import java.io.*;
import java.util.*;


/** A class that prompts the user for a URL, then goes through
the, presumably HTML, content of that URL checking for links
to other WWW content and making sure that the documents those
links connect to actually exist and that all THEIR links are
valid.  This is recursive and potentially time-wasting.
```

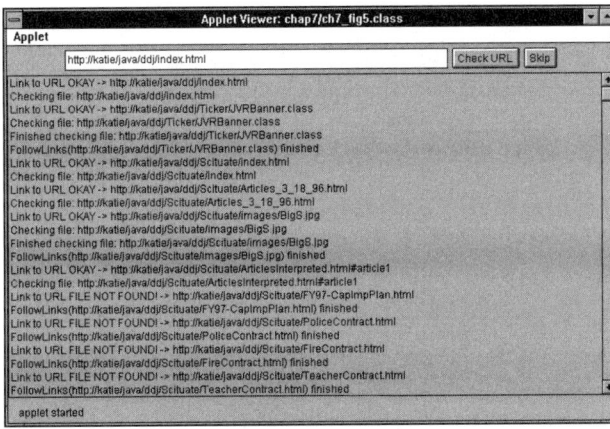

Figure 13.3   Line checker running against a Web page.

```
@author John Rodley
@version 1.0 1/1/1996
@see TextField
@see Button
@see Panel
*/
public class ch7_fig5 extends Applet {

  public static ch7_fig5 c7;

  TextField urlEntryField;
  Button checkButton;
  Button skipButton;
  public List lineList;
  Panel topPanel;
  public boolean bSkip = false;
  String buttonLabel = new String( "Check URL" );
  String skipLabel = new String( "Skip" );

  /** Set up a text field for entering the URL to check, a button
  to start the check, and a button to interrupt an undesired
  check.
  @see Panel
  @see Button
  @see TextField
  */
  public void init() {
    c7 = this;

    setLayout( new BorderLayout());
    topPanel = new Panel();
    urlEntryField = new TextField( "http://", 60 );
```

```
    urlEntryField.setEditable( true );
    topPanel.add( urlEntryField );
    checkButton = new Button(buttonLabel);
    topPanel.add( checkButton );
    skipButton = new Button(skipLabel);
    topPanel.add( skipButton );
    lineList = new List(10, false);
    add( "North", topPanel );
    add( "Center", lineList );
    resize( 700, 400 );
    }


/** Handle the start and skip buttons, starting a new search
if the start button is pushed, and breaking out a scan every
time the skip button is pressed.
*/
public boolean handleEvent(Event e) {
   if (e.id == Event.ACTION_EVENT) {
     if( e.target instanceof Button )
       {
       Button b = (Button )e.target;
       System.out.println( "button "+b );
       if( b.getLabel().compareTo( buttonLabel ) == 0 )
         clicked();
       if( b.getLabel().compareTo( skipLabel ) == 0 ) {
         System.out.println( "skip button clicked" );
         bSkip = true;
         }
       }
     }
   return( false );
   }


/** Actually start the search, getting the URL from the
text field, and setting off a recursive LinkFollower object.
@see LinkFollower
*/
public void clicked() {
   System.out.println( "Starting check run" );

   String stringURL = urlEntryField.getText();
   if( stringURL == null ) {
     showStatus( "URL ENTRY FIELD CAN NOT BE EMPTY!!" );
     return;
     }
   if( stringURL.compareTo("" ) == 0 )
     {
     showStatus( "URL ENTRY FIELD CAN NOT BE EMPTY!!" );
     return;
     }
```

```
      LinkFollower lf = new LinkFollower( this, stringURL );
      lf.start();
      }
}
```

```
/** A class that recursively follows all the links in a HTML
page to the very end.  This has circularity problems that are
not entirely solved, hence the skip button.  A HashTable
contains the list of all links that have been checked, and no
link should be checked twice.
@see HashTable
@author John Rodley
@version 1.0 1/10/1996
*/
class LinkFollower extends Thread {
String stringURL;
ch7_fig3 c;
static Hashtable hash;
String linkStrings[];
```

```
/** Constructor - creates the checked-link HashTable, and an
array of "keys" that we use to find links - HREF, IMG, and
applet.
@see HashTable
*/
public LinkFollower( ch7_fig3 ch, String url ) {
  hash = new Hashtable();
  linkStrings = new String[3];
  linkStrings[0] = new String("<A HREF=");
  linkStrings[1] = new String("<IMG SRC=");
  linkStrings[2] = new String("<applet code=");
  c = ch;
  stringURL = new String( url );
  }
```

```
/** The run loop for this LinkFollower thread.  This makes the
first call to the recursive method, FollowLinks.
@see FollowLinks
*/
public void run() {
  FollowLinks( stringURL );
  showOutput( "Check finished" );
  }
```

```
/** The recursive method that opens a stream from a URL, and
calls FindLinks with that stream as an arg.  FindLinks then
calls back to FollowLinks for each found link.  For each link,
add a line to the list box in the user interface describing
whether or not the link is valid.
```

```
@see URL
@see InputStream
*/
public void FollowLinks( String stringURL ) {
  String s;
  try {
    URL u = new URL(stringURL);
    Enumeration en = hash.elements();
    for( int i = 0; i < hash.size(); i++ ) {
                URL storedU = (URL)en.nextElement();
      if( u.sameFile(storedU) == true ) {
        s = new String( "already checked -> "+u );
        System.out.println( s );
        showOutput( s );
        return;
        }
      }
    hash.put( u.toString(), u );
    try {
      try {
        InputStream is = u.openStream();
        showOutput( "Link to URL OKAY -> "+u );
        FindLinks( u.toString(), is );
      }
      catch( FileNotFoundException e ) {
        showOutput( "Link to URL FILE NOT FOUND! -> "+u );
      }
    } catch( IOException e ) {
      showOutput( "Link to URL Error! -> "+u );
    }
   }
  catch( MalformedURLException e1 ) {
    showOutput( "Bad URL "+stringURL );
    }
  showOutput( "FollowLinks("+stringURL+") finished" );
}


/** Given an InputStream, grab each CRLF delimited line and
scan it for links to other URLs.  Calls FollowLinks for each
found URL.
@see InputStream
@see DataInputStream
@see FollowLinks
@see StringTokenizer
*/
void FindLinks( String url, InputStream is ) {
  int lineNo = 1;

  showOutput( "Checking file: "+url );
```

```
// First get the base directory of this HTML doc
int index = url.lastIndexOf( "/" );
String baseDir = new String(url.substring( 0, index ));

DataInputStream dis = new DataInputStream( is );
while( true ) {
  try {
    if( c.bSkip == true ) {
      showOutput( "Interrupting "+url );
      c.bSkip = false;
      break;
      }
    String line = dis.readLine();
    if( line == null )
      break;
    for( int i = 0; i < linkStrings.length; i++ ) {
      int startIndex = 0;
      while( true ) {
        int ret = line.indexOf(linkStrings[i],startIndex);
        if( ret == -1 )
          break;
        String subLine = new String( line.substring(ret));
        StringTokenizer st =
              new StringTokenizer(subLine,"<>");
        String element = (String)st.nextElement();
        st = new StringTokenizer( element, "=" );
        st.nextElement();
        st = new StringTokenizer( (String)st.nextElement());
        String ourLink =
              new String( (String )st.nextElement());
        int colon = ourLink.indexOf(":");
        int first = ourLink.indexOf("\"");
        int last = ourLink.lastIndexOf("\"");
        if( first != -1 && last != -1 && first != last ){
          ourLink =
              new String( ourLink.substring(first+1,last));
          }
        if( colon == -1 ) { // relative URL
          char ca[] = new char[1];
          ourLink.getChars( 0, 1, ca, 0);
          if( ca[0] == '#' ) {
            showOutput("skipping name relative link "+ourLink );
            startIndex = ret+1;
            continue;
            }
          else
            System.out.println("relative url baseDir = "+
                        baseDir+" ourLink = "+ourLink );
```

```
                ourLink = new String(baseDir+"/"+ourLink );
                }
             FollowLinks( ourLink );
             startIndex = ret+1;
             }
          }
       lineNo++;
       } catch( IOException e ) {break;}
     }
   showOutput( "Finished checking file: "+url );
   }

void showOutput( String s ) {
  c.lineList.addItem( s );
  System.out.println( s );
  }
 }
```

To make this applet check the links on a Web site, we enter the URL of a Web page in the text field, then press the start button to start it checking links. When the user presses the start button, the applet creates a **LinkFollower** object passing the **Applet** and **String** URL to the constructor. Once running (via **Thread.start**), the new **LinkFollower** object goes through the following steps:

1. Connect to the URL specified in the text field.

2. Download the document found there.

3. Scan the document **InputStream** for any of the strings that indicate a hyperlink.

4. If it finds one:

   a. Pull the target of the hyperlink from the text.

   b. Turn that hyperlink target into a URL.

   c. Go back to step 2, using the new URL.

As you can see, this is clearly recursive. **FindLinks** calls **FollowLinks**, which calls back to **FindLinks**.

In parsing the HTML, we use the same basic technique we used in the word searches of Listing 13.1 and 13.3. Instead of the single search word, we look for any of three strings that indicate hyperlinks. These specific strings are defined in the **linkStrings** array, which we create in the **LinkFollower** constructor shown here:

```
linkStrings = new String[3];
  linkStrings[0] = new String("<A HREF=");
  linkStrings[1] = new String("<IMG SRC=");
  linkStrings[2] = new String("<applet code=");
```

This brute force parsing works surprisingly well, although it's a far cry from the kind of rigorous syntax checking a commercial product would need to do.

One of the biggest problems in writing an applet like this is a by-product of the structure of the Web itself—circular references. In the most basic case, if you have two pages that contain links to one another, an unsophisticated Web crawler will sit spinning in an endless loop.

Our checker takes a number of steps to try to prevent this. One is to store the URL of each site we visit, so that we never visit any page more than once. That's the purpose of the **HashTable** hash. In **FollowLinks**, we check each element of the **HashTable** against the URL we're about to check as follows:

```
URL u = new URL(stringURL);
    Enumeration en = hash.elements();
    for( int i = 0; i < hash.size(); i++ ) {
                URL storedU = (URL)en.nextElement();
      if( u.sameFile(storedU) == true ) {
        s = new String( "already checked -> "+u );
        System.out.println( s );
        showOutput( s );
        return;
        }
    }
    hash.put( u.toString(), u );
```

Now we could have just used **HashTable.contains** to see if this URL was already there. However, there are a number of different URLs that describe the same file. We try to cover this by calling **URL.sameFile**.

We also have to have a mechanism for breaking out of any unwanted branches in the Web site hyperlink structure. In my own Web site, I have links to both java.sun.com and microsoft.com. I certainly don't want to check the links to those Web sites along with my own. The simplest way to do that is to provide a skip button, that breaks you out of the lowest level of link-checking—the loop in **FindLinks** where lines are read and parsed.

The skip button is created in the **init** method, and as you would expect, clicking it causes an event that gets passed to **handleEvent**. When we detect a skip button press in **handleEvent**, we simply set the boolean, **bSkip**. The **LinkFollower** runs asynchronously in its own thread. When **bSkip** is set, the **LinkFollower** could be executing anywhere in the **run**, **FollowLinks**, or **FindLinks** methods, but more than likely it will be down in the **for** loop of **FindLinks**. Thus, we let **FindLinks** finish dealing with whatever line it's on, then check **bSkip** before starting the next line. If **bSkip** is set, we clear it and skip the rest of this document.

Using Sockets

Sockets are a form of interprocess communication that allows processes on different network hosts to communicate. They originated with Berkeley Unix and have spread to become the defacto standard for Internet communication. A form of sockets, Winsock, has also taken hold in the Windows world to the point that most Internet-capable Windows applications conform to some version of Winsock.

Sockets are actually an interface—a set of function calls that your application can call and be guaranteed a particular response. Each operating system that supports sockets implements them in its own way, but all present the same interface to applications that wish to use those sockets. Thus, socket libraries in both the System V and BSD versions of Unix provide a function called **gethostname**, though each implements it differently.

Socket libraries generally consist of about two dozen functions, but there are really only a few functions you need to understand to get going with sockets. Table 13.1 lists the key socket functions.

Two connected sockets make a point-to-point communications channel. Each side of the conversation creates a socket (via **socket**). The server side **bind**s to a host name and port number, **listen**s for connections, and **accept**s them as they occur. The client side simply **connect**s to the hostname and portnumber. When the **connect** returns, the two sides can then call **send** and **recv** to read and write the connection.

Sockets are at the heart of almost every instance of Internet communication. When, for instance, you point your Web browser at http://java.sun.com, the browser uses the socket interface to connect to a port on java.sun.com. Sockets are a simple, old, tried-and-true technology that make network programming fairly easy.

Table 13.1   Key Socket Functions

Message	Direction	Meaning
QueryAgentList	AgentLauncher -> dispatching AgentServer	Send me the list of agents that this AgentServer can dispatch.
AgentList	dispatching AgentServer -> AgentLauncher	Here is the list of agents that this AgentServer can dispatch.
Dispatch	AgentLauncher-> dispatching AgentServer	Dispatch the named class to all your servers.
Load	AgentServer-> AgentServer	Load and run the supplied class.
Kill	AgentLauncher-> AgentServer	Kill the named agent.
Start	AgentServer-> dispatching AgentServer -> AgentLauncher	The named agent has started work.
Result	AgentServer-> dispatching AgentServer -> AgentLauncher	The named agent is reporting results in the named URL.

Socket Basics

There are two ends to each Java socket conversation: server and client. The server end is embodied in the **ServerSocket** class, while the client end is embodied in **Socket**. These two ends go through a specific set of steps to setup, conduct, and terminate a conversation, as shown here.

1. The server instantiates **ServerSocket** passing a local port number. This creates the socket and binds it to that local port number:

```
ServerSocket ServerS = new ServerSocket( 1037 );
```

2. We accept connections to this server socket by calling **accept**.

```
Socket AcceptedS = ServerS.accept();
```

3. The client instantiates **Socket**, passing a server name and port number. This creates a client end socket and connects it to the named port, on the named host. When this call returns, the two ends are connected.

```
Socket ClientSocket = new Socket( "www.mymachine.com", 1037 );
```

4. **ServerSocket.accept** returns a **Socket**, that can now be used for I/O. Most applications will spawn a new thread to read and write this socket. The **ServerSocket** can continue to "accept" connections on the original socket.

```
byte b[] = new byte[100];
AcceptedS.getOutputStream().write( b );
```

From this point on, both server app and client applet can read and write the connected sockets. This is a compression/simplification of the steps C programs using the socket interface would go through. On the server side, Java's **ServerSocket** class compresses the socket creation, address binding, and listen calls into the constructor. On the client side, the **Socket** class compresses socket creation and connect into the constructor.

How does one side know when the conversation is over? Many protocols call for there to be a "goodbye," but depending on something like that won't get you very far. Lost connections are a fact of life. Fortunately, Java throws an **IOException** in almost any case where the network connection has been interrupted. You must catch and handle **IOException**s properly to write usable network communications code.

The Snitcher Applet

With those basic ideas well in hand, let's construct an application/applet combo that does some very simple socket communication. The purpose of this combination is to record the date/time, URL, and IP address of the user whenever someone accesses the HTML page in which this applet is embedded. This is one of the holy grails of Web publishers: to be able to know who is hitting their page and when. This applet, Snitcher, is unusual in that it has *no* user interface. The user never sees it.

The theory behind the system is simple enough. The server Java application (Snitch), is running all the time on the server accepting connections on port 1038. When a user loads the page with our applet in it, the applet starts up, gets the page URL, the host name, and IP address, and packages all that information in a message. Then it connects to the server socket and sends the message to the server, which stores it in a file from where it can be retrieved and analyzed. Listing 13.6 shows the Snitcher applet.

LISTING 13.6 THE SNITCHER APPLET

```
package chap7;

import java.awt.Graphics;
import java.awt.*;
import java.applet.Applet;
import java.net.*;
import java.lang.*;
import java.io.*;
import java.util.*;

/** An applet that reports the hostname and IP address of the
machine reading the HTML page back to the server from which
the HTML page was loaded.
@author John Rodley
@version 1.0 12/1/11996
*/
public class ch7_fig6 extends Applet {
boolean bAlreadyRan = false;
int port = 1038;

/** Resize the applet to almost nothing, and change the port
number that the applet will connect to, if the port parameter
is set in the applet tag.
*/
public void init() {
```

```
    String sPort = getParameter( "port" );
    if( sPort != null ) {
      Integer iPort = new Integer( sPort );
      port = iPort.intValue();
      }
    resize( 10, 10 );
    }


/** Check if the snitcher has already informed on this user and only
   contact the server if we haven't run yet.  Tries to guarantee that
  we only get one report for each time the page is loaded.
  */
public void start() {
    if( bAlreadyRan == false ) {
      snitch();
      bAlreadyRan = true;
      }
    }
/** Report the hostname and IP address of this machine to the
  server.
  @see InetAddress
  @see URL
  @see PrintStream
  @see Socket
  @see Snitch
  */
void snitch() {
    // Get the local hostname and IP address
    String sIpaddr = "Unknown ipaddr";
    try {
      InetAddress in = InetAddress.getLocalHost();
      sIpaddr = in.toString();
    } catch( UnknownHostException e )
      {System.out.println("exception "+e );;}

    // Now get the URL of the HTML page we're running
    URL u = getDocumentBase();
    String sHost = new String( u.getHost());
    try {
      String snitchInfo = new String( u+" :::: "+sIpaddr);
      System.out.println( "reporting snitchinfo "+snitchInfo );
      Socket s = new Socket( sHost, port );
      PrintStream p = new PrintStream( s.getOutputStream());
      p.println( snitchInfo );
      s.close();
    } catch( IOException e )
      {System.out.println( "ioexception "+e ); }
    }
  }
```

This applet is deceptively simple. Let's look at it in detail.

The applet needs to create a **Socket** that is connected to a **ServerSocket**. This means that we need to know the name of the server host and the port number it's accepting connections on. The port number is easy. We set that via a parameter in the **<applet>** HTML tag. The host name is a little trickier. As we've stated before (and will again), a security feature of some browsers requires that the server application run on the same host that the client applet is loaded from. This represents the "least-common-denominator" in network communication. Thus, we can get the name of the host simply by getting the URL of the HTML page, and then pulling the hostname from that, as shown here:

```
// Now get the URL of the HTML page we're running
 URL u = getDocumentBase();
 String sHost = new String( u.getHost());
```

getDocumentBase, an **Applet** method, returns the URL of the HTML document and **URL.getHost** gives the **String** version of the host to which the URL points.

Using InetAddress

Now that we're all set up to communicate with the server, we need to get the IP address and host name of the machine the browser (and the Snitcher applet) is running on so that we can create the message we'll actually send to the server. To do that, we need to use the **InetAddress** class. **InetAddress** is the interface between Java and the network name service. You can use it to turn a host name into an IP address or vice versa. The Snitcher applet uses the static method **InetAddress.getLocalHost** to get a complete description of the machine that the applet is running on. Notice that all we need do to get the hostname/IP address is call **InetAddress.toString**. This is a recurring theme in Java. It is also what happens if you append a non-**String** object to a **String** via the + operator as in:

```
InetAddress in = InetAddress.getLocalHost();
String s = "blah blah blah"+in;
```

Java calls **in.toString** in order to append it to the first string. Since we know where to connect, and what we want to say, the network communication boils down to four lines in the snitch method:

```
Socket s = new Socket( sHost, port );
    PrintStream p = new PrintStream( s.getOutputStream());
    p.println( snitchInfo );
    s.close();
```

As in other I/O examples, we take a bare **OutputStream** returned by **Socket.getOutputStream**, turn it into a more capable Stream—in this case, a **PrintStream** just like **System.out**—and use that new Stream to write a **String** to the **Socket**.

The Snitch Application

That covers the client Snitcher applet, but we still need a server Snitch application for the Snitcher applet to talk to. Listing 13.7 shows the server Snitch application.

LISTING 13.7 STANDALONE SERVER SNITCH APPLICATION

```
package chap7;

import java.awt.*;
import java.lang.*;
import java.util.*;
import java.net.*;
import java.io.*;


/** A standalone socket connection server that simply writes
everything it receives over the socket connection to a
day file. When the date changes, the server opens a new file.
The intent is that applets will connect, report the HTML
page's URL, date/time and the clients ip host name and IP
address allowing Web page owner to know who hits his
page and when.

@version 1.0
@author John Rodley
@see ch7_fig4
*/


public class Snitch extends Thread {
public static ServerFrame f;
```

```
static public boolean bRun = true;
static Panel p;
MenuBar m;
SrvSocket s;
Acceptor acceptor;
public static Snitch currentSnitch;
String filename = "Report.web";
PrintStream ps;

/** The main function for this standalone application.
Corresponds directly to the main function in a C application.
@param  argv The arguments to this application.  Currently
takes none.
*/
public static void main(String argv[] ) {
  Snitch as = new Snitch();
  Properties p = System.getProperties();

  try {
  p.load(
   new FileInputStream("/users/default/.hotjava/properties"));
  } catch( IOException e ) {System.out.println("except "+e ); }
  System.out.println( "system properties "+p );

    String topDirectory = System.getProperty( "acl.read" );
    if( topDirectory == null ) {
      System.out.println( "can't read this machine" );
      }
    else
      System.out.println( "got "+topDirectory+" for acl.read");
  as.start();
  }

/** Constructor.  Creates a unique file via switchFiles for
logging, an acceptor thread for accepting connections on the
port, and a main window for user interaction.  Currently just
runs, and exits on command.
@see switchFiles
@see ServerFrame
@see Acceptor
@see awt.Frame
@see awt.MenuBar
@see awt.Panel
@see awt.Layout
@see awt.Menu
@see awt.MenuItem
*/
public Snitch() {
  switchFiles();
```

```
      currentSnitch = this;
      f = new ServerFrame();
      f.resize(300, 300);
      f.show();
      p = new Panel();
      p.reshape( 0, 0, 300, 300 );
      p.setLayout( new FlowLayout());
      f.add( p );
      m = new MenuBar();
      f.setMenuBar( m );
      Menu m1 = new Menu("File");
      m.add(m1);
      MenuItem m2 = new MenuItem( "Exit" );
      m1.add( m2 );
      acceptor = new Acceptor( this );
      acceptor.start();
      }


/** Reports a line of text received over the socket connection
to the unique log file created by switchFiles. Synchronized
so that entire entries are written as one lump.
@see Date
@see PrintStream
@see OutputStream
*/
public synchronized void Report( String msg ) {
  if( ps == null )
    return;
  Date d = new Date();
  ps.println( new String(d+" ::::: "+msg) );
  }


/** Create a log file with a unique name formatted as:
  "M" The letter M
  mm  One or two digit month 1-12
  "D" The letter D
  dd  One or two digit day of month
  "Y" The letter Y
  yy  One or two digit year offset from 1900
  ".w"  Dot and letter w
  hh  One or two digit hour
  mm  One or two digit minute
This gives us a file that's guaranteed to be unique both to
the day, and within the day so that the server can be stopped
and restarted within a day.
@see Date
@see File
@see FileOutputStream
@see PrintStream
```

```
*/
public void switchFiles() {
  Date d = new Date();

  filename = new String( "M"+(d.getMonth()+1)+"D"+d.getDate()+
      "Y"+d.getYear()+".w"+d.getHours()+""+d.getMinutes() );
  try {
    File fi = new File( filename );
    ps = new PrintStream( new FileOutputStream(fi) );
  } catch( IOException e )
    { System.out.println( "ioexception e "+e );}


  }

/** The run loop for the the snitcher thread.  Wakes up once
per second and checks the date to see if we should switch log
files. This is far too often for the date checking, but
message processing is on hold while we sleep.  Thus, if we
change the sleep time to 1 minute, when the user closes
Snitch, it sits for a whole minute before closing the app -
unacceptable.
@see switchFiles
@see Date
@see Acceptor
*/
public void run() {
  boolean bLast = false;
  Date d = new Date();
  int lastday;
  int today;
  today = d.getDay();
  lastday = today;
  f.setTitle( "Snitch" );
  while( bRun == true ) {
    d = new Date();
    today = d.getDay();
    if( today != lastday )
      switchFiles();
    lastday = today;
    // Wake up once per minute and check the time
    try {Thread.sleep( 1000 );} catch( Exception e ) { }
    }
  acceptor.stop();
  System.out.println( "out of run loop" );
  f.dispose();
  System.exit(0);
  }
}
```

```
/** The frame window for this standalone application.  Exists
only to provide a way to kill the server.  Handles kill via
the system menu and the file menu.
@author John Rodley
@version 1.0
*/
class ServerFrame extends Frame {

/** Handle close from the system menu.
*/
    public synchronized boolean handleEvent(Event evt) {
   if( evt.id == Event.MOUSE_UP ) {
    return( true );
      }
    else
      {
    if( evt.target instanceof Frame ) {
      if( evt.id == Event.WINDOW_DESTROY ) {
        Snitch.currentSnitch.bRun = false;
        System.out.println( "window destroy "+evt );
        return( true );
        }
      else
        return super.handleEvent(evt);
      }
    else
      return super.handleEvent(evt);
      }
   }

/** Handle exit from the file menu.
*/
public boolean action( Event evt, Object o ) {
  if( evt.target instanceof MenuItem )
    {
    if( evt.arg.toString().compareTo( "Exit" ) == 0 )
      {
      Snitch.currentSnitch.bRun = false;
      System.out.println( "action event "+evt );
      }
    else
      {
      }
    }
  return( true );
   }
}
```

```
/** Handle reading and closing a socket which has already been
accepted.
@see Report
@see Thread
@see AcceptedSocket
@author John Rodley
@version 1.0
*/
class SocketHandler extends Thread {
  public AcceptedSocket as;
  FileOutputStream outputFile;
  boolean bDispatcher = false;
  boolean bContinue = true;
/** Simply saves the Socket that's passed as an argument.
@arg  Socket  This socket is saved and used within the run method to
read from.
@see AcceptedSocket
@see Socket
*/
  public SocketHandler( Socket so ) {
   as = new AcceptedSocket( so );
  }


/** The run loop for this thread.  Does a single blocking read
from the Socket that was supplied to the constructor for a
maximum of 1024 bytes and then closes the socket and exits the
thread.  Passes whatever is read to Report for logging in the
day file.  The small, single read is done for security
purposes.  A malicious app could still flood the log, but it
would have to re-connect every time—an expensive and
dangerous proposition.
@see Report
*/
  public void run() {
    int ret;
    byte buffer[] = new byte[1024];

    if(( ret = as.readLine( buffer )) != 0 )
      {
      Snitch.currentSnitch.Report( new String(buffer,0,0,ret ));
      System.out.println( "read "+ new String(buffer,0,0,ret));
      }
    as.close();
    }

}


/** A thread that simply sits in a loop accepting connections
on the port and spawning other threads to read the accepted
```

```
socket.
@author John Rodley
@version 1.0
@see SrvSocket
@see SocketHandler
@see Snitch
*/
class Acceptor extends Thread {
  Snitch as;
  SrvSocket s;
/** Constructor - daemonize this thread and save the Snitch
for later use.
*/
  public Acceptor( Snitch a ) {
    setDaemon( true );
    as = a;
    }

/** The run loop for this thread.  Sits in a loop accepting
connections.  Whenever a client connects, we create a
SocketHandler thread using that accepted Socket and start the
thread up.  Runs until "stopped" from above.
@see Socket
@see SrvSocket
@see SocketHandler
*/
  public void run() {
    // set up the server socket
    s = new SrvSocket( 1038 );
    while( true ) {
      Socket newS = s.Accept();
      SocketHandler a = new SocketHandler( newS );
      a.start();
      }
    }
}


/** Class representing a server socket bound to a local port.
@see ServerSocket
@version 1.0 August 1, 1995
@author John Rodley
*/
class SrvSocket {
ServerSocket s;
Socket newS;

/** Constructor creates a ServerSocket bound to a local port.
@arg  port  The integer local port number that this socket will
be bound to.
```

```
@see ServerSocket
*/
public SrvSocket( int port ) {
  s = null;
  while( s == null ) {
    System.out.println( "Accepting on host port:"+port );
    try {
      s = new ServerSocket( port );
      } catch( IOException e )
        { System.out.println( "exception "+e ); }
    }
  }

/** Accept a connection on this port and return the new
socket.  Swallow any exceptions.
@see Socket
@see Socket.accept
*/
public Socket Accept() {
  try {
    newS = s.accept();
    System.out.println( "Accepted on host port" );
    } catch( IOException e )
      { System.out.println( "exception "+e ); }
  return( newS );
  }
}

/** A socket that has been accepted, meaning that there is a
client now attached to it.
@see InputStream
@see OutputStream
@author John Rodley
@version 1.0
*/
class AcceptedSocket {
public InputStream inputStream;
public OutputStream outputStream;
public DataInputStream dis;
Socket s;

/** Constructor - creates input and output streams that read
and write can use.
@arg  so  The accepted Socket, saved for further use.
@see InputStream
@see OutputStream
*/
public AcceptedSocket( Socket so ) {
  s = so;
```

```java
   try {
     inputStream = s.getInputStream();
     outputStream = s.getOutputStream();
     } catch( IOException e )
       { System.out.println( "exception "+e); }
   }

/** Read a line terminated by one of the usual suspects - \r
and/or \n.  Accomplish this by making a DataInputStream from
our base InputStream.
@see DataInputStream
*/
public int readLine( byte buffer[] ) {
  int ret = -1;
  String s = new String("");

  try {
    dis = new DataInputStream(inputStream);
    s = dis.readLine();
    s.getBytes( 0, s.length(), buffer, 0 );
    } catch( IOException e )
     { System.out.println("exception "+e); return( -1 );}
  return( s.length());
  }

/** Read an array of bytes from the socket.
@return The number of bytes read.
*/
public int read(byte buffer[], int length) {
  try {
    return( inputStream.read(buffer));
    } catch( IOException e )
      { System.out.println("exception "+e); return( -1 ); }
  }

/** Write an array of bytes to the socket. */
public void write(byte buffer[], int length) {
  try {
    outputStream.write(buffer, 0, length);
    } catch( IOException e )
      { System.out.println( "exception "+e); }
  }

/** Close the socket. */
public void close() {
  try {
    s.close();
    } catch( IOException e )
      { System.out.println( "exception "+e); }
  }
}
```

The starting point for any standalone application is the **main** method. Snitch's **main** method accomplishes the following tasks:

◆ Loads a set of "properties" into the **System**'s properties list

◆ Gets the path of the directory in which the day file will be created by querying the property "*acl.read*"

◆ Instantiates the Snitch class

◆ Starts the new **Snitch** instance by calling **Thread.start**

A close look at **Snitch.java** reveals a basic skeleton that all server applications follow. The top level thread does almost nothing except create a **Frame** object (window) for accepting user input, and create another thread to accept connections to a **ServerSocket**. This is what happens in the Snitch constructor. We create our frame window and populate it with child windows, in this case a menu and some menu items. We also create an acceptor thread, and set it running.

The **Acceptor** class merely creates a **ServerSocket** on the local host bound to port number 1038. Each time a client applet connects to this server socket, the acceptor thread creates a new thread to read the port and deal with whatever the client sends us, in this case, writing a line of text to the day-file.

Like the **File** class, the **Socket** class provides two methods, **getInputStream** and **getOutputStream**, that provide a base object through which we can do whatever style of I/O we wish. The AgentServer, for the most part, does non-delimited, byte-level I/O using the bare **InputStream**. Snitch, on the other hand, receives CRLF-delimited lines of text from its client applets. Thus, it needs to create a **DataInputStream** from the **Socket**'s bare **InputStream**, and use **DataInputStream.readLine** rather than **InputStream.read**. You will find that almost all I/O operates this way. You take a bare **InputStream** or **OutputStream**, then create a more sophisticated, higher-level stream, like **DataInputStream**, using that bare stream.

The other big difference between Snitch and more complicated server applications like AgentServer is that we do only a single **readLine** before closing the socket; most servers keep reading the socket until the client applet disconnects.

File I/O

Something in the server Snitch application that we haven't seen before is file I/O via the **File** class. File I/O is not useful to applets because the browser **SecurityManagers** generally do not allow applets to use it. Period. When you're writing a Java standalone application like Snitch, on the other hand, you're free to do whatever I/O you might want. Snitch's use of file I/O is limited to:

◆ Creating a new day file

◆ Writing whatever lines come over the **Socket** into that day file

◆ Creating the new day file is embodied in the **switchFiles** method

```
public void switchFiles() {
  Date d = new Date();

  filename = new String( "M"+(d.getMonth()+1)+"D"+d.getDate()+
      "Y"+d.getYear()+".w"+d.getHours()+""+d.getMinutes() );
  try {
    File fi = new File( filename );
    ps = new PrintStream( new FileOutputStream(fi) );
  } catch( IOException e )
    { System.out.println( "ioexception e "+e );}

}
```

The point of **switchFiles** is to create a file that will be unique and have a name that will indicate what date it is associated with. In normal operation, the system would create one day file for each day. Since the day file name also contains an hour/minute indicator, you can stop and restart the server within a day and end up with two day files for one day. As with all I/O, we create the basic I/O object, get a base Stream object (in this case, a **FileOutputStream**) and create a higher-level Stream (in this case, a **PrintStream**) to do our actual I/O against.

When does **switchFiles** get called? Well, it gets called once at startup. What happens in normal running then is that the main loop of Snitch simply sleeps for a second, then wakes up and checks the time. If we've rolled past midnight, the main loop calls **switchFiles** to create a new day file.

To Block, or Not to Block

One of the key characteristics of any I/O operation is whether or not it blocks. If you call **InputStream.readLine**, no matter how many bytes it does read, it will not return until it reads a line terminator. It "blocks" until the line terminator is read. If **readLine** were non-blocking, it would return immediately whether or not it had read a line terminator.

Many coders, especially those who grew up in the bad old days of single threading, prefer to write their communication code as non-blocking. In single-threaded systems, there are very good reasons for this, one being that code that blocks, often fails to unblock.

That reasoning doesn't hold up in Java. Any thread that has blocked should be able to be unblocked by calling **Thread.stop** (throwing a **ThreadDeath** at it). Java also doesn't support many of the system calls (**select** and **available**, to name two) that Unix coders used to rely on to write non-blocking I/O.

Almost all Java I/O calls block, including socket connect, stream read, and stream write. Some allow the operation to timeout, but for the most part, you are literally required to thread and block.

Conclusion

Java makes network communication easy, through a set of simple classes—**URL**, **ServerSocket**, **Socket**, and **InetAddress**—that abstract the important concepts in Internetworking. While URLs provide some high-level functionality through **getContent**, you can easily program right down to the lowest levels using the **Socket** class.

Using these basic tools, we can easily construct functional systems of cooperating Java objects. While security restrictions often force some inelegance in the design this goal can still be achieved with modular, portable, and fairly readable implementations.

Handling Exceptions

John Rodley

14

In this chapter, you'll learn ways of throwing, catching, and bypassing exceptions and get a sneak preview of the latest support for exceptions in the Café debugger.

*I*like to think of programming as drawing a circle of solution around a problem. Each bit of code is another little arc in the circle. A bugless, deliverable program would be a complete circle around the problem; every aspect of the problem encompassed by the solution.

Unfortunately, there's no such thing as a bugless program. Parts of the problem always "seep" through the solution. How a program deals with errors often marks the difference between a usable, commercial program and an interesting-but-useless programming exercise.

In Java, the notion of programmatic error is encapsulated in *exceptions*. **Exception** is a Java class that embodies everything you need to pinpoint where (and often why) an exception occurred. In this chapter we'll first talk about what exceptions are, then we'll talk about how they're used and what effect they have on a program's flow of execution. We'll finish up by taking a quick look at new debugger enhancement in the Café 1.2 Prerelease, which was designed to make debugging with exceptions easier.

The Exception Class

The **Exception** class is a subclass of **Throwable**. Strictly speaking, it is not exceptions, but throwables that get thrown in a Java program. In normal use though, you will almost always throw and catch exceptions. Figure 14.1 shows the class hierarchy for the **Throwable** class and its descendants.

In the earlier test versions of Java, all of the functionality of exceptions resided solely in the **Exception** class. The release version, however, split **Exception** into two classes: the superclass **Throwable**, which contains the **toString** and **StackTrace** methods, and a subclass, **Exception**, which contains only the two constructors. This approach makes a lot of sense because, as we will see later, not all that is throwable is necessarily an exception.

What information does an exception really need to embody? Under Java, an exception stores two pieces of information: a *detail message* describing

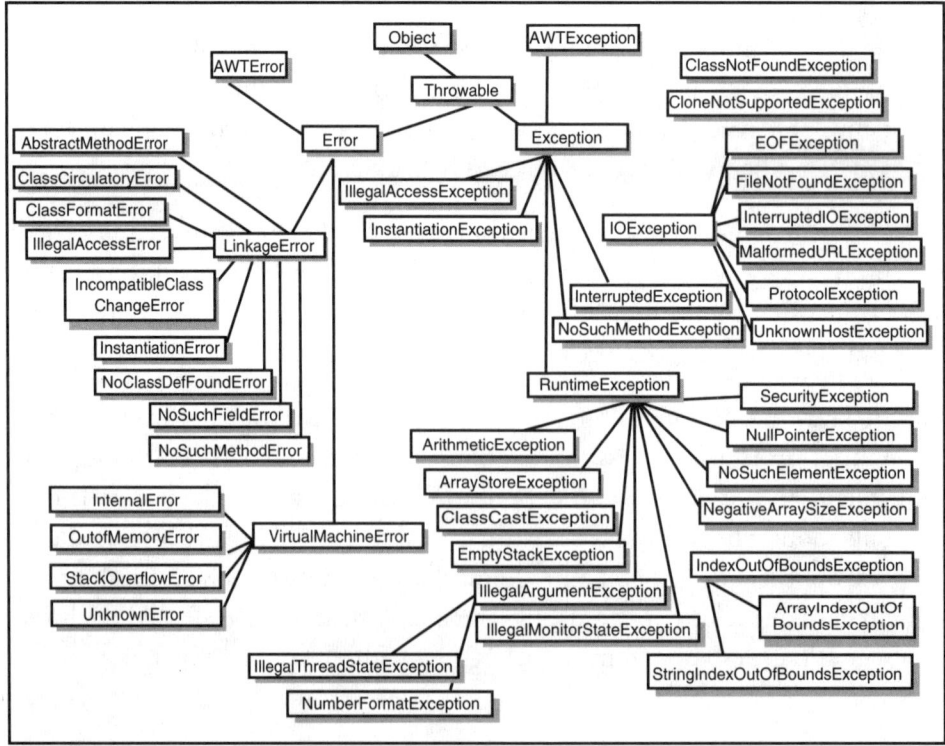

Figure 14.1   The Throwable class hierarchy.

the problem, and a *stack trace* that describes where in the program's source code the exception occurred. All the methods included in the **Exception**, **Error**, and **Throwable** classes are devoted to storing and displaying these two pieces of information.

The Error Class

Exception has a mirror image, an "evil twin," if you will: the **Error** class. Functionally, **Error** is identical to **Exception**. It exists mainly to provide exception throwers with a way around your exception-handling code. At first glance, this seems outrageous. You go to all the trouble of catching and dealing with exceptions, and somebody goes and throws an error just to get around you. In practice, it turns out that there are some problems from which you just can't recover. A classic example of this is when your program runs out of memory. Literally anything you do after running out of memory will only make the problem worse because you can't instantiate anything. You end up in a spiral of exception-handling code because your exception handler itself causes more exceptions. It's just not worth it.

As the Sun documentation for **Error** says: only catch errors if you really know what you're doing. Error handling, as you might have guessed, is beyond the scope of this book. All you really have to remember about errors is that the base **Error** class is identical in function to the **Exception** class. It exists as a separate entity solely to get around statements like the one in the following code line:

```
catch( Exception e ) { ... }
```

Anything we say about exceptions applies equally to errors, unless otherwise noted.

Throwables In Detail

As you can see in Tables 14.1, 14.2, and 14.3, the line of inheritance for errors and exceptions goes **Object-Throwable-Error/Exception**. Thus, all the functionality of exceptions is embodied in the **Throwable** and **Exception** classes. Table 14.1 shows the methods and constructors for the **Throwable** class, while Tables 14.2 and 14.3 show the methods and constructors for **Throwable**'s two subclasses, **Error** and **Exception** (there are no public variables).

Table 14.1 The Throwable Class.

Return Type	Method	Description
None	Throwable()	Constructs a Throwable with no detail message.
None	Throwable(String DetailMessage)	Constructs a Throwable with the specified detail message.
String	getMessage()	Returns the detail message.
String	toString()	Returns a description of the Throwable.
void	printStackTrace()	Prints the Throwable and its stack trace on standard output.
void specified.	printStackTrace (PrintStream s)	Prints the Throwable and its stack trace on the PrintStream.
Throwable	fillInStackTrace()	Fills in the stack trace; must be used whenever you rethrow a Throwable.

Table 14.2 The Exception Class.

Constructor	Description
Exception()	Constructs an exception with no detail message.
Exception(String DetailMessage)	Constructs an exception where the detail message is specified by the DetailMessage parameter.

Table 14.3 The Error Class.

Constructor	Description
Error()	Constructs an error with no detail message.
Error(String DetailMessage)	Constructs an error where the detail message is specified by the DetailMessage parameter.

Exceptions are designed to accomplish the following tasks:

◆ *Break the flow of execution.* The **throw** mechanism, which we'll discuss shortly, accomplishes this task.

◆ *Preserve and display the call stack at the exception point.* The **StackTrace** methods, **fillInStackTrace** and **printStackTrace** deal with this task.

◆ *Preserve and display a "label" that names the exception and gives a description that would be meaningful to debuggers who don't have access to the source code.* The constructors store the label, while **toString** and **getMessage** return it.

As we said, **Error** and **Exception** contain only the two constructors—one that sets the detail message, and one that doesn't. Within the superclass **Throwable**, **getMessage**, and **toString** both give you a **String** that describes the exception. This **String** is the detail message that the exception designer attached to this exception. **getMessage** returns only the detail message, while **toString** prepends the class name to the **detailMessage**.

FillInStackTrace loads the exception with a description of the call stack at the time the **fillInStackTrace** was called. The call stack is simply the list of method invocations that the applet took to get to a particular source line. If methodA calls methodB, and methodB calls methodC, which then calls **fillInStackTrace**, the call stack will contain methodA, methodB, and methodC. **fillInStackTrace** loads the exception with this information. **PrintStackTrace** prints it back out again.

Pre-Defined Exceptions and Errors

Java and its accompanying packages define a number of exceptions and errors, which are detailed in Tables 14.4 and 14.5. Additional views of thse exceptions and errors classes, seen from Café's Hierarchy Editor, are shown in Figures 14.2 and 14.3.

Table 14.4   A Comprehensive List of Java Exceptions.

Exception Name	Description
ArithmeticException	Divide by zero/mod by zero.
ArrayIndexOutOfBounds	Tried to access past current bounds of array.
ExceptionArrayStoreException	Tried to put the wrong class of Object into an array.
AWTException	Exception occurred somewhere in the window toolkit.
ClassCastException	Tried to cast between classes that are not related.
ClassNotFoundException	ClassLoader failed to load class (See Chapter 9).
CloneNotSupportedException	Tried to clone an Object that doesn't support it.
EmptyStackException	Tried to use an empty stack.
EOFException	File I/O reached end of file.
Exception	Base Exception class; never thrown.
FileNotFoundException	Tried to create a File object from a file that doesn't exist.
IllegalAccessException	Tried to invoke a method that couldn't be found.
IllegalArgumentException	Invoked method detected a bad argument.
IllegalMonitorStateException	Tried to notify a monitor that you don't own.
IllegalThreadStateException	Tried to set daemon status on a Thread that was already running.
IndexOutOfBoundsException	Generic bad index.
InstantiationException	Problem in new.
InterruptedException	The receiving thread has been interrupted by another thread.
InterruptedIOException	A blocking I/O operation has been interrupted.
IOException	I/O device (socket or file) broke while in use; often socket connection lost.
MalformedURLException	String URL passed to URL constructor was nonsense.
NegativeArraySizeException	Tried to create an array with negative size "int j[] = new int[-5]."
NoSuchElementException	Tried to access Vector element < 0 or beyond size() of Vector.
NoSuchMethodException	Method that existed during compile no longer exists.
NullPointerException	Tried to use an uninitialized object.
NumberFormatException	Tried to make a number from a non-numeric string.
ProtocolException	Problem in protocol handler.

Continued

Table 14.4   A Comprehensive List of Java Exceptions (Continued).

Exception Name	Description
RuntimeException	Base class for exceptions generated by the interpreter; never thrown.
SecurityException	Operation failed security check.
SocketException	Generic socket use problem.
StringIndexOutOfBoundsException	Tried to access character at index < 0 or beyond length()of String.
UnknownHostException	Host name couldn't be resolved to an IP address.
UnknownServiceException	There is no handler for the Stream type.
UTFDataFormatException	Malformed string encountered in a DataInputStream.

Table 14.5   A Comprehensive List of Java Errors.

Error Name	Description
AbstractMethodError	Tried to invoke abstract method.
AWTError	Unexpected error in window toolkit.
ClassCircularityError	Circular dependence detected while loading class.
ClassFormatError	Bad file format detected by implicit class loader.
Error	Base Error class; never thrown.
IllegalAccessError	Non-permitted access.
IncompatibleClassChange Error	Bad type cast.
InstantiationError	Tried to instantiate abstract class or interface via new.
InternalError	Catch-all for interpreter problems.
LinkageError	Base class for indicating that interdependent classes have changed incompatiblly.
NoClassDefFoundError	Class that was available at compile-time is no longer available.
NoSuchFieldError	Field could not be found.
NoSuchMethodError	Invoked method that couldn't be found.
OutOfMemoryError	System is out of memory.
StackOverflowError	Ran out of stack; possibly unterminated recursion.
UnknownError	Error of unknown nature.
UnsatisfiedLinkError	Unsatisfied link.
VerifyError	Class bytecode file failed security check during class load operation.
VirtualMachineError	The virtual machine has a problem.

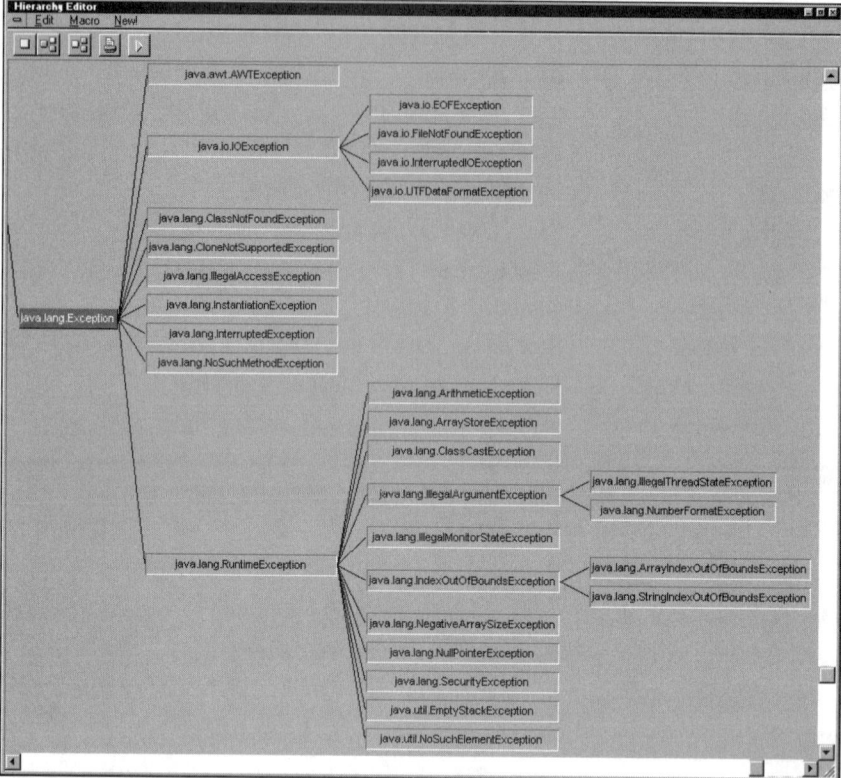

Figure 14.2   Hierarchy of Java Exceptions.

Many of the exceptions and errors listed in the tables and figures—especially **RunTimeException**s, such as **NullPointerException** and**IllegalAccess Exception**, and **VirtualMachineError**s, like **OutOfMemoryError** and **StackOverflowError**—should be familiar to C and C++ coders. Others, like **ArrayIndexOutOfBoundsException** and **NoSuchMethodError**, are designed specifically to implement new features of the Java language.

The thing to remember about all these exceptions and errors is that they usually differ *only* in the information contained in their detail message. Exceptions, in general, do not implement new methods or public variables. Given that any exception is going to go traveling up the call stack, and get caught who knows where, there is no additional functionality that it makes any sense for **Exception** to provide.

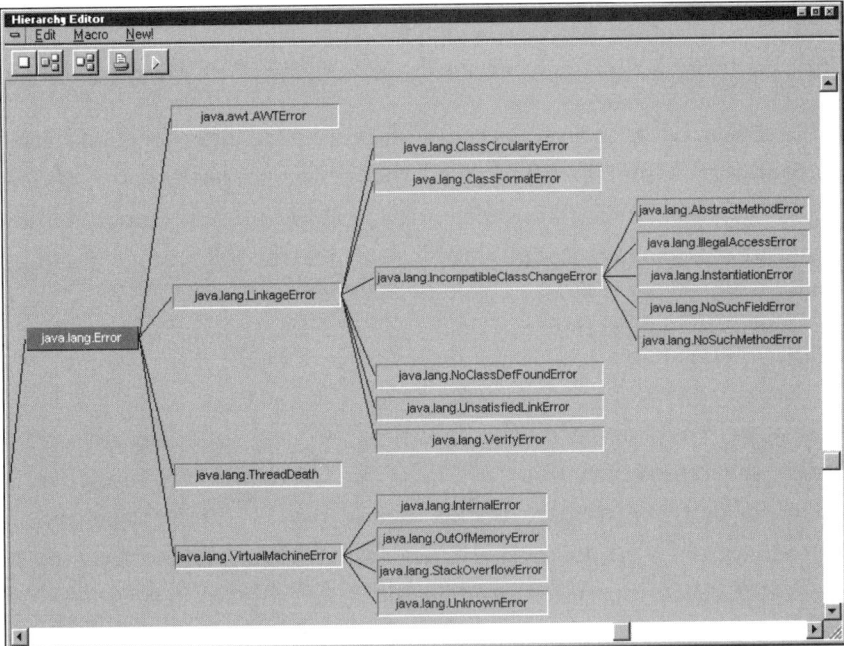

Figure 14.3 **Hierarchy of Java Errors.**

Exceptions and The Flow of Execution

The purpose of an exception is to break the normal flow of execution. To understand how a thrown exception affects the flow of execution, we have to think back to our discussion of threads. Everything that happens within a thread is within the scope of the **Thread** object's **run** method. At any point in the execution of the program, you'll be executing somewhere within a set of nested scopes with the **run** method being the outermost scope. When you throw an exception, Java stops execution of the current method. Then it checks the current scope to see if the object is caught there; that is, whether or not the current scope is bracketed by a **try-catch** block. If the throw occurs within a **try-catch** block, then the **catch** clause is checked to see whether the exception thrown is the same class (or some subclass) as the exception being caught. If it is, the method continues execution at the start of the **catch** block. If there is no matching **catch** clause in this scope, Java exits that scope and runs the same check on the next scope out. This process continues until the exception is caught. By traveling back through the call stack this way, an uncaught exception effectively terminates the thread.

There are two ends to any exception: the **throw** statement, which starts the exception traveling up through all the nested scopes,and the **try-catch** control structure, which stops this runaway object from traveling up through any more scopes. The general form is shown in the following code snippet:

```
try { set of expressions }
catch ( exception ) { expressions to run if we catch an exception. }
```

The syntax really describes the function. We "try" the block of code, and "catch" the named exception class if it occurs. In fact, the **try** block describes a scope of its own. In order for this pseudo-code to catch the exception, it must be thrown within the **try** block (set of curly braces following **try**). The **catch** clause is easiest to understand if you think of it as almost a sub-method that takes an argument. In the **catch** clause, you can name a single exception type, then follow it with a block of code to execute if that exception is caught. Listing 14.1 shows an actual exception-handling block.

LISTING 14.1 AN EXCEPTION HANDLING BLOCK

```
public void readit( Socket s ) {
  int ret;
  try {
        ret = s.getInputStream().read(); }
  catch( IOException ourExc ) {
        System.out.println( "Socket error "+ourExc ); }
  }
```

In this example, if **s.getInputStream().read** throws an **IOException**, the variable **ourExc** is initialized with the specifics of the exception. Then, the block attached to the **catch** clause executes, printing a message to standard output. In order to throw this exception, somewhere in the source for **InputStream.read** must be a statement that reads something like:

```
throw( new IOException());
```

If an **IOException** is *not* thrown by **s.getInputStream().read**, the **catch** block never executes. This is a simple, but illustrative example. Let's take a look at a complete example, shown in Listing 14.2, that generates an exception two levels down the call stack. Listing 14.3 shows the output from Café's Output window that gets generated when you run the applet.

LISTING **14.2** GENERATING AN EXCEPTION

```
package chap14;

import java.awt.Graphics;
import java.awt.*;
import java.applet.Applet;
import java.net.*;
import java.lang.*;
import java.io.*;
import java.util.*;

/** A class for demonstrating a thrown-exceptions effect on the
flow of execution.
*/
public class ch14 extends Applet implements Runnable {

public Thread myThread;

public void start() {
  if( myThread == null ) {
    myThread = new Thread( this );
    myThread.start();
  }
}

/** Override of Thread.run. */
public void run() {
  System.out.println( "run invoked" );
  try {
    while( true ) {
      System.out.println( "run-while-1" );
      myMethodA();
      myMethodB();
      System.out.println( "run-while-2" );
    }
  }
  catch( Exception e )
    { System.out.println( "run caught exception "+e ); }
  }

/** A method that gets called by run, which calls another
method that generates an exception.
*/
```

```java
public void myMethodA() throws Exception {
 try {
      System.out.println( "\tmyMethodA invoked" );
      lastMethod();
      System.out.println( "\tmyMethodA-2" );
 }
 catch( Exception e ) {
    System.out.println( "\tmyMethodA caught Exception" );
    e.printStackTrace( System.out );
    throw (Exception)e.fillInStackTrace();
 }
}


/** A method, called by myMethodA, that calls another method
that generates an exception.
*/
public void myMethodB() throws MalformedURLException {
 try {
    System.out.println( "\tmyMethodB invoked" );
    lastMethod();
    System.out.println( "\tmyMethodB-2" );
 }
 catch( Exception e ) {
    System.out.println( "\tmyMethodB caught Exception" );
    throw (MalformedURLException)e.fillInStackTrace();
 }
 finally { System.out.println( "\tmyMethodB finally" ); }
 }


/** A method that generates an MalformedURLException. */
public void lastMethod() throws MalformedURLException {
  int ret;
  int j = 0;
  System.out.println( "\t\tlastMethod invoked" );
  URL u = new URL( "JohnHost" );
  System.out.println( "\t\tlastMethod-2" );
  j++;
}
```

LISTING 14.3   THE CALL STACK PRINTOUT FROM LISTING 14.2

```
thread applet-chap14/ch14.class find class chap14.ch14
Opening stream to: file:/C:/agent/classes/rel/chap14/ch14.class to
 get chap14.ch14
run invoked
run-while-1
 myMethodA invoked
      lastMethod invoked
```

```
myMethodA caught Exception
java.net.MalformedURLException: no protocol: JohnHost
 at java.net.URL.<init>(URL.java:157)
 at java.net.URL.<init>(URL.java:107)
 at chap14.ch14.lastMethod(ch14.java:78)
 at chap14.ch14.myMethodA(ch14.java:47)
 at chap14.ch14.run(ch14.java:32)
 at java.lang.Thread.run(Thread.java:289)
```

Here we've intentionally passed a bad string URL to the **URL** constructor in order to make it throw a **MalformedURLException**. We've also placed **println**'s throughout the code to show where the generated exception breaks the normal flow of execution. As you can see from Listing 14.2, the methods **run**, **myMethodA**, and **lastMethod** get invoked. Taking it from the bottom up, let's see what these methods do:

◆ **lastMethod**'s first **println** ("... invoked") executes, but then the invocation of the **URL** constructor throws an exception, so **lastMethod**'s second **println** never gets called.

◆ **myMethodA**'s initial **println** ("... invoked") gets executed, but then the invocation of **lastMethod** throws an exception, so the second **println** ("myMethodA-2") never gets called. The **catch** clause matches the exception, so our **catch** block gets executed, printing out the "caught exception" method, then generating the stack trace (via**printStack Trace**) that tells us which lines in the source code we were at when the exception blew through. **myMethodA** then rethrows the exception.

◆ **run**'s initial **println** ("... invoked") executes and we fall into the **while** loop and execute the second **println** ("run-while-1"). **myMethodA** is then invoked, which throws an exception. The exception bounces us straight out of the **while** loop without executing either **myMethodB** or the third **println** ("run-while-2"), then it matches the **catch** clause and executes the **println** there.

Using Finally

If you're only catching a single exception type, you'll probably end up writing a lot of code like this:

```
try { expressions }
catch( exception ) {
```

```
Do cleanup;
rethrow the Exception
}
```

The fact is, most code can't really do anything with caught exceptions, but merely needs to do some housekeeping if an exception should break the method at an inconvenient spot. To deal with this situation, Java allows a shortcut using the **try-finally** syntax. Using this technique, our pseudo-code **try-catch-rethrow** example then becomes:

```
try { expressions }
finally {
 Do cleanup;
 }
```

The effect is similar: any caught throwable gets rethrown, but some unneccessary source code is eliminated. Where **try-finally** really differs from **try-catch** is that in **try-catch**, the **catch** block *only gets executed if a thrown object is caught, while a finally block is always executed whether or not a throw occurs.* To illustrate, consider the following blocks:

```
try {
  myMethod();
}
catch( Exception e ) { System.out.println( "myMethod is done" );  }

try {
  myMethod();
}
finally { System.out.println( "myMethod is done" );  }
```

The first block prints out "myMethod is done" only if **myMethod** throws an **Exception**, while the second block prints out "myMethod is done" whether or not **myMethod** throws an **Exception**. The **finally** block executes no matter what happens, whether or not any kind of object gets thrown.

Catching Multiple Exceptions

Each **catch** clause specifies a single class/interface to catch, but **catch** clauses can be cascaded as shown in Listing 14.4. The **catch** clauses are evaulated in order. When an object is thrown, it passes through each of the **catch** clauses and the first **catch** clause that it happens to match gets executed.

LISTING 14.4 CASCADED CATCH CLAUSES

```
try {
  MyClass.doSomeFtpStuff();
}
catch( FtpLoginException fe ) { System.out.println( "FTP login
  exception" ); }
catch( FtpProtocolException fpe ) { System.out.println( "FTP protocol
  exception" ); }
```

Thus, you can write a **try-catch** block to do one thing for a particular exception and something else for all the other exceptions, as shown in Listing 14.5.

LISTING 14.5 SIFTING EXCEPTIONS USING SUBCLASSES

```
try {
  MyClass.myMethod();
}
catch( ParticularException pe) { System.out.println("particular
  exception" ); }
catch( Exception e) { System.out.println( "Some other exception" ); }
finally { System.out.println( "The try block has finished." ); }
```

ParticularException is caught by the first clause, while all others fall through to the second clause. Note the **finally** clause cascaded with the **catch** clauses.

Exceptions and Scope

Java's object orientation not only encourages proper scoping of variables, but in some not-so-subtle ways, it actually enforces proper scoping. One of the places where you see this most clearly is in the development of exception-handling code. The code in Listing 14.6 attempts to connect to a URL and get the contents of the file located there.

LISTING 14.6 CONNECTING TO A URL

```
public void start() {
URL u = new URL("http://www.myhouse.com/images/image.gif" );
Object o = u.getContent();
System.out.println( "connected to "+u+" and got object "+o);
}
```

If you compile this code, it bombs with two messages saying you need to catch **MalformedURLException** and **IOException**. So you rewrite the code as in Listing 14.7.

LISTING 14.7   CONNECTING TO A URL, TAKE 2

```
public void start() {
try {
 URL u = new URL("http://www.myhouse.com/images/image.gif" );
} catch( MalformedURLException e ){ System.out.println( "url
 exception "+e ); }
try {
 Object o = u.getContent();
} catch( IOException e ) { System.out.println( "io exception "+e ); }

System.out.println( "connected to "+u+" and got object "+o);
}
```

When you recompile this code, it bombs again, complaining that the identifiers **u** and **o** are undefined. You berate yourself for being so stupid and rewrite it, taking the declaration of *u* and *o* out to the next scope as in Listing 14.8.

LISTING 14.8   CONNECTING TO A URL, TAKE 3

```
public void start() {
URL u;
Object o;
try {
 u = new URL("http://www.myhouse.com/images/image.gif" );
} catch( MalformedURLException e ){ System.out.println( "url
 exception "+e ); }
try {
  o = u.getContent();
} catch( IOException e ) { System.out.println( "io exception "+e ); }

System.out.println( "connected to "+u+" and got object "+o);
}
```

When you compile this one, Java complains that **u** and **o** are uninitialized when they get printed out. At this point, you could just set **u** and **o** to something such as **null**: the applet would compile, and in the best case, it would run okay. But all you've really accomplished is to work around the compiler's best efforts to guide you in the right direction. What you really want to end up with is the code shown in Listing 14.9.

LISTING 14.9 CONNECTING TO A *URL*, THE FINAL CHAPTER

```
public void start() {
try {
 URL u = new URL("http://www.myhouse.com/images/image.gif" );
 try {
      Object o = u.getContent();
      System.out.println( "connected to "+u+" and got object "+o);
 } catch( IOException e ) { System.out.println( "io exception "+e );
 }
} catch( MalformedURLException e ){ System.out.println( "url
 exception "+e ); }

}
```

As you can see, Java strives mightily to encourage and enforce good coding practices, but our first instincts and old habits of mind can often lead us astray.

When to Catch Exceptions

Exceptions are like grenades: don't catch one unless you know what to do with it. Fortunately, we don't have to catch every exception, or keep every exception we catch. The trick is knowing which ones to ignore, which to catch and keep, and which to pass through.

What often makes exceptions/errors confusing to Java novices is that some of them can be ignored, and others can't. If a method declares itself as throwing a particular exception, then any method that calls that method must either catch, or declare itself as throwing that exception. For example, consider the method shown in the following code snippet:

```
void myRead( InputStream is ) {
  int myInt = is.read();
}
```

This method will not compile because we haven't accounted for the **IOException** that **InputStream.read** throws. We have only two options for dealing with this. The first option is to catch the exception ourselves, as in Listing 14.10. The second is to pass the exception through, as shown in Listing 14.11.

LISTING 14.10 CATCHING THE EXCEPTION

```
void myRead( InputStream is ) {
  try {
    int myInt = is.read();
  } catch( IOException e )
    { System.out.println( "bad read "+e ); }
}
```

LISTING 14.11 PASSING THE EXCEPTION THROUGH

```
void myRead( InputStream is ) throws IOException {
  int myInt = is.read();
}
```

This situation arises only because **InputStream.read** contains a **throw** statement like

```
throw (new IOException());.
```

and declares itself as throwing **IOException** as in:

```
public int read() throws Exception { ...
```

Within an applet, if you call a method that declares itself as throwing an exception, then that exception *must* eventually be caught within your code. This is not so obvious, unless you think about it awhile. Any method that calls an exception-throwing method must either catch the exception or pass it through. So assume that all of our methods pass the exception through. Thus, all these methods will be declared as **throws Exception**. Eventually, there will be an applet override that has to call a method that throws an exception. That applet override either has to catch the exception or pass it through. But it can't pass the exception through because none of the applet's methods are declared as throwing an exception. Thus, any exceptions must be caught at least at the applet level.

Runtime Exceptions

It should be clear that if exceptions are thrown by a method that declares itself as throwing an exception, then they are part of a closed loop; they must eventually be caught. However, there is another type of exception that occurs outside this closed loop: this type of exception doesn't necessarily have to be caught. These are the exceptions/errors that emanate from the interpreter itself. In the class hierarchy diagram shown earlier in Figure 14.1, three huge branches—**LinkageError**, **VirtualMachineError**, and **RuntimeException** (as well as a few other exceptions)—fall into this category. These exceptions/errors can be thrown by such innocuous statements as:

```
Integer I = new Integer(1) or Integer I = (Integer)j.
```

In fact, almost any statement can result in one of these exceptions. Java does not expect us to catch or deal with interpreter-generated exceptions/errors. In general, you should not try to catch errors at all, and the only exceptions you should try to catch are those that you are forced to catch because they're declared as being thrown by a method you've called.

For example, consider how **NumberFormatException** is used in the code in listing 14.12, below. In this code, given a message string that has a price within it, we start with a byte array from the price field of the message and turn it into a number representing the price. In C or C++, we'd have scanned the string for illegal characters, flagging an error if we found one. To do the same thing in Java, you'd write something like Listing 14.12.

LISTING 14.12 NUMBER FROM DUBIOUS STRING, THE HARD WAY

```
if( s.compareTo( PRICE_PREFIX ) == 0 )
    {
    String s1 = new String( b, 0, currentOffset,PRICELEN_SIZE);
    currentOffset += PRICELEN_SIZE;
    Integer length = new Integer( s1 );
    System.out.println( "got price of length "+length );
    bprice = new byte[length.intValue()];

    boolean bError = false;
    for( int i = 0; i < length.intValue(); i++ ) {
      bprice[i] = b[currentOffset++];
      if( bprice[i] < '0' || bprice[i] > '9' )
        bError = true;
      }
    String sprice = new String( bprice, 0 );
    if( bError == true )
      System.out.println( "price number format error" );
    else {
```

```
        Integer J = new Integer( sprice );
        price = J.intValue();
        }
    }
  else
    System.out.println( "out of sync at price" );
```

See the grief we go through to check each member of the byte array. Listing 14.13 does it the Java way, simply passing the **String** to the **Number** constructor and catching the **NumberFormatException** the constructor throws if there is any problem converting the **String**.

LISTING 14.13   NUMBER FROM DUBIOUS STRING

```
  if( s.compareTo( PRICE_PREFIX ) == 0 )
    {
    String s1 = new String( b, 0, currentOffset,PRICELEN_SIZE);
    currentOffset += PRICELEN_SIZE;
    Integer length = new Integer( s1 );
    System.out.println( "got price of length "+length );
    bprice = new byte[length.intValue()];
    for( int i = 0; i < length.intValue(); i++ ) {
      bprice[i] = b[currentOffset++];
      }
    String sprice = new String( bprice, 0 );
    try {
      Integer J = new Integer( sprice );
      price = J.intValue();
      }
    catch( NumberFormatException e ) {
        System.out.println( "price number format error" );
        }
    }
  else
    System.out.println( "out of sync at price" );
```

Essentially, the format checking we did in Listing 14.12 to see whether each byte was a valid number, was redundant. The **Integer** constructor already does this checking. All we need to do is catch the exception.

When to Throw Exceptions

Never, never, never use method return values to pass errors back up the call stack. If you find yourself thinking of implementing a return value for an error condition, this is where you need to throw an exception.

When throwing exceptions there are three rules by which you need to abide:

1. If a method throws an exception, it must declare it in the method declaration.

2. If a method overrides a method in a superclass or interface, it can only throw exceptions that the overridden method has declared.

   This rule is very restrictive, but there is good reason for it. Java is a language for distributed computing, where there are millions of programmers writing large numbers of small-ish objects that interact via interfaces. The percentage of reused code in the Java environment is some large multiple of that experienced with C and C++. In order to make code reuse a viable option, the published APIs (including thrown exceptions) for public methods must be reliable, and immutable. If you were to override a public method, and then go throwing exceptions that users of your method weren't prepared for (because it wasn't part of the published API), you'd end up breaking perfectly good code, and the writers of that perfectly good code would have much less confidence in that published API. It is for this reason that the compiler enforces this rule. Remember, your applets are traveling over the network and executing within applications you could never have envisioned.

3. If a method overrides a method in a superclass or interface, it must catch any exception that the overridden method doesn't throw, if that exception is thrown by a method that it calls. In other words, the method can't allow any disallowed exception from proceeding up the call stack through it. As an example, the **run** method from the **Runnable** interface declares no exceptions, but **Thread.sleep** throws the**Interrupted Exception**. So if we call **Thread.sleep**, we must catch**Interrupted Exception**.

These three rules help close a large hole in our coding methodology. The fact that interface declarations specify the exceptions that emanate from implementations will limit the actual number of exceptions that coders can throw (and define). Forcing coders to catch any disallowed exceptions limits the propagation of exceptions through the call stack, and declaring thrown exceptions in the method declaration guarantees that there will never be undocumented exceptions. The hope is that Java applets will be "closed" systems where problems that arise within the system are handled gracefully within the system.

Native Exceptions

Generating exceptions within native methods is easy and good practice. The mechanism you use is signals. On Window NT, Windows 95 or Sun Solaris, for example, you would use the **SignalError** system call to send a signal as in Listing 14.14.

LISTING 14.14 USING THE SIGNALERROR SYSTEM CALL TO THROW A JAVA EXCEPTION

```
SignalError(0, "java/io/IOException", "Out of Disk space");
```

Calling **SignalError** does not actually throw the exception. What happens is that the exception is "recorded" when **SignalError** is called, but doesn't get thrown until your native method returns to the interpreter. After the native method returns, the native method invoker simply checks whether or not an exception has been recorded, and, if it has, throws it. This has one important side effect. If you throw two exceptions within a single native method (probably bad practice in any case), the second exception will overwrite the first and upon return to the interpreter only the second exception will be thrown. Thus, any native method can only throw one exception per invocation.

Debugging with Exceptions in Café

As it was noted in Chapter 10, one of the latest new features of the Café debugger is a sophisticated way of telling the debugger how to respond when exceptions get raised. This feature is relatively new to Café, and since I am working with Prerelease 1.2 of Café, things may look a little different in the final release. But the concepts should remain the same. Therefore, let's now take a look at this powerful Café debugger enhancement and see how it will help us to debug Java exceptions.

As we mentioned earlier, Java generates certain exceptions that you are not required to catch. One such exception, as we noted above, is the **NumberFormatException**. In Listing 14.13, we added code to catch a **NumberFormatException**. We may find that in some situations we are not sure why an exception is being razed. By simply catching the exception, we are no further along in understanding what caused the exception to be raised in the first place.

The Café debugger changes that. As of Prerelease 1.2, you can now *tell* the Café debugger what to do when it encounters either Java exceptions or your own exceptions. Using this feature, you can tell the debugger to actually stop in the code that threw the exception, thereby allowing you to see what the code objected to.

Let's now use this debugging feature to find out what actually happens when a **NumberFormatException** gets raised in some code. Consider the code in Listing 14.15.

LISTING *14.15* *A SIMPLE APPLET THAT RAISES A* *NUMBERFORMATEXCEPTION*

```
public class except extends java.applet.Applet {
    public void init() {
        super.init();
        Integer j= new Integer("Hi");
    }
}
```

Since "Hi" is certainly not a valid value for an integer, and since there is no code to handle the situation when an integer cannot be created because of a bad argument, a **NumberFormatException** is going to be raised when this applet runs. Try it, create a new project in Café called "except", type the above code into a source file named except.java, add it to the project and then run it.

After you run this code in Café, you get the following output in Café's Output window.

```
java.lang.NumberFormatException: Hi
        at java.lang.Integer.parseInt(Integer.java:147)
        at java.lang.Integer.<init>(Integer.java:217)
```

```
at except.init(except.java:6)
at sun.applet.AppletPanel.run(AppletPanel.java:251)
at java.lang.Thread.run(Thread.java:297)
```

Let's now tell the Café debugger to stop when the **NumberFormatException** gets raised.

From the Debug menu select Settings. Then select the "Exceptions" tab. You will see a screen that looks similar to Figure 14.4 (note: this feature of the debugger is only available in Café 1.2 and higher).

What you see here is a complete list of the Java system exceptions, some buttons for adding, deleting and working with these exceptions and a list box to change the debuggers behavior when it encounters an particular exception.

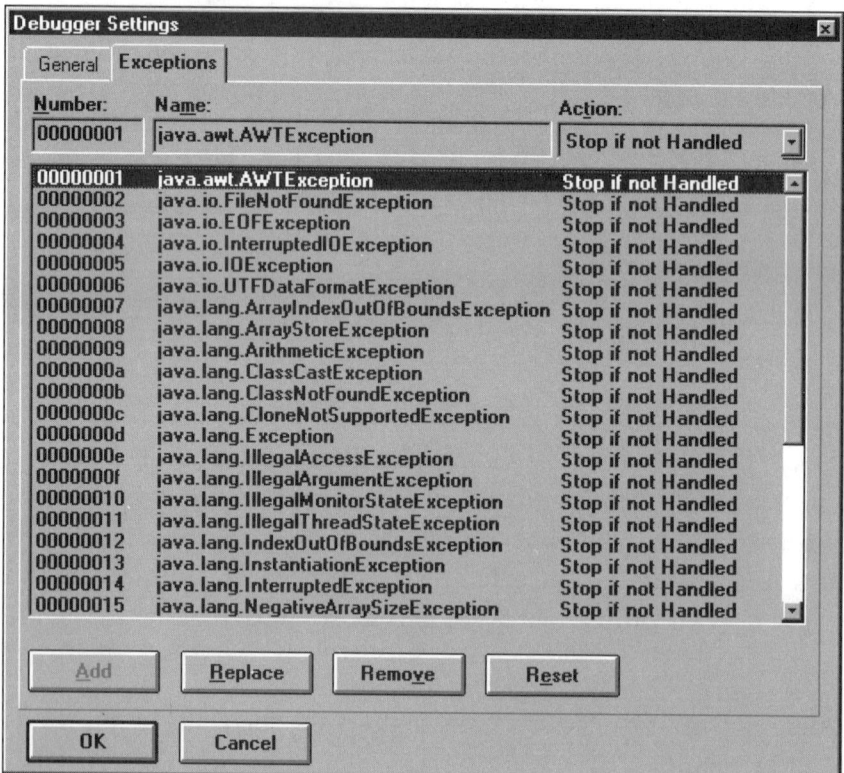

Figure 14.4   Exceptions Tab in Debug Settings.

Scroll down to the entry for **NumberFormatException**. As you can see, the current action that the compiler will take when it encounters this exception is to "Stop if not Handled." This is the default behavior. Click on the list box on the top right portion of this window and select "Always Stop." Next, click on the button named "Replace". You should now see the entry for **NumberFormatException** updated, as in Figure 14.5.

Click on OK. Lets now set a breakpoint in the code. Go to the second line of the init() method, which reads **super.init**(). Right-click and select "Set/ Clear Breakpoint." Now, from the Debug menu, select "Go until Breakpoint." When the line, **super.init**(), gets highlighted, select "Debug | Step Over" or simply press **F10**. You are now on the line that will produce a **NumberFormatException**. Again, step over this line by selecting "Debug | Step Over."

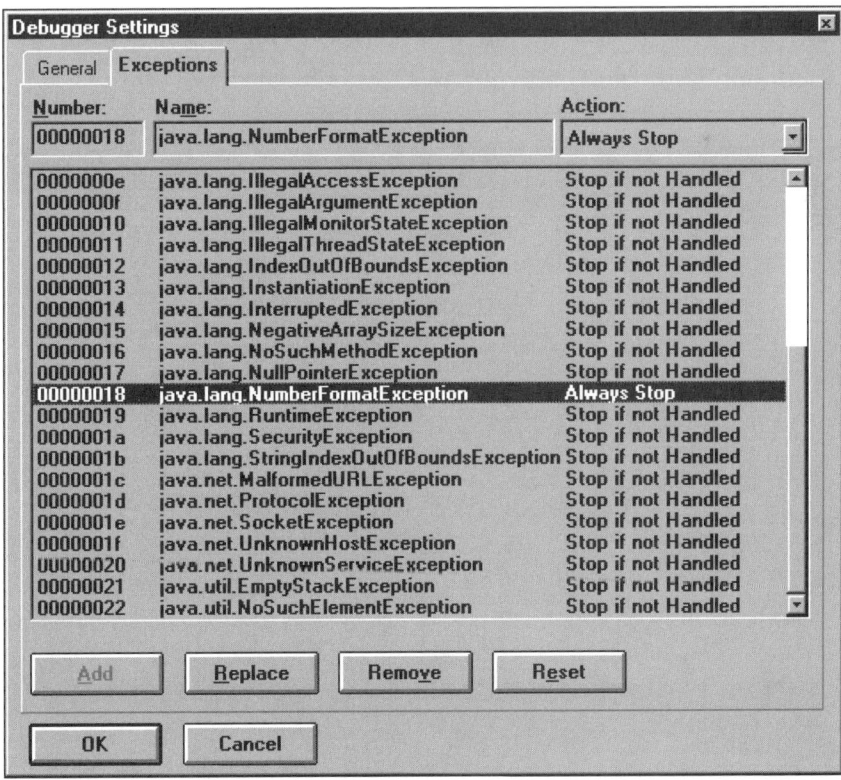

Figure 14.5   Updated NumberFormatException entry.

You will now see a source code window pop up, highlighting the line of code from which the **NumberFormatException** will be thrown. This window is pictured in Figure 14.6

In Café's Output window, you will see the following messages:

```
Exception raised:  "java.lang.NumberFormatException: Hi"
(You may press F5 to continue with default exception handling)
```

As the message states, you may press F5, which corresponds to "Debug | Go until Breakpoint." By doing this, you can walk the call chain from which the exception was raised, eventually returning to the offending line of code in this applet.

That concludes our demonstration and discussion of one of the newest debugging features to be added to Café. The added control you obtain with this new feature should make your debugging experiences with exceptions, both Java's and your own, a whole lot easier.

```
d:\cafepre\java\src\java\lang\Integer.java
 File  Edit  Goto  Macro  New!

      */
      public static int parseInt(String s, int radix) throws NumberForma
         if (s == null) {
            throw new NumberFormatException("null");
         }
      int result = 0;
      boolean negative = false;
      int i=0, max = s.length();
      if (max > 0) {
         if (s.charAt(0) == '-') {
         negative = true;
         i++;
         }
         while (i < max) {
         int digit = Character.digit(s.charAt(i++),radix);
         if (digit < 0)
            throw new NumberFormatException(s);
         result = result * radix + digit;
         }
      } else
         throw new NumberFormatException(s);
      if (negative)
         return -result;
      else
         return result;
      }

      /**
       * Assuming the specified String represents an integer, returns th
```

Figure 14.6   Origin of NumberFormatException.

Conclusion

We've spent a lot of time talking about how to use throwable objects in general and exceptions in particular. I've focused on this aspect of Java because proper use of exceptions (and other thrown objects) allows us to write more efficient and readable Java code. Learning to work within the bounds imposed by Java exception handling will also make our applets better and more respected citizens of the global applet society Java has spawned.

Security

John Rodley

Since it impacts how Java code will be used by the real world, security is a vital issue for the Java community. Now we'll explore some ways to add custom security managers to your applications and applets.

15

Security is a hard topic to deal with because Sun and the browser designers are still wrestling with the issue themselves. Within Java itself, security is pretty much a settled issue. The mechanism for implementing security (the **SecurityManager** class) is in place. What remains unsettled, at this writing, is how browsers will use this mechanism to protect their users.

The question is one of risk and reward. How much risk are users willing to risk to enjoy the, as yet undetermined, benefit of running Java applets?

Netscape has taken a very cautious approach to the subject, with the result that applets under Netscape are severely restricted. The security rules that Netscape applies to applets are:

◆ Applets cannot read or write files on the local file system.

◆ Applets can only open network connections to the host from which they were loaded.

◆ When an applet opens a pop-up window (such as a dialog box), Netscape will warn the user that it's an applet window. You currently see an "Untrusted" message on the bottom part of the window.

Properties

Java supports the concept of a *"property."* A property is essentially a global variable that Java programs (applet or application) can read or write via the **System.getProperty** and **System.setProperty** methods. A group of "system" properties exist that have a value in every situation, whether your code is standalone, runs from Netscape, Cafe or the appletviewer, or HotJava. Table 15.1 shows the system properties and describes their purpose.

As you can see, most of the system properties deal with the environment in which the browser operates—current directory, user name, operating system version, and so on. There can also be any number of "user" properties, which are essentially private properties that are meaningful only to specific applications or applets.

Table 15.1   The System Properties.

Property	Description
java.class.path	Value of "classpath:" the toplevel directory under which all classes to be loaded via the primordial class loader will be found.
java.class.version	Version of the Java packages.
java.home	Directory where the Java executables live.
java.vendor	Name of the vendor of this Java interpreter.
java.vendor.url	URL of the vendor's home page.
java.version	Version of Java in use.
file.separator	Character that separates files in a multi-file string.
line.separator	Character sequence that indicates the end of a line in this operating system.
path.separator	Character that separates directories in this operating system.
os.arch	"Architecture" of this machine;. for Intel Pentium and 486 this will be "x86."
os.name	Name of the operating system;. for Windows NT, this will be "Windows NT."
os.version	Version of the operating system.
user.dir	Current directory.
user.home	Name of the user's home directory.
user.name	User's login name.

The Properties File

For HotJava and appletviewer, you can set properties for your computer via the ~/.hotjava/properties file, where ~ stands for your home directory. For reasons of its own, Netscape does not use the properties file. All properties must be set using dialog boxes within Netscape.

All Windows programmers are familiar with the idea of initialization files such as WIN.INI. These files usually contain a series of statements of the form:

```
key=value
```

where *key* is the name of something, and *value* is the value we want to initialize this something to. Java supports the same concept in the properties file. Listing 15.1 shows the properties file I use locally for applet development.

LISTING 15.1   MY PROPERTIES FILE

```
#AppletViewer
#Fri Feb 09 12:04:35  1996
firewallSet=false
appletviewer.version=1.0
package.restrict.access.netscape=false
proxySet=false
firewallHost=
package.restrict.access.sun=false
acl.read.applet=true
acl.write.applet=true
acl.read=/temp/
firewallPort=80
appletviewer.security.mode=unrestricted
acl.write=/temp/
```

As you can see, I've defined thirteen variables, and set each to some string value. All of these variables are meaningful to appletviewer, though I could have easily defined my own variables and set them here manually. Table 15.2 shows some of the properties that are unique to appletviewer and HotJava.

The most interesting of these, and the most important from a security standpoint, are the **acl.read** and **acl.write** properties. acl stands for Access Control List, and that's just what these properties are—lists of directories

Table 15.2   appletviewer and HotJava Properties.

Property	Description
awt.toolkit	Package name of the AWT package in use.
acl.read	Directory that applets are allowed to read; all subdirectories of this directory are readable too.
acl.write	Directory that applets are allowed to write; all subdirectories are writeable too.
appletviewer.version	Version of the appletviewer.
firewallSet	Set to "true" if we're behind a firewall.
firewallProxyPort	Set to the http port number of the firewall proxy.
firewallProxyHost	Set to the host name of the firewall proxy.
firewallPort	Set to the http port number of the firewall.
firewallHost	Set to the host name of the firewall.
proxySet	Set to true if we're using a proxy.
cachingProxyPort	Set to the port number of the caching proxy.
cachingProxyHost	Set to the host name of the caching proxy.
appletviewer.security.mode	Set to the security mode of the appletviewer; appletviewer supports restricted and unrestricted class loading.

that an applet can access. Let's take a look at an example. What if our properties file contained the following lines:

```
acl.read=/home/johnr;/temp;/usr/ajr
acl.write=/temp;/usr/ajr
```

Applets loaded on a computer that had this property file would be allowed to read the directories /home/johnr, /temp, and /usr/ajr directories, *and* all the subdirectories beneath them. They would be able to write to /temp and /usr/ajr, *and* all the subdirectories beneath them. It's as easy as that.

Querying Properties

Having persistent properties is a wonderful thing, but how do we get at these properties from within an applet? Listing 15.2 shows a simple applet that gets the value of each of these properties.

LISTING 15.2 A PROPERTY-READING APPLET

```java
import java.awt.*;
import java.applet.Applet;
import java.lang.*;
import java.util.*;

/** An applet that tries to read and display various
properties. Displays the properties in a list.
@author John Rodley
@version 1.0
*/
public class security extends Applet {

  Vector props = new Vector(1);

/** Set the screen in border layout, put a list in the center,
and then display all the properties in the list.
*/
  public void init() {
    setLayout( new BorderLayout());
    List l = new List();
    add( "Center", l );
    props.addElement( new String( "firewallSet" ));
    props.addElement( new String( "appletviewer.version" ));
    props.addElement(
        new String("package.restrict.access.netscape"));
    props.addElement( new String( "proxySet" ));
    props.addElement( new String( "firewallHost" ));
    props.addElement(
        new String("package.restrict.access.sun"));
    props.addElement( new String( "acl.read.applet" ));
    props.addElement( new String( "acl.write.applet" ));
    props.addElement( new String( "acl.read" ));
    props.addElement( new String( "firewallPort" ));
    props.addElement(new String("appletviewer.security.mode"));
    props.addElement( new String( "acl.write" ));
    props.addElement( new String( "xyzabc" ));

    for( int i = 0; i < props.size(); i++ ) {
      try {
        l.addItem((String)props.elementAt(i)+
          "="+System.getProperty((String)props.elementAt(i)));
        System.out.println( (String)props.elementAt(i)+
          "="+System.getProperty((String)props.elementAt(i)));
      }
      catch( Exception e ) {
          l.addItem( "Unable to read property "+
              (String)props.elementAt(i));
```

```
        System.out.println("Unable to read property "+
            (String)props.elementAt(i));
        }
      }
    }
  }
```

In the **init** method we build a Vector of Strings containing all the variable names we expect to find in the properties file. Then we run through this Vector calling **System.getProperty** for each variable name. If the **getProperty** call throws an exception, we catch it and print a message declaring that the property is somehow inaccessible.

If we run this applet against this properties file in appletviewer, we get the application window and standard output shown in Listing 15.3.

LISTING 15.3   A PROPERTY-READING APPLET

```
firewallSet=false
appletviewer.version=1.0
package.restrict.access.netscape=false
proxySet=false
firewallHost=
package.restrict.access.sun=false
acl.read.applet=true
acl.write.applet=true
acl.read=/home/johnr;/temp;/usr/ajr
firewallPort=80
appletviewer.security.mode=unrestricted
acl.write=/temp;/usr/ajr
xyzabc=null
```

The SecurityManager Class

A standalone Java executable, such as HotJava, implements security by subclassing **SecurityManager** and attaching an instance of the new class to the **System** via **System.setSecurityManager**. **setSecurityManager** can only be called once in the life of the JVM, so that once a browser sets the **SecurityManager**, a rogue applet cannot reset it. By the time an applet executes, the browser will already have set the **SecurityManager**. Table 15.3 shows the **SecurityManager** class.

As you can see, there are protective methods guarding each of the resources that is vulnerable to abuse by misbehaved applets—properties, class loading, windows, network I/O, file I/O, and thread processes. Let's look at how the protective methods of **SecurityManager** guard these resources.

Table 15.3   The Methods of the SecurityManager Class.

Method Name	Arguments	Description
HELPER METHODS		
classDepth	String	Returns the index into the current class stack where the specified class is located; 0 is top of stack.
currentClassLoader		Returns the class loader or null if the primordial class loader is current.
getClassContext		Returns an array of classes that is the list of classes on the stack.
inClass	String	Returns true if the String argument is in the class.
inClassLoader		Returns true if there is a ClassLoader, false if the primordial class loader in use.
THE NETWORK		
CheckAccept	String, int	Can we accept connections on a socket?
CheckConnect	String, int	Can we connect to the specified network socket?
CheckListen	int	Can we listen to the specified local socket?
checkAccess	Thread or ThreadGroup	Can the specified Thread/ThreadGroup modify this ThreadGroup?
checkExec	String	Can we execute the specified system command?
checkExit	int	Has the system exited the virtual machine?
checkLink	String	Can we use the specified linked library?
THE FILE		
SystemcheckRead	int or String	Can we read from the specified file name or file descriptor?
checkWrite	int or String	Can we write to the specified file name or file descriptor?

Continued

Table 15.3 The Methods of the SecurityManager Class (continued)

Method Name	Arguments	Description
TOP-LEVEL WINDOWS		
checkTopLevelWindow		Can we create a window with no warning on it?
CLASSES AND CLASS LOADING		
checkCreateClassLoade		Can we create a ClassLoader?
checkPackageAccess	String	Can we use classes from the specified package?
checkPackage	Definition	Can we define a new package?
PROPERTIES		
checkProperties	Access	Can we read the list of properties?
checkPropertyAccess	String	Can we read the value of the specified property?

SecurityManager is an abstract class. An application that implements security, such as a browser, must define its own subclass of **SecurityManager**. We can divide the **SecurityManager** into two big sections: check methods and helper methods. The helper methods are utilities that security managers will find useful, and which we'll talk more about later. As for the check methods, Java puts all the sensitive resources in the system (file I/O, network I/O and so on) behind a lockable security door. The **SecurityManager's** check methods are the dead-bolt lock of Java security.

Whenever the interpreter runs into an instruction that accesses a protected resource, it turns that instruction into two distinct operations:

◆ Check if the access in the instruction is allowed

◆ Execute the instruction

To check if the access is allowed, the interpreter calls the check method that protects that resource. If the check method returns, the access is allowed. If the check method throws a **SecurityException**, the next operation (execute the instruction) doesn't happen because (as you may remember from Chapter 14) the thrown exception has broken the flow of execution. By design, there is nothing we (or any hacker) can do to get around this restriction.

Writing a SecurityManager

So much for the theory of **SecurityManagers**. What does a real **SecurityManager** look like? In the code below we will actually create one and then integrate it with an AppExpress generated Java application, which is called **manager**. Using the application you will be able to configure the security manager as you like. Figures 15.1 and 15.2 show the application in action. Listing 15.4 contains the source code for the application as well as the **SecurityManager**, which is called AgentServerSecurityManager.

LISTING 15.4 A SECURITY MANAGER CONFIGURATION APPLICATION

```
/*
    This class is an extension of the Frame class for use as the
    main window of an application.

    You can add controls or menus to manager with Cafe Studio.
*/
```

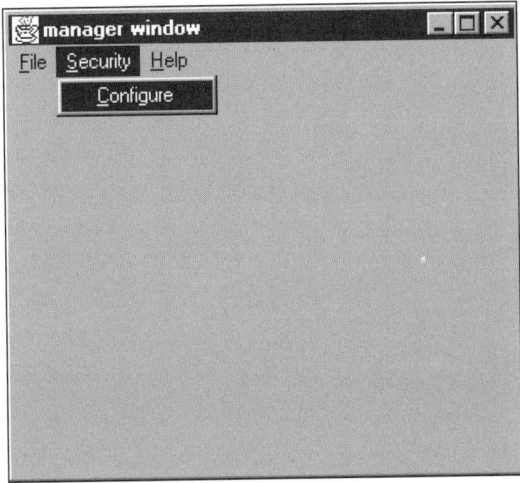

Figure 15.1   The Security Manager Configuration Application.

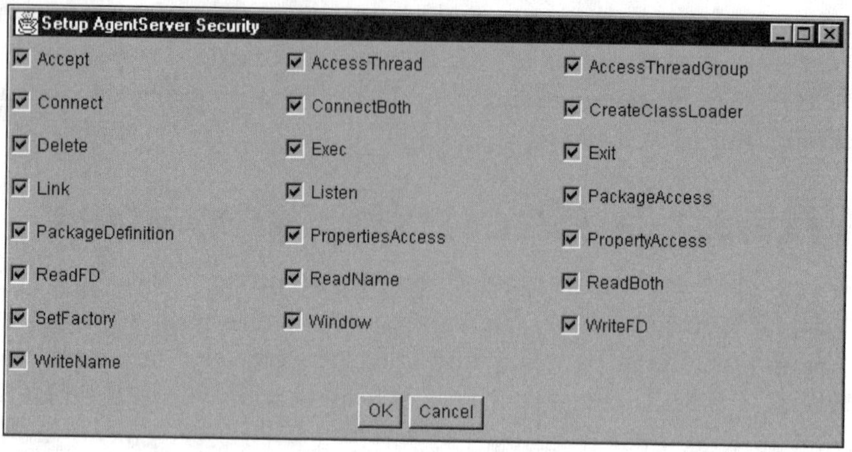

Figure 15.2   The Security Manager Configuration Screen.

```java
import java.awt.*;
import java.util.*;
import java.io.*;

public class manager extends Frame {
    private AgentServerSecurityManager assm;

    public manager() {

        super("manager window");
        assm = new AgentServerSecurityManager(this);
        try
        {
          System.setSecurityManager(assm);
        }
        catch (SecurityException se)
        {
          // this means a security manager was already set!
          System.out.println("Security Manager Already Set!");
        }

        //{{INIT_MENUS
        MenuBar mb = new MenuBar();
        fileMenu = new Menu("&File");
        fileMenu.add(new MenuItem("E&xit"));
        mb.add(fileMenu);
        securityMenu = new Menu("&Security");
        securityMenu.add(new MenuItem("&Configure "));
        mb.add(securityMenu);
        helpMenu = new Menu("&Help");
        helpMenu.add(new MenuItem("&About..."));
```

```
      mb.add(helpMenu);
      setMenuBar(mb);
      //}}

      //{{INIT_CONTROLS
      setLayout(null);
      addNotify();
      resize(insets().left + insets().right + 302, insets().top +
      insets().bottom + 250);
      //}}

      show();
   }

   public synchronized void show() {
move(50, 50);
super.show();
   }

   public boolean handleEvent(Event event) {

if (event.id == Event.WINDOW_DESTROY) {
         hide();           // hide the Frame
         dispose();        // tell windowing system to free
resources
         System.exit(0); // exit
         return true;
}
return super.handleEvent(event);
   }

   public boolean action(Event event, Object arg) {
      if (event.target instanceof MenuItem) {
         String label = (String) arg;
         if (label.equalsIgnoreCase("&Configure ")) {
                  selectedConfigure();
                  return true;
              } else if (label.equalsIgnoreCase("&Configure"))
{
               selectedConfigure();
               return true;
           } else if (label.equalsIgnoreCase("&About...")) {
             selectedAbout();
             return true;
         } else if (label.equalsIgnoreCase("E&xit")) {
             selectedExit();
             return true;
         } else if (label.equalsIgnoreCase("&Open...")) {
             selectedOpen();
```

```
                            return true;
                    }
            }
            return super.action(event, arg);
    }

    public static void main(String args[]) {
        new manager();
    }

    //{{DECLARE_MENUS
    Menu fileMenu;
    Menu securityMenu;
    Menu helpMenu;
    //}}

    //{{DECLARE_CONTROLS
    //}}

    public void selectedOpen() {
        (new FileDialog(this, "Open...")).show();
    }
    public void selectedExit() {
        QuitBox theQuitBox;
        theQuitBox = new QuitBox(this);
        theQuitBox.show();
    }
    public void selectedAbout() {
        AboutBox theAboutBox;
        theAboutBox = new AboutBox(this);
        theAboutBox.show();
    }
    public void selectedConfigure() {
        assm.configure();
    }
}


/*
This class is a basic extension of the Dialog class.  It can be used
by subclasses of Frame.  To use it, create a reference to the class,
then instantiate an object of the class (pass 'this' in the
constructor), and call the show() method.

    example:

    AboutBox theAboutBox;
    theAboutBox = new AboutBox(this);
    theAboutBox.show();
```

```
    You can add controls to AboutBox with Cafe Studio.
    (Menus can be added only to subclasses of Frame.)
*/

class AboutBox extends Dialog {

    public AboutBox(Frame parent) {

      super(parent, "About", true);
  setResizable(false);

  //{{INIT_CONTROLS
        setLayout(null);
        addNotify();
        resize(insets().left + insets().right + 288, insets().top +
        insets().bottom + 85);
        label1=new Label("A Security Manager");
        label1.setFont(new Font("Dialog",Font.BOLD,14));
        add(label1);
        label1.reshape(insets().left + 15,insets().top + 18,165,16);
        OKButton=new Button("OK");
        add(OKButton);
        OKButton.reshape(insets().left + 194,insets().top +
        18,73,23);
        //}}
    }

    public synchronized void show() {
  Rectangle bounds = getParent().bounds();
  Rectangle abounds = bounds();

  move(bounds.x + (bounds.width - abounds.width)/ 2,
        bounds.y + (bounds.height - abounds.height)/2);

  super.show();
    }

    public synchronized void wakeUp() {
  notify();
    }

    public boolean handleEvent(Event event) {
  if (event.id == Event.ACTION_EVENT && event.target == OKButton) {
        clickedOKButton();
        return true;
  }
  else

  if (event.id == Event.WINDOW_DESTROY) {
```

```
        hide();
        return true;
    }
  return super.handleEvent(event);
    }


    //{{DECLARE_CONTROLS
    Label label1;
    Button OKButton;
    //}}

    public void clickedOKButton() {
        handleEvent(new Event(this, Event.WINDOW_DESTROY, null));
    }
}


/*
This class is a basic extension of the Dialog class.  It can be used
by subclasses of Frame.  To use it, create a reference to the class,
then instantiate an object of the class (pass 'this' in the
constructor), and call the show() method.

    example:

    QuitBox theQuitBox;
    theQuitBox = new QuitBox(this);
    theQuitBox.show();

    You can add controls, but not menus, to QuitBox with Cafe Studio.
    (Menus can be added only to subclasses of Frame.)
*/

class QuitBox extends Dialog {

    public QuitBox(Frame parent) {

      super(parent, "Quit Application?", true);
    setResizable(false);

  //{{INIT_CONTROLS
        setLayout(null);
        addNotify();
        resize(insets().left + insets().right + 257, insets().top +
        insets().bottom + 68);
        yesButton=new Button("Yes");
        add(yesButton);
        yesButton.reshape(insets().left + 68,insets().top +
        10,46,23);
```

```
        noButton=new Button("No");
        add(noButton);
        noButton.reshape(insets().left + 135,insets().top +
        10,47,23);
        //}}
    }

    public synchronized void show() {
Rectangle bounds = getParent().bounds();
Rectangle abounds = bounds();

move(bounds.x + (bounds.width - abounds.width)/ 2,
      bounds.y + (bounds.height - abounds.height)/2);

super.show();
    }

    public synchronized void wakeUp() {
notify();
    }

    public boolean handleEvent(Event event) {
if (event.id == Event.ACTION_EVENT && event.target == noButton) {
        clickedNoButton();
        return true;
}
else
if (event.id == Event.ACTION_EVENT && event.target == yesButton) {
        clickedYesButton();
        return true;
}
else

if (event.id == Event.WINDOW_DESTROY) {
    hide();
    return true;
}
return super.handleEvent(event);
    }

    //{{DECLARE_CONTROLS
    Button yesButton;
    Button noButton;
    //}}

    public void clickedYesButton() {
        System.exit(0);
    }
    public void clickedNoButton() {
```

```
            handleEvent(new Event(this, Event.WINDOW_DESTROY, null));
        }
    }
```

```
/** A class that implements security for the AgentServer.
Brute-force strategy that simply uses a flag for each of the
methods in SecurityManager.  Can configure itself using a
SecurityDialog. Initializes with ALL ACCESS ALLOWED.
*/
class AgentServerSecurityManager extends SecurityManager {
    public static Vector v = new Vector(1);
    private Frame mainApp;

/** Build a vector of SecurityItems, one for each of the check
methods in SecurityManager.  Initialize each SecurityItem to
true (access allowed).  Can be changed later using configure.
*/
    public AgentServerSecurityManager(Frame f) {
        mainApp = f;
        v.addElement( new SecurityItem( "Accept", true ));
        v.addElement( new SecurityItem( "AccessThread", true ));
        v.addElement( new SecurityItem( "AccessThreadGroup", true ));
        v.addElement( new SecurityItem( "Connect", true ));
        v.addElement( new SecurityItem( "ConnectBoth", true ));
        v.addElement( new SecurityItem( "CreateClassLoader", true ));
        v.addElement( new SecurityItem( "Delete", true ));
        v.addElement( new SecurityItem( "Exec", true ));
        v.addElement( new SecurityItem( "Exit", true ));
        v.addElement( new SecurityItem( "Link", true ));
        v.addElement( new SecurityItem( "Listen", true ));
        v.addElement( new SecurityItem( "PackageAccess", true ));
        v.addElement( new SecurityItem( "PackageDefinition", true ));
        v.addElement( new SecurityItem( "PropertiesAccess", true ));
        v.addElement( new SecurityItem( "PropertyAccess", true ));
        v.addElement( new SecurityItem( "ReadFD", true ));
        v.addElement( new SecurityItem( "ReadName", true ));
        v.addElement( new SecurityItem( "ReadBoth", true ));
        v.addElement( new SecurityItem( "SetFactory", true ));
        v.addElement( new SecurityItem( "Window", true ));
        v.addElement( new SecurityItem( "WriteFD", true ));
        v.addElement( new SecurityItem( "WriteName", true ));
    }

/** Change the state of a SecurityItem based on the name of the
item.  This is called for each SecurityItem by the
SecurityDialog when the the OK button is hit.
@param   name   The name of the SecurityItem.
```

```
@param  state The state true/false we want to set the
SecurityItem to.
*/
  public void setFlagState( String name, boolean state ) {
    for( int i = 0; i < v.size(); i++ ) {
      SecurityItem si = (SecurityItem)v.elementAt(i);
      if( si.name.compareTo(name) == 0 ) {
        si.state = state;
        break;
        }
      }
    }
/** Return the true/false state of the named SecurityItem.
@param  name  The name of the item we want to query.
*/
  boolean isSet( String name ) {
    for( int i = 0; i < v.size(); i++ ) {
      SecurityItem si = (SecurityItem)v.elementAt(i);
      if( si.name.compareTo(name) == 0 )
        return si.state;
      }
    return( false );
    }

/** Allow the user to configure this security manager by
filling out a SecurityDialog.
*/
  public void configure() {
  // dumpContext();
    SecurityDialog sd = new SecurityDialog(mainApp, this);
    sd.ShowAndLayout();
    }


/**  Generic check routine
*/
  public void checkIt(String whatToCheck) {
    if( isSet( whatToCheck )) return;
    throw new AgentServerSecurityException();
  }


/**  Checks to see if a socket connection to the specified
port on the specified host has been accepted.
*/
  public void checkAccept(String host, int port)
  { checkIt("Accept");}
```

```
/** Checks to see if the specified Thread is allowed to
modify the Thread group.
*/
  public void checkAccess(Thread t)
  { checkIt("AccessThread"); }

/**     Checks to see if the specified Thread group is allowed
to modify this group.
*/
  public void checkAccess(ThreadGroup tg)
  { checkIt("AccessThreadGroup"); }

/**     Checks to see if a socket has connected to the specified
port on the the specified host.
*/
  public void checkConnect(String host, int port)
  { checkIt("Connect" ); }

/**     Checks to see if the current execution context and the
indicated execution context are both allowed to connect to the
    indicated host and port.
*/
  public void checkConnect(String host, int port, Object o)
  { checkIt("ConnectBoth" ); }

/**     Checks to see if the ClassLoader has been created.
*/
  public void checkCreateClassLoader()
  { checkIt("CreateClassLoader" ); }

/**     Checks to see if a file with the specified system
dependent file name can be deleted.
*/
  public void checkDelete(String filename)
  { checkIt("Delete" ); }

/**     Checks to see if the system command is executed by
trusted code.
*/
  public void checkExec(String cmdname)
  { checkIt("Exec" ); }

/**     Checks to see if the system has exited the virtual
machine with an exit code.
*/
  public void checkExit(int i)
  { checkIt("Exit" ); }
```

```
/**     Checks to see if the specified linked library exists.
*/
 public void  checkLink(String libname)
   { checkIt("Link" ); }

/**     Checks to see if a server socket is listening to the
specified local port that it is bounded to.
*/
   public void  checkListen(int port)
   { checkIt("Listen" ); }

/**     Checks to see if an applet can access a package.
*/
   public void  checkPackageAccess(String pkgname)
   { checkIt("PackageAccess" ); }

/**     Checks to see if an applet can define classes in a
package.
*/
   public void  checkPackageDefinition(String pkgname)
   { checkIt("PackageDefinition" ); }

/**     Checks to see who has access to the System properties.
*/
   public void  checkPropertiesAccess()
   { checkIt("PropertiesAccess" ); }

/**     Checks to see who has access to the System property
named by key.
*/
   public void  checkPropertyAccess(String property)
   { checkIt("PropertyAccess" ); }

/**     Checks to see who has access to the System property
named by key and def.
*/
   public void  checkPropertyAccess(String property, String s)
   { checkIt("PropertyAccess" ); }

/**     Checks to see if an input file with the specified file
descriptor object gets created.
*/
   public void  checkRead(FileDescriptor fd)
   { checkIt("ReadFD" ); }

/**     Checks to see if an input file with the specified
system dependent file name gets created.
*/
```

```
  public void  checkRead(String filename)
  { checkIt("ReadName" ); }

/**     Checks to see if the current context or the indicated
context are both allowed to read the given file name.
*/
  public void  checkRead(String filename, Object o)
  { checkIt("ReadBoth" ); }

/**     Checks to see if an applet can set a
networking-related object factory.
*/
  public void  checkSetFactory()
  { checkIt("SetFactory" ); }

/**     Checks to see if top-level windows can be created by
the caller.
*/
  public boolean  checkTopLevelWindow(Object o)
  {
    if ( isSet( "Window" ))
      return true;
    throw new AgentServerSecurityException();
  }

/**     Checks to see if an output file with the specified
file descriptor object gets created.
*/
  public void  checkWrite(FileDescriptor fd)
  { checkIt("WriteFD" ); }

/**     Checks to see if an output file with the specified
system dependent file name gets created.
*/
  public void  checkWrite(String filename)
  { checkIt("WriteName" ); }
}

/** A class representing a violation of the AgentServer's
security strategy.
*/
class AgentServerSecurityException
                   extends SecurityException {
  public AgentServerSecurityException() {
    super( "AgentServerSecurityException" );
    }
  }
```

```
/** A class for holding the name and current state of a
Security property.
*/
class SecurityItem {
/** The name of the resource this security item is protecting. */
  public String name;
/** Set to true if the access to this resource is ALLOWED. */
  public boolean state;

/** constructor - force the user to initialize the name and
state of this property.
@param  label The name of this property.
@param  initState The initial state of this property.
*/
  public SecurityItem( String label, boolean initState ) {
    name = new String( label );
    state = initState;
    }
  }


/** A modal dialog box that allows the user to set the security
strategy
@version 1.0 1/4/1996
@author John Rodley
*/
class SecurityDialog extends Dialog {
  int selectIndex = -1;
  Frame parent;
  Panel ButtonPanel;
  public boolean bFinished = false;
    Vector cbV = new Vector(1);
    AgentServerSecurityManager assm;

 /** Constructor.
 */
  public SecurityDialog(Frame p, AgentServerSecurityManager assm) {
  super(p, "Setup AgentServer Security", true);
    parent = p;
    this.assm = assm;

    // Set up all the graphical elements
    // Split the dialog main panel into three elements, top,
    // bottom and middle, via the BorderLayout.  The top and
    // bottom size themselves according to the preferred sizes
    // of the text on the top and the buttons on the bottom.
    // The Center panel, which the List fills, uses all the
    // space left in the middle.
    setLayout(new BorderLayout());
```

```
ButtonPanel = new Panel();
add( "South", ButtonPanel );

Panel checkPanel = new Panel();
checkPanel.setLayout( new GridLayout( 8, 3 ));

Vector v = AgentServerSecurityManager.v;
for( int i = 0; i < v.size(); i++ ) {
  Checkbox cb = new Checkbox(
    ((SecurityItem)v.elementAt(i)).name,
    null, ((SecurityItem)v.elementAt(i)).state);
  checkPanel.add( cb );
  cbV.addElement(cb );
  }

add( "Center", checkPanel );

Button okbutton = new Button("OK");
ButtonPanel.add( okbutton );
Button cancelbutton = new Button( "Cancel" );
ButtonPanel.add( cancelbutton );
}


/** Size the dialog to something appropriate, then make it
non-resizeable so that users don't go resizing it themselves.
*/
public void ShowAndLayout() {
show();
resize( 600, 300 );
layout();
setResizable(false);
}


/** Process the OK and cancel buttons.  This also gets called
every time the user changes the state of one of our Checkboxes
so we explicitly ignore that case.  When OK is hit, roll
through the SecurityItem Vector setting the state of each of
the items based on the checkbox state.
*/
public boolean action(Event e, Object o) {

  if( e.target instanceof Checkbox ) {
    return false;
    }
  if( e.target instanceof Button ) {
    if( ((Button)e.target).getLabel().compareTo("OK") == 0 ) {
      for( int i = 0; i < cbV.size(); i++ ) {
        assm.setFlagState(
```

```
            ((Checkbox)cbV.elementAt(i)).getLabel(),
              ((Checkbox)cbV.elementAt(i)).getState());
        }
      }
       }
 bFinished = true;
 dispose();
 return true;
 }
}
```

In Listing 15.4, we define a class, **SecurityItem**, that holds the name of the resource, and a **boolean**, state, that tells whether or not access to the resource is allowed. In the **AgentServerSecurityManager** constructor, we build a **Vector** of these **SecurityItem**s, one for each resource, and set its initial state. Each check method merely reads the current state of "its" **SecurityItem**, returning if the access is allowed, or throwing an exception if the access is not allowed. To facilitate our use of **SecurityItem**s, we define two of our own methods, **isSet** and **setFlagState**, which allow us to set and check the state of a **SecurityItem** based on its name.

All these "locks" would be useless without some way to turn them on and off. Thus, we define a dialog box, SecurityDialog, that simply allows us to set or clear each of the **SecurityItem.state** booleans. Users of the application select Security from the main menu and then select Configure to bring up the dialog box.

Up in class manager's constructor, we instantiate our **SecurityManager**, then call **System.setSecurityManager** to make our **SecurityManager** the one, and only one, that Java will use for this application. *Once invoked, setSecurityManager can never be called again for the life of the application.* Once we've set our **SecurityManager**, Java will begin automatically calling its check methods whenever any security issues arise. Listing 15.5 shows you the code that sets up our **SecurityManager**.

LISTING 15.5 SETTING UP A SECURITY MANAGER

```
assm = new AgentServerSecurityManager(this);
try
{
```

```
    System.setSecurityManager(assm);
}
catch (SecurityException se)
{
  // this means a security manager was already set!
  System.out.println("Security Manager Already Set!");
}
```

Selective Access Restriction

Another security issue along the same lines is one of file I/O. What if we wanted to disallow programs from doing direct file I/O?

I had this very situation come up in my Agent and AgentServer programs from my book **Writing Java Applets**, by Coriolis Group Books. Essentially, my task was to let a server called AgentServer write to files, but prevent a client, called **Agent**, from performing writes. In addition, the example was taken a step further to allow **Agents** to be allowed to write to a file *only when using* what was called the **AgentContext** interface.

In Listing 15.6, you'll see methods that were implemented called **checkWrite**, which were placed in a custom **SecurityManager**. The **checkWrite** methods became responsible for restricting direct agent writes, but allowing AgentServer writes, and agent writes via the **AgentContext** interface.

LISTING 15.6 THE CHECKWRITE METHODS, AND THEIR HELPER METHODS

```
/**    Checks to see if an output file with the specified
file descriptor object gets created.
*/
  public void  checkWrite(FileDescriptor fd)  {
if( isAgent()) {
      if( isAgentGoingThroughAgentContext())
        return;
      }
    else
      return;
//    if( isSet( "WriteFD" ))
//        return;
    throw new AgentServerSecurityException();
    }

/**    Checks to see if an output file with the specified
system dependent file name gets created.
*/
```

```
    public void  checkWrite(String filename)  {
      if( isAgent()) {
        if( isAgentGoingThroughAgentContext())
          return;
        }
      else
        return;
      throw new AgentServerSecurityException();
      }

  }
/** Return true if Agent is on the stack. This means we were
called from somewhere within an Agent.
@return true if an instance of Agent is somewhere on the stack.
*/
boolean isAgent() {
  Class c[] = getClassContext();
  for( int i = 0; i < c.length; i++ ) {
    if( subclassesAgent( c[i] )) {
      int AgentIndex = classDepth( c[i].getName() );
      if( AgentIndex >= 0 )
        return( true );
      }
    }
  return( false );
  }

/** Return true if the specified class subclasses
agent.Agent.Agent. All agents run over the Net should subclass
Agent. Runs through all the superclasses of c checking their
name against agent.Agent.Agent.
@param  c The class we're inquiring about.
@return true if c is a subclass of Agent, false otherwise.
*/
boolean subclassesAgent( Class c ) {
  Class cNext = c;
  while( true ) {
    Class c1 = cNext.getSuperclass();
    if( c1 == null )
      break;
    if( c1.getName().compareTo( "agent.Agent.Agent" ) == 0 )
      return( true );
    cNext = c1;
    }
  return( false );
  }

/** Return true if the Agent is calling us through the
AgentContext, false otherwise. Accomplish this by looking at
```

```
the stack. If the "classDepth" of the Agent is lower than that
of the AgentContext, or if the AgentContext isn't on the stack,
then the Agent is trying to go around us.
*/
boolean isAgentGoingThroughAgentContext() {
  Class c[] = getClassContext();
  for( int i = 0; i < c.length; i++ ) {
    if( subclassesAgent( c[i] )) {
      int AContextIndex = classDepth( "agent.Server.SepContext" );
      int AgentIndex = classDepth( c[i].getName() );
      // This is where we should catch an agent calling
      // File.write directly.
      if( AContextIndex < 0 )
        return( false );

      // This should never happen. Indicates SepContext
      // calling back to Agent!!
      if( AgentIndex < AContextIndex )
        return( false );
      else
        return( true );
    }
  }
  System.out.println( "NO AGENT!!" );
  return( true );
}
```

The **checkWrite** methods are fairly simple, in themselves. First, we call **isAgent**, which tells us whether this call emanates from an instance of one of our **Agents**. If the call doesn't come from an **Agent**, we allow it. If the call does come from an **Agent**, we call **isAgentGoingThroughAgentContext**, to see if the call goes through the **AgentContext**. If it does, we allow the call. If not, we throw an exception. Pretty easy, huh?

The real work here is done by the two methods: **isAgent** and **isAgentGoing ThroughAgentContext**. **isAgent** gets the list of classes on the stack by calling **SecurityManager.getClassContext**. This gives us an array of classes. We go through these classes one by one, checking to see if they subclass **Agent**. If any subclass of **Agent** is on the stack, we were called, somehow, by **Agent** and we return true.

At this point, we know that an instance of **Agent** caused this call to **checkWrite**. That's all we know. It could have been caused by a direct call to **FileOutputStream.write**, or it could have been some more convoluted invocation chain. What we need to know now is whether the **AgentContext** was between the invocation by **Agent** and the call to **writeCheck**. This is where **isAgentGoingThroughAgentContext** comes in. Like **isAgent**, we get the list of classes on the stack from **getClassContext**. Then we run through the array looking for the class that subclasses **Agent**. When we find it, we call **SecurityManager.classDepth** to find out where on the stack the **AgentContext** and the **Agent** reside. As methods call each other, Java builds a stack of classes. At the top of the stack (index 0) is the class you're in when you look at the stack. At index 1 is the class whose method called the current class, and so on .... So, when we call **classDepth**, at the top of the stack (index 0), **AgentServerSecurityManager** is at the top of the stack (index 0). All we need to know now is whether there's an **AgentContext** on the stack between our **Agent** and our **SecurityManager**. So, we compare the **classDepth** of our **Agent** against the **classDepth** of our **AgentContext** (**SepContext**). If there is no **AgentContext** (**AContextIndex** < 0) or its **classDepth** is greater than the **Agent**'s, we return false (operation disallowed).

The only method we haven't talked about is **subclassesAgent**. This method takes a class and determines whether that class subclasses **agent.Agent.Agent**. We do this by repeatedly calling **getSuperclass** until we reach the base class and **getSuperclass** returns null. We compare each superclass name to the string name for our **Agent** class, "**agent.Agent.Agent**".

Using this technique, the desired behavior for File I/O was achieved. You can use the same techniques on your programs as well.

Conclusion

Java applet security is a work-in-progress. In many cases, applet security restrictions are so severe that applets need to connect to a server daemon to get any useful work done at all. In this chapter, we've seen how applets are restricted, and how they can tell what those restrictions are by querying the system properties.

We've seen the mechanism, the **SecurityManager** class, that browsers use to protect the system against rogue applets. We've implemented our own **SecurityManager** to allow users to define how security should be implemented.

You may use the code from this chapter as a starting point to implement your own custom **SecurityManagers** and to restrict access on particular system privileges. With a little hard work, you can make your applets and applications have only the privileges that you specify.

Index